Yukon Ho!

A Calvin and Hobbes Collection
by Bill Watterson

Andrews and McMeel
A Universal Press Syndicate Company
Kansas City • New York

ISBN: 0-8362-1835-3

Library of Congress Catalog Card Number: 88-83874

The Yukon Song

My tiger friend has got the sled,
And I have packed a snack.
We're all set for the trip ahead.
We're never coming back!

We're abandoning this life we've led!
So long, Mom and Pop!
We're sick of doing what you've said,
And now it's going to stop!

We're going where it snows all year,
Where life can have real meaning.
A place where we won't have to hear,
"Your room could stand some cleaning."

The Yukon is the place for us!
That's where we want to live.
Up there we'll get to yell and cuss,
And act real primitive.

We'll never have to go to school,
Forced into submission,
By monstrous, crabby teachers who'll
Make us learn addition.

We'll never have to clean a plate,
Of veggie glops and goos.
Messily we'll masticate,
Using any fork we choose!

The timber wolves will be our friends.
We'll stay up late and howl,
At the moon, till nighttime ends,
Before going on the prowl.

Oh, what a life! We cannot wait,
To be in that arctic land,
Where we'll be masters of our fate,
And lead a life that's grand!

No more of parental rules!
We're heading for some snow!
Good riddance to those grown-up ghouls!
We're leaving! *Yukon Ho!*

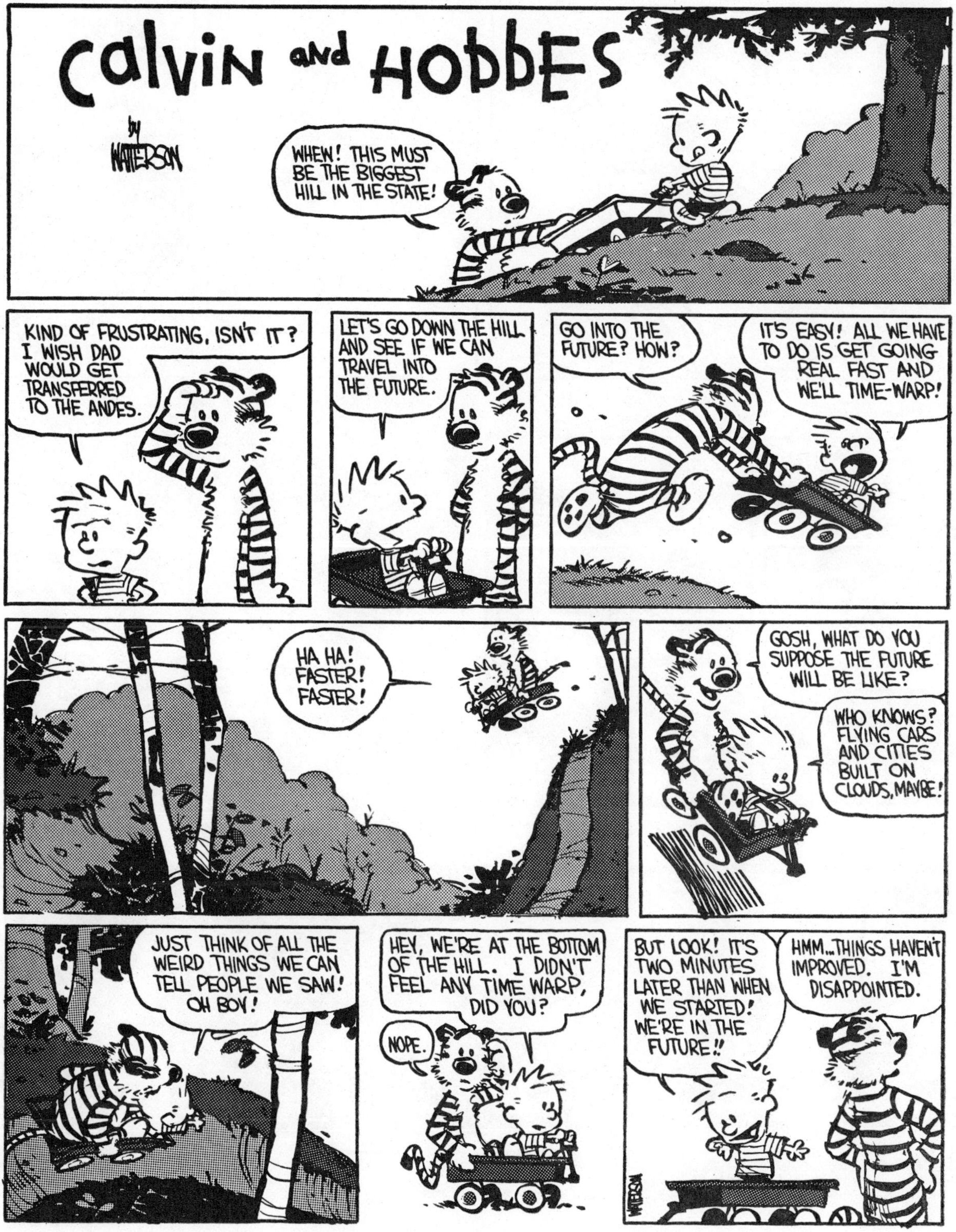
Calvin and HOBBES
by WATTERSON
WHEW! THIS MUST BE THE BIGGEST HILL IN THE STATE!
KIND OF FRUSTRATING, ISN'T IT? I WISH DAD WOULD GET TRANSFERRED TO THE ANDES.
LET'S GO DOWN THE HILL AND SEE IF WE CAN TRAVEL INTO THE FUTURE.
GO INTO THE FUTURE? HOW?
IT'S EASY! ALL WE HAVE TO DO IS GET GOING REAL FAST AND WE'LL TIME-WARP!
HA HA! FASTER! FASTER!
GOSH, WHAT DO YOU SUPPOSE THE FUTURE WILL BE LIKE?
WHO KNOWS? FLYING CARS AND CITIES BUILT ON CLOUDS, MAYBE!
JUST THINK OF ALL THE WEIRD THINGS WE CAN TELL PEOPLE WE SAW! OH BOY!
HEY, WE'RE AT THE BOTTOM OF THE HILL. I DIDN'T FEEL ANY TIME WARP, DID YOU?
NOPE.
BUT LOOK! IT'S TWO MINUTES LATER THAN WHEN WE STARTED! WE'RE IN THE FUTURE!!
HMM...THINGS HAVEN'T IMPROVED. I'M DISAPPOINTED.
WATTERSON

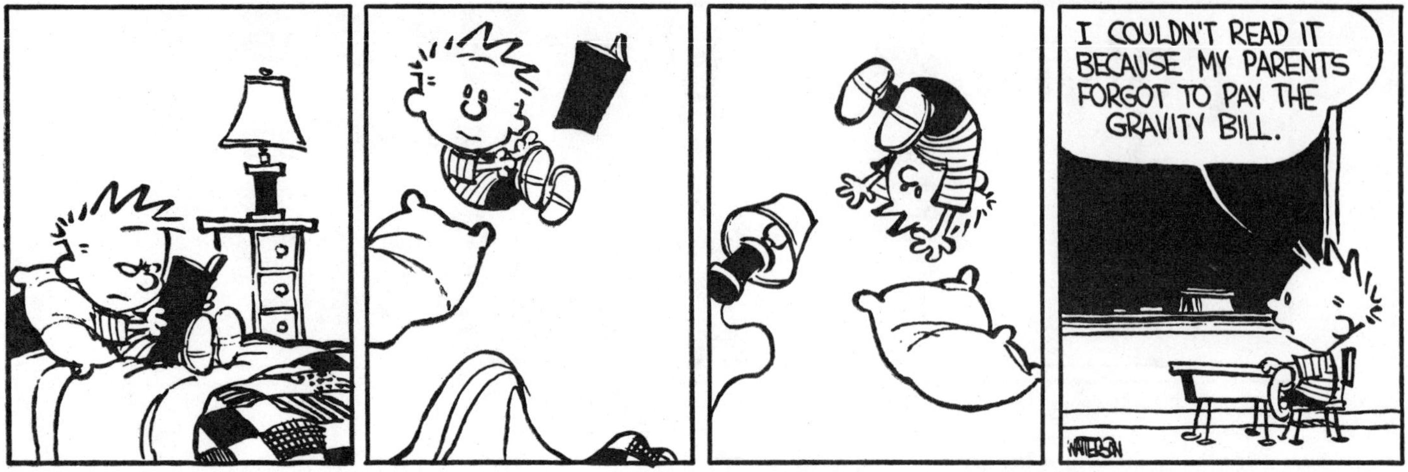
I COULDN'T READ IT BECAUSE MY PARENTS FORGOT TO PAY THE GRAVITY BILL.
WATTERSON

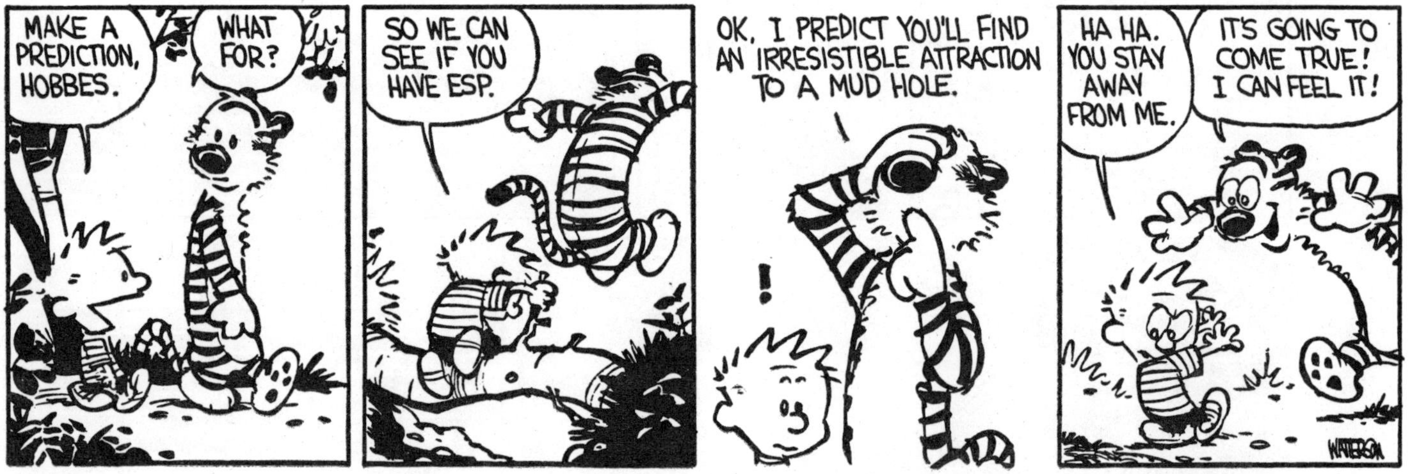
MAKE A PREDICTION, HOBBES.
WHAT FOR?
SO WE CAN SEE IF YOU HAVE ESP.
OK, I PREDICT YOU'LL FIND AN IRRESISTIBLE ATTRACTION TO A MUD HOLE.
!
HA HA. YOU STAY AWAY FROM ME.
IT'S GOING TO COME TRUE! I CAN FEEL IT!
WATTERSON

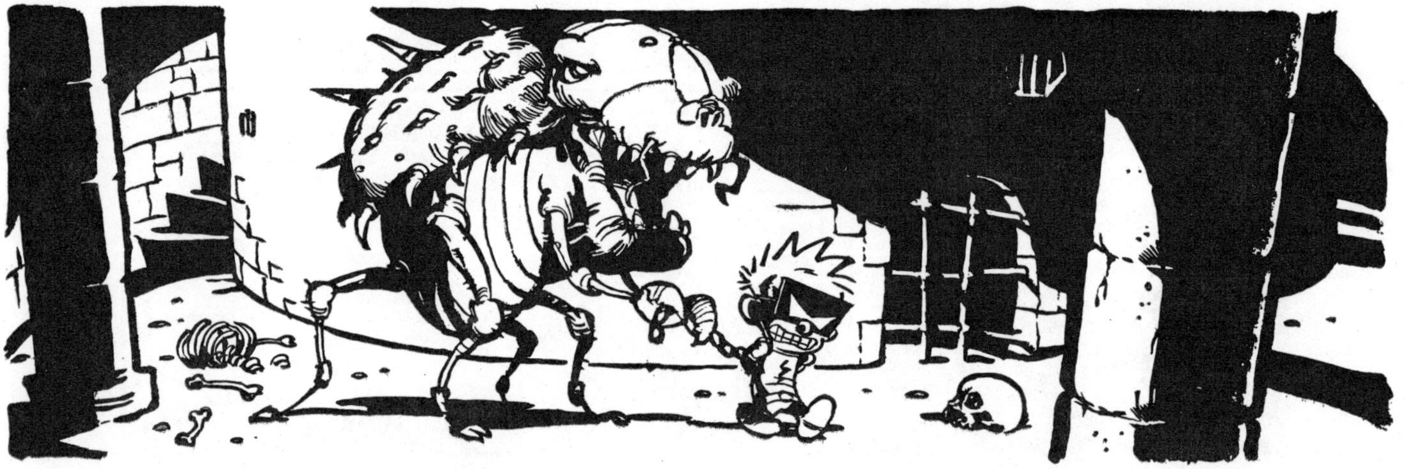

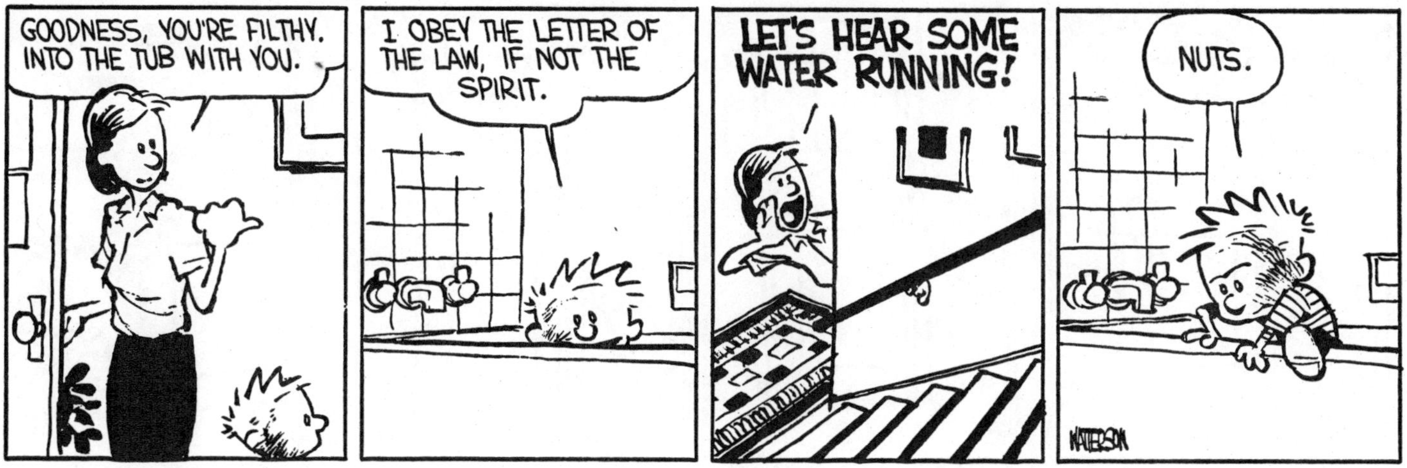
GOODNESS, YOU'RE FILTHY. INTO THE TUB WITH YOU.
I OBEY THE LETTER OF THE LAW, IF NOT THE SPIRIT.
LET'S HEAR SOME WATER RUNNING!
NUTS.

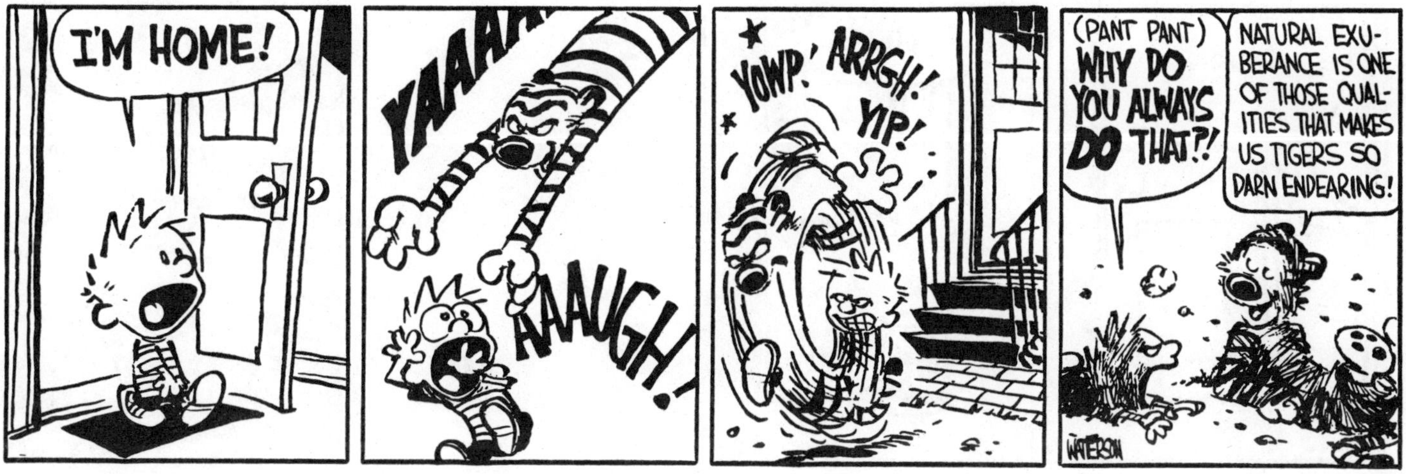
I'M HOME!
YAAAH
AAAUGH!
YOWP!
ARRGH!
YIP!
(PANT PANT) WHY DO YOU ALWAYS DO THAT?!
NATURAL EXUBERANCE IS ONE OF THOSE QUALITIES THAT MAKES US TIGERS SO DARN ENDEARING!

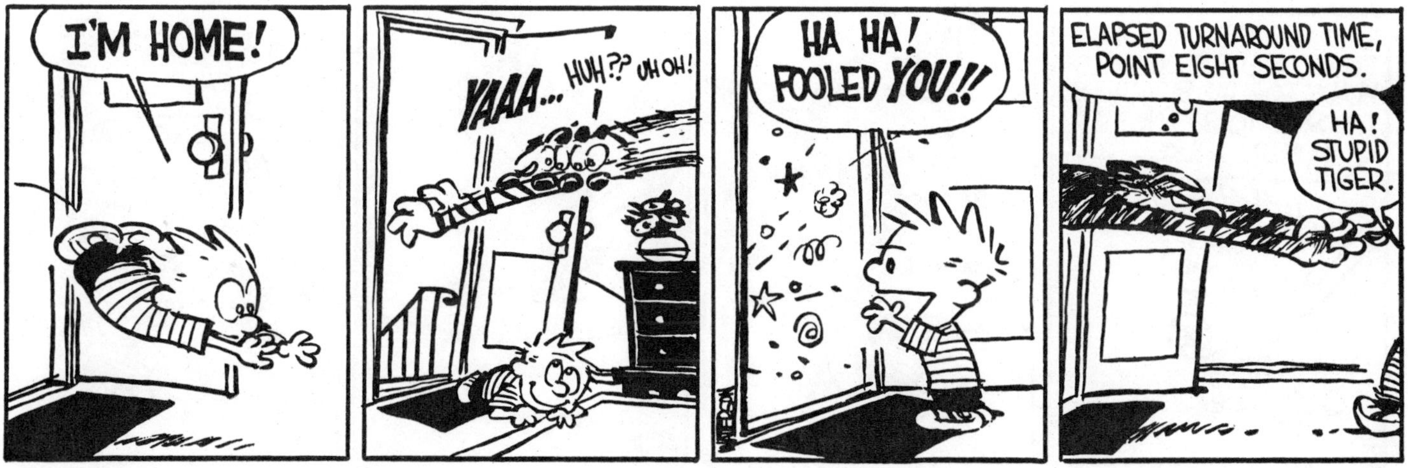
I'M HOME!
YAAA...
HUH?!?
UH OH!
HA HA! FOOLED YOU!!
ELAPSED TURNAROUND TIME, POINT EIGHT SECONDS.
HA! STUPID TIGER.

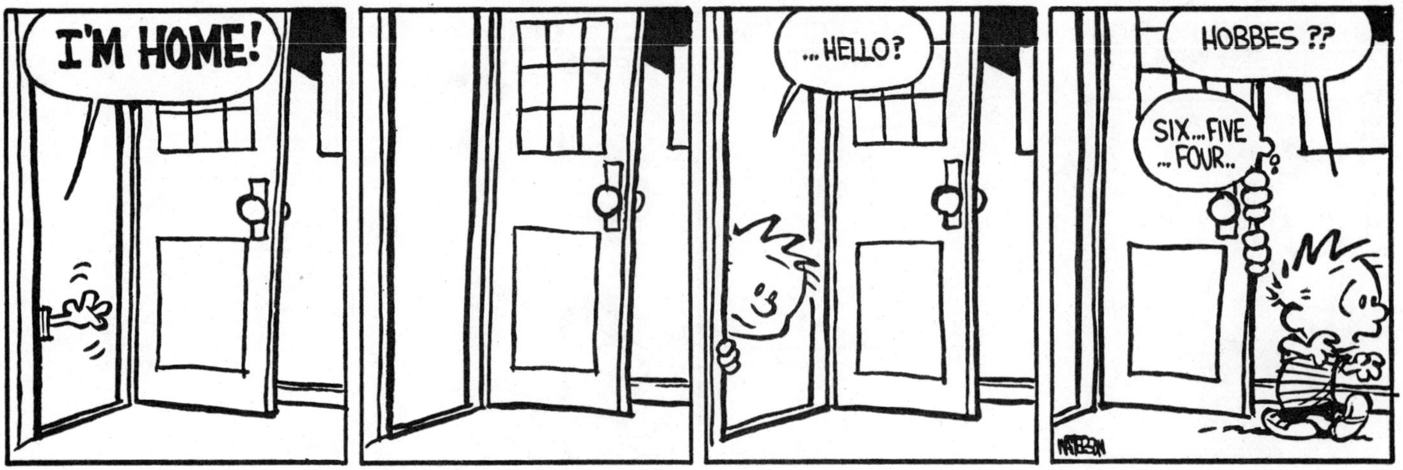
I'M HOME!
...HELLO?
HOBBES ??
SIX...FIVE ...FOUR..
WATTERSON

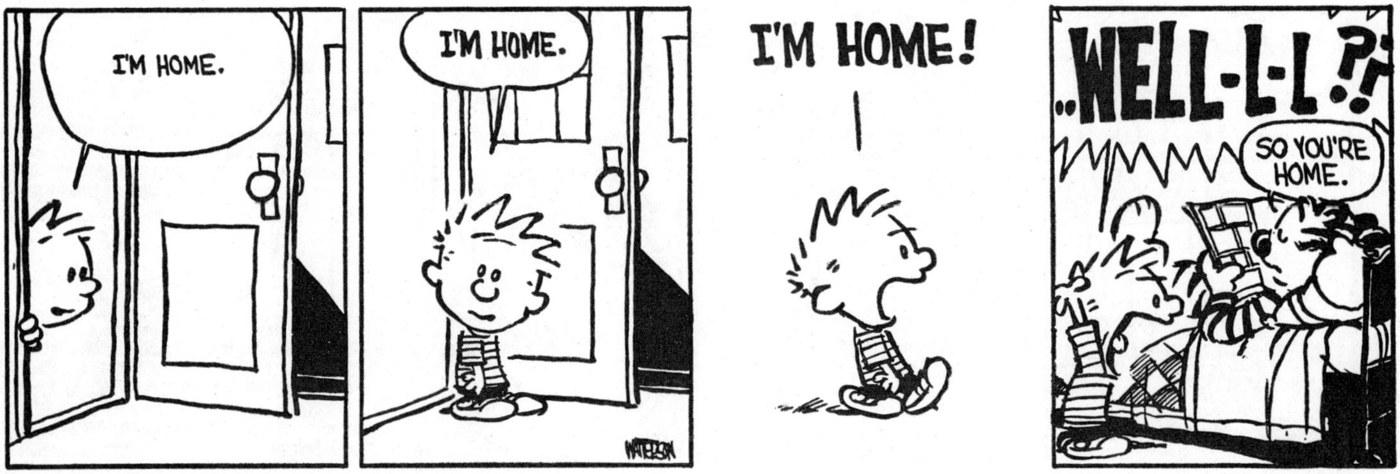
I'M HOME.
I'M HOME.
I'M HOME!
..WELL-L-L ?!?
SO YOU'RE HOME.
WATTERSON

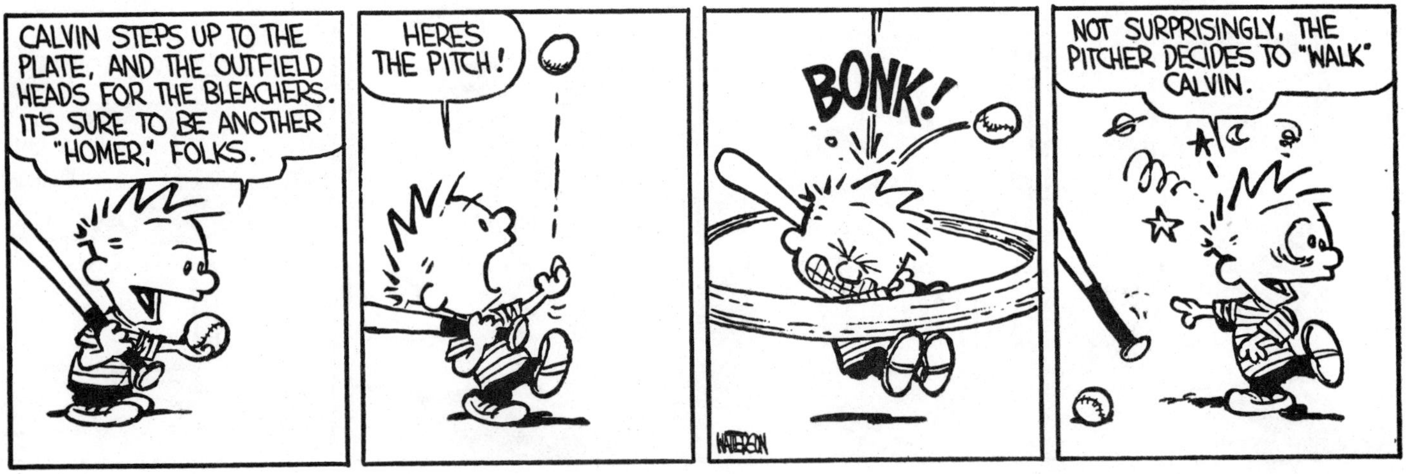
CALVIN STEPS UP TO THE PLATE, AND THE OUTFIELD HEADS FOR THE BLEACHERS. IT'S SURE TO BE ANOTHER "HOMER," FOLKS.
HERE'S THE PITCH!
BONK!
NOT SURPRISINGLY, THE PITCHER DECIDES TO "WALK" CALVIN.
WATTERSON

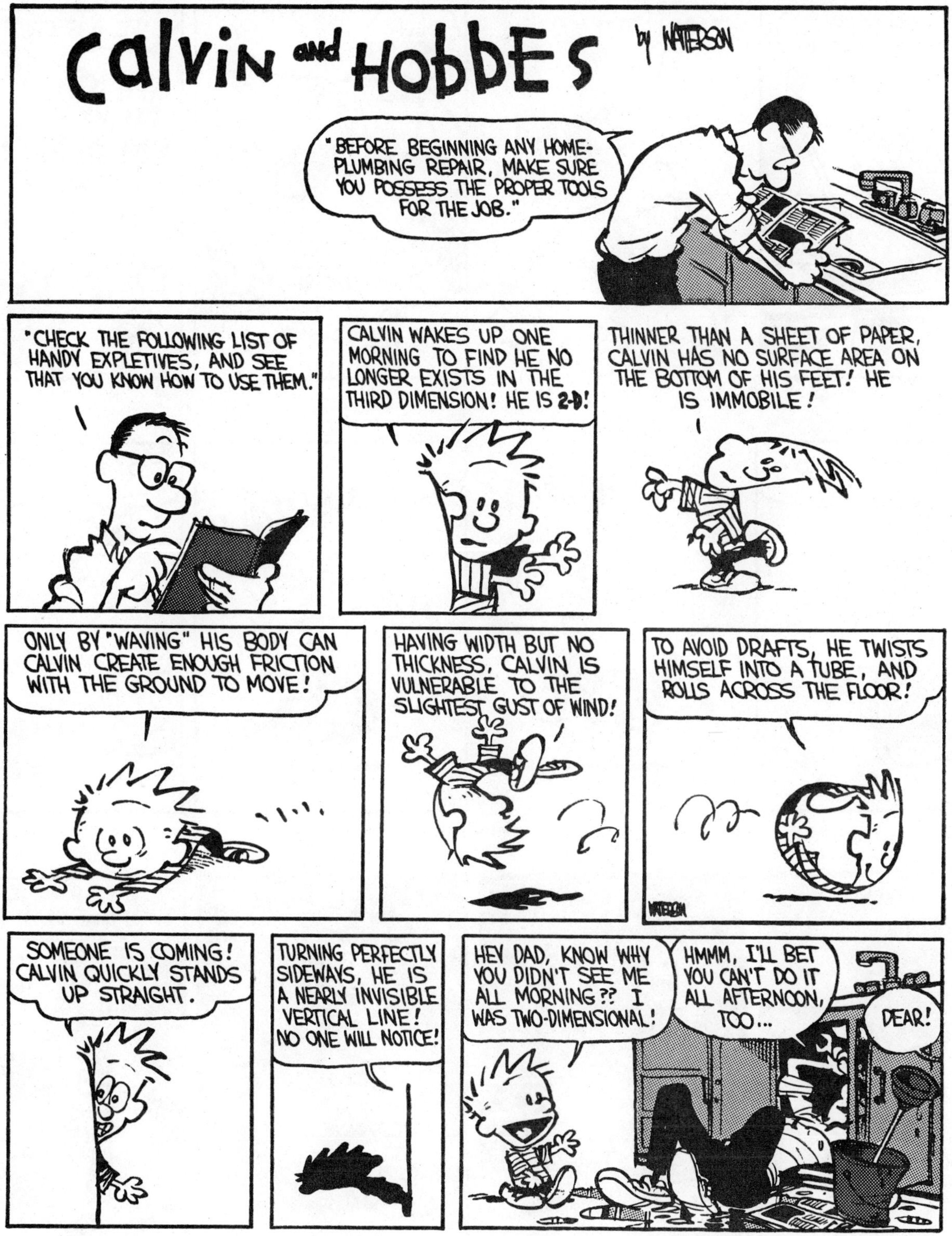
Calvin and HOBBES
by WATTERSON
"BEFORE BEGINNING ANY HOME-PLUMBING REPAIR, MAKE SURE YOU POSSESS THE PROPER TOOLS FOR THE JOB."
"CHECK THE FOLLOWING LIST OF HANDY EXPLETIVES, AND SEE THAT YOU KNOW HOW TO USE THEM."
CALVIN WAKES UP ONE MORNING TO FIND HE NO LONGER EXISTS IN THE THIRD DIMENSION! HE IS 2-D!
THINNER THAN A SHEET OF PAPER, CALVIN HAS NO SURFACE AREA ON THE BOTTOM OF HIS FEET! HE IS IMMOBILE!
ONLY BY "WAVING" HIS BODY CAN CALVIN CREATE ENOUGH FRICTION WITH THE GROUND TO MOVE!
HAVING WIDTH BUT NO THICKNESS, CALVIN IS VULNERABLE TO THE SLIGHTEST GUST OF WIND!
TO AVOID DRAFTS, HE TWISTS HIMSELF INTO A TUBE, AND ROLLS ACROSS THE FLOOR!
WATTERSON
SOMEONE IS COMING! CALVIN QUICKLY STANDS UP STRAIGHT.
TURNING PERFECTLY SIDEWAYS, HE IS A NEARLY INVISIBLE VERTICAL LINE! NO ONE WILL NOTICE!
HEY DAD, KNOW WHY YOU DIDN'T SEE ME ALL MORNING?? I WAS TWO-DIMENSIONAL!
HMMM, I'LL BET YOU CAN'T DO IT ALL AFTERNOON, TOO...
DEAR!

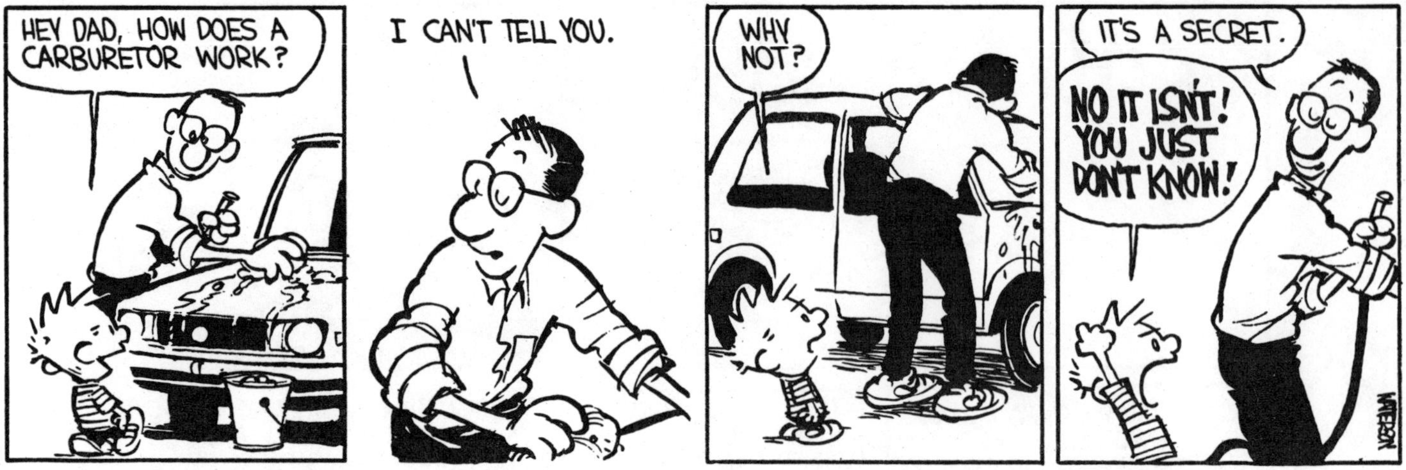
HEY DAD, HOW DOES A CARBURETOR WORK?
I CAN'T TELL YOU.
WHY NOT?
IT'S A SECRET.
NO IT ISN'T! YOU JUST DON'T KNOW!

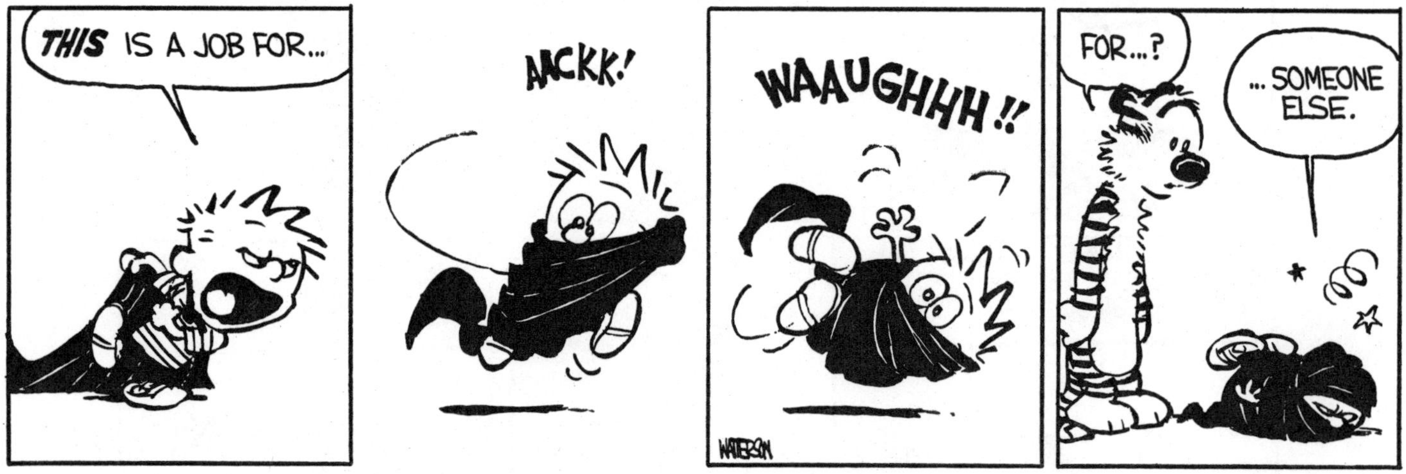
THIS IS A JOB FOR...
AACKK!
WAAUGHHH!!
FOR...?
...SOMEONE ELSE.

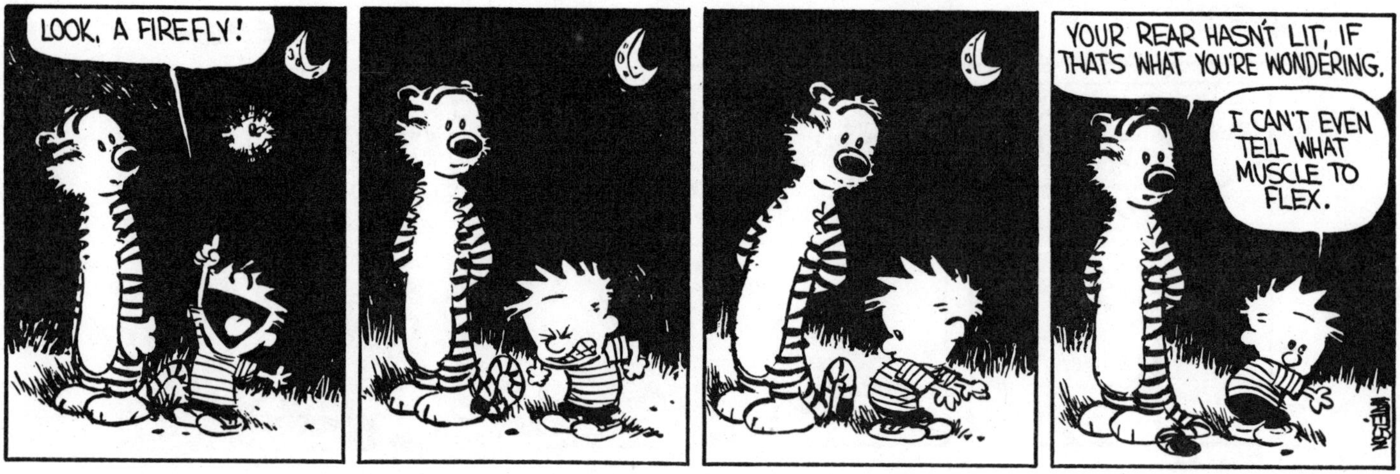
LOOK, A FIREFLY!
YOUR REAR HASN'T LIT, IF THAT'S WHAT YOU'RE WONDERING.
I CAN'T EVEN TELL WHAT MUSCLE TO FLEX.

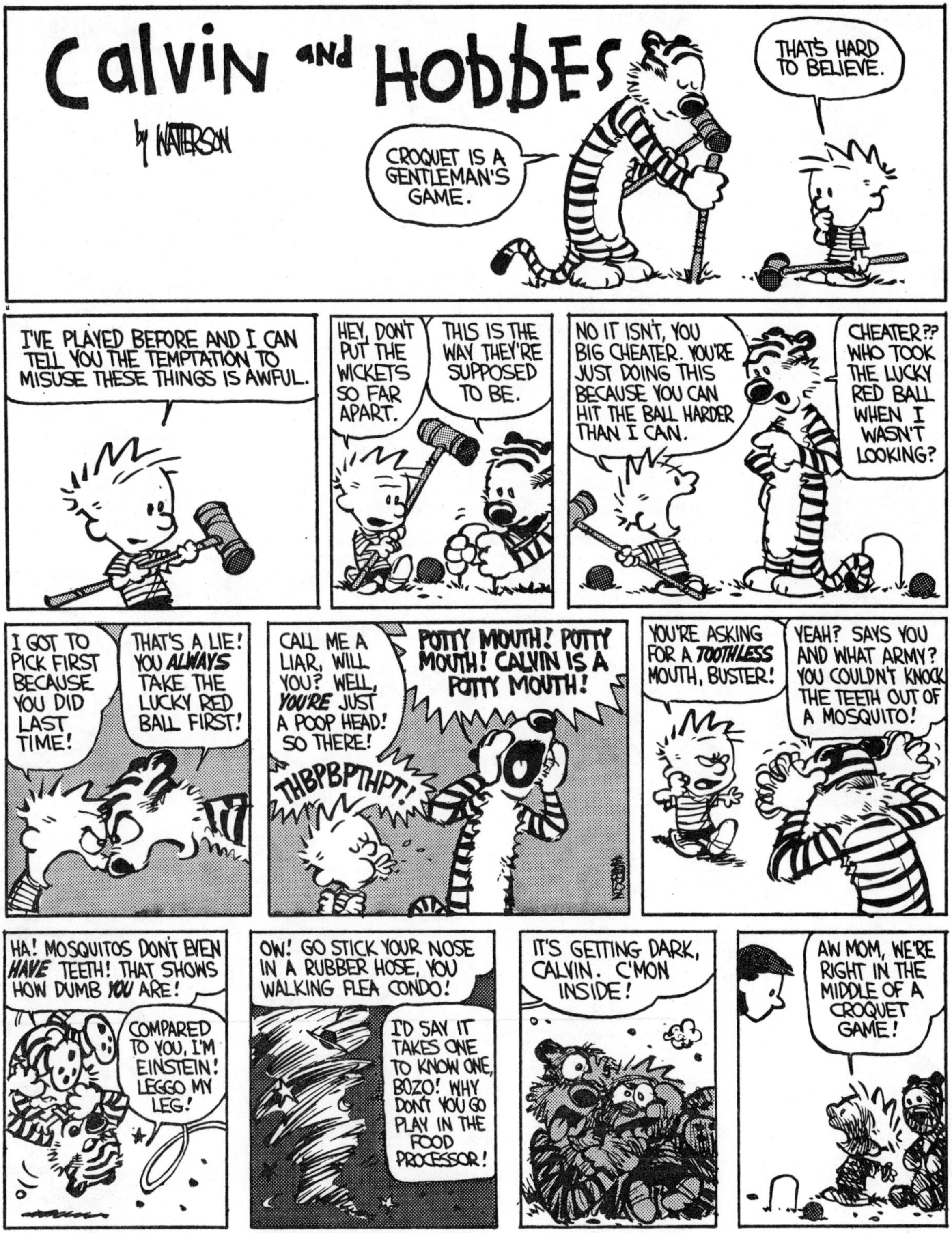
Calvin and HOBBES
by WATTERSON
CROQUET IS A GENTLEMAN'S GAME.
THAT'S HARD TO BELIEVE.
I'VE PLAYED BEFORE AND I CAN TELL YOU THE TEMPTATION TO MISUSE THESE THINGS IS AWFUL.
HEY, DON'T PUT THE WICKETS SO FAR APART.
THIS IS THE WAY THEY'RE SUPPOSED TO BE.
NO IT ISN'T, YOU BIG CHEATER. YOU'RE JUST DOING THIS BECAUSE YOU CAN HIT THE BALL HARDER THAN I CAN.
CHEATER?? WHO TOOK THE LUCKY RED BALL WHEN I WASN'T LOOKING?
I GOT TO PICK FIRST BECAUSE YOU DID LAST TIME!
THAT'S A LIE! YOU ALWAYS TAKE THE LUCKY RED BALL FIRST!
CALL ME A LIAR, WILL YOU? WELL, YOU'RE JUST A POOP HEAD! SO THERE!
THBPBPTHPT!
POTTY MOUTH! POTTY MOUTH! CALVIN IS A POTTY MOUTH!
YOU'RE ASKING FOR A TOOTHLESS MOUTH, BUSTER!
YEAH? SAYS YOU AND WHAT ARMY? YOU COULDN'T KNOCK THE TEETH OUT OF A MOSQUITO!
HA! MOSQUITOS DON'T EVEN HAVE TEETH! THAT SHOWS HOW DUMB YOU ARE!
COMPARED TO YOU, I'M EINSTEIN! LEGGO MY LEG!
OW! GO STICK YOUR NOSE IN A RUBBER HOSE, YOU WALKING FLEA CONDO!
I'D SAY IT TAKES ONE TO KNOW ONE, BOZO! WHY DON'T YOU GO PLAY IN THE FOOD PROCESSOR!
IT'S GETTING DARK, CALVIN. C'MON INSIDE!
AW MOM, WE'RE RIGHT IN THE MIDDLE OF A CROQUET GAME!

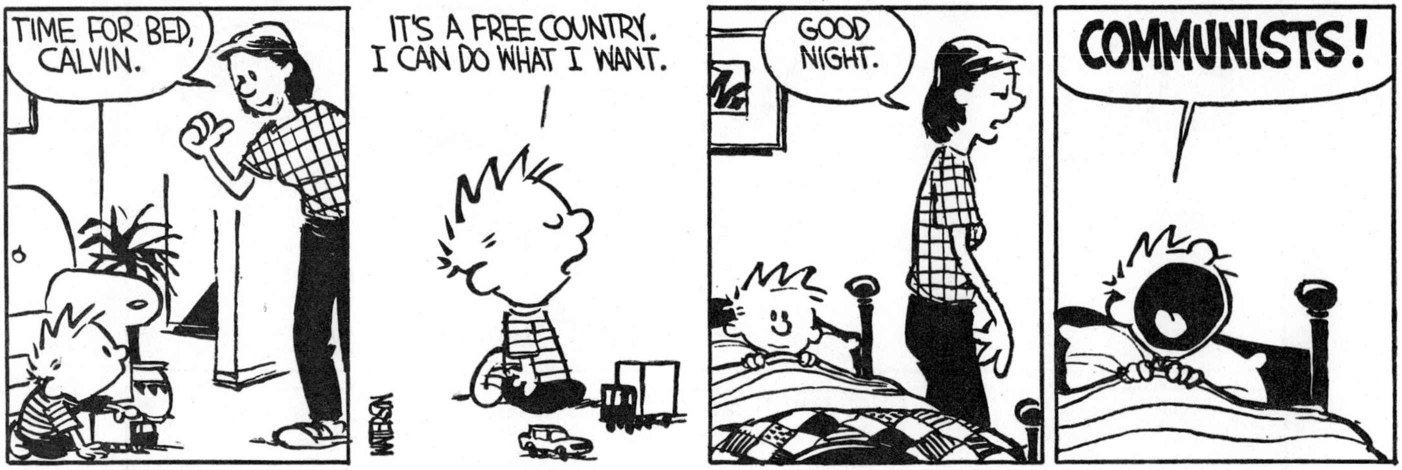
TIME FOR BED, CALVIN.
IT'S A FREE COUNTRY. I CAN DO WHAT I WANT.
GOOD NIGHT.
COMMUNISTS!

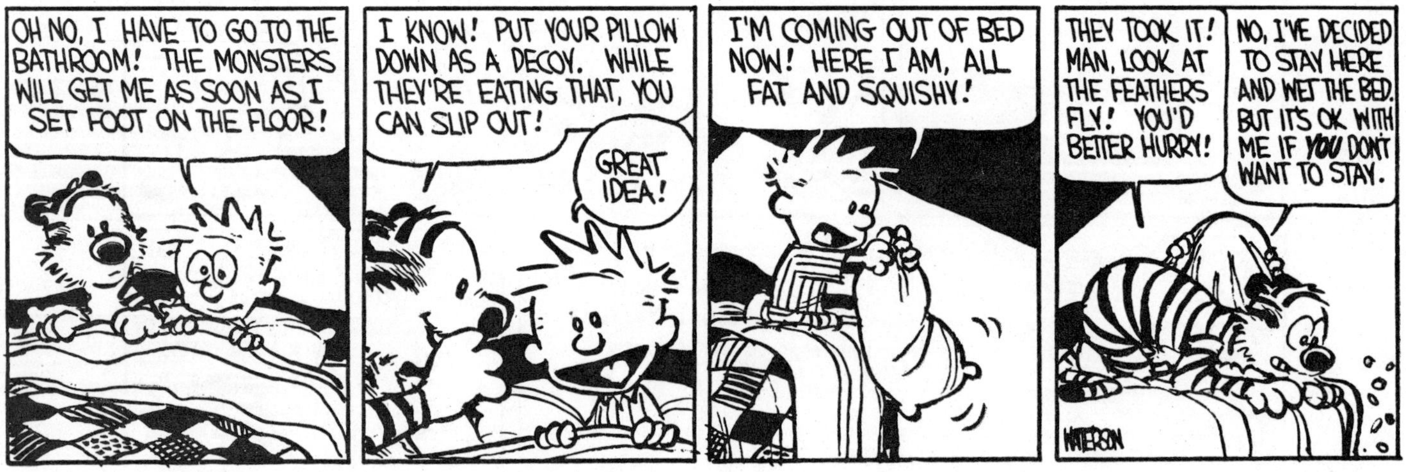
OH NO, I HAVE TO GO TO THE BATHROOM! THE MONSTERS WILL GET ME AS SOON AS I SET FOOT ON THE FLOOR!
I KNOW! PUT YOUR PILLOW DOWN AS A DECOY. WHILE THEY'RE EATING THAT, YOU CAN SLIP OUT!
GREAT IDEA!
I'M COMING OUT OF BED NOW! HERE I AM, ALL FAT AND SQUISHY!
THEY TOOK IT! MAN, LOOK AT THE FEATHERS FLY! YOU'D BETTER HURRY!
NO, I'VE DECIDED TO STAY HERE AND WET THE BED. BUT IT'S OK WITH ME IF YOU DON'T WANT TO STAY.

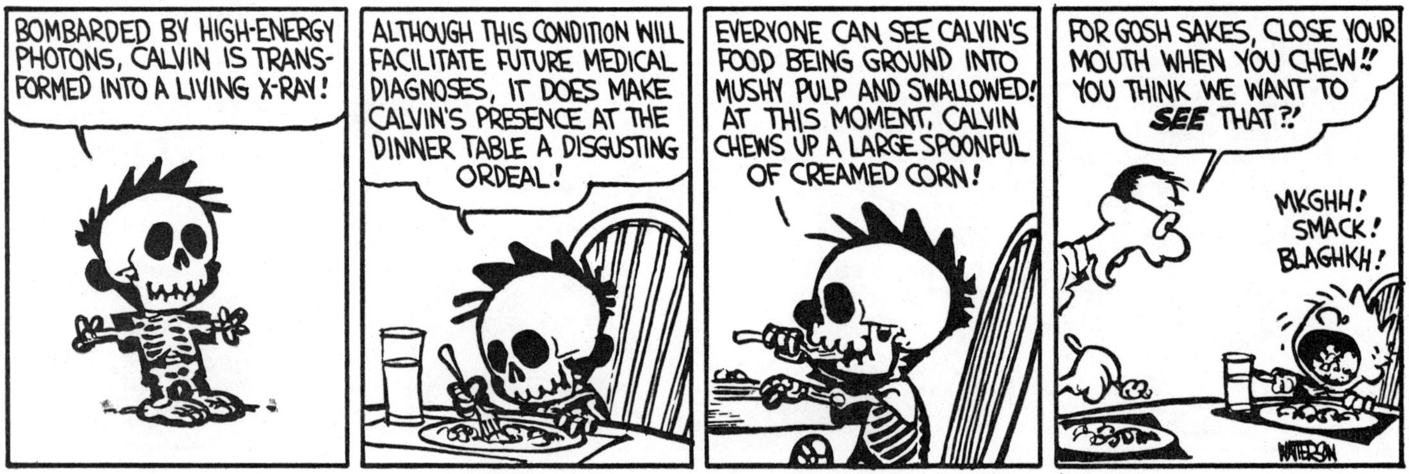
BOMBARDED BY HIGH-ENERGY PHOTONS, CALVIN IS TRANSFORMED INTO A LIVING X-RAY!
ALTHOUGH THIS CONDITION WILL FACILITATE FUTURE MEDICAL DIAGNOSES, IT DOES MAKE CALVIN'S PRESENCE AT THE DINNER TABLE A DISGUSTING ORDEAL!
EVERYONE CAN SEE CALVIN'S FOOD BEING GROUND INTO MUSHY PULP AND SWALLOWED! AT THIS MOMENT, CALVIN CHEWS UP A LARGE SPOONFUL OF CREAMED CORN!
FOR GOSH SAKES, CLOSE YOUR MOUTH WHEN YOU CHEW!! YOU THINK WE WANT TO SEE THAT?!
MKGHH! SMACK! BLAGHKH!

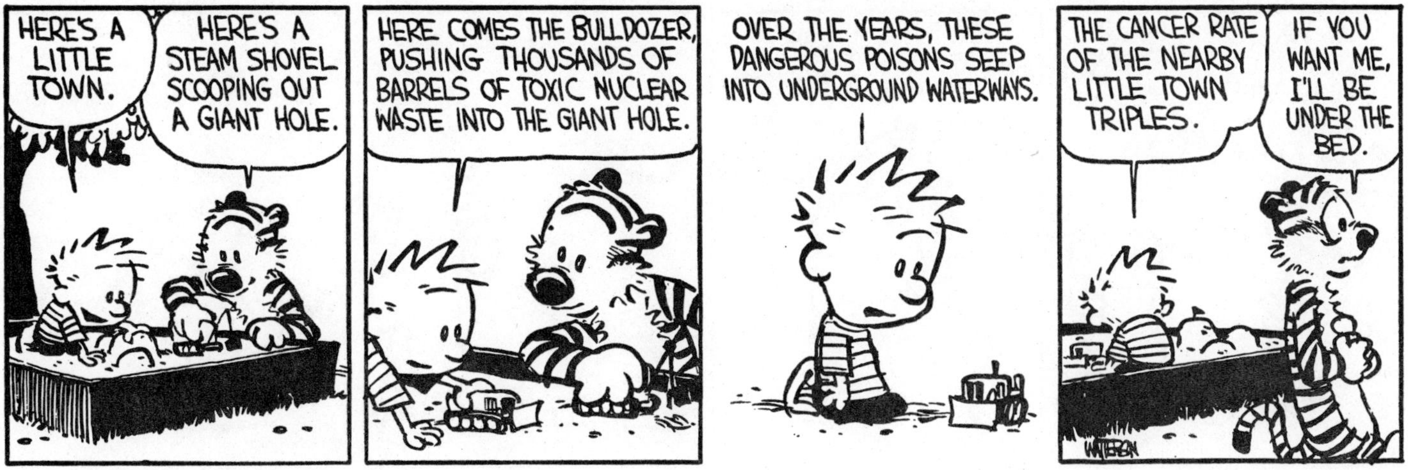
HERE'S A LITTLE TOWN.
HERE'S A STEAM SHOVEL SCOOPING OUT A GIANT HOLE.
HERE COMES THE BULLDOZER, PUSHING THOUSANDS OF BARRELS OF TOXIC NUCLEAR WASTE INTO THE GIANT HOLE.
OVER THE YEARS, THESE DANGEROUS POISONS SEEP INTO UNDERGROUND WATERWAYS.
THE CANCER RATE OF THE NEARBY LITTLE TOWN TRIPLES.
IF YOU WANT ME, I'LL BE UNDER THE BED.

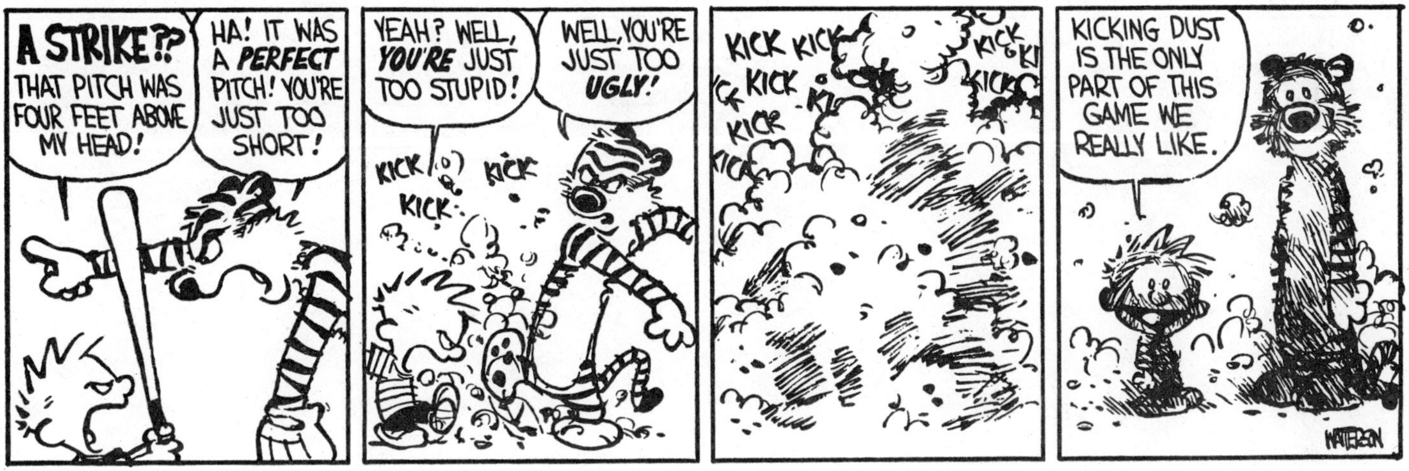
A STRIKE?!? THAT PITCH WAS FOUR FEET ABOVE MY HEAD!
HA! IT WAS A ***PERFECT*** PITCH! YOU'RE JUST TOO SHORT!
YEAH? WELL, ***YOU'RE*** JUST TOO STUPID!
WELL, YOU'RE JUST TOO ***UGLY!***
KICK KICK KICK
KICK KICK KICK KICK KICK
KICKING DUST IS THE ONLY PART OF THIS GAME WE REALLY LIKE.

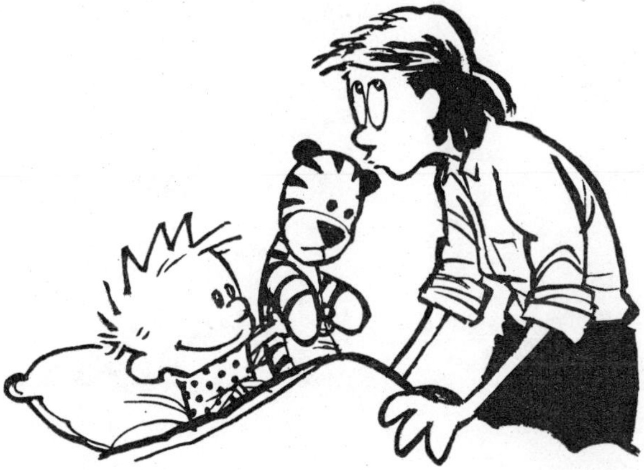

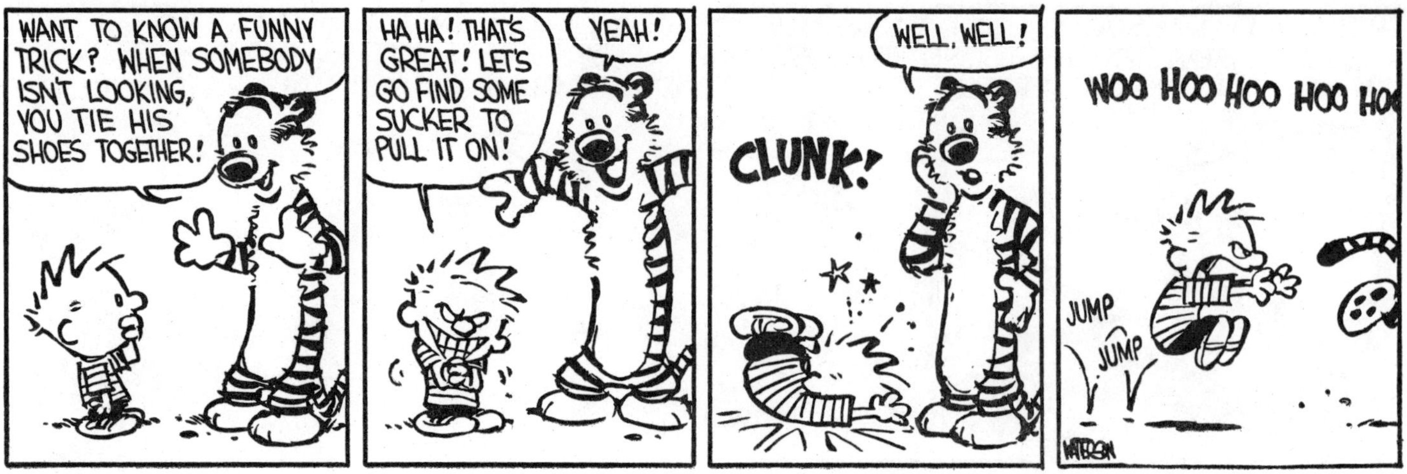
WANT TO KNOW A FUNNY TRICK? WHEN SOMEBODY ISN'T LOOKING, YOU TIE HIS SHOES TOGETHER!
HA HA! THAT'S GREAT! LET'S GO FIND SOME SUCKER TO PULL IT ON!
YEAH!
WELL, WELL!
CLUNK!
WOO HOO HOO HOO HO
JUMP
JUMP

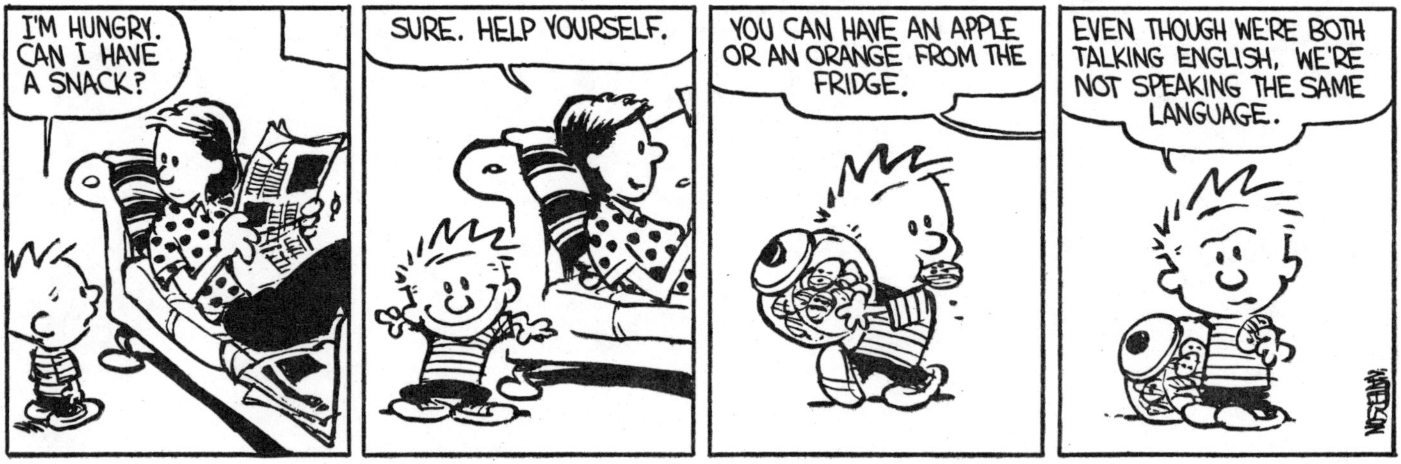
I'M HUNGRY. CAN I HAVE A SNACK?
SURE. HELP YOURSELF.
YOU CAN HAVE AN APPLE OR AN ORANGE FROM THE FRIDGE.
EVEN THOUGH WE'RE BOTH TALKING ENGLISH, WE'RE NOT SPEAKING THE SAME LANGUAGE.

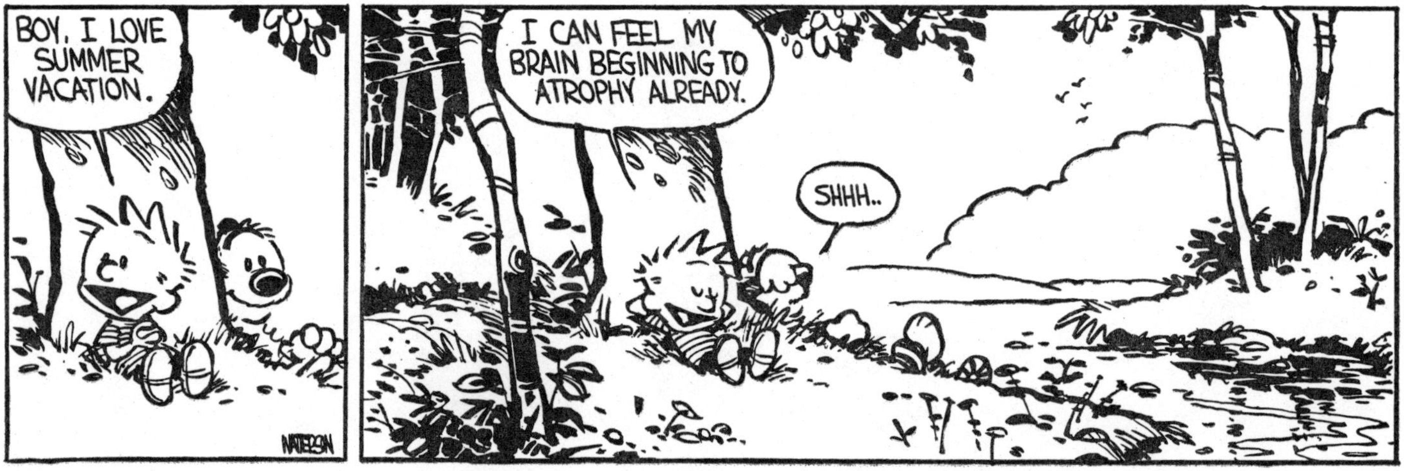
BOY, I LOVE SUMMER VACATION.
I CAN FEEL MY BRAIN BEGINNING TO ATROPHY ALREADY.
SHHH..

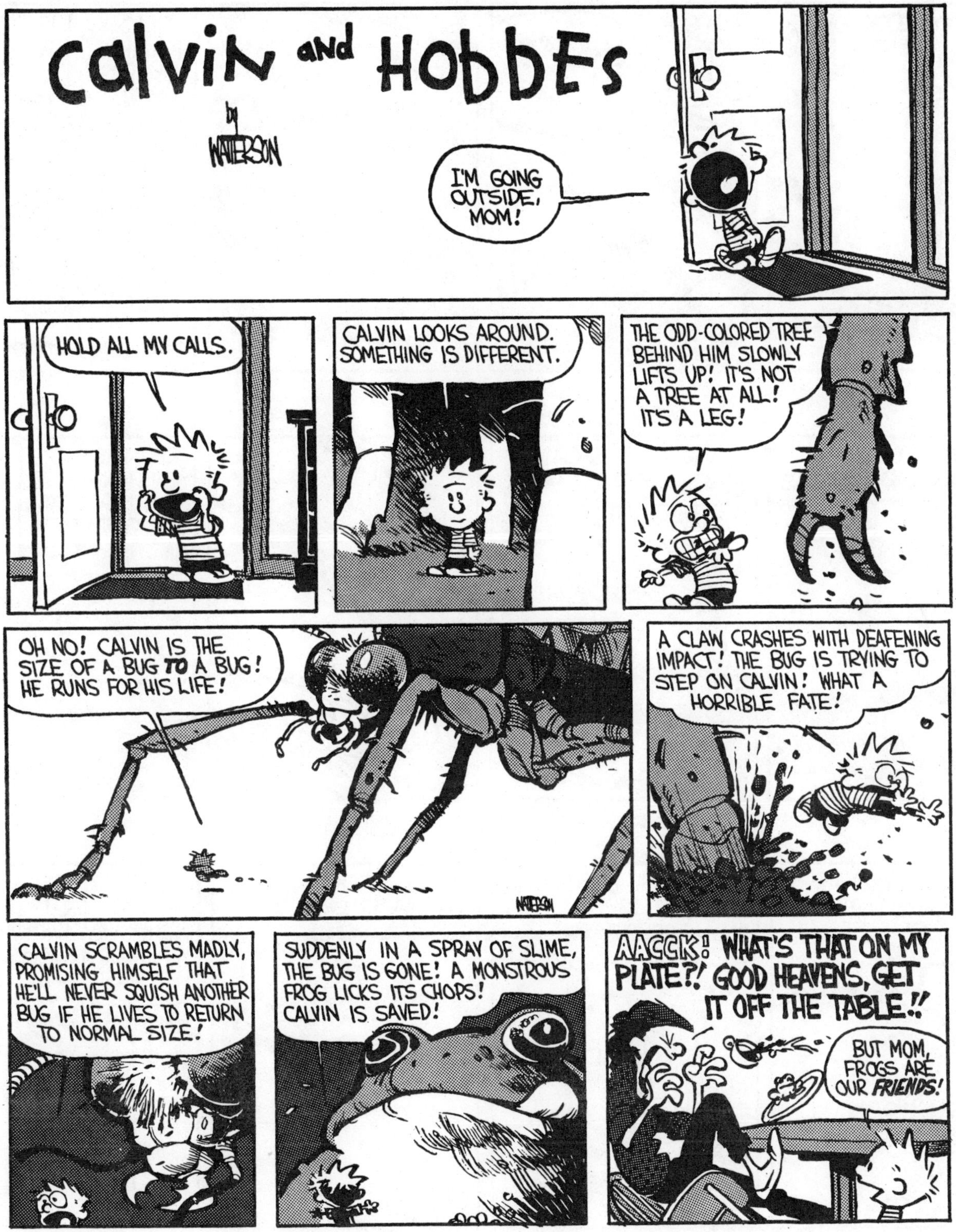
Calvin and HOBBES
by WATTERSON
I'M GOING OUTSIDE, MOM!
HOLD ALL MY CALLS.
CALVIN LOOKS AROUND. SOMETHING IS DIFFERENT.
THE ODD-COLORED TREE BEHIND HIM SLOWLY LIFTS UP! IT'S NOT A TREE AT ALL! IT'S A LEG!
OH NO! CALVIN IS THE SIZE OF A BUG TO A BUG! HE RUNS FOR HIS LIFE!
WATTERSON
A CLAW CRASHES WITH DEAFENING IMPACT! THE BUG IS TRYING TO STEP ON CALVIN! WHAT A HORRIBLE FATE!
CALVIN SCRAMBLES MADLY, PROMISING HIMSELF THAT HE'LL NEVER SQUISH ANOTHER BUG IF HE LIVES TO RETURN TO NORMAL SIZE!
SUDDENLY IN A SPRAY OF SLIME, THE BUG IS GONE! A MONSTROUS FROG LICKS ITS CHOPS! CALVIN IS SAVED!
AACCK! WHAT'S THAT ON MY PLATE?! GOOD HEAVENS, GET IT OFF THE TABLE!!
BUT MOM, FROGS ARE OUR FRIENDS!

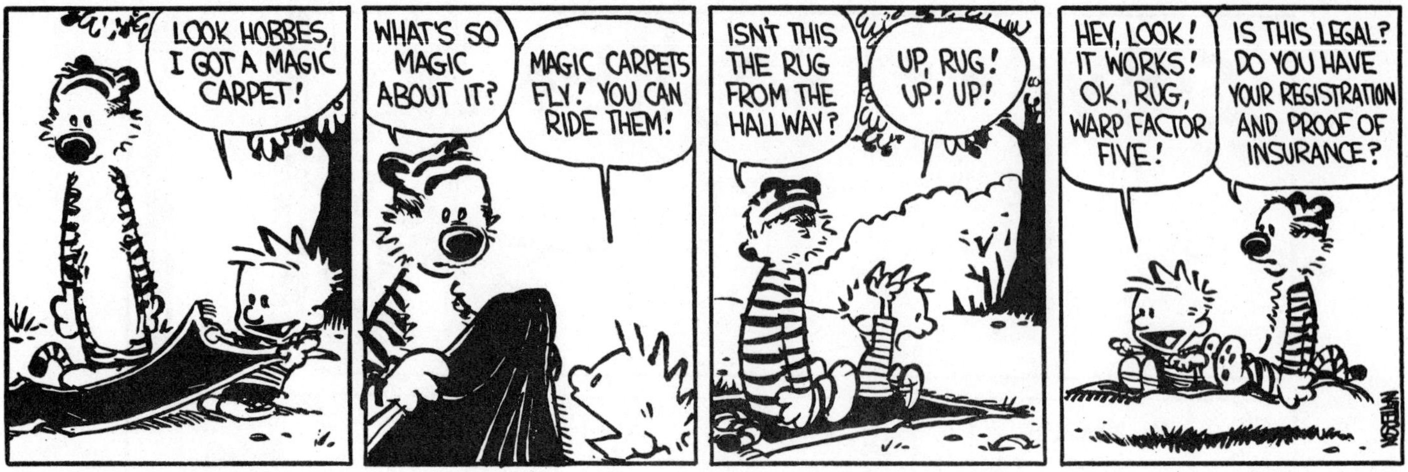
LOOK HOBBES, I GOT A MAGIC CARPET!
WHAT'S SO MAGIC ABOUT IT?
MAGIC CARPETS FLY! YOU CAN RIDE THEM!
ISN'T THIS THE RUG FROM THE HALLWAY?
UP, RUG! UP! UP!
HEY, LOOK! IT WORKS! OK, RUG, WARP FACTOR FIVE!
IS THIS LEGAL? DO YOU HAVE YOUR REGISTRATION AND PROOF OF INSURANCE?

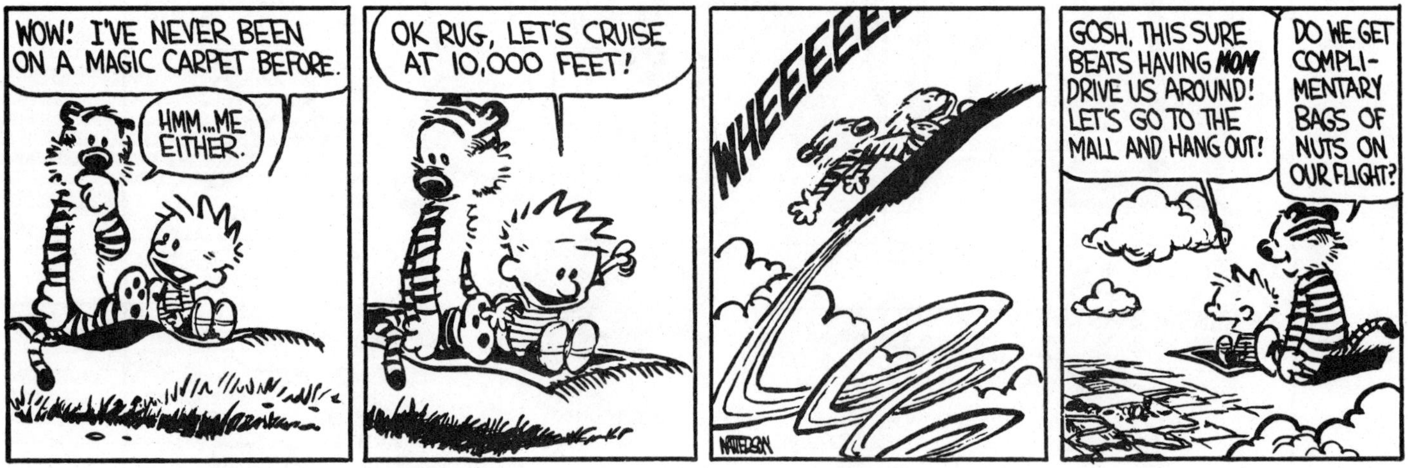
WOW! I'VE NEVER BEEN ON A MAGIC CARPET BEFORE.
HMM...ME EITHER.
OK RUG, LET'S CRUISE AT 10,000 FEET!
WHEEEEEE
GOSH, THIS SURE BEATS HAVING MOM DRIVE US AROUND! LET'S GO TO THE MALL AND HANG OUT!
DO WE GET COMPLIMENTARY BAGS OF NUTS ON OUR FLIGHT?

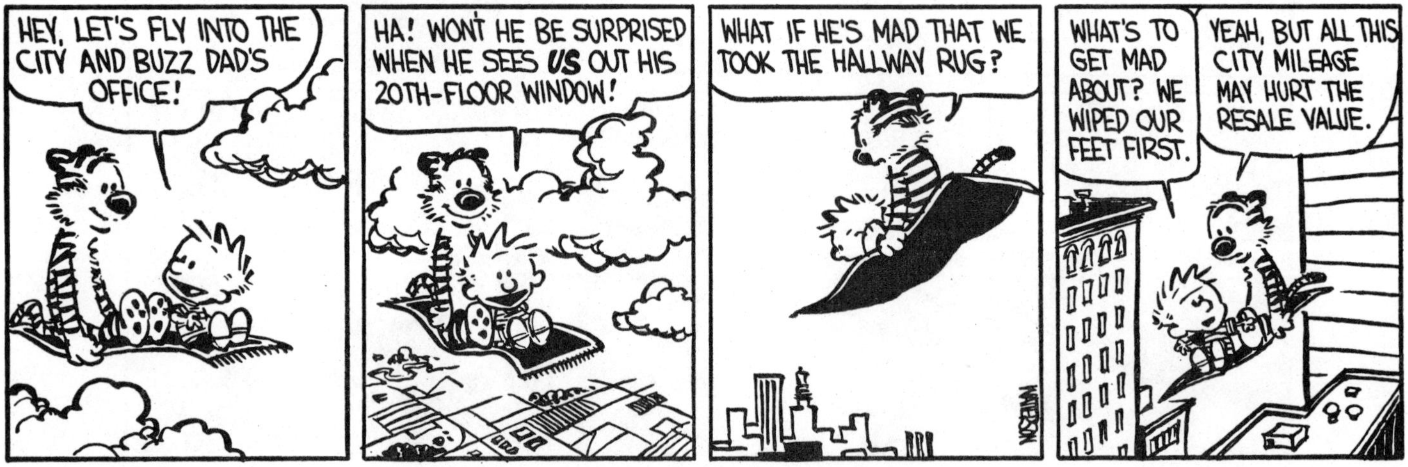
HEY, LET'S FLY INTO THE CITY AND BUZZ DAD'S OFFICE!
HA! WON'T HE BE SURPRISED WHEN HE SEES US OUT HIS 20TH-FLOOR WINDOW!
WHAT IF HE'S MAD THAT WE TOOK THE HALLWAY RUG?
WHAT'S TO GET MAD ABOUT? WE WIPED OUR FEET FIRST.
YEAH, BUT ALL THIS CITY MILEAGE MAY HURT THE RESALE VALUE.

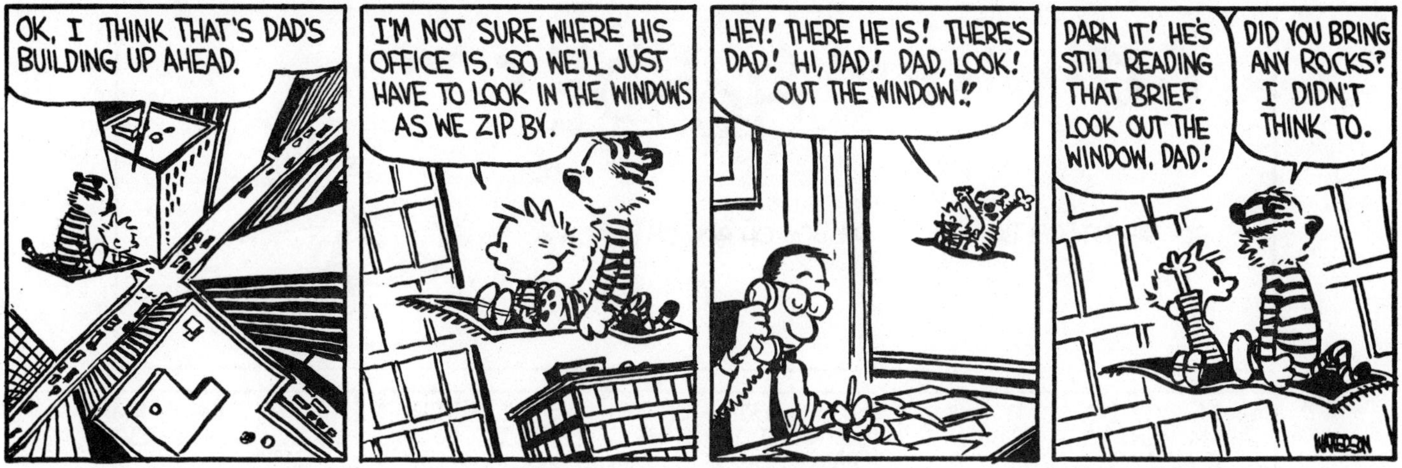
OK, I THINK THAT'S DAD'S BUILDING UP AHEAD.
I'M NOT SURE WHERE HIS OFFICE IS, SO WE'LL JUST HAVE TO LOOK IN THE WINDOWS AS WE ZIP BY.
HEY! THERE HE IS! THERE'S DAD! HI, DAD! DAD, LOOK! OUT THE WINDOW!!
DARN IT! HE'S STILL READING THAT BRIEF. LOOK OUT THE WINDOW, DAD!
DID YOU BRING ANY ROCKS? I DIDN'T THINK TO.

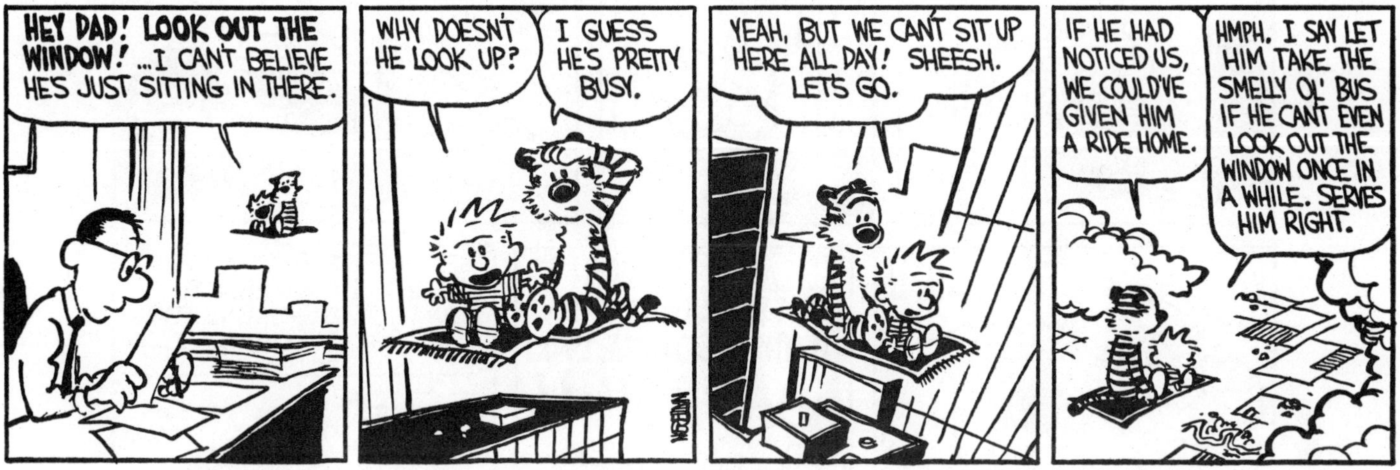
HEY DAD! LOOK OUT THE WINDOW! ...I CAN'T BELIEVE HE'S JUST SITTING IN THERE.
WHY DOESN'T HE LOOK UP?
I GUESS HE'S PRETTY BUSY.
YEAH, BUT WE CAN'T SIT UP HERE ALL DAY! SHEESH. LET'S GO.
IF HE HAD NOTICED US, WE COULD'VE GIVEN HIM A RIDE HOME.
HMPH. I SAY LET HIM TAKE THE SMELLY OL' BUS IF HE CAN'T EVEN LOOK OUT THE WINDOW ONCE IN A WHILE. SERVES HIM RIGHT.

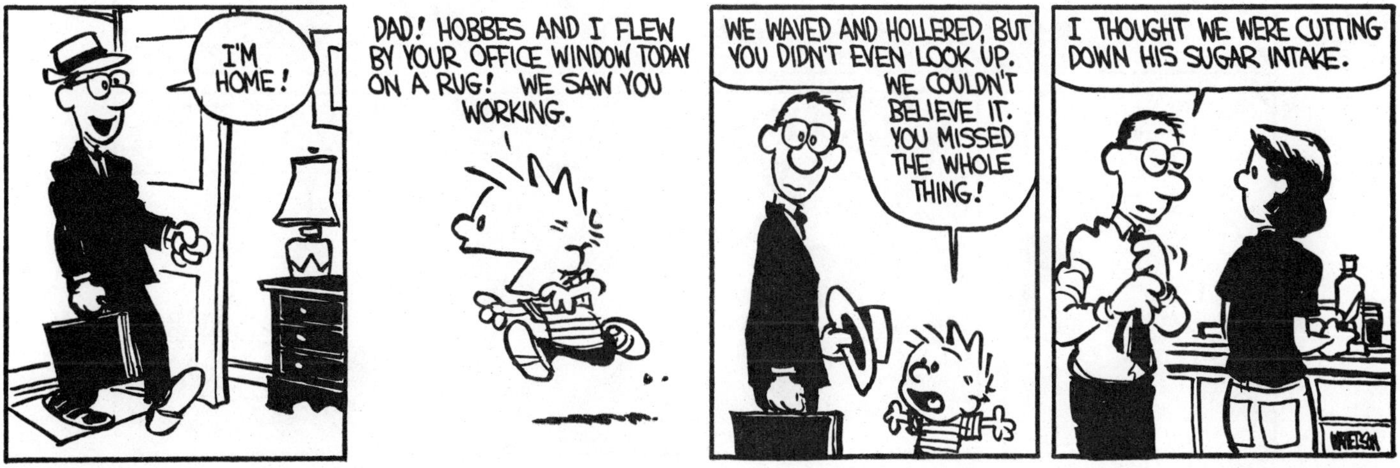
I'M HOME!
DAD! HOBBES AND I FLEW BY YOUR OFFICE WINDOW TODAY ON A RUG! WE SAW YOU WORKING.
WE WAVED AND HOLLERED, BUT YOU DIDN'T EVEN LOOK UP.
WE COULDN'T BELIEVE IT. YOU MISSED THE WHOLE THING!
I THOUGHT WE WERE CUTTING DOWN HIS SUGAR INTAKE.

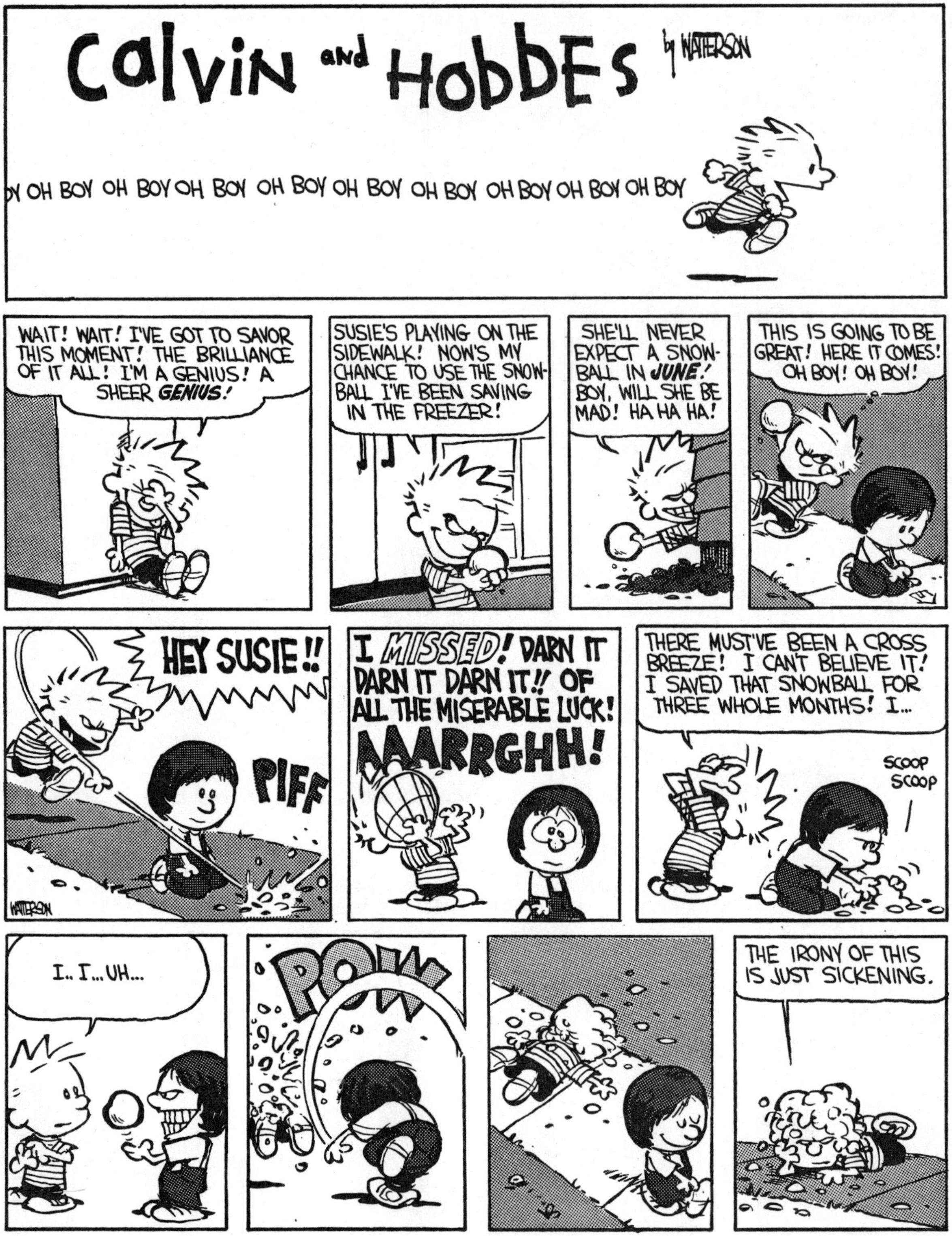
Calvin and Hobbes
by WATTERSON
OY OH BOY OH BOY OH BOY OH BOY OH BOY OH BOY OH BOY OH BOY OH BOY OH BOY
WAIT! WAIT! I'VE GOT TO SAVOR THIS MOMENT! THE BRILLIANCE OF IT ALL! I'M A GENIUS! A SHEER GENIUS!
SUSIE'S PLAYING ON THE SIDEWALK! NOW'S MY CHANCE TO USE THE SNOWBALL I'VE BEEN SAVING IN THE FREEZER!
SHE'LL NEVER EXPECT A SNOWBALL IN JUNE! BOY, WILL SHE BE MAD! HA HA HA!
THIS IS GOING TO BE GREAT! HERE IT COMES! OH BOY! OH BOY!
HEY SUSIE!!
PIFF
WATTERSON
I MISSED! DARN IT DARN IT DARN IT!! OF ALL THE MISERABLE LUCK!
AAARRGHH!
THERE MUST'VE BEEN A CROSS BREEZE! I CAN'T BELIEVE IT! I SAVED THAT SNOWBALL FOR THREE WHOLE MONTHS! I...
SCOOP SCOOP
I.. I... UH...
POW
THE IRONY OF THIS IS JUST SICKENING.

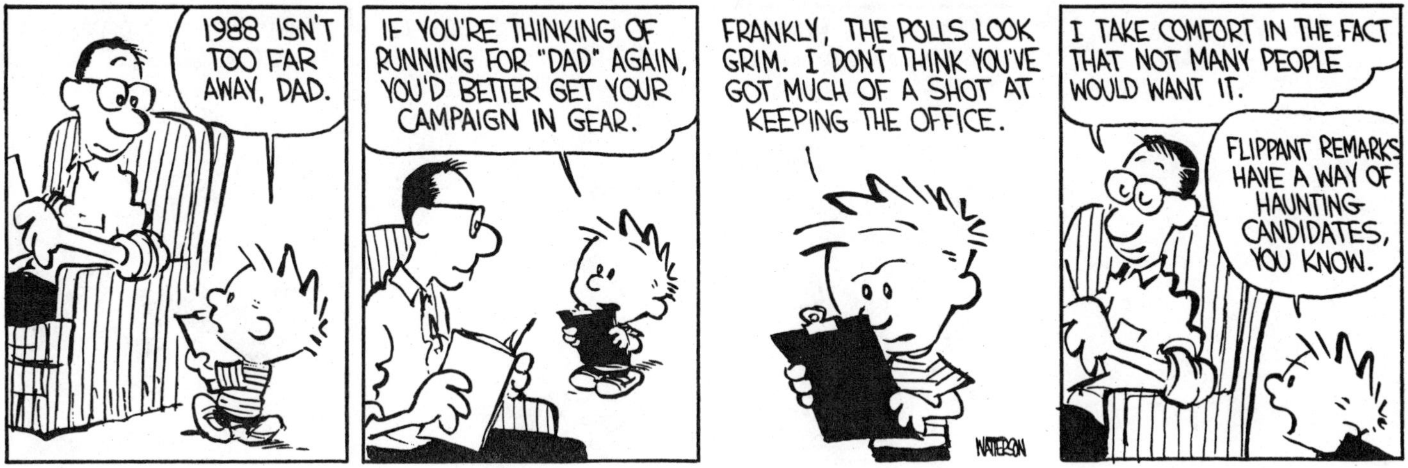
1988 ISN'T TOO FAR AWAY, DAD.
IF YOU'RE THINKING OF RUNNING FOR "DAD" AGAIN, YOU'D BETTER GET YOUR CAMPAIGN IN GEAR.
FRANKLY, THE POLLS LOOK GRIM. I DON'T THINK YOU'VE GOT MUCH OF A SHOT AT KEEPING THE OFFICE.
WATTERSON
I TAKE COMFORT IN THE FACT THAT NOT MANY PEOPLE WOULD WANT IT.
FLIPPANT REMARKS HAVE A WAY OF HAUNTING CANDIDATES, YOU KNOW.

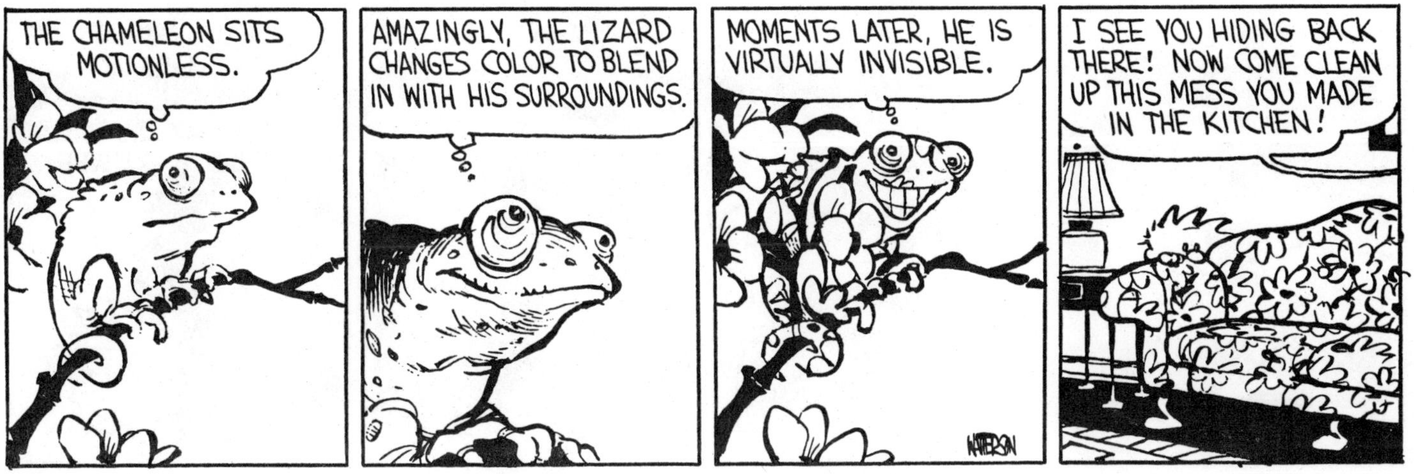
THE CHAMELEON SITS MOTIONLESS.
AMAZINGLY, THE LIZARD CHANGES COLOR TO BLEND IN WITH HIS SURROUNDINGS.
MOMENTS LATER, HE IS VIRTUALLY INVISIBLE.
WATTERSON
I SEE YOU HIDING BACK THERE! NOW COME CLEAN UP THIS MESS YOU MADE IN THE KITCHEN!

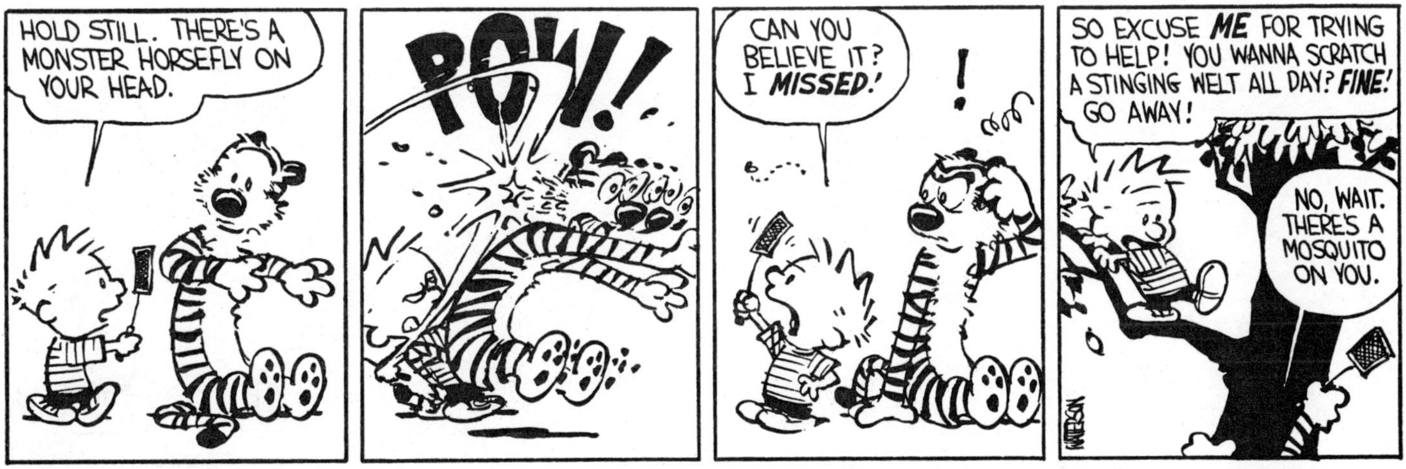
HOLD STILL. THERE'S A MONSTER HORSEFLY ON YOUR HEAD.
POW!!
CAN YOU BELIEVE IT? I *MISSED*!
!
SO EXCUSE *ME* FOR TRYING TO HELP! YOU WANNA SCRATCH A STINGING WELT ALL DAY? *FINE!* GO AWAY!
NO, WAIT. THERE'S A MOSQUITO ON YOU.
WATTERSON

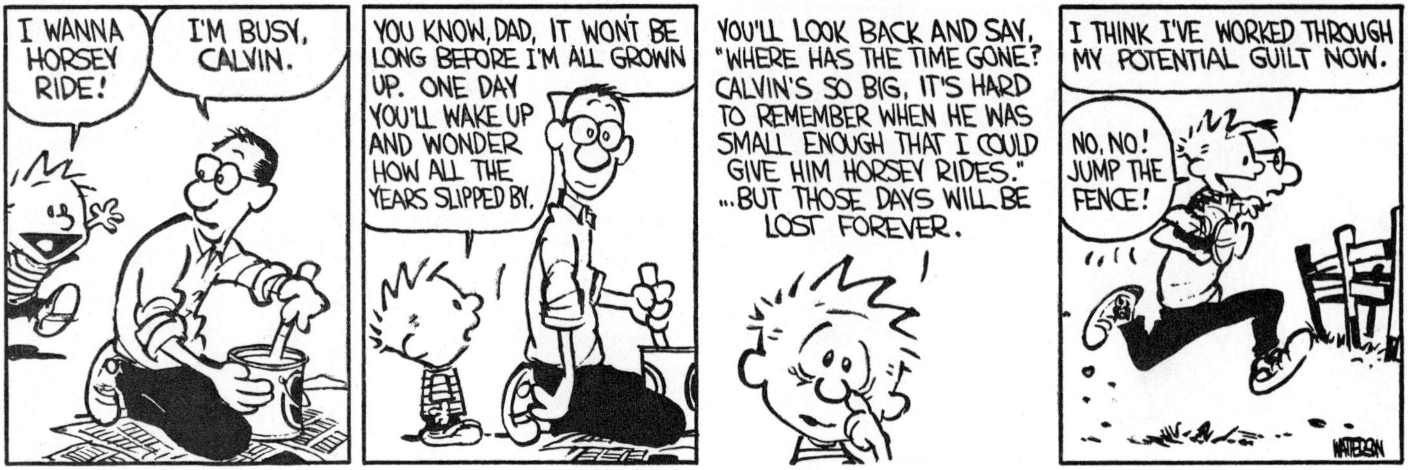
I WANNA HORSEY RIDE!
I'M BUSY, CALVIN.
YOU KNOW, DAD, IT WON'T BE LONG BEFORE I'M ALL GROWN UP. ONE DAY YOU'LL WAKE UP AND WONDER HOW ALL THE YEARS SLIPPED BY.
YOU'LL LOOK BACK AND SAY, "WHERE HAS THE TIME GONE? CALVIN'S SO BIG, IT'S HARD TO REMEMBER WHEN HE WAS SMALL ENOUGH THAT I COULD GIVE HIM HORSEY RIDES." ...BUT THOSE DAYS WILL BE LOST FOREVER.
I THINK I'VE WORKED THROUGH MY POTENTIAL GUILT NOW.
NO, NO! JUMP THE FENCE!
WATTERSON

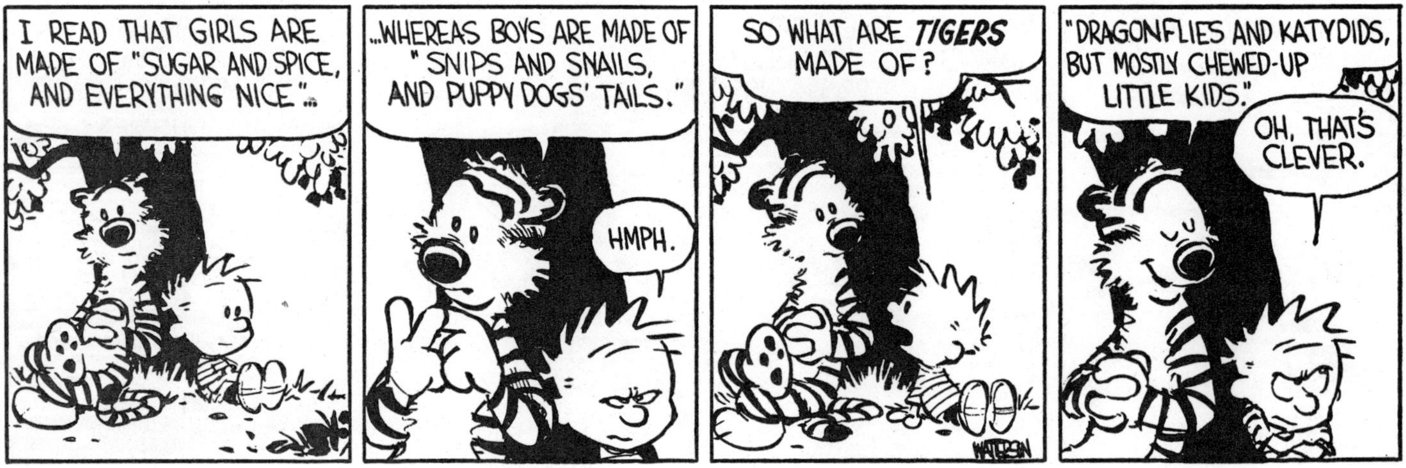
I READ THAT GIRLS ARE MADE OF "SUGAR AND SPICE, AND EVERYTHING NICE"...
...WHEREAS BOYS ARE MADE OF "SNIPS AND SNAILS, AND PUPPY DOGS' TAILS."
HMPH.
SO WHAT ARE *TIGERS* MADE OF?
WATTERSON
"DRAGONFLIES AND KATYDIDS, BUT MOSTLY CHEWED-UP LITTLE KIDS."
OH, THAT'S CLEVER.

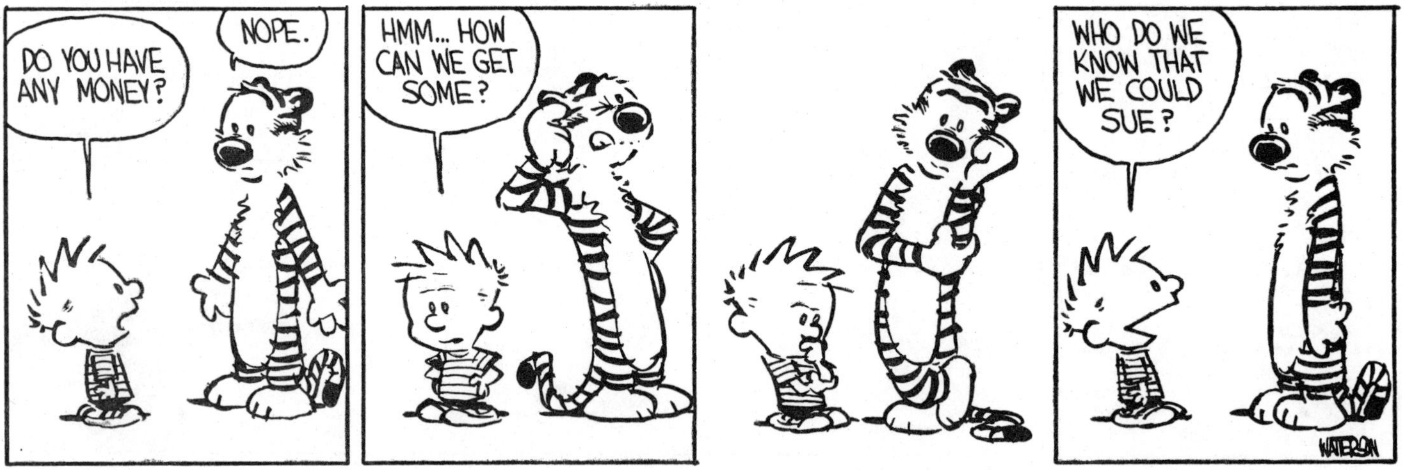
DO YOU HAVE ANY MONEY?
NOPE.
HMM... HOW CAN WE GET SOME?
WHO DO WE KNOW THAT WE COULD SUE?
WATTERSON

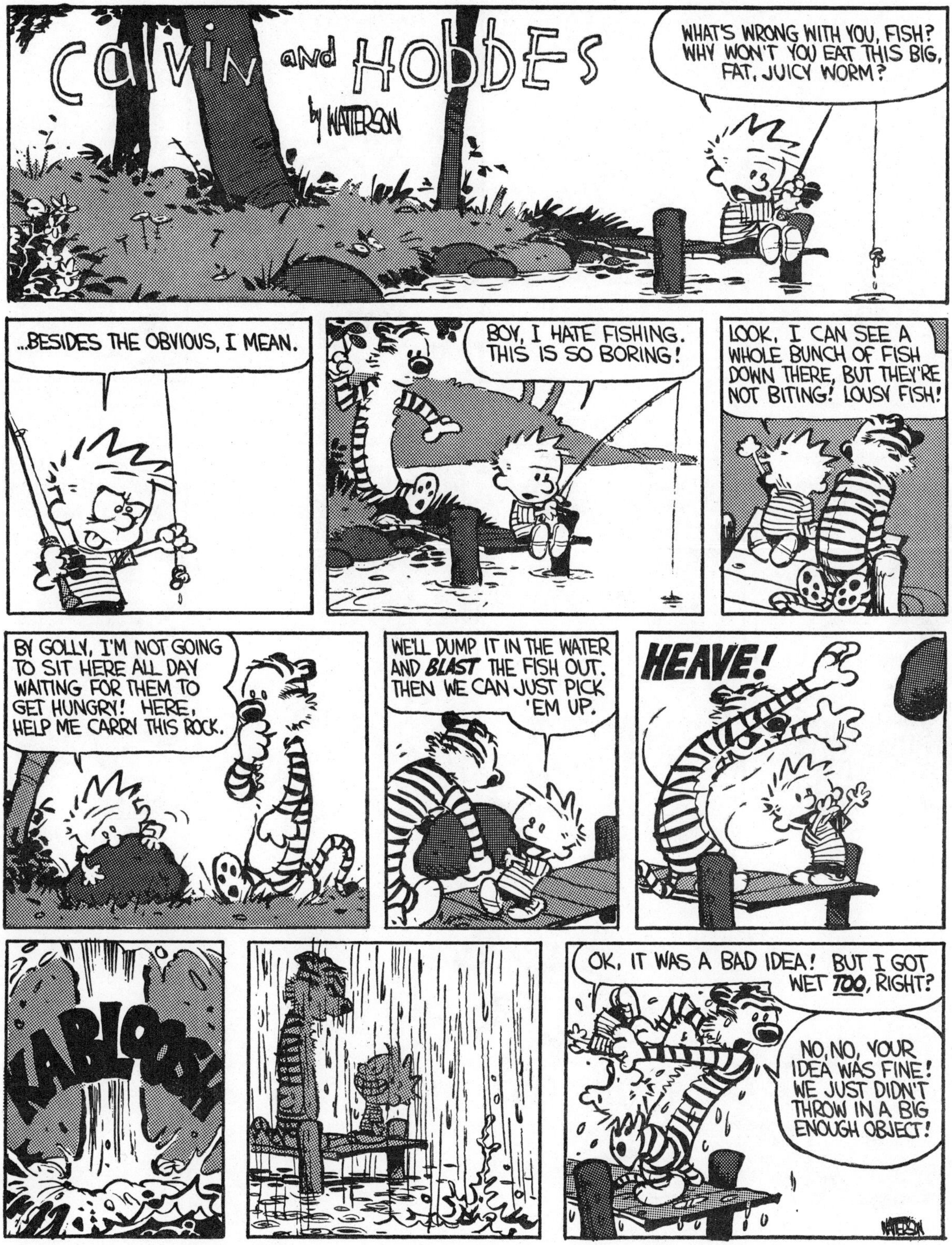
Calvin and HOBBES
by WATTERSON
WHAT'S WRONG WITH YOU, FISH? WHY WON'T YOU EAT THIS BIG, FAT, JUICY WORM?
...BESIDES THE OBVIOUS, I MEAN.
BOY, I HATE FISHING. THIS IS SO BORING!
LOOK, I CAN SEE A WHOLE BUNCH OF FISH DOWN THERE, BUT THEY'RE NOT BITING! LOUSY FISH!
BY GOLLY, I'M NOT GOING TO SIT HERE ALL DAY WAITING FOR THEM TO GET HUNGRY! HERE, HELP ME CARRY THIS ROCK.
WE'LL DUMP IT IN THE WATER AND BLAST THE FISH OUT. THEN WE CAN JUST PICK 'EM UP.
HEAVE!
KABLOOSH
OK, IT WAS A BAD IDEA! BUT I GOT WET TOO, RIGHT?
NO, NO, YOUR IDEA WAS FINE! WE JUST DIDN'T THROW IN A BIG ENOUGH OBJECT!
WATTERSON

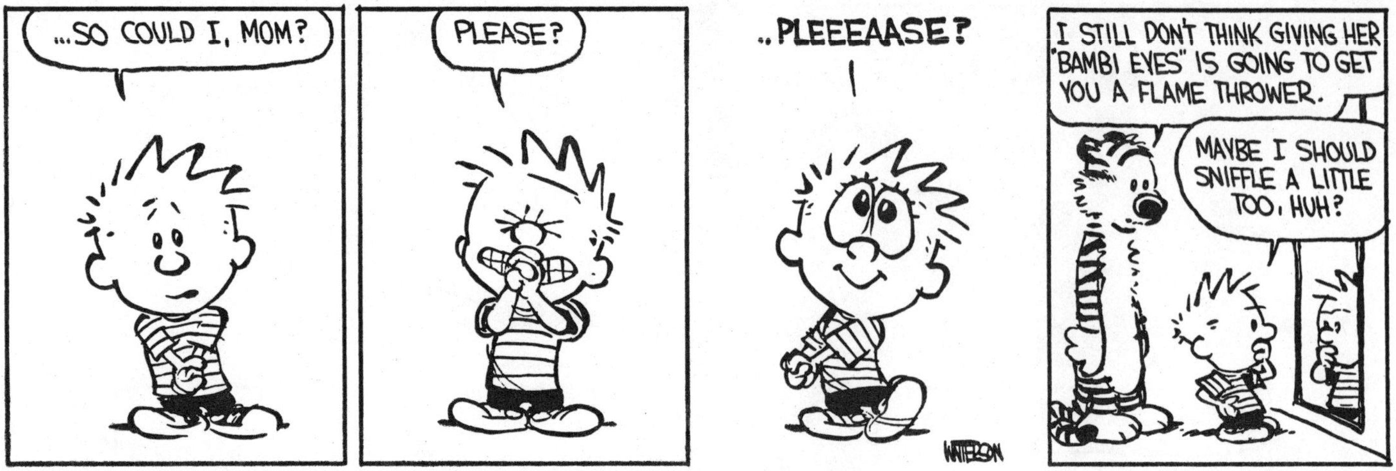
...SO COULD I, MOM?
PLEASE?
..PLEEEAASE?
I STILL DON'T THINK GIVING HER "BAMBI EYES" IS GOING TO GET YOU A FLAME THROWER.
MAYBE I SHOULD SNIFFLE A LITTLE TOO, HUH?

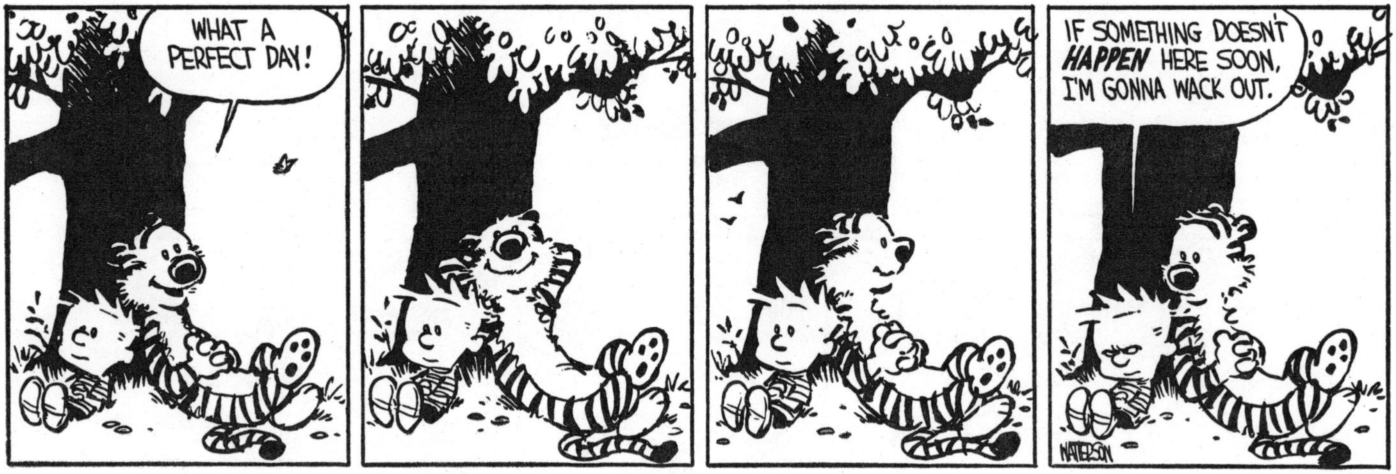
WHAT A PERFECT DAY!
IF SOMETHING DOESN'T HAPPEN HERE SOON, I'M GONNA WACK OUT.

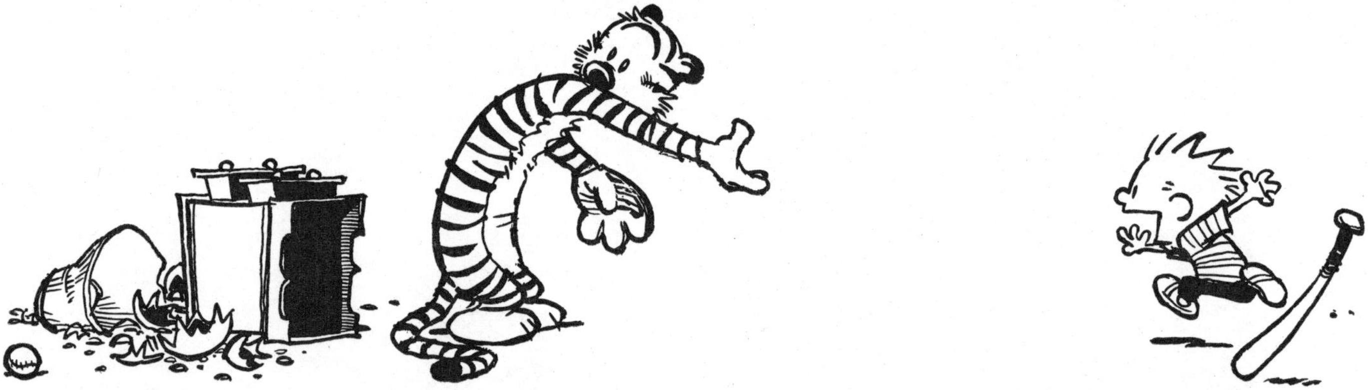

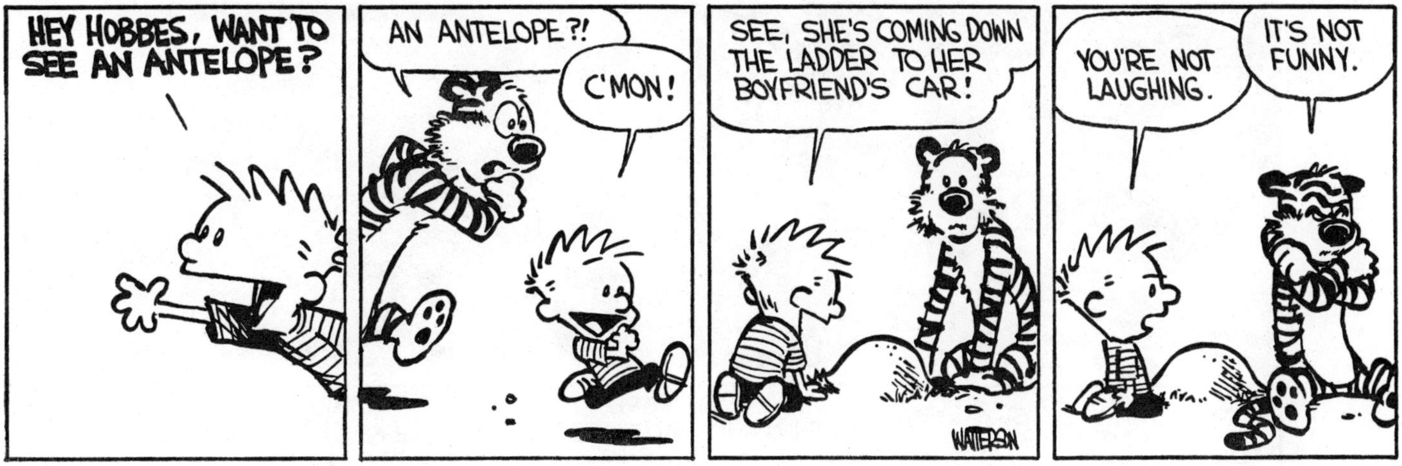
HEY HOBBES, WANT TO SEE AN ANTELOPE?
AN ANTELOPE?!
C'MON!
SEE, SHE'S COMING DOWN THE LADDER TO HER BOYFRIEND'S CAR!
WATTERSON
YOU'RE NOT LAUGHING.
IT'S NOT FUNNY.

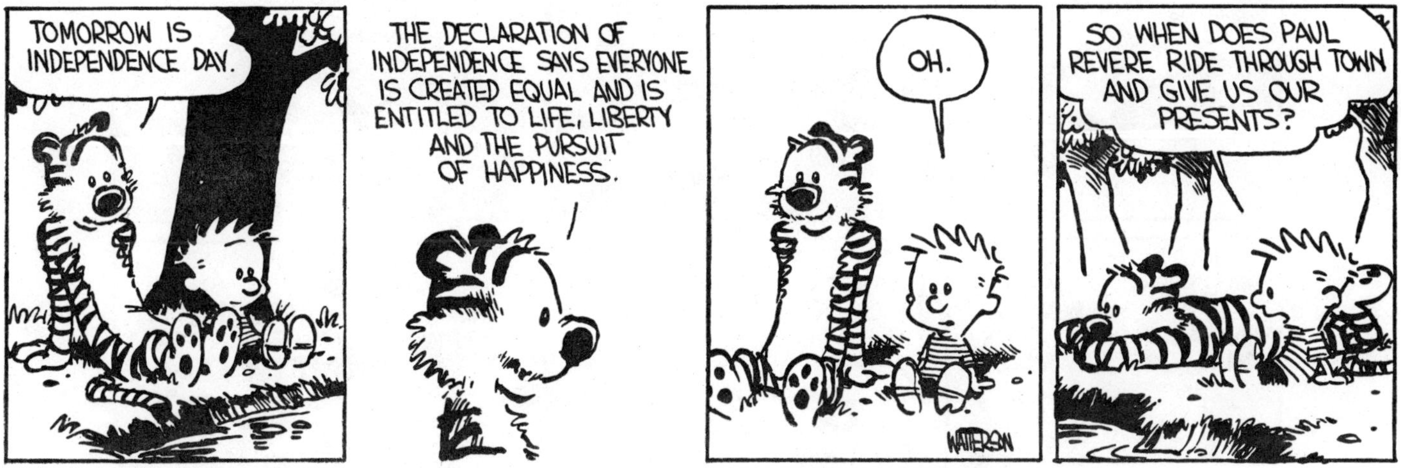
TOMORROW IS INDEPENDENCE DAY.
THE DECLARATION OF INDEPENDENCE SAYS EVERYONE IS CREATED EQUAL AND IS ENTITLED TO LIFE, LIBERTY AND THE PURSUIT OF HAPPINESS.
OH.
WATTERSON
SO WHEN DOES PAUL REVERE RIDE THROUGH TOWN AND GIVE US OUR PRESENTS?

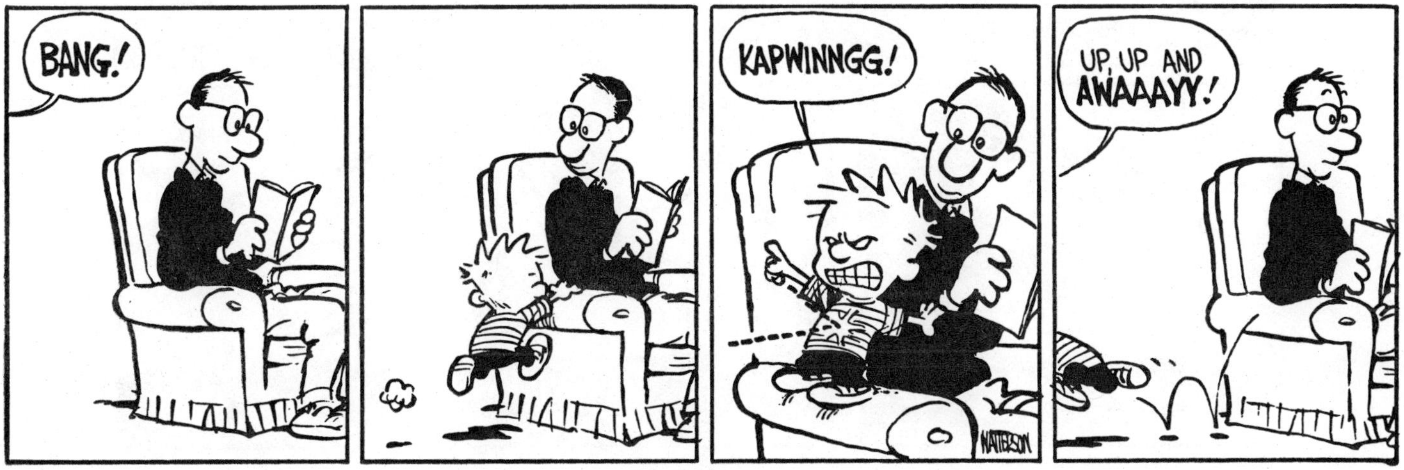
BANG!
KAPWINNGG!
WATTERSON
UP, UP AND AWAAAYY!

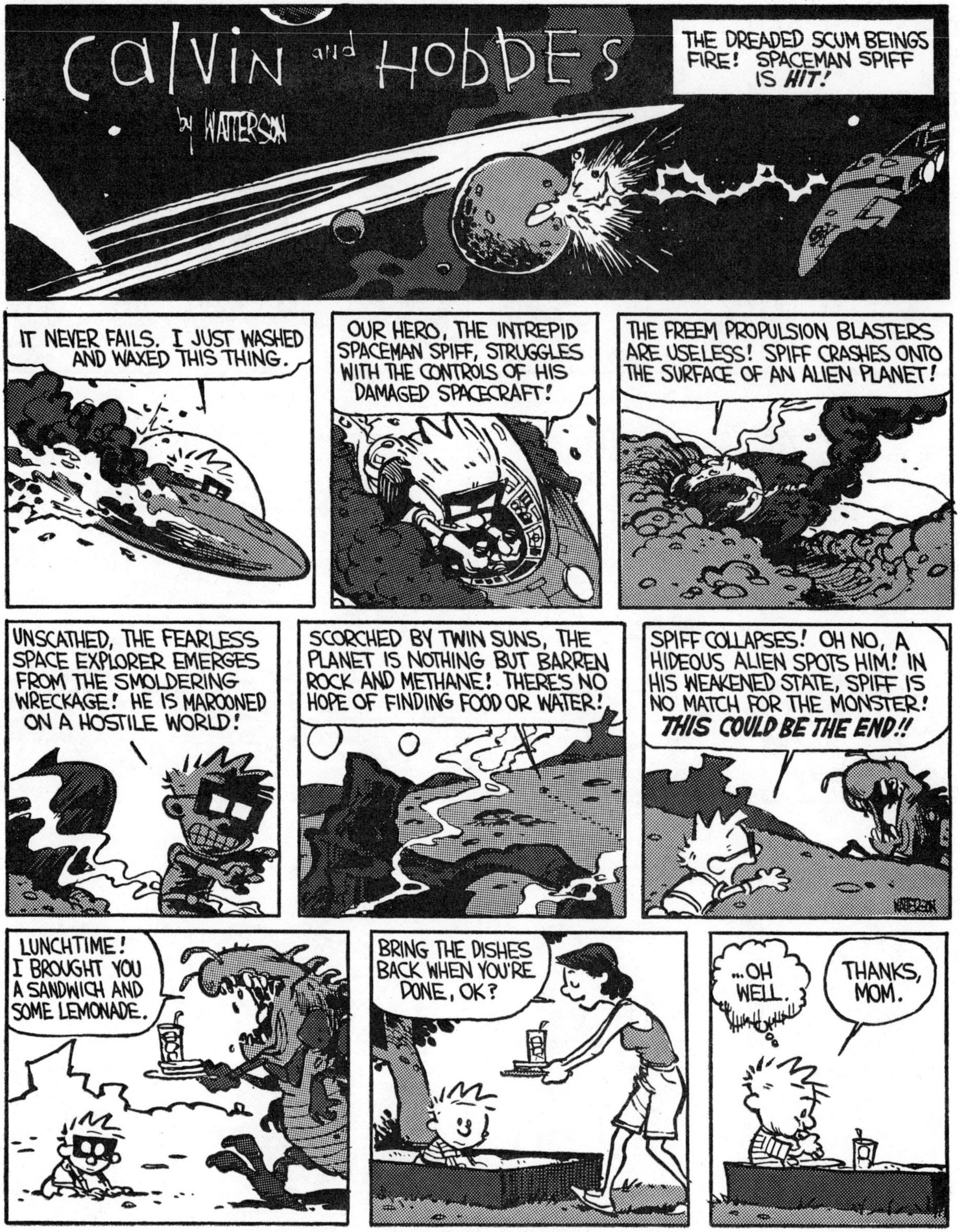
Calvin and HobbES
by WATTERSON
THE DREADED SCUM BEINGS FIRE! SPACEMAN SPIFF IS HIT!
IT NEVER FAILS. I JUST WASHED AND WAXED THIS THING.
OUR HERO, THE INTREPID SPACEMAN SPIFF, STRUGGLES WITH THE CONTROLS OF HIS DAMAGED SPACECRAFT!
THE FREEM PROPULSION BLASTERS ARE USELESS! SPIFF CRASHES ONTO THE SURFACE OF AN ALIEN PLANET!
UNSCATHED, THE FEARLESS SPACE EXPLORER EMERGES FROM THE SMOLDERING WRECKAGE! HE IS MAROONED ON A HOSTILE WORLD!
SCORCHED BY TWIN SUNS, THE PLANET IS NOTHING BUT BARREN ROCK AND METHANE! THERE'S NO HOPE OF FINDING FOOD OR WATER!
SPIFF COLLAPSES! OH NO, A HIDEOUS ALIEN SPOTS HIM! IN HIS WEAKENED STATE, SPIFF IS NO MATCH FOR THE MONSTER! THIS COULD BE THE END!!
WATTERSON
LUNCHTIME! I BROUGHT YOU A SANDWICH AND SOME LEMONADE.
BRING THE DISHES BACK WHEN YOU'RE DONE, OK?
...OH WELL.
THANKS, MOM.

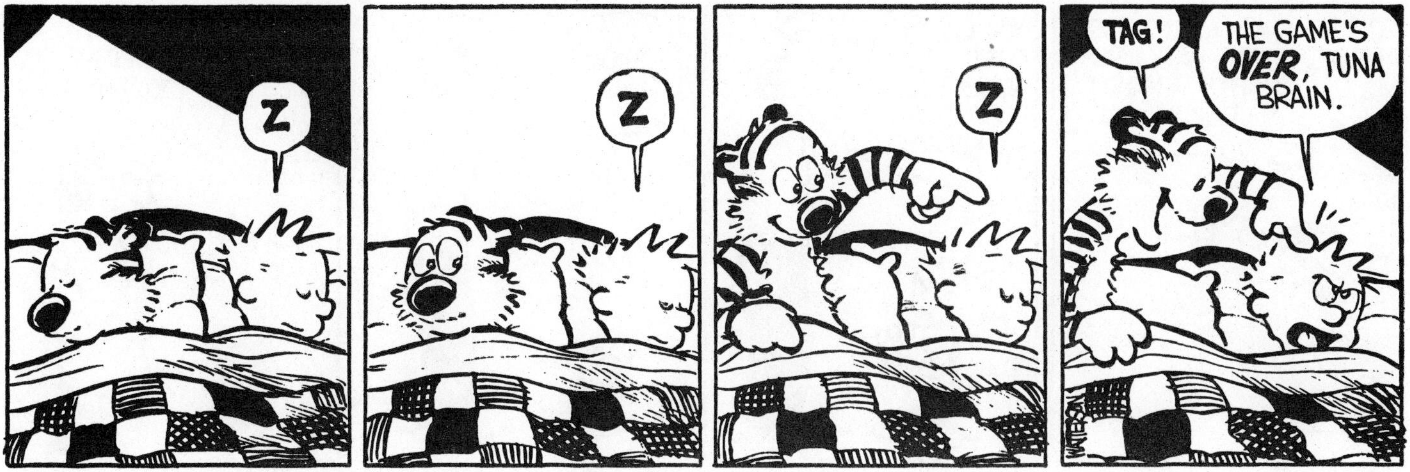
Z
Z
Z
TAG!
THE GAME'S **OVER**, TUNA BRAIN.

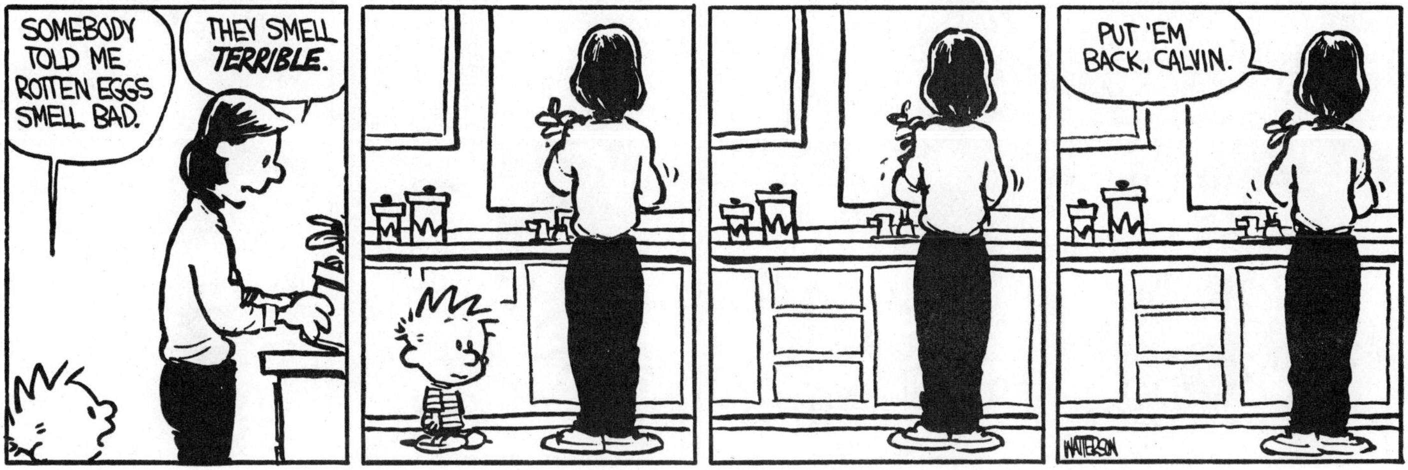
SOMEBODY TOLD ME ROTTEN EGGS SMELL BAD.
THEY SMELL **TERRIBLE**.
PUT 'EM BACK, CALVIN.
WATTERSON

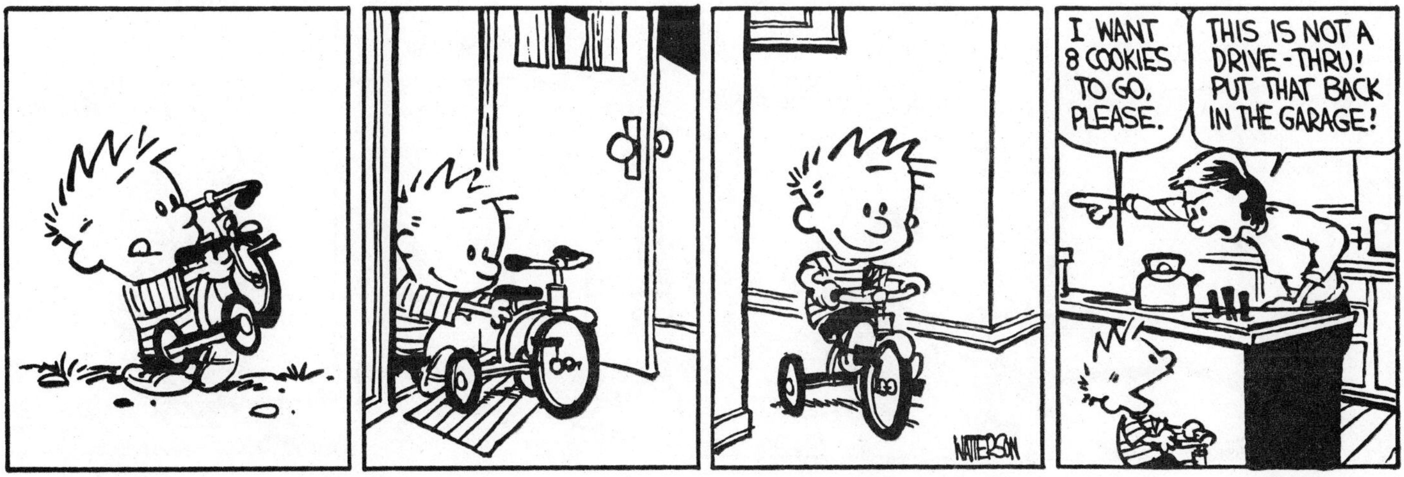
WATTERSON
I WANT 8 COOKIES TO GO, PLEASE.
THIS IS NOT A DRIVE-THRU! PUT THAT BACK IN THE GARAGE!

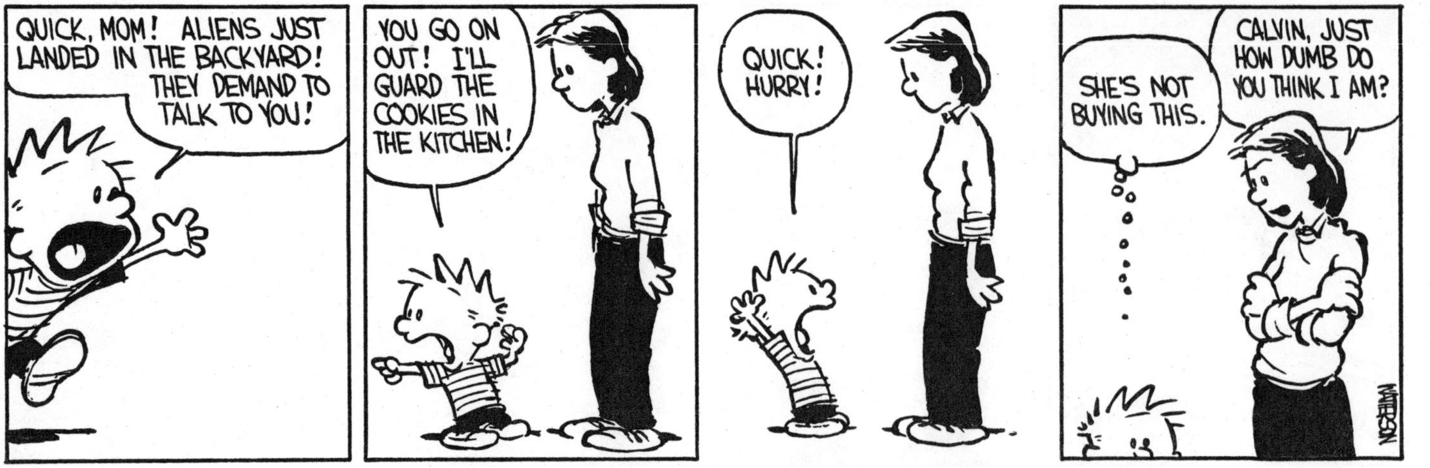
QUICK, MOM! ALIENS JUST LANDED IN THE BACKYARD! THEY DEMAND TO TALK TO YOU!
YOU GO ON OUT! I'LL GUARD THE COOKIES IN THE KITCHEN!
QUICK! HURRY!
SHE'S NOT BUYING THIS.
CALVIN, JUST HOW DUMB DO YOU THINK I AM?
WATTERSON

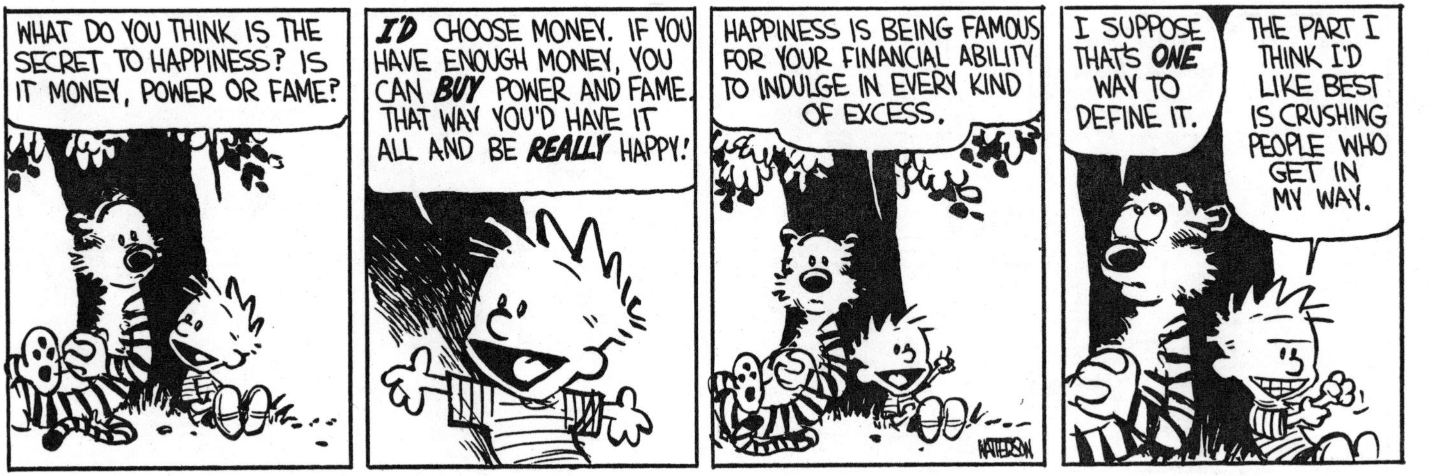
WHAT DO YOU THINK IS THE SECRET TO HAPPINESS? IS IT MONEY, POWER OR FAME?
I'D CHOOSE MONEY. IF YOU HAVE ENOUGH MONEY, YOU CAN BUY POWER AND FAME. THAT WAY YOU'D HAVE IT ALL AND BE REALLY HAPPY!
HAPPINESS IS BEING FAMOUS FOR YOUR FINANCIAL ABILITY TO INDULGE IN EVERY KIND OF EXCESS.
WATTERSON
I SUPPOSE THAT'S ONE WAY TO DEFINE IT.
THE PART I THINK I'D LIKE BEST IS CRUSHING PEOPLE WHO GET IN MY WAY.

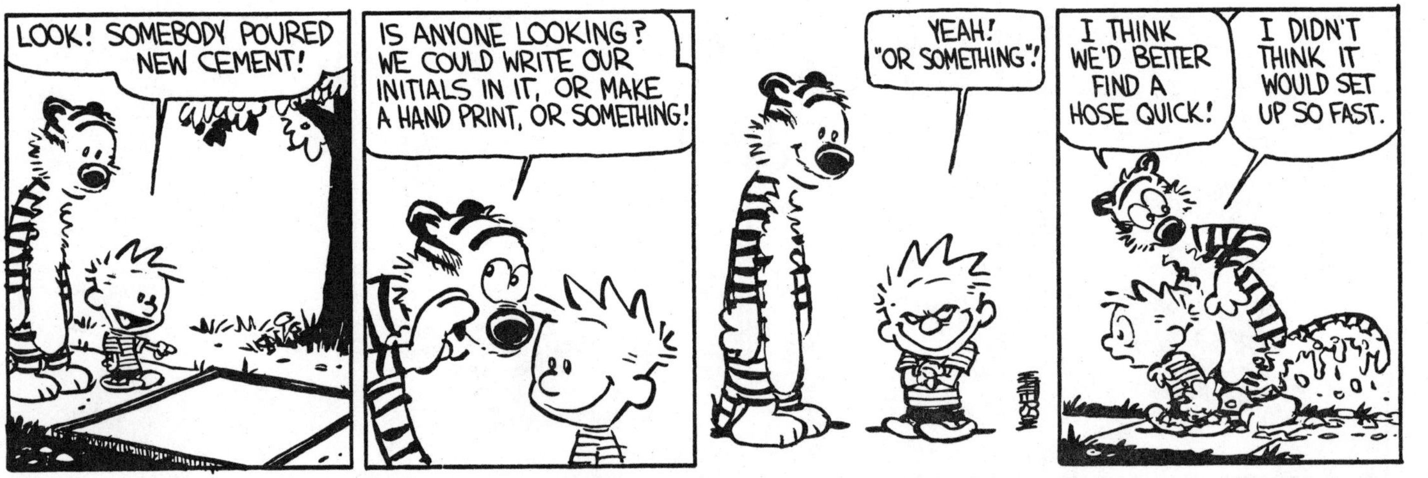
LOOK! SOMEBODY POURED NEW CEMENT!
IS ANYONE LOOKING? WE COULD WRITE OUR INITIALS IN IT, OR MAKE A HAND PRINT, OR SOMETHING!
YEAH! "OR SOMETHING"!
WATTERSON
I THINK WE'D BETTER FIND A HOSE QUICK!
I DIDN'T THINK IT WOULD SET UP SO FAST.

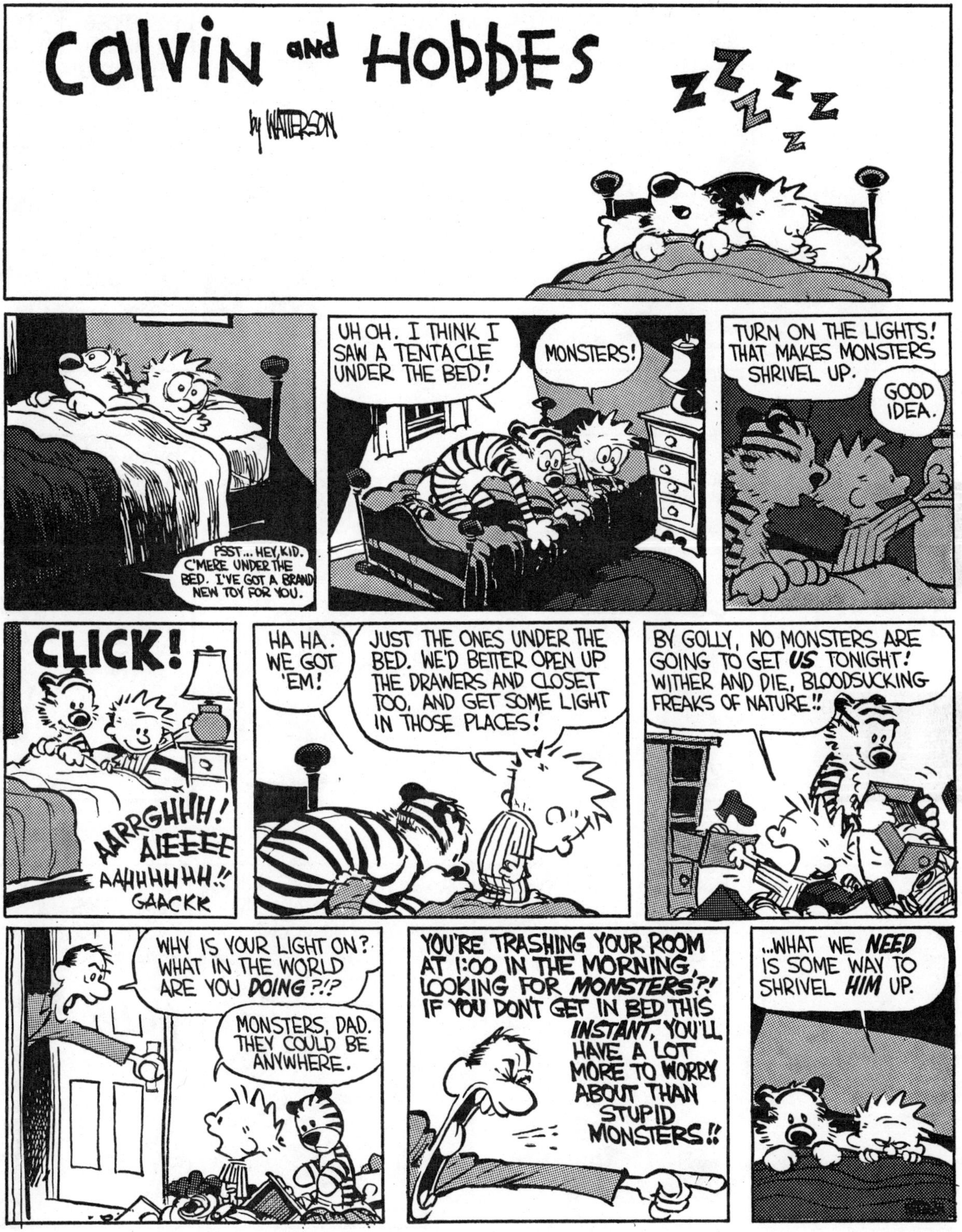
Calvin and HOBBES
by WATTERSON
ZZZZZZZ
PSST... HEY, KID. C'MERE UNDER THE BED. I'VE GOT A BRAND NEW TOY FOR YOU.
UH OH. I THINK I SAW A TENTACLE UNDER THE BED!
MONSTERS!
TURN ON THE LIGHTS! THAT MAKES MONSTERS SHRIVEL UP.
GOOD IDEA.
CLICK!
AARRGHHH! AIEEEEE AAHHHHHH!! GAACKK
HA HA. WE GOT 'EM!
JUST THE ONES UNDER THE BED. WE'D BETTER OPEN UP THE DRAWERS AND CLOSET TOO, AND GET SOME LIGHT IN THOSE PLACES!
BY GOLLY, NO MONSTERS ARE GOING TO GET US TONIGHT! WITHER AND DIE, BLOODSUCKING FREAKS OF NATURE!!
WHY IS YOUR LIGHT ON? WHAT IN THE WORLD ARE YOU DOING ?!?
MONSTERS, DAD. THEY COULD BE ANYWHERE.
YOU'RE TRASHING YOUR ROOM AT 1:00 IN THE MORNING, LOOKING FOR MONSTERS ?! IF YOU DON'T GET IN BED THIS INSTANT, YOU'LL HAVE A LOT MORE TO WORRY ABOUT THAN STUPID MONSTERS!!
...WHAT WE NEED IS SOME WAY TO SHRIVEL HIM UP.

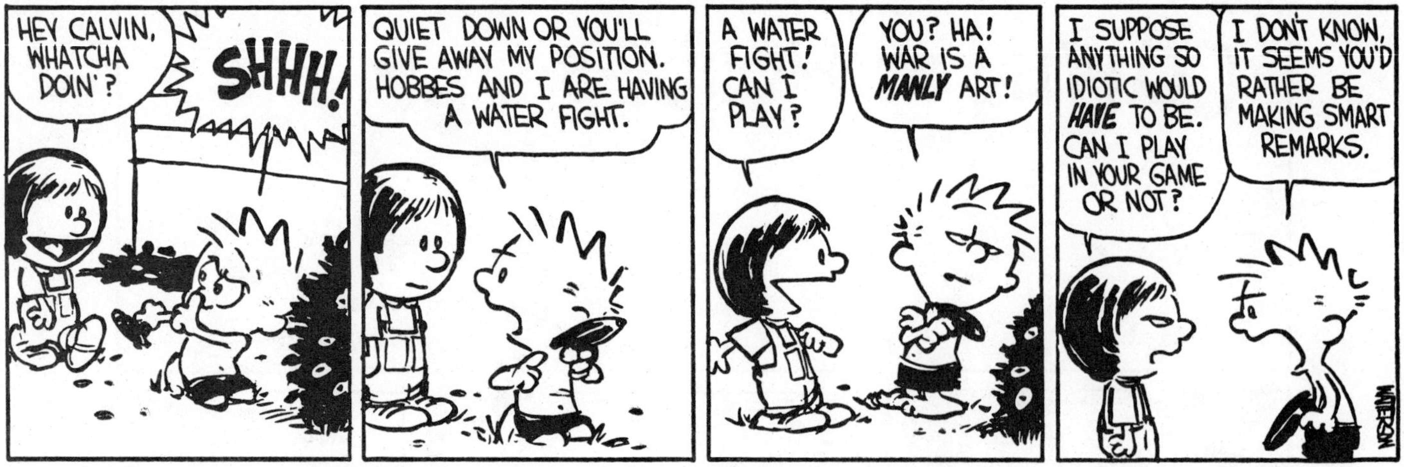
HEY CALVIN, WHATCHA DOIN'?
SHHH!
QUIET DOWN OR YOU'LL GIVE AWAY MY POSITION. HOBBES AND I ARE HAVING A WATER FIGHT.
A WATER FIGHT! CAN I PLAY?
YOU? HA! WAR IS A MANLY ART!
I SUPPOSE ANYTHING SO IDIOTIC WOULD HAVE TO BE. CAN I PLAY IN YOUR GAME OR NOT?
I DON'T KNOW, IT SEEMS YOU'D RATHER BE MAKING SMART REMARKS.
WATTERSON

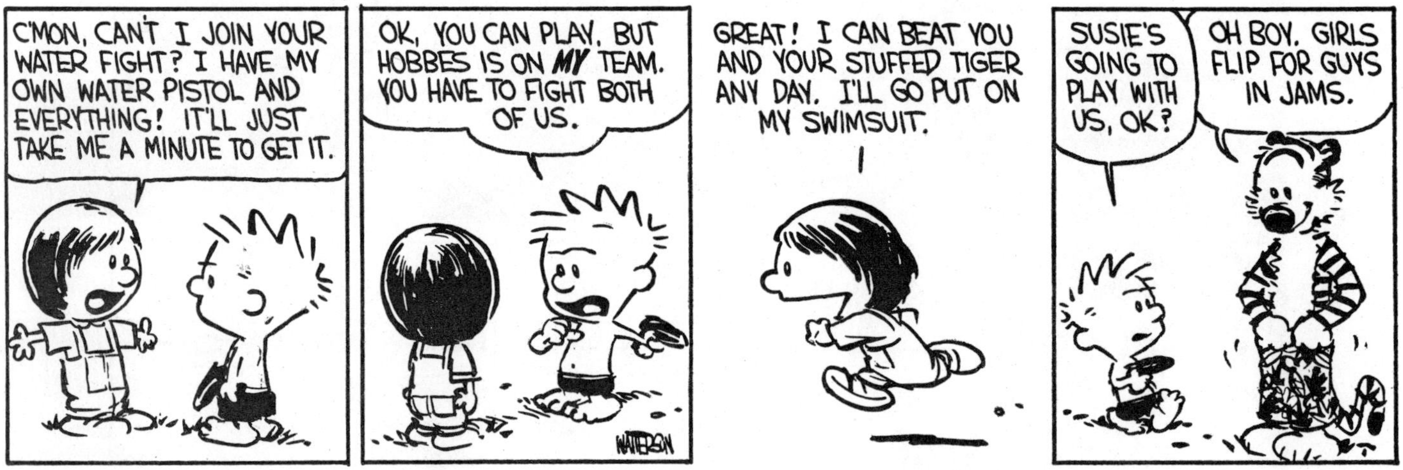
C'MON, CAN'T I JOIN YOUR WATER FIGHT? I HAVE MY OWN WATER PISTOL AND EVERYTHING! IT'LL JUST TAKE ME A MINUTE TO GET IT.
OK, YOU CAN PLAY, BUT HOBBES IS ON MY TEAM. YOU HAVE TO FIGHT BOTH OF US.
WATTERSON
GREAT! I CAN BEAT YOU AND YOUR STUFFED TIGER ANY DAY. I'LL GO PUT ON MY SWIMSUIT.
SUSIE'S GOING TO PLAY WITH US, OK?
OH BOY. GIRLS FLIP FOR GUYS IN JAMS.

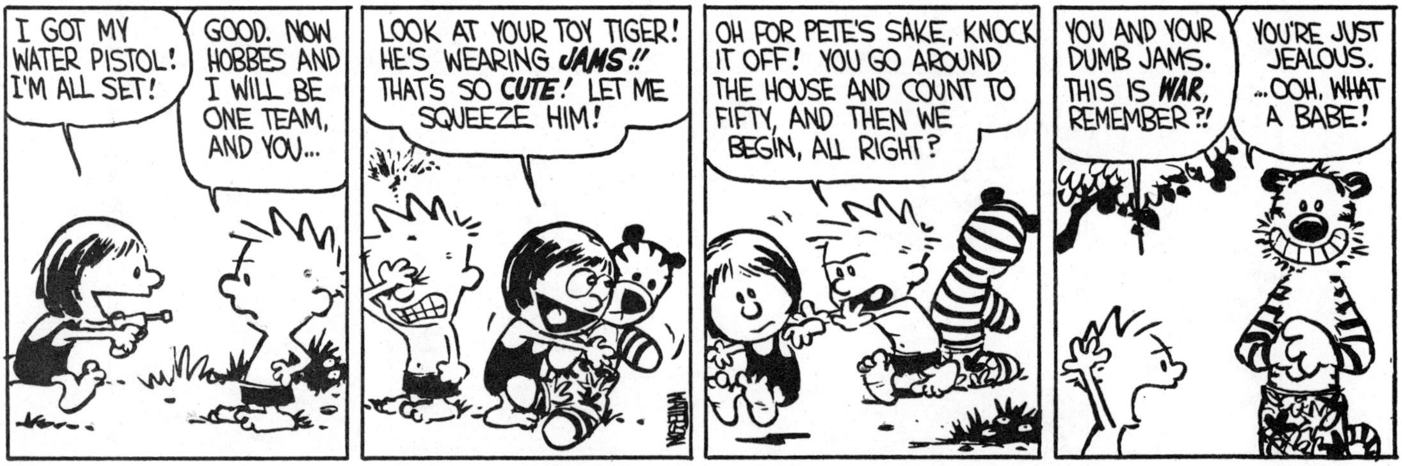
I GOT MY WATER PISTOL! I'M ALL SET!
GOOD. NOW HOBBES AND I WILL BE ONE TEAM, AND YOU...
LOOK AT YOUR TOY TIGER! HE'S WEARING JAMS!! THAT'S SO CUTE! LET ME SQUEEZE HIM!
WATTERSON
OH FOR PETE'S SAKE, KNOCK IT OFF! YOU GO AROUND THE HOUSE AND COUNT TO FIFTY, AND THEN WE BEGIN, ALL RIGHT?
YOU AND YOUR DUMB JAMS. THIS IS WAR, REMEMBER?!
YOU'RE JUST JEALOUS. ...OOH, WHAT A BABE!

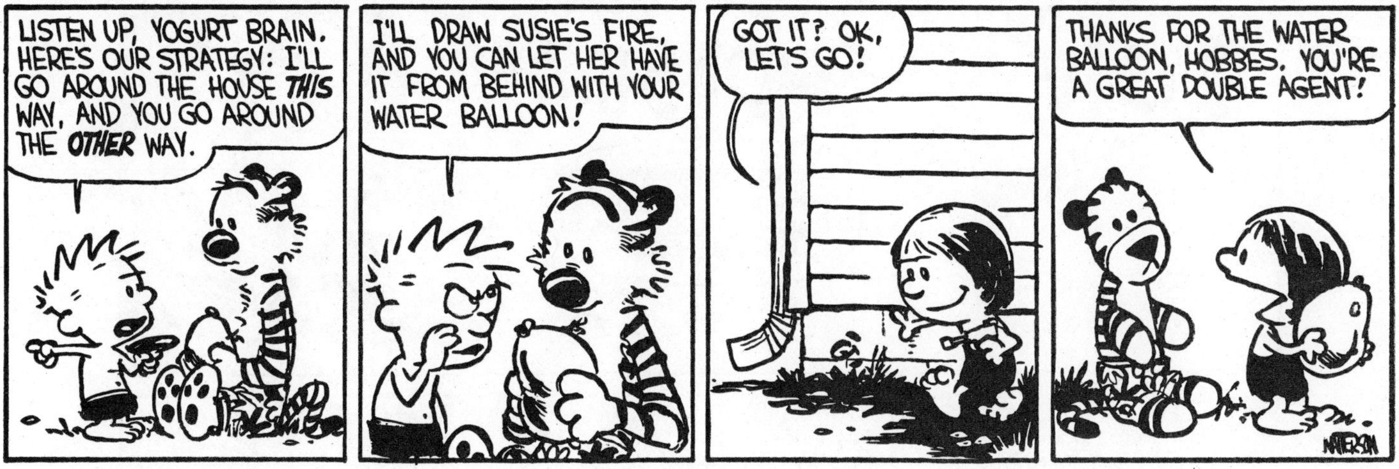
LISTEN UP, YOGURT BRAIN. HERE'S OUR STRATEGY: I'LL GO AROUND THE HOUSE *THIS* WAY, AND YOU GO AROUND THE *OTHER* WAY.
I'LL DRAW SUSIE'S FIRE, AND YOU CAN LET HER HAVE IT FROM BEHIND WITH YOUR WATER BALLOON!
GOT IT? OK, LET'S GO!
THANKS FOR THE WATER BALLOON, HOBBES. YOU'RE A GREAT DOUBLE AGENT!
WATERSON

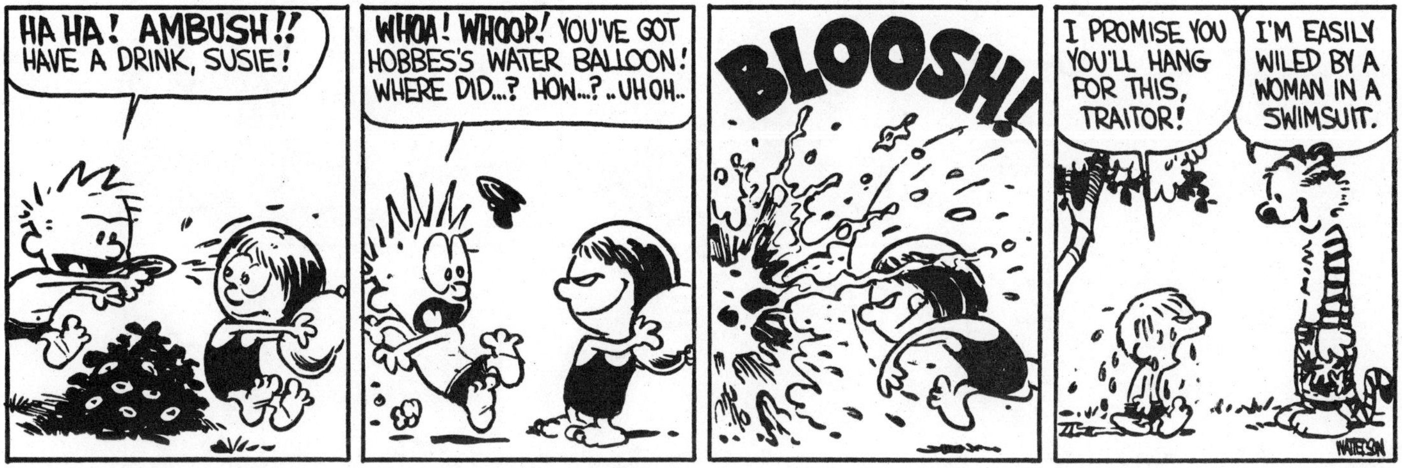
HA HA! AMBUSH!! HAVE A DRINK, SUSIE!
WHOA! WHOOP! YOU'VE GOT HOBBES'S WATER BALLOON! WHERE DID...? HOW...? ..UH OH..
BLOOSH!
I PROMISE YOU YOU'LL HANG FOR THIS, TRAITOR!
I'M EASILY WILED BY A WOMAN IN A SWIMSUIT.
WATERSON

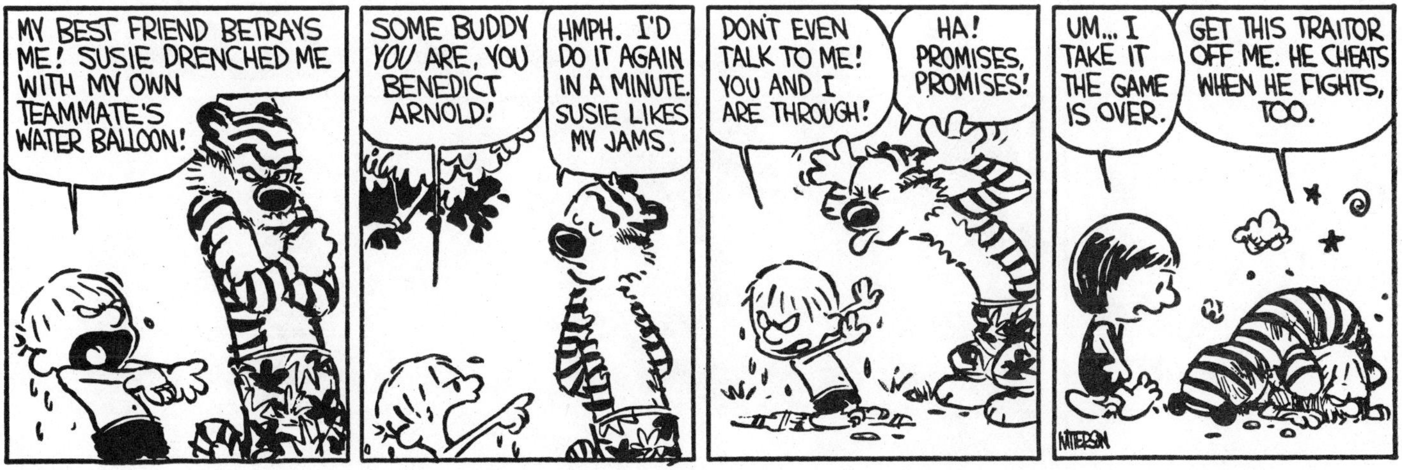
MY BEST FRIEND BETRAYS ME! SUSIE DRENCHED ME WITH MY OWN TEAMMATE'S WATER BALLOON!
SOME BUDDY *YOU* ARE, YOU BENEDICT ARNOLD!
HMPH. I'D DO IT AGAIN IN A MINUTE. SUSIE LIKES MY JAMS.
DON'T EVEN TALK TO ME! YOU AND I ARE THROUGH!
HA! PROMISES, PROMISES!
UM... I TAKE IT THE GAME IS OVER.
GET THIS TRAITOR OFF ME. HE CHEATS WHEN HE FIGHTS, TOO.
WATERSON

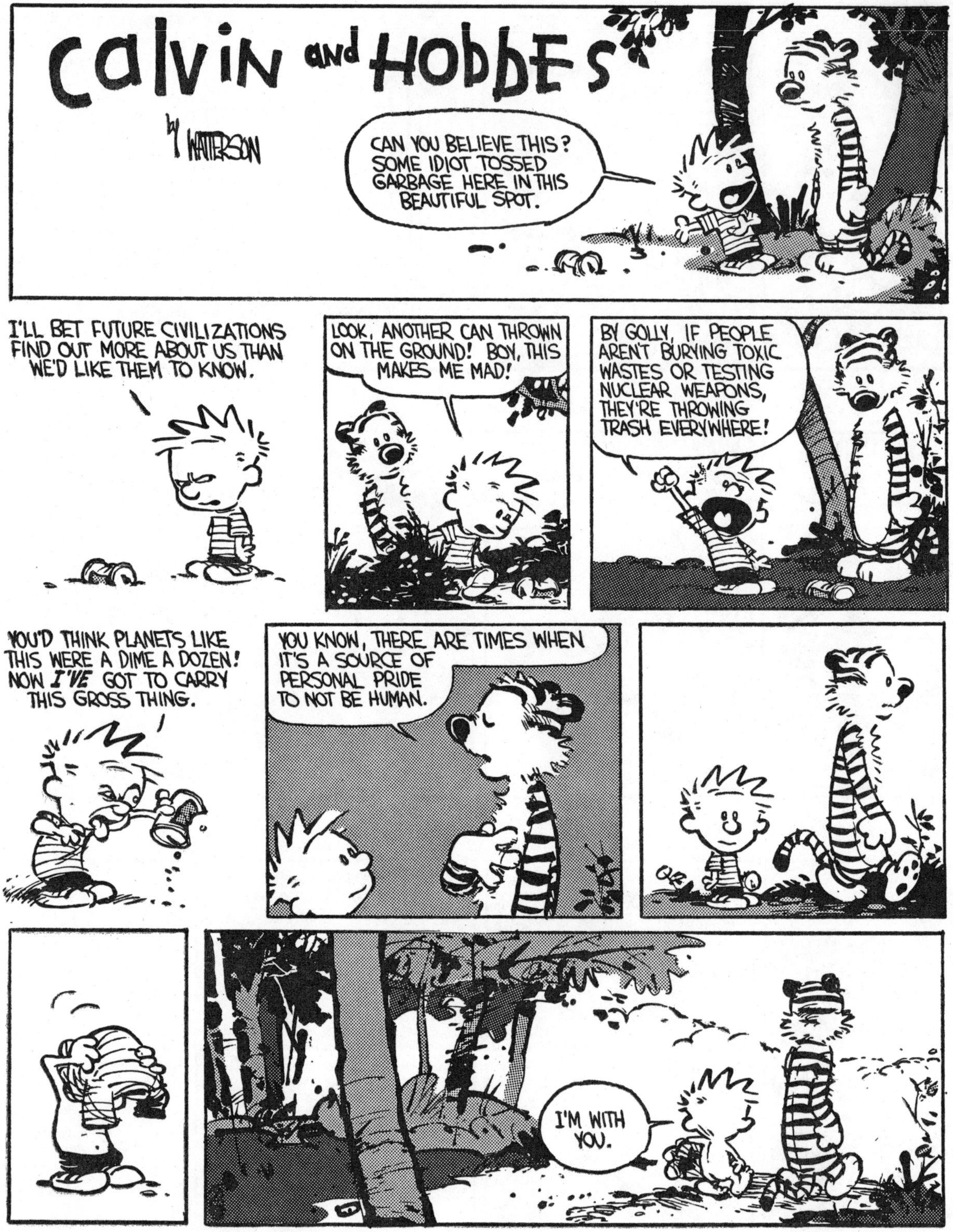
Calvin and HOBBES
by WATTERSON
CAN YOU BELIEVE THIS? SOME IDIOT TOSSED GARBAGE HERE IN THIS BEAUTIFUL SPOT.
I'LL BET FUTURE CIVILIZATIONS FIND OUT MORE ABOUT US THAN WE'D LIKE THEM TO KNOW.
LOOK, ANOTHER CAN THROWN ON THE GROUND! BOY, THIS MAKES ME MAD!
BY GOLLY, IF PEOPLE AREN'T BURYING TOXIC WASTES OR TESTING NUCLEAR WEAPONS, THEY'RE THROWING TRASH EVERYWHERE!
YOU'D THINK PLANETS LIKE THIS WERE A DIME A DOZEN! NOW I'VE GOT TO CARRY THIS GROSS THING.
YOU KNOW, THERE ARE TIMES WHEN IT'S A SOURCE OF PERSONAL PRIDE TO NOT BE HUMAN.
I'M WITH YOU.

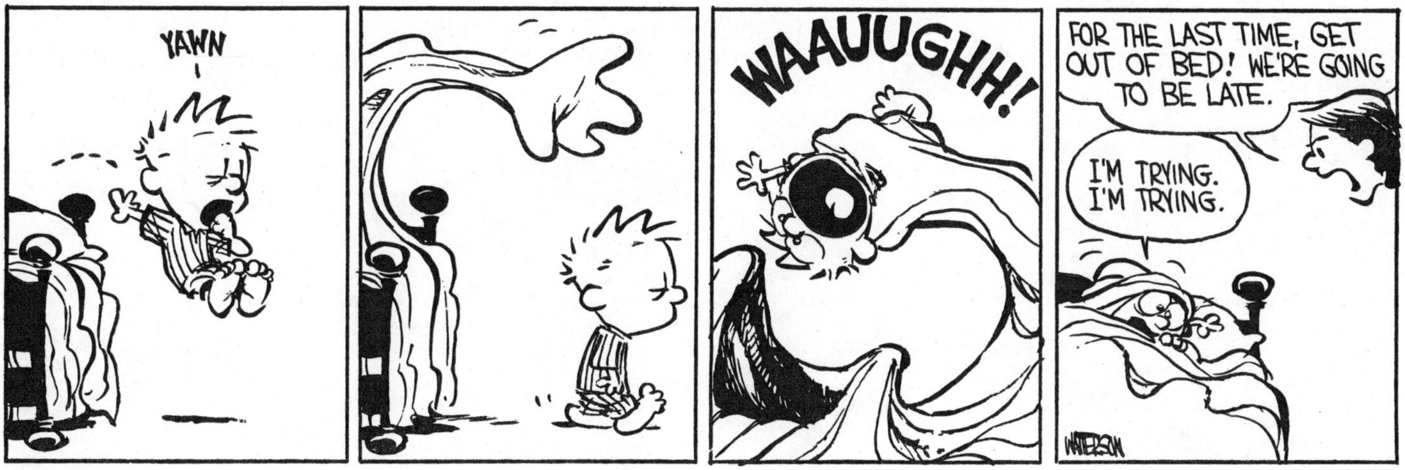
YAWN
WAAUUGHH!
FOR THE LAST TIME, GET OUT OF BED! WE'RE GOING TO BE LATE.
I'M TRYING. I'M TRYING.
WATTERSON

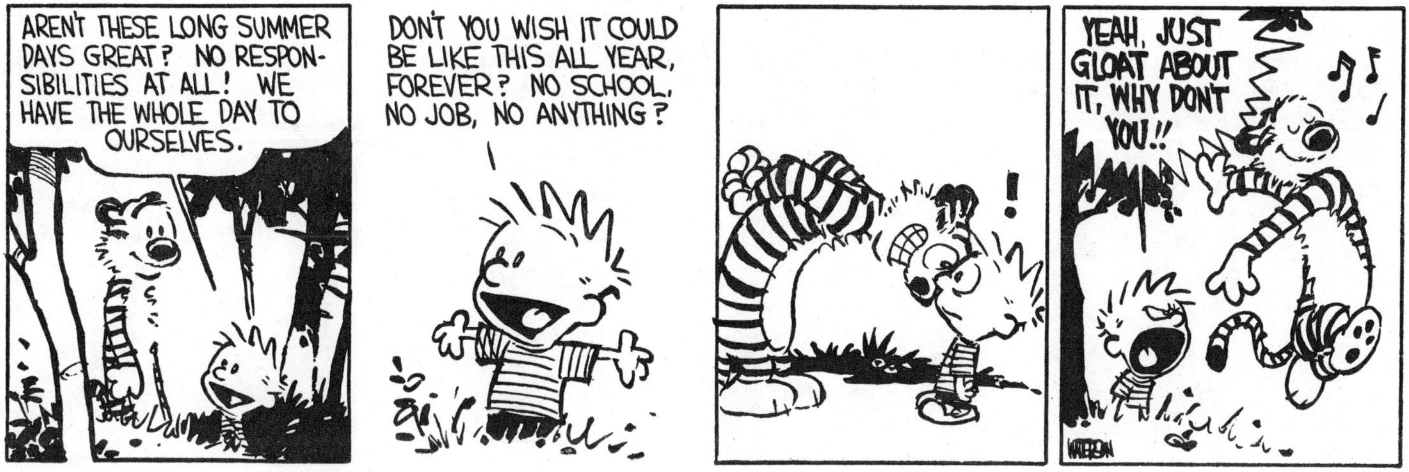
AREN'T THESE LONG SUMMER DAYS GREAT? NO RESPONSIBILITIES AT ALL! WE HAVE THE WHOLE DAY TO OURSELVES.
DON'T YOU WISH IT COULD BE LIKE THIS ALL YEAR, FOREVER? NO SCHOOL, NO JOB, NO ANYTHING?
!
YEAH, JUST GLOAT ABOUT IT, WHY DON'T YOU!!
WATTERSON

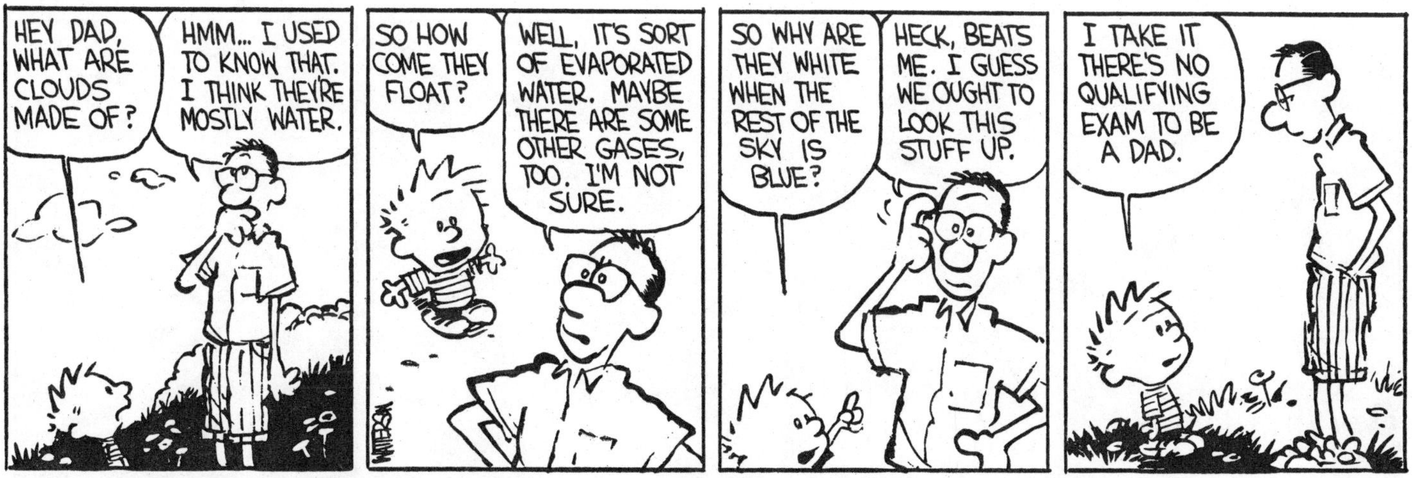
HEY DAD, WHAT ARE CLOUDS MADE OF?
HMM... I USED TO KNOW THAT. I THINK THEY'RE MOSTLY WATER.
WATTERSON
SO HOW COME THEY FLOAT?
WELL, IT'S SORT OF EVAPORATED WATER. MAYBE THERE ARE SOME OTHER GASES, TOO. I'M NOT SURE.
SO WHY ARE THEY WHITE WHEN THE REST OF THE SKY IS BLUE?
HECK, BEATS ME. I GUESS WE OUGHT TO LOOK THIS STUFF UP.
I TAKE IT THERE'S NO QUALIFYING EXAM TO BE A DAD.

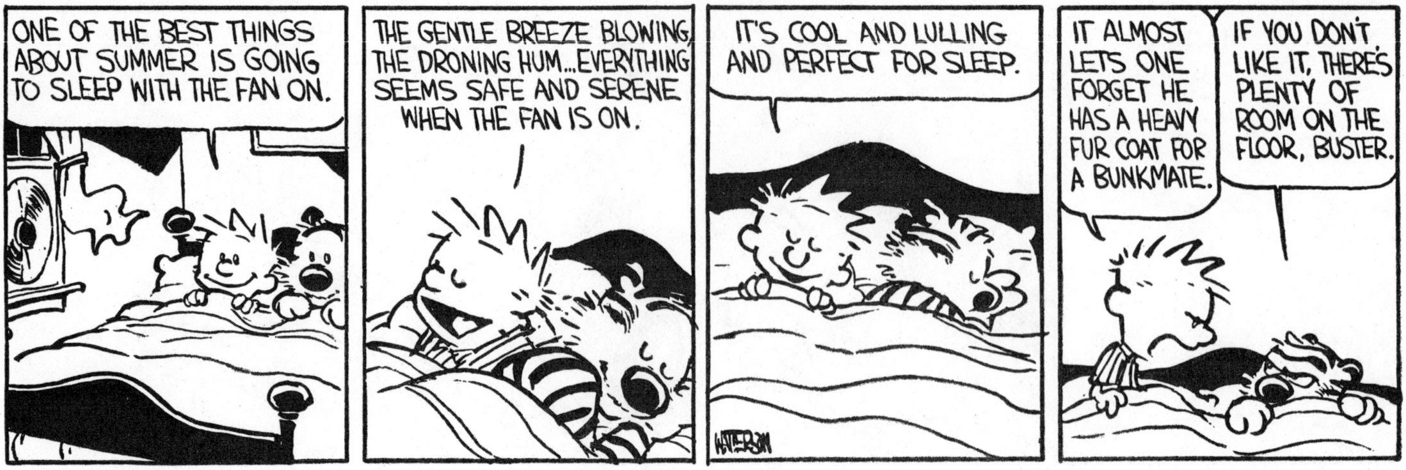
ONE OF THE BEST THINGS ABOUT SUMMER IS GOING TO SLEEP WITH THE FAN ON.
THE GENTLE BREEZE BLOWING, THE DRONING HUM...EVERYTHING SEEMS SAFE AND SERENE WHEN THE FAN IS ON.
IT'S COOL AND LULLING AND PERFECT FOR SLEEP.
IT ALMOST LETS ONE FORGET HE HAS A HEAVY FUR COAT FOR A BUNKMATE.
IF YOU DON'T LIKE IT, THERE'S PLENTY OF ROOM ON THE FLOOR, BUSTER.

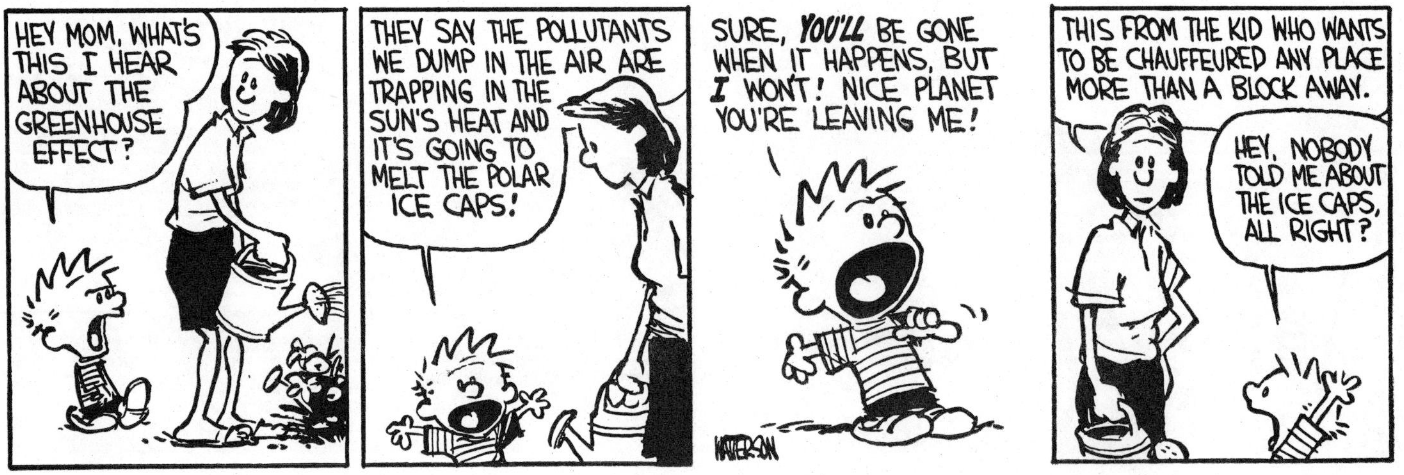
HEY MOM, WHAT'S THIS I HEAR ABOUT THE GREENHOUSE EFFECT?
THEY SAY THE POLLUTANTS WE DUMP IN THE AIR ARE TRAPPING IN THE SUN'S HEAT AND IT'S GOING TO MELT THE POLAR ICE CAPS!
SURE, YOU'LL BE GONE WHEN IT HAPPENS, BUT I WON'T! NICE PLANET YOU'RE LEAVING ME!
THIS FROM THE KID WHO WANTS TO BE CHAUFFEURED ANY PLACE MORE THAN A BLOCK AWAY.
HEY, NOBODY TOLD ME ABOUT THE ICE CAPS, ALL RIGHT?

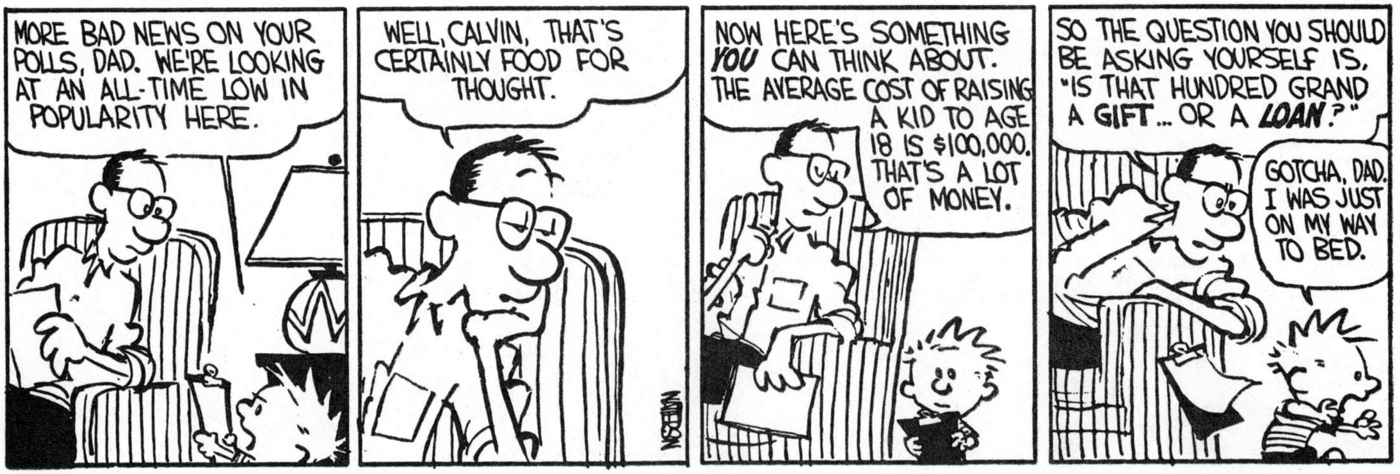
MORE BAD NEWS ON YOUR POLLS, DAD. WE'RE LOOKING AT AN ALL-TIME LOW IN POPULARITY HERE.
WELL, CALVIN, THAT'S CERTAINLY FOOD FOR THOUGHT.
NOW HERE'S SOMETHING YOU CAN THINK ABOUT. THE AVERAGE COST OF RAISING A KID TO AGE 18 IS $100,000. THAT'S A LOT OF MONEY.
SO THE QUESTION YOU SHOULD BE ASKING YOURSELF IS, "IS THAT HUNDRED GRAND A GIFT... OR A LOAN?"
GOTCHA, DAD. I WAS JUST ON MY WAY TO BED.

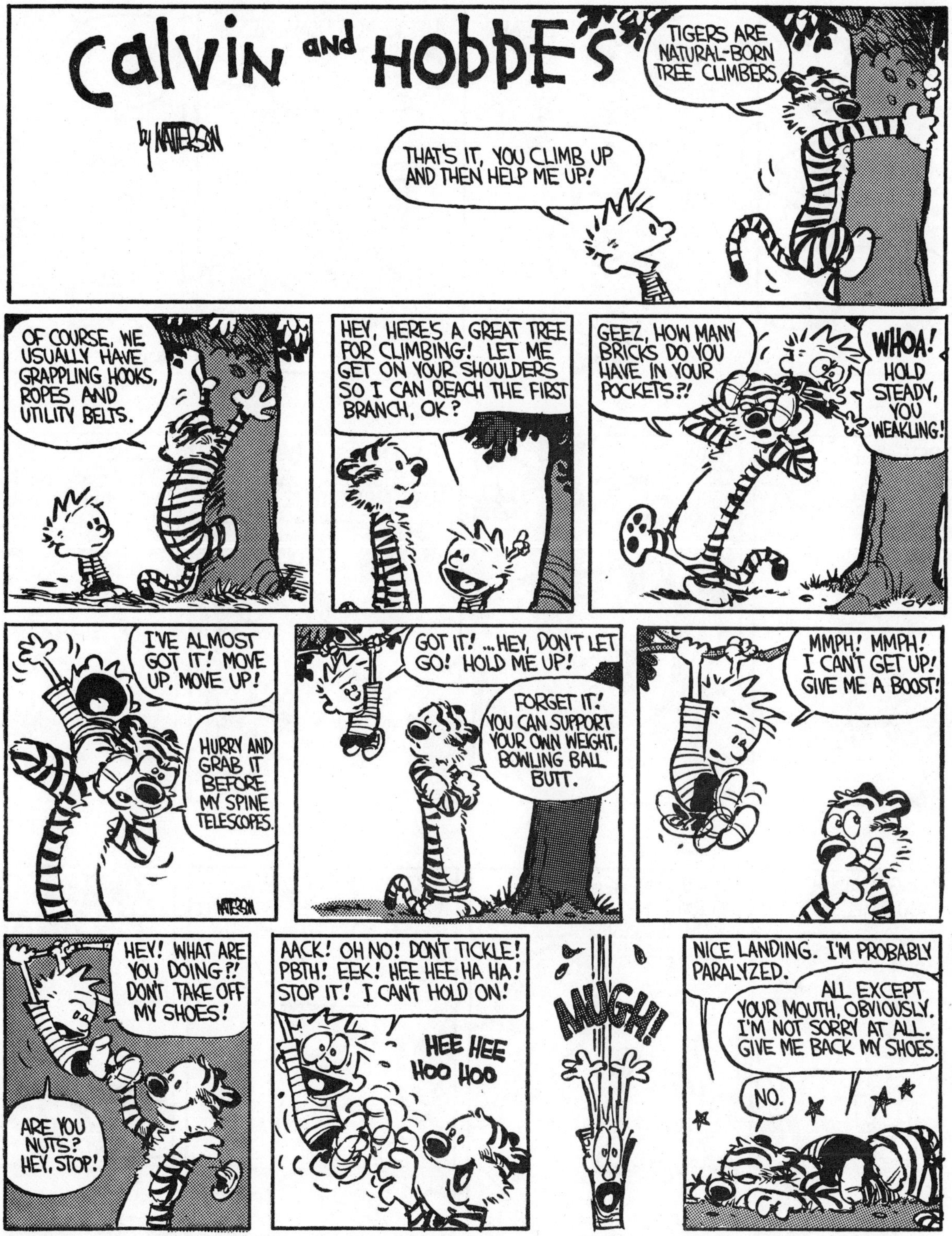
Calvin and HOBBES
by WATTERSON
TIGERS ARE NATURAL-BORN TREE CLIMBERS.
THAT'S IT, YOU CLIMB UP AND THEN HELP ME UP!
OF COURSE, WE USUALLY HAVE GRAPPLING HOOKS, ROPES AND UTILITY BELTS.
HEY, HERE'S A GREAT TREE FOR CLIMBING! LET ME GET ON YOUR SHOULDERS SO I CAN REACH THE FIRST BRANCH, OK?
GEEZ, HOW MANY BRICKS DO YOU HAVE IN YOUR POCKETS?!
WHOA! HOLD STEADY, YOU WEAKLING!
I'VE ALMOST GOT IT! MOVE UP, MOVE UP!
HURRY AND GRAB IT BEFORE MY SPINE TELESCOPES.
WATTERSON
GOT IT! ...HEY, DON'T LET GO! HOLD ME UP!
FORGET IT! YOU CAN SUPPORT YOUR OWN WEIGHT, BOWLING BALL BUTT.
MMPH! MMPH! I CAN'T GET UP! GIVE ME A BOOST!
HEY! WHAT ARE YOU DOING?! DON'T TAKE OFF MY SHOES!
ARE YOU NUTS? HEY, STOP!
AACK! OH NO! DON'T TICKLE! PBTH! EEK! HEE HEE HA HA! STOP IT! I CAN'T HOLD ON!
HEE HEE HOO HOO
MUGH!
NICE LANDING. I'M PROBABLY PARALYZED.
ALL EXCEPT YOUR MOUTH, OBVIOUSLY. I'M NOT SORRY AT ALL. GIVE ME BACK MY SHOES.
NO.

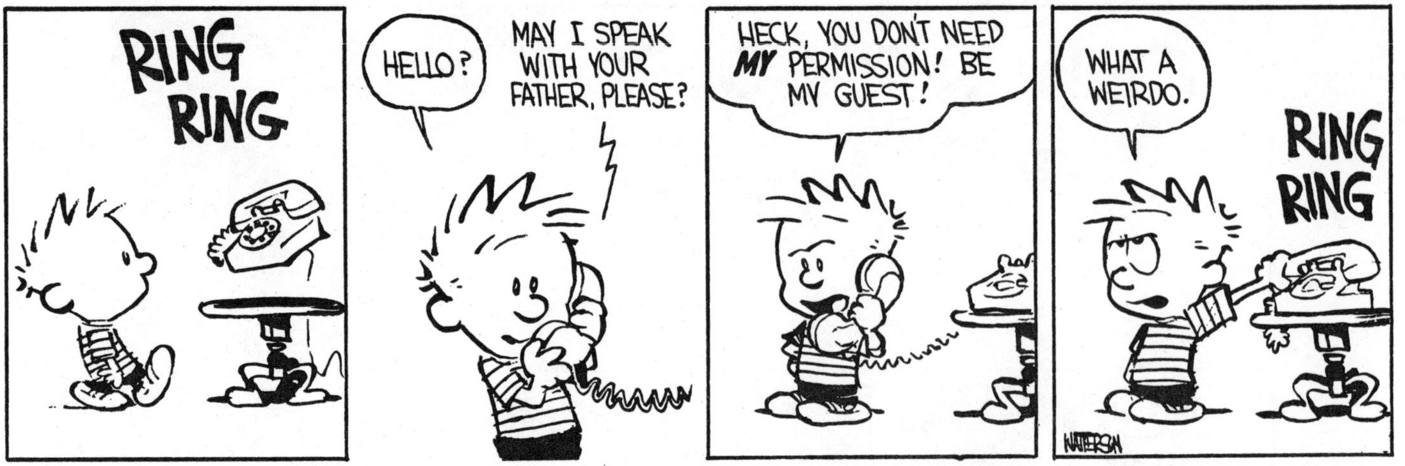
RING RING
HELLO?
MAY I SPEAK WITH YOUR FATHER, PLEASE?
HECK, YOU DON'T NEED MY PERMISSION! BE MY GUEST!
WHAT A WEIRDO.
RING RING

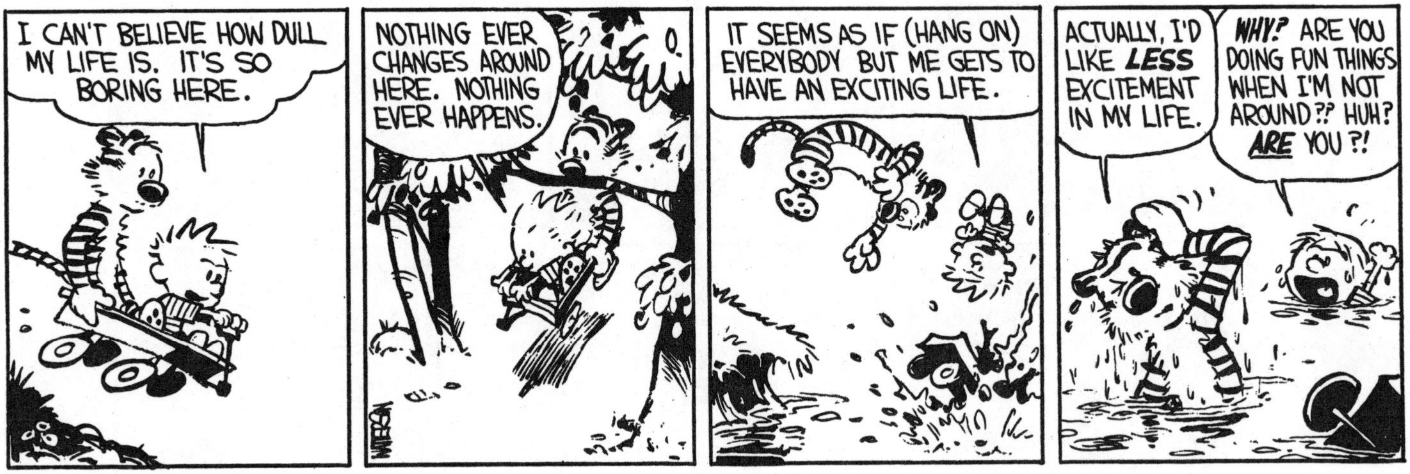
I CAN'T BELIEVE HOW DULL MY LIFE IS. IT'S SO BORING HERE.
NOTHING EVER CHANGES AROUND HERE. NOTHING EVER HAPPENS.
IT SEEMS AS IF (HANG ON) EVERYBODY BUT ME GETS TO HAVE AN EXCITING LIFE.
ACTUALLY, I'D LIKE LESS EXCITEMENT IN MY LIFE.
WHY? ARE YOU DOING FUN THINGS WHEN I'M NOT AROUND?? HUH? ARE YOU?!

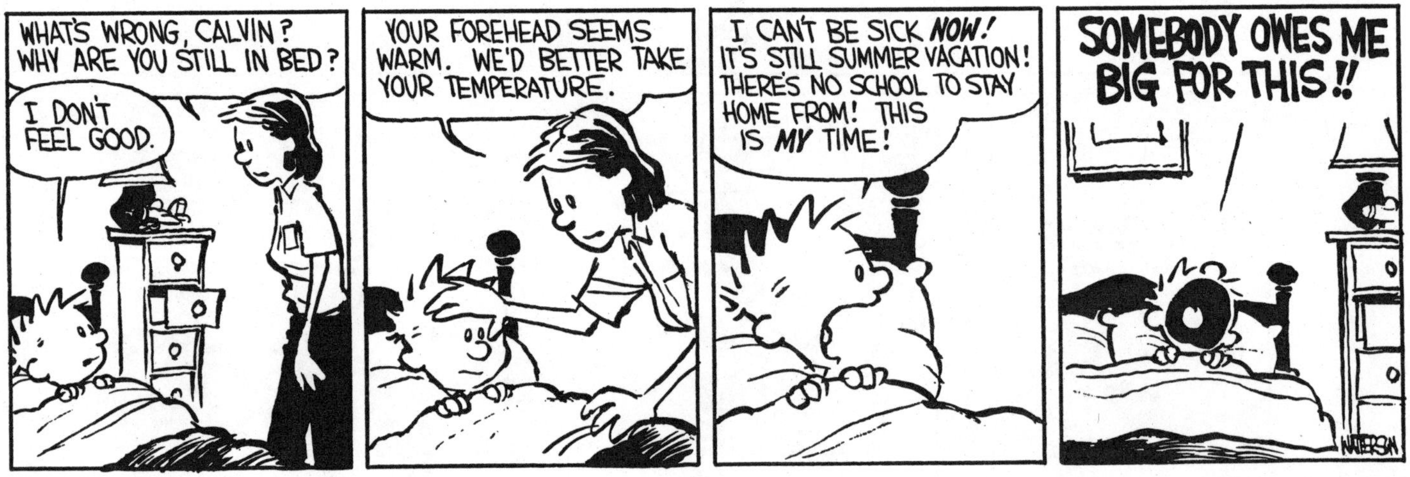
WHAT'S WRONG, CALVIN? WHY ARE YOU STILL IN BED?
I DON'T FEEL GOOD.
YOUR FOREHEAD SEEMS WARM. WE'D BETTER TAKE YOUR TEMPERATURE.
I CAN'T BE SICK NOW! IT'S STILL SUMMER VACATION! THERE'S NO SCHOOL TO STAY HOME FROM! THIS IS MY TIME!
SOMEBODY OWES ME BIG FOR THIS!!

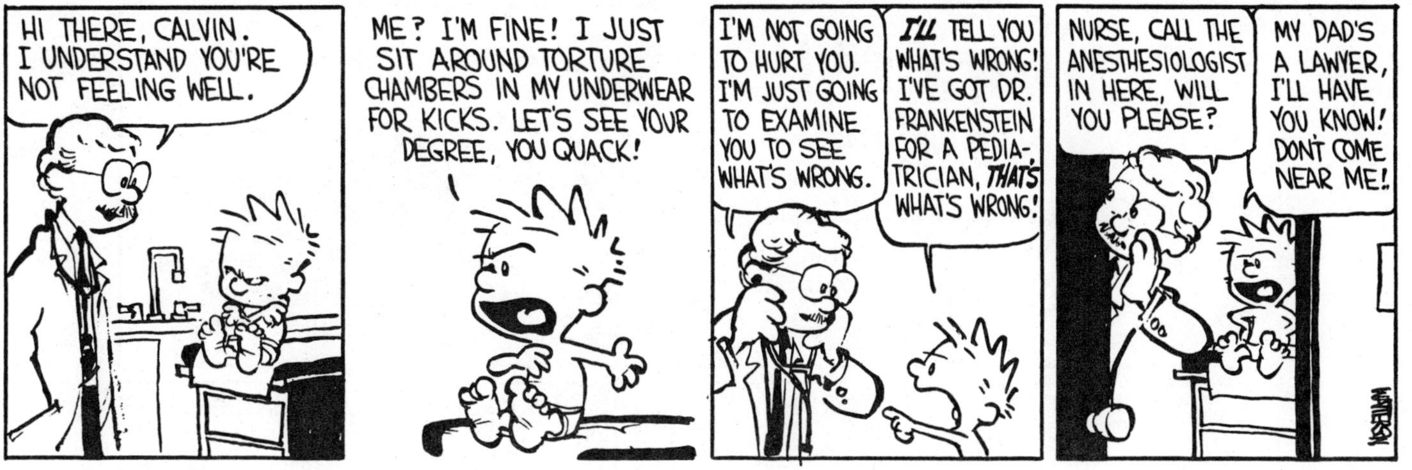
HI THERE, CALVIN. I UNDERSTAND YOU'RE NOT FEELING WELL.
ME? I'M FINE! I JUST SIT AROUND TORTURE CHAMBERS IN MY UNDERWEAR FOR KICKS. LET'S SEE YOUR DEGREE, YOU QUACK!
I'M NOT GOING TO HURT YOU. I'M JUST GOING TO EXAMINE YOU TO SEE WHAT'S WRONG.
I'LL TELL YOU WHAT'S WRONG! I'VE GOT DR. FRANKENSTEIN FOR A PEDIATRICIAN, **THAT'S** WHAT'S WRONG!
NURSE, CALL THE ANESTHESIOLOGIST IN HERE, WILL YOU PLEASE?
MY DAD'S A LAWYER, I'LL HAVE YOU KNOW! DON'T COME NEAR ME!

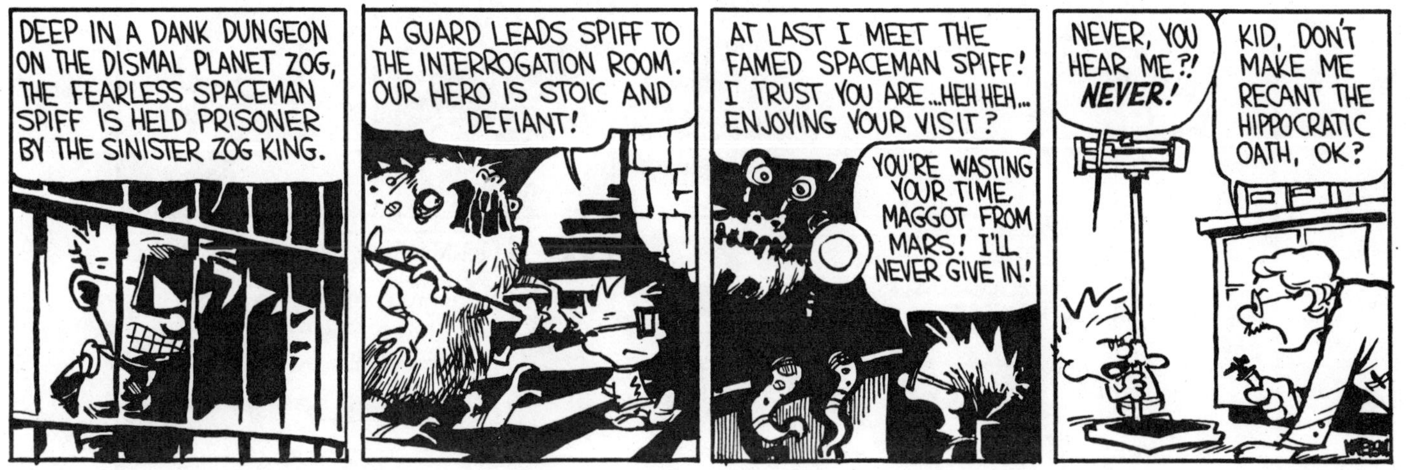
DEEP IN A DANK DUNGEON ON THE DISMAL PLANET ZOG, THE FEARLESS SPACEMAN SPIFF IS HELD PRISONER BY THE SINISTER ZOG KING.
A GUARD LEADS SPIFF TO THE INTERROGATION ROOM. OUR HERO IS STOIC AND DEFIANT!
AT LAST I MEET THE FAMED SPACEMAN SPIFF! I TRUST YOU ARE...HEH HEH... ENJOYING YOUR VISIT?
YOU'RE WASTING YOUR TIME, MAGGOT FROM MARS! I'LL NEVER GIVE IN!
NEVER, YOU HEAR ME?! **NEVER!**
KID, DON'T MAKE ME RECANT THE HIPPOCRATIC OATH, OK?

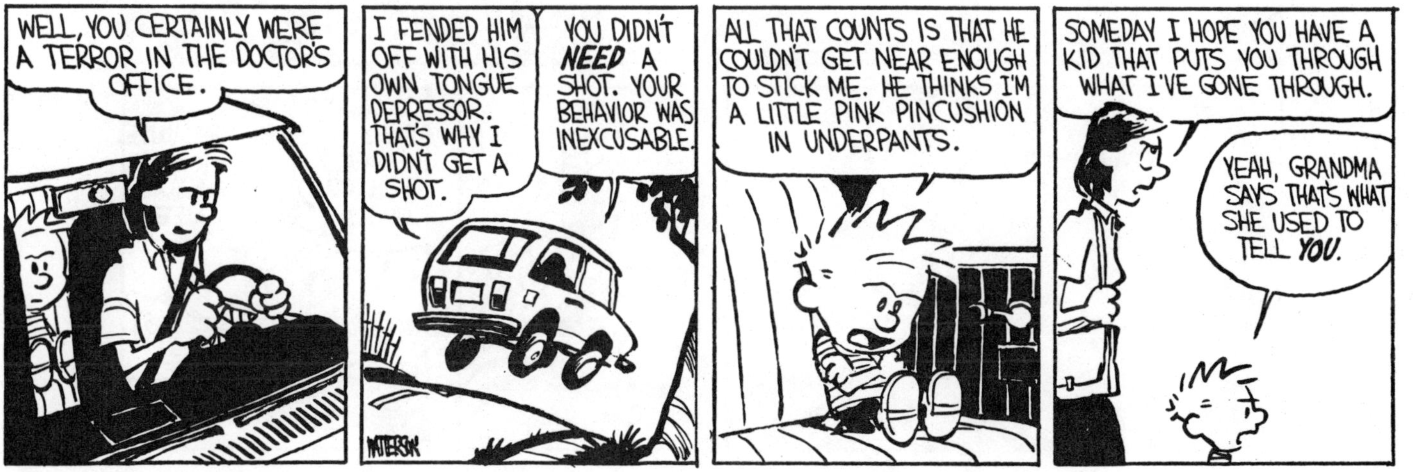
WELL, YOU CERTAINLY WERE A TERROR IN THE DOCTOR'S OFFICE.
I FENDED HIM OFF WITH HIS OWN TONGUE DEPRESSOR. THAT'S WHY I DIDN'T GET A SHOT.
YOU DIDN'T **NEED** A SHOT. YOUR BEHAVIOR WAS INEXCUSABLE.
ALL THAT COUNTS IS THAT HE COULDN'T GET NEAR ENOUGH TO STICK ME. HE THINKS I'M A LITTLE PINK PINCUSHION IN UNDERPANTS.
SOMEDAY I HOPE YOU HAVE A KID THAT PUTS YOU THROUGH WHAT I'VE GONE THROUGH.
YEAH, GRANDMA SAYS THAT'S WHAT SHE USED TO TELL **YOU**.

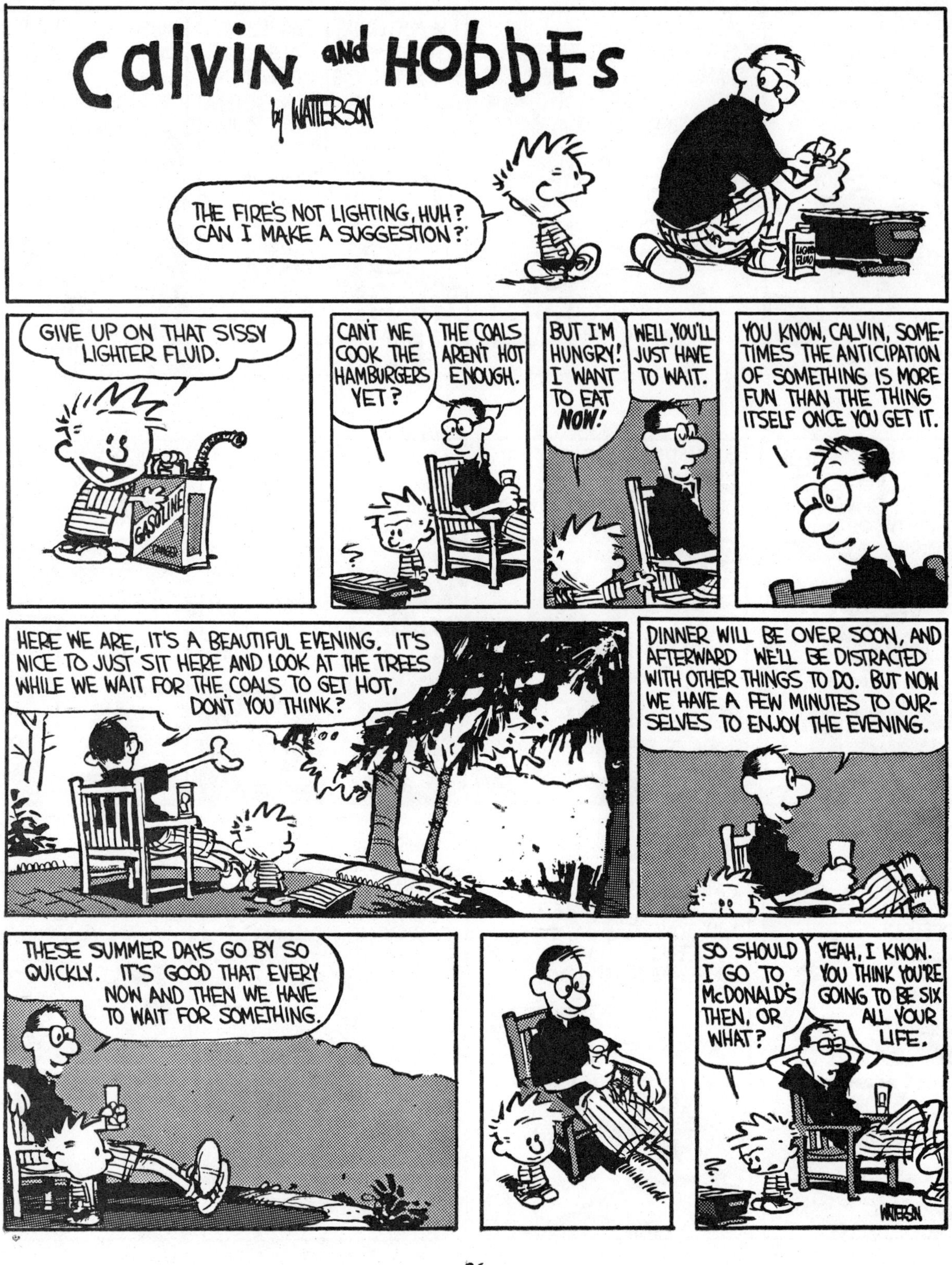
Calvin and HOBBES
by WATTERSON
THE FIRE'S NOT LIGHTING, HUH? CAN I MAKE A SUGGESTION?
GIVE UP ON THAT SISSY LIGHTER FLUID.
GASOLINE
CAN'T WE COOK THE HAMBURGERS YET?
THE COALS AREN'T HOT ENOUGH.
BUT I'M HUNGRY! I WANT TO EAT NOW!
WELL, YOU'LL JUST HAVE TO WAIT.
YOU KNOW, CALVIN, SOMETIMES THE ANTICIPATION OF SOMETHING IS MORE FUN THAN THE THING ITSELF ONCE YOU GET IT.
HERE WE ARE, IT'S A BEAUTIFUL EVENING. IT'S NICE TO JUST SIT HERE AND LOOK AT THE TREES WHILE WE WAIT FOR THE COALS TO GET HOT, DON'T YOU THINK?
DINNER WILL BE OVER SOON, AND AFTERWARD WE'LL BE DISTRACTED WITH OTHER THINGS TO DO. BUT NOW WE HAVE A FEW MINUTES TO OURSELVES TO ENJOY THE EVENING.
THESE SUMMER DAYS GO BY SO QUICKLY. IT'S GOOD THAT EVERY NOW AND THEN WE HAVE TO WAIT FOR SOMETHING.
SO SHOULD I GO TO McDONALD'S THEN, OR WHAT?
YEAH, I KNOW. YOU THINK YOU'RE GOING TO BE SIX ALL YOUR LIFE.
WATTERSON

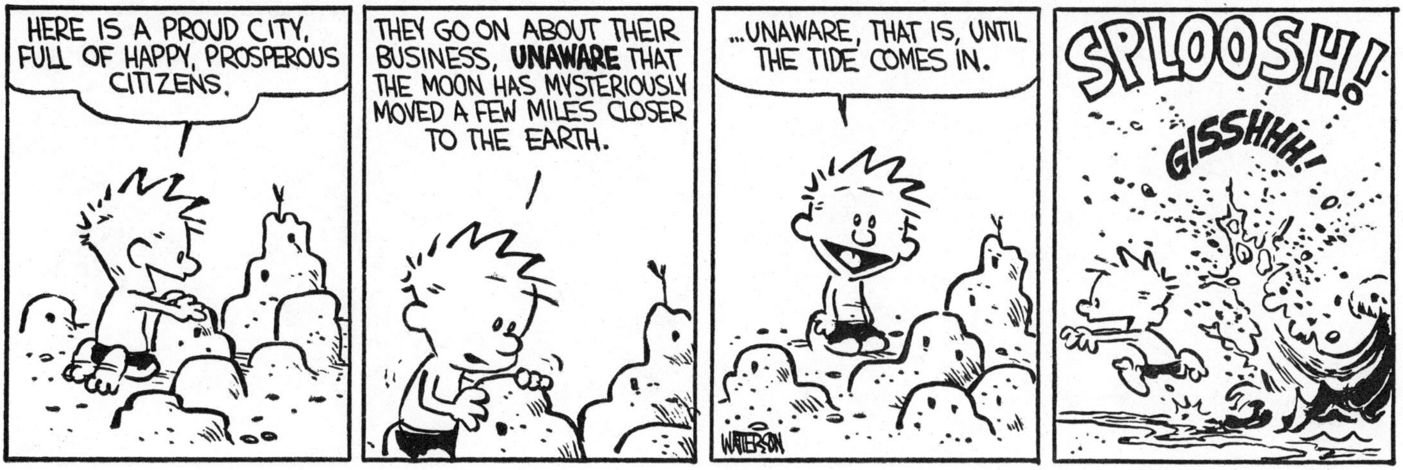
HERE IS A PROUD CITY, FULL OF HAPPY, PROSPEROUS CITIZENS.
THEY GO ON ABOUT THEIR BUSINESS, **UNAWARE** THAT THE MOON HAS MYSTERIOUSLY MOVED A FEW MILES CLOSER TO THE EARTH.
...UNAWARE, THAT IS, UNTIL THE TIDE COMES IN.
SPLOOSH!
GISSHHH!

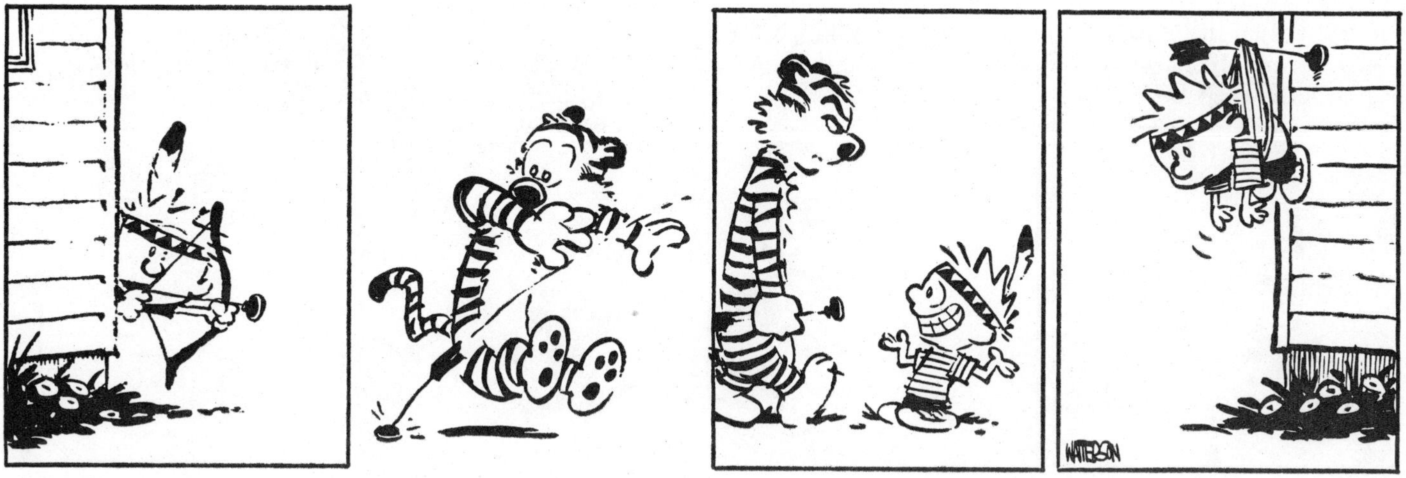

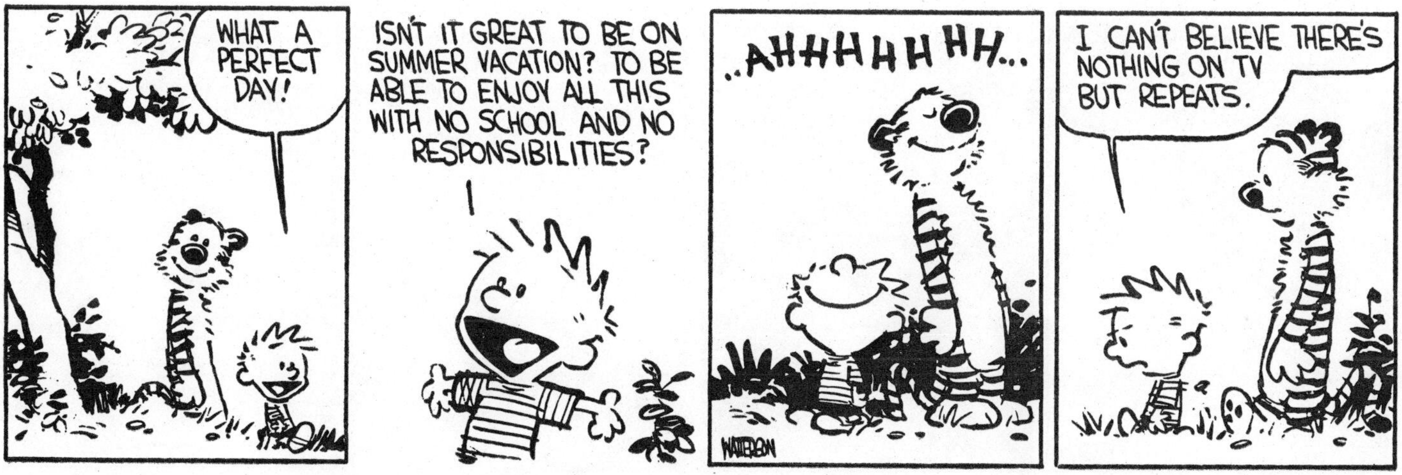
WHAT A PERFECT DAY!
ISN'T IT GREAT TO BE ON SUMMER VACATION? TO BE ABLE TO ENJOY ALL THIS WITH NO SCHOOL AND NO RESPONSIBILITIES?
..AHHHHHHH...
I CAN'T BELIEVE THERE'S NOTHING ON TV BUT REPEATS.

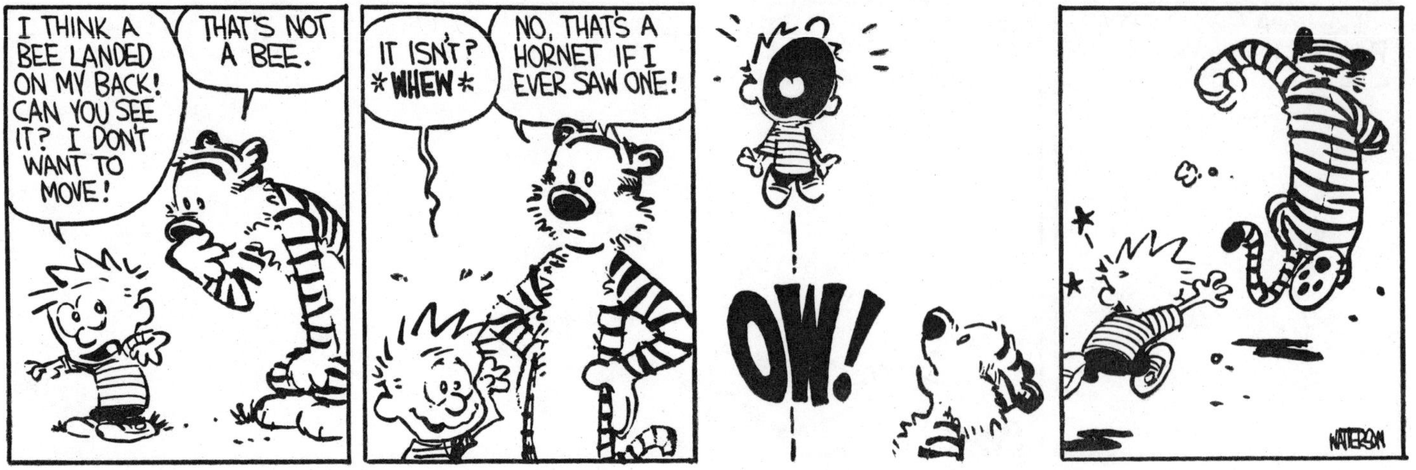
I THINK A BEE LANDED ON MY BACK! CAN YOU SEE IT? I DON'T WANT TO MOVE!
THAT'S NOT A BEE.
IT ISN'T? *WHEW*
NO, THAT'S A HORNET IF I EVER SAW ONE!
OW!
WATTERSON

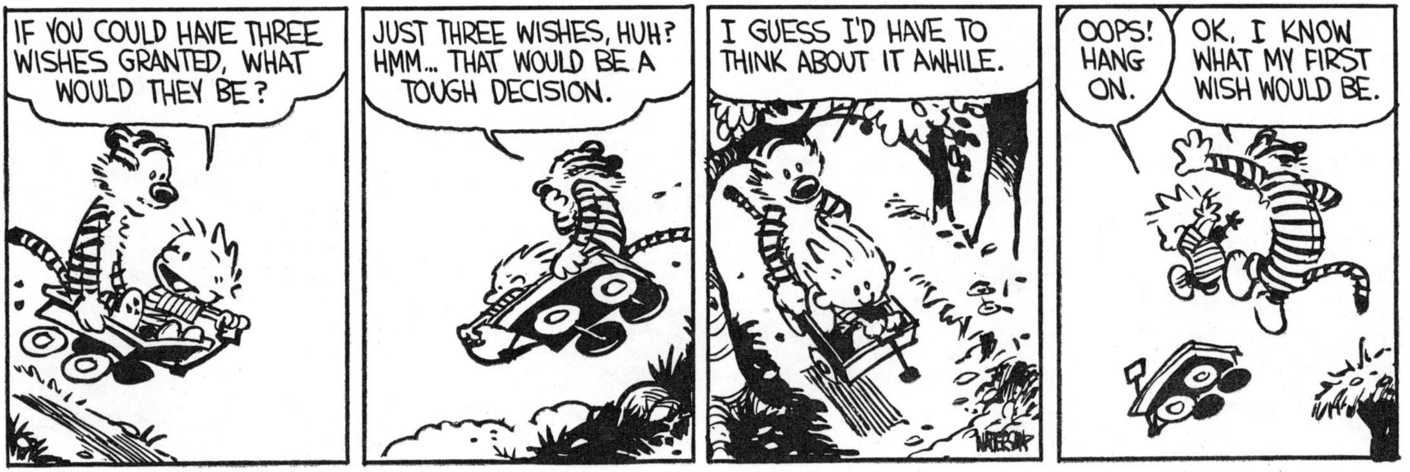
IF YOU COULD HAVE THREE WISHES GRANTED, WHAT WOULD THEY BE?
JUST THREE WISHES, HUH? HMM... THAT WOULD BE A TOUGH DECISION.
I GUESS I'D HAVE TO THINK ABOUT IT AWHILE.
OOPS! HANG ON.
OK, I KNOW WHAT MY FIRST WISH WOULD BE.

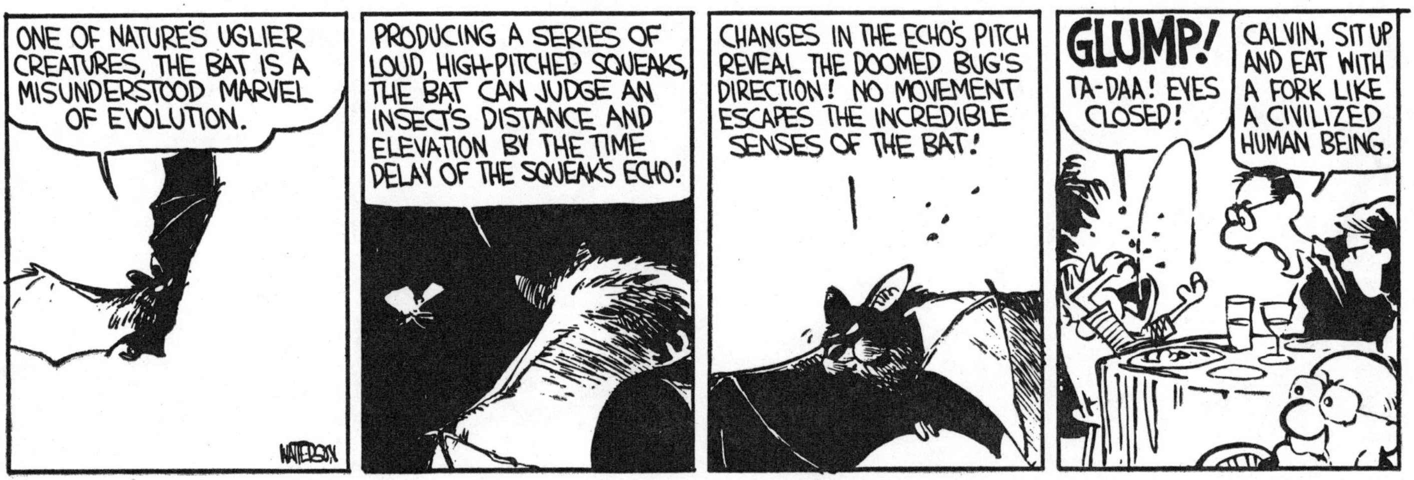
ONE OF NATURE'S UGLIER CREATURES, THE BAT IS A MISUNDERSTOOD MARVEL OF EVOLUTION.
PRODUCING A SERIES OF LOUD, HIGH-PITCHED SQUEAKS, THE BAT CAN JUDGE AN INSECT'S DISTANCE AND ELEVATION BY THE TIME DELAY OF THE SQUEAK'S ECHO!
CHANGES IN THE ECHO'S PITCH REVEAL THE DOOMED BUG'S DIRECTION! NO MOVEMENT ESCAPES THE INCREDIBLE SENSES OF THE BAT!
GLUMP!
TA-DAA! EYES CLOSED!
CALVIN, SIT UP AND EAT WITH A FORK LIKE A CIVILIZED HUMAN BEING.

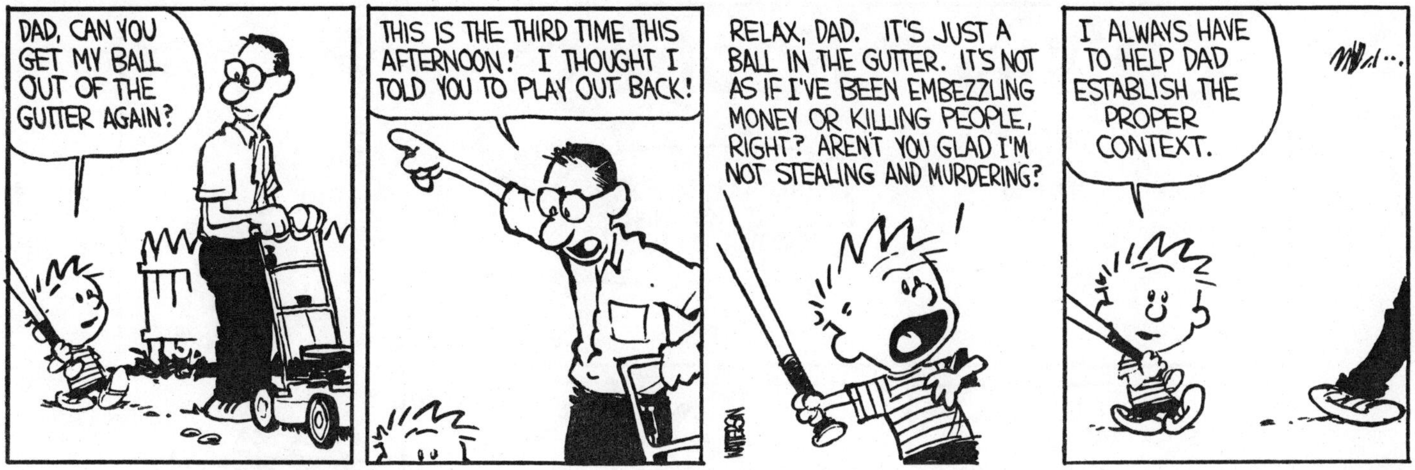
DAD, CAN YOU GET MY BALL OUT OF THE GUTTER AGAIN?
THIS IS THE THIRD TIME THIS AFTERNOON! I THOUGHT I TOLD YOU TO PLAY OUT BACK!
RELAX, DAD. IT'S JUST A BALL IN THE GUTTER. IT'S NOT AS IF I'VE BEEN EMBEZZLING MONEY OR KILLING PEOPLE, RIGHT? AREN'T YOU GLAD I'M NOT STEALING AND MURDERING?
I ALWAYS HAVE TO HELP DAD ESTABLISH THE PROPER CONTEXT.

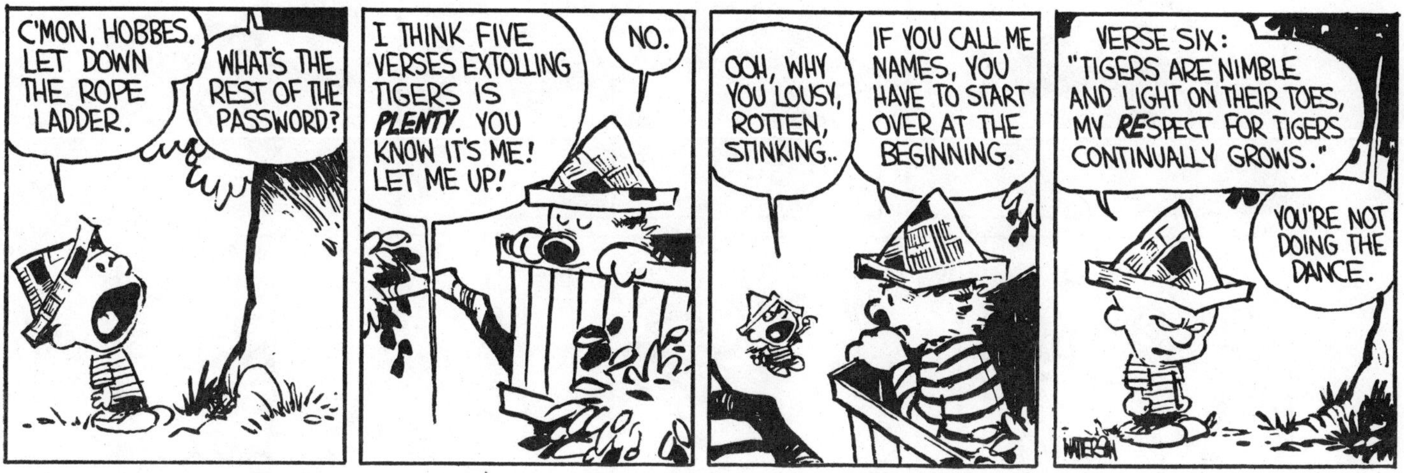
C'MON, HOBBES. LET DOWN THE ROPE LADDER.
WHAT'S THE REST OF THE PASSWORD?
I THINK FIVE VERSES EXTOLLING TIGERS IS PLENTY. YOU KNOW IT'S ME! LET ME UP!
NO.
OOH, WHY YOU LOUSY, ROTTEN, STINKING..
IF YOU CALL ME NAMES, YOU HAVE TO START OVER AT THE BEGINNING.
VERSE SIX: "TIGERS ARE NIMBLE AND LIGHT ON THEIR TOES, MY RESPECT FOR TIGERS CONTINUALLY GROWS."
YOU'RE NOT DOING THE DANCE.

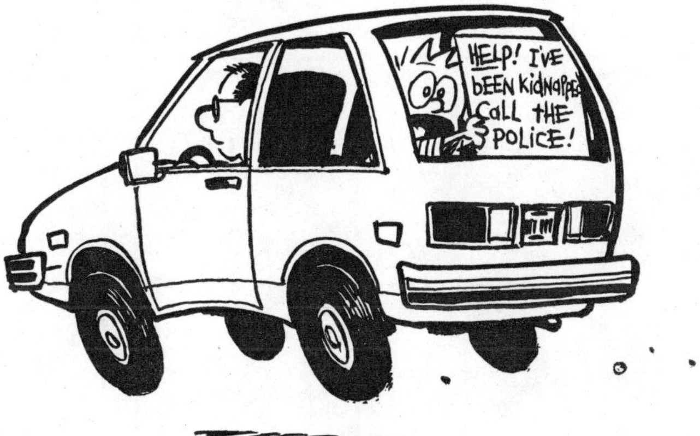
HELP! I'VE bEEN kidNapped Call THE POLICE!

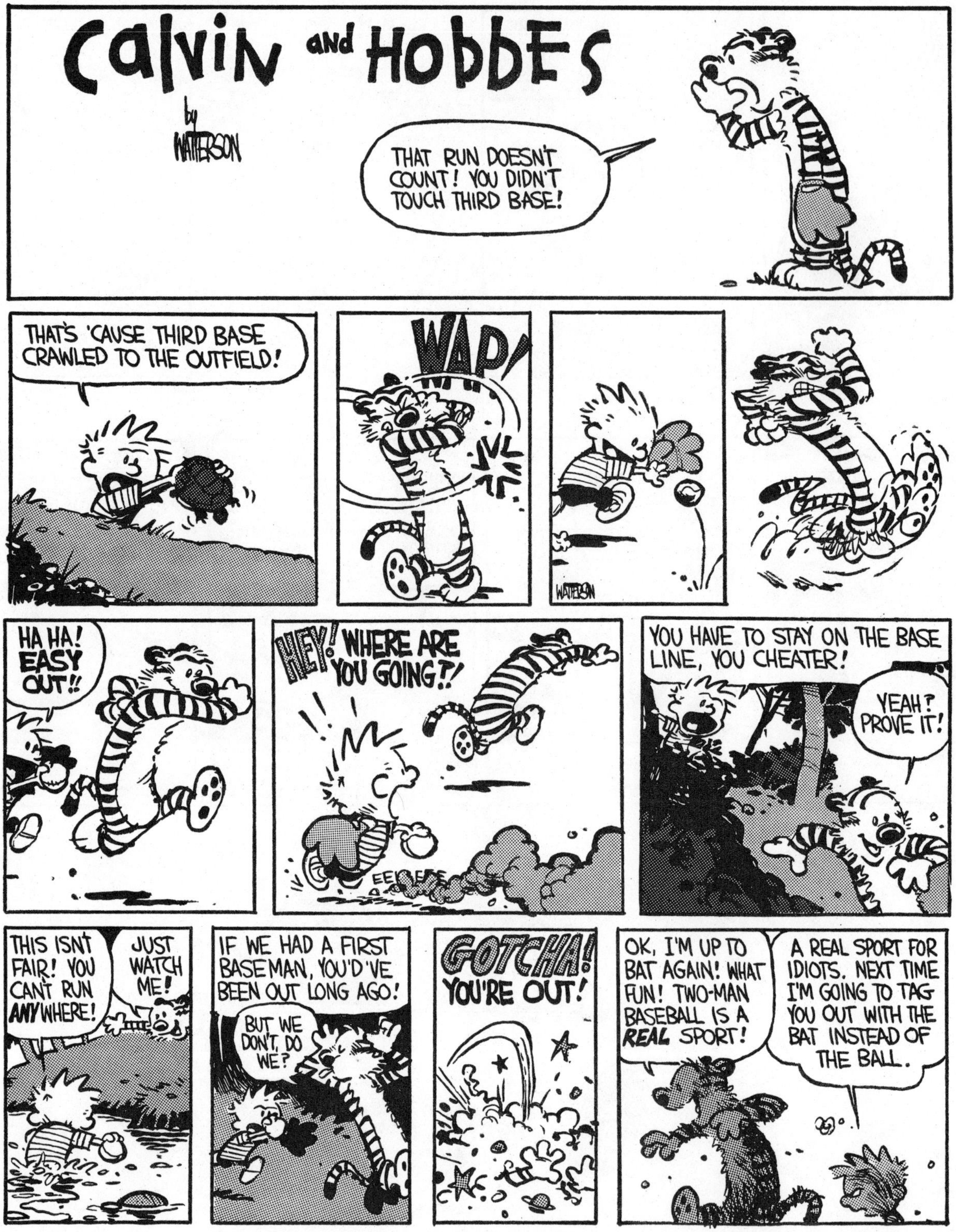
Calvin and HOBBES
by WATTERSON
THAT RUN DOESN'T COUNT! YOU DIDN'T TOUCH THIRD BASE!
THAT'S 'CAUSE THIRD BASE CRAWLED TO THE OUTFIELD!
WAP!
WATTERSON
HA HA! EASY OUT!!
HEY! WHERE ARE YOU GOING?!
EEEEEEE
YOU HAVE TO STAY ON THE BASE LINE, YOU CHEATER!
YEAH? PROVE IT!
THIS ISN'T FAIR! YOU CAN'T RUN ANYWHERE!
JUST WATCH ME!
IF WE HAD A FIRST BASEMAN, YOU'D'VE BEEN OUT LONG AGO!
BUT WE DON'T, DO WE?
GOTCHA! YOU'RE OUT!
OK, I'M UP TO BAT AGAIN! WHAT FUN! TWO-MAN BASEBALL IS A REAL SPORT!
A REAL SPORT FOR IDIOTS. NEXT TIME I'M GOING TO TAG YOU OUT WITH THE BAT INSTEAD OF THE BALL.

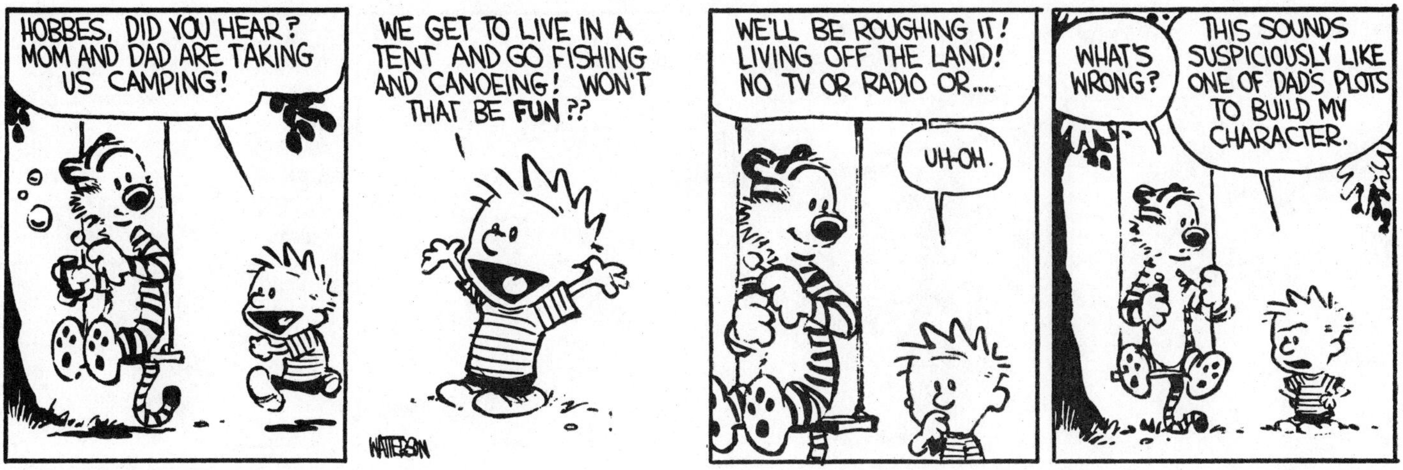
HOBBES, DID YOU HEAR? MOM AND DAD ARE TAKING US CAMPING!
WE GET TO LIVE IN A TENT AND GO FISHING AND CANOEING! WON'T THAT BE FUN??
WATTERSON
WE'LL BE ROUGHING IT! LIVING OFF THE LAND! NO TV OR RADIO OR....
UH-OH.
WHAT'S WRONG?
THIS SOUNDS SUSPICIOUSLY LIKE ONE OF DAD'S PLOTS TO BUILD MY CHARACTER.

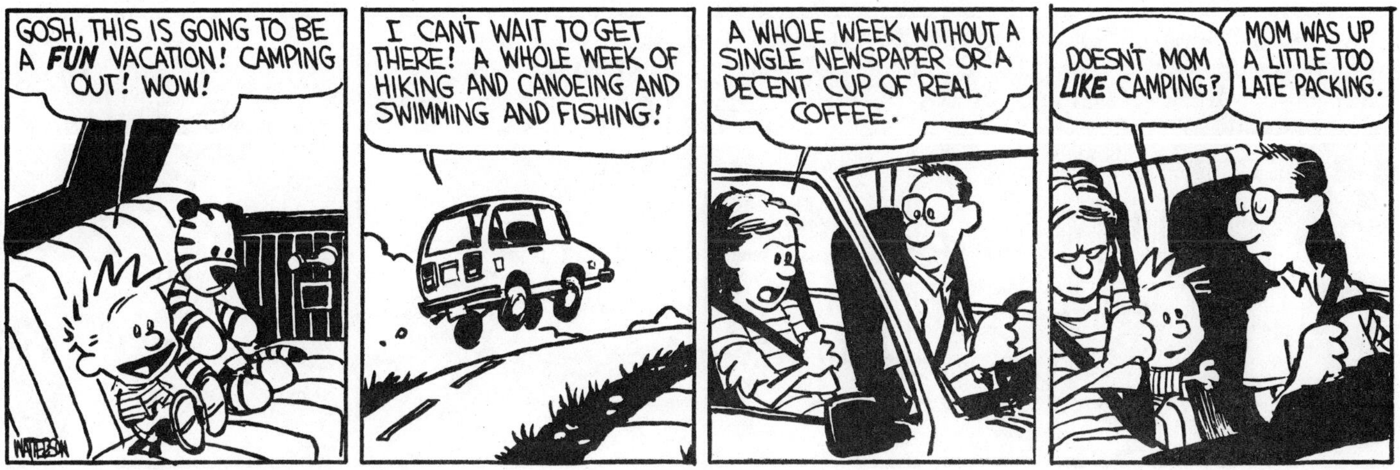
GOSH, THIS IS GOING TO BE A FUN VACATION! CAMPING OUT! WOW!
WATTERSON
I CAN'T WAIT TO GET THERE! A WHOLE WEEK OF HIKING AND CANOEING AND SWIMMING AND FISHING!
A WHOLE WEEK WITHOUT A SINGLE NEWSPAPER OR A DECENT CUP OF REAL COFFEE.
DOESN'T MOM LIKE CAMPING?
MOM WAS UP A LITTLE TOO LATE PACKING.

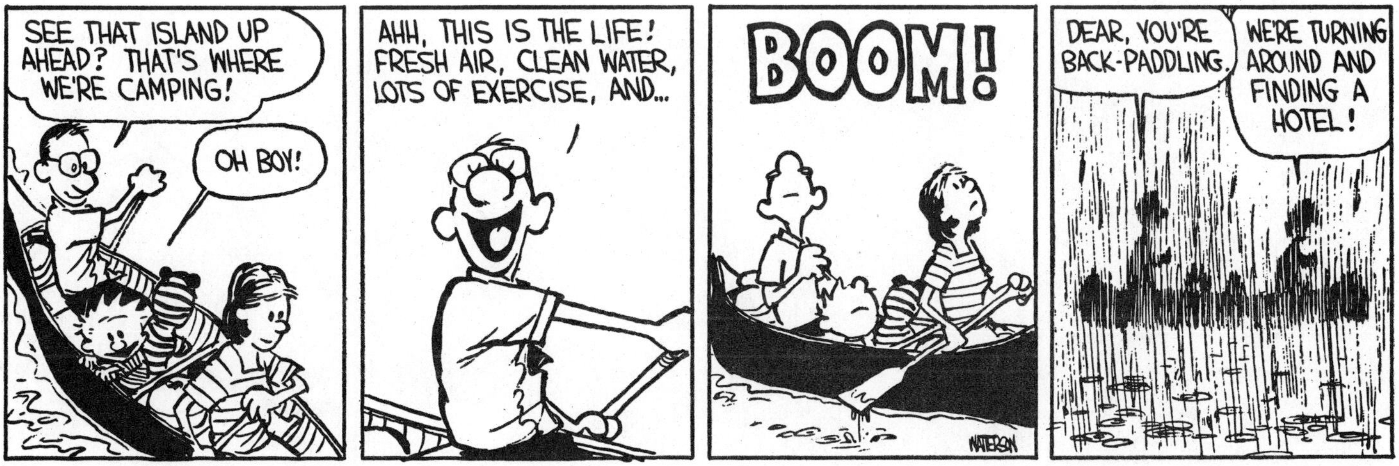
SEE THAT ISLAND UP AHEAD? THAT'S WHERE WE'RE CAMPING!
OH BOY!
AHH, THIS IS THE LIFE! FRESH AIR, CLEAN WATER, LOTS OF EXERCISE, AND...
BOOM!
WATTERSON
DEAR, YOU'RE BACK-PADDLING.
WE'RE TURNING AROUND AND FINDING A HOTEL!

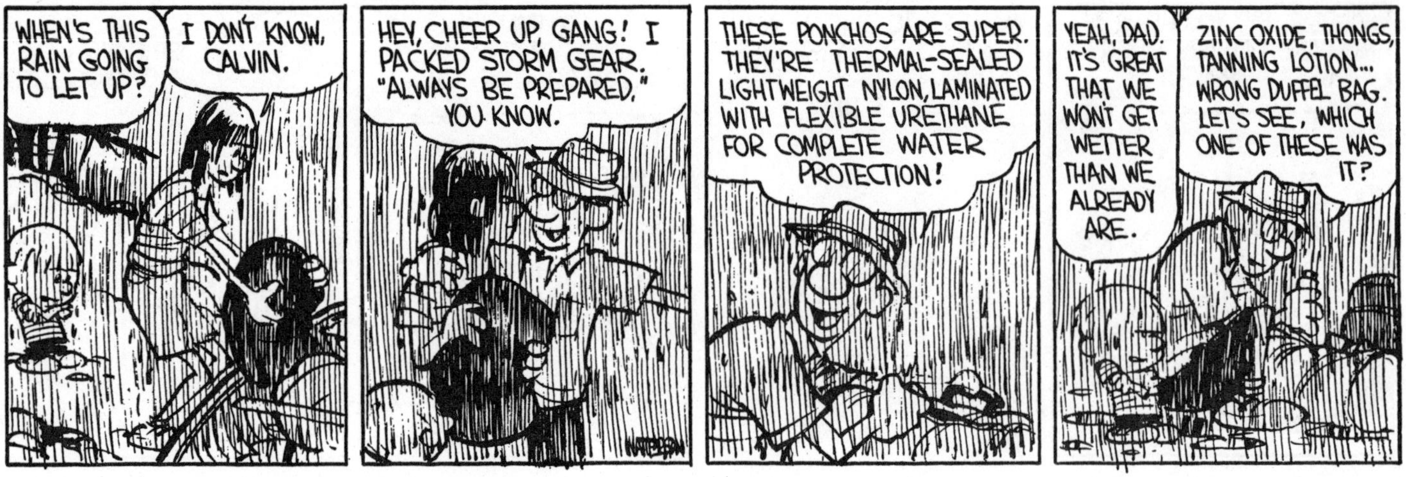
WHEN'S THIS RAIN GOING TO LET UP?
I DON'T KNOW, CALVIN.
HEY, CHEER UP, GANG! I PACKED STORM GEAR. "ALWAYS BE PREPARED," YOU KNOW.
THESE PONCHOS ARE SUPER. THEY'RE THERMAL-SEALED LIGHTWEIGHT NYLON, LAMINATED WITH FLEXIBLE URETHANE FOR COMPLETE WATER PROTECTION!
YEAH, DAD. IT'S GREAT THAT WE WON'T GET WETTER THAN WE ALREADY ARE.
ZINC OXIDE, THONGS, TANNING LOTION... WRONG DUFFEL BAG. LET'S SEE, WHICH ONE OF THESE WAS IT?

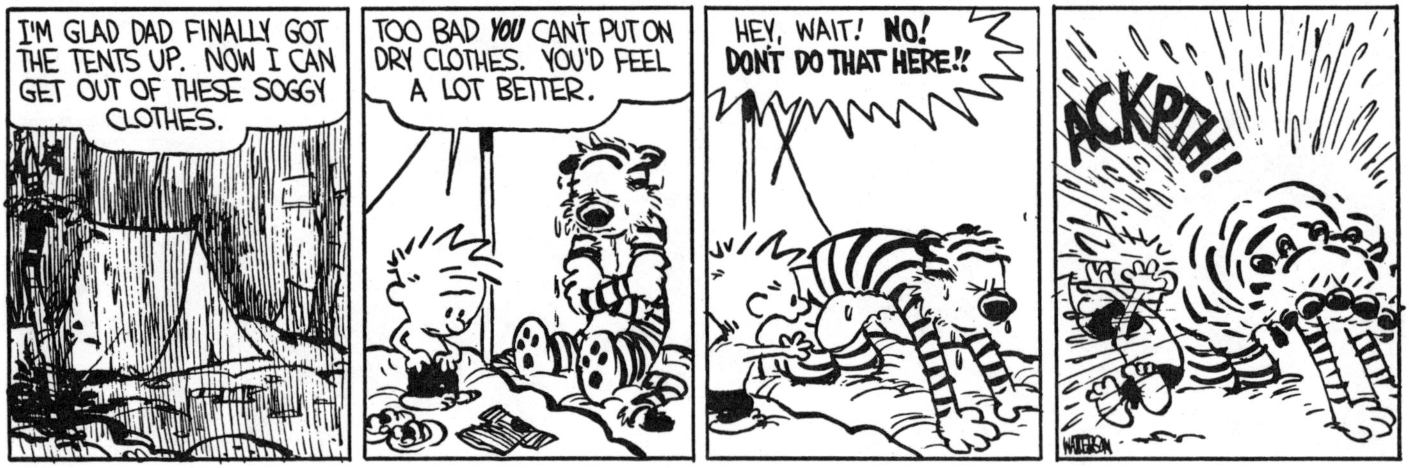
I'M GLAD DAD FINALLY GOT THE TENTS UP. NOW I CAN GET OUT OF THESE SOGGY CLOTHES.
TOO BAD YOU CAN'T PUT ON DRY CLOTHES. YOU'D FEEL A LOT BETTER.
HEY, WAIT! NO! DON'T DO THAT HERE!!
ACKPTH!

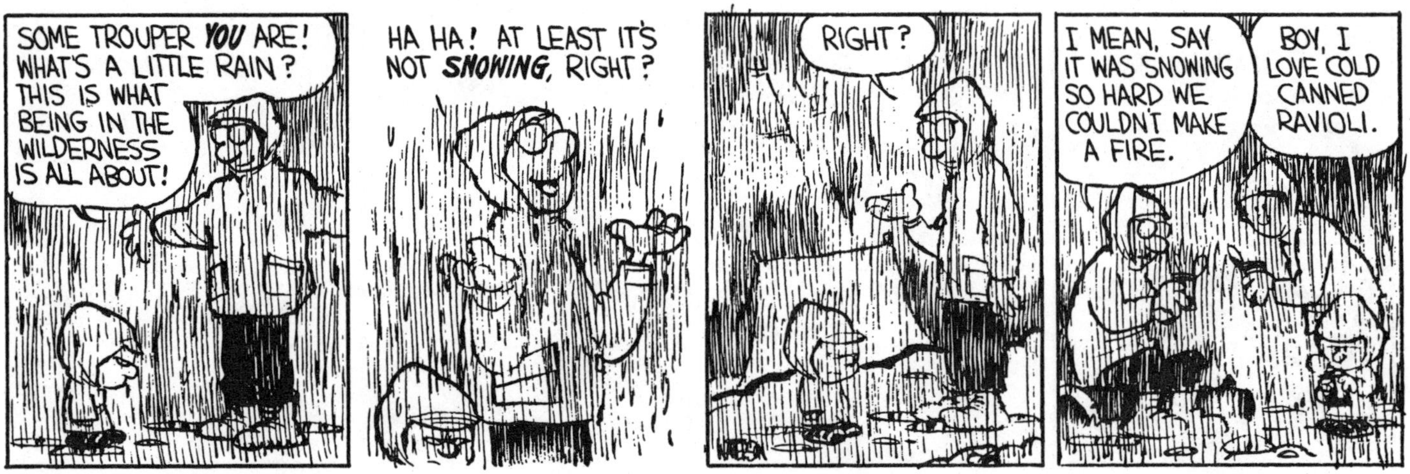
SOME TROUPER YOU ARE! WHAT'S A LITTLE RAIN? THIS IS WHAT BEING IN THE WILDERNESS IS ALL ABOUT!
HA HA! AT LEAST IT'S NOT SNOWING, RIGHT?
RIGHT?
I MEAN, SAY IT WAS SNOWING SO HARD WE COULDN'T MAKE A FIRE.
BOY, I LOVE COLD CANNED RAVIOLI.

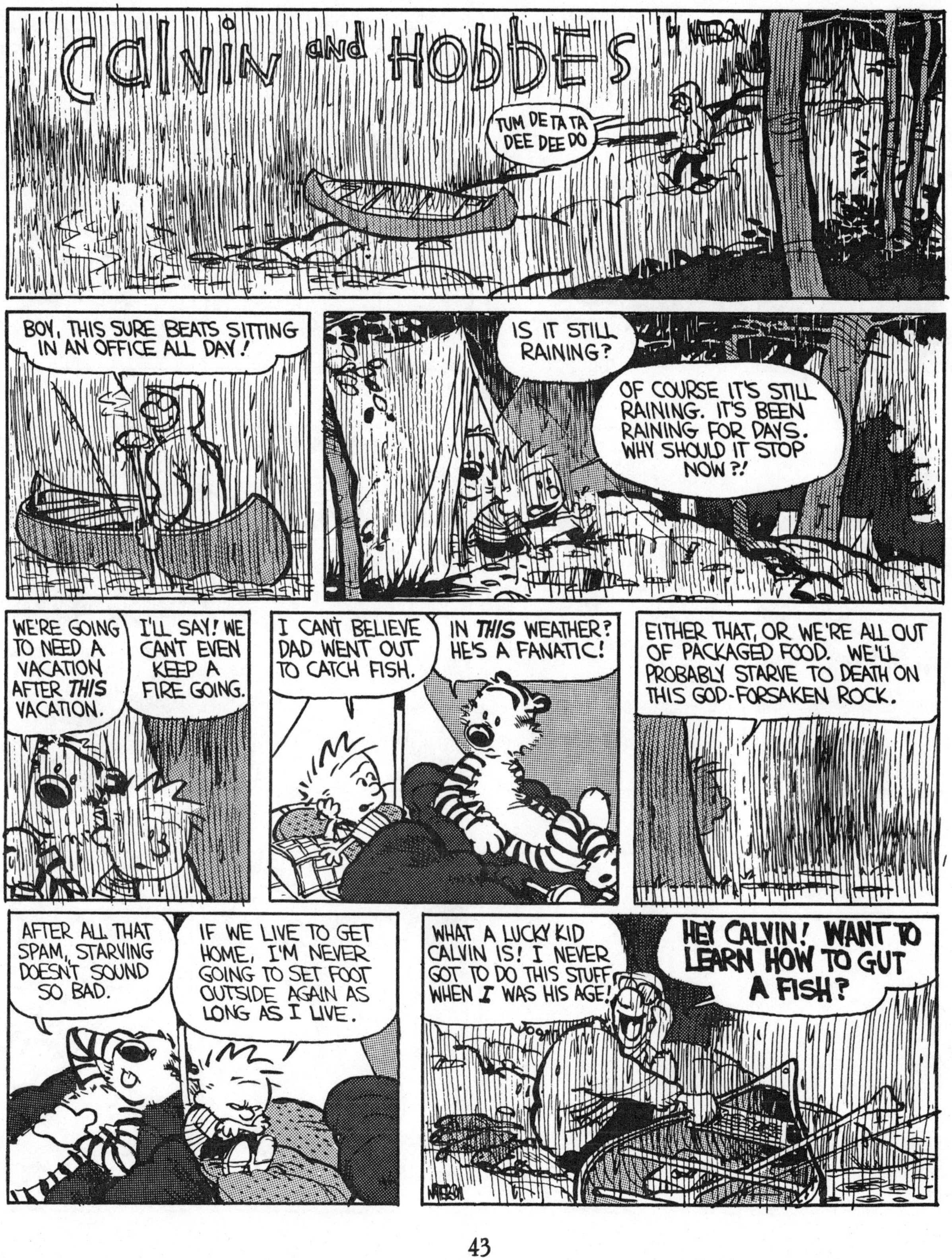
Calvin and Hobbes
by WATTERSON
TUM DE TA TA DEE DEE DO
BOY, THIS SURE BEATS SITTING IN AN OFFICE ALL DAY!
IS IT STILL RAINING?
OF COURSE IT'S STILL RAINING. IT'S BEEN RAINING FOR DAYS. WHY SHOULD IT STOP NOW?!
WE'RE GOING TO NEED A VACATION AFTER THIS VACATION.
I'LL SAY! WE CAN'T EVEN KEEP A FIRE GOING.
I CAN'T BELIEVE DAD WENT OUT TO CATCH FISH.
IN THIS WEATHER? HE'S A FANATIC!
EITHER THAT, OR WE'RE ALL OUT OF PACKAGED FOOD. WE'LL PROBABLY STARVE TO DEATH ON THIS GOD-FORSAKEN ROCK.
AFTER ALL THAT SPAM, STARVING DOESN'T SOUND SO BAD.
IF WE LIVE TO GET HOME, I'M NEVER GOING TO SET FOOT OUTSIDE AGAIN AS LONG AS I LIVE.
WHAT A LUCKY KID CALVIN IS! I NEVER GOT TO DO THIS STUFF WHEN I WAS HIS AGE!
HEY CALVIN! WANT TO LEARN HOW TO GUT A FISH?
WATERSON

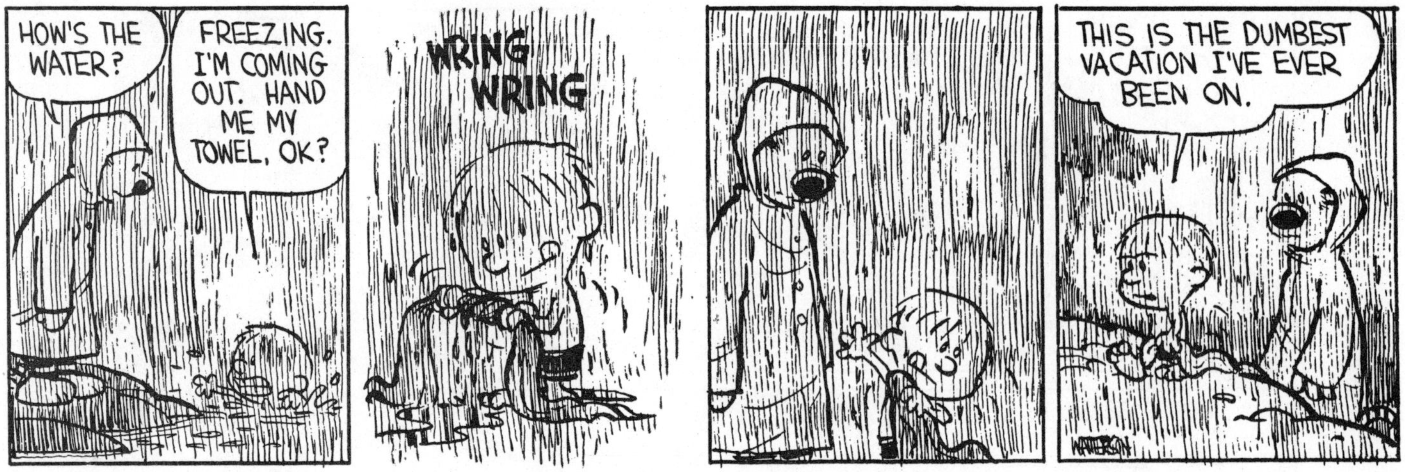
HOW'S THE WATER?
FREEZING. I'M COMING OUT. HAND ME MY TOWEL, OK?
WRING WRING
THIS IS THE DUMBEST VACATION I'VE EVER BEEN ON.

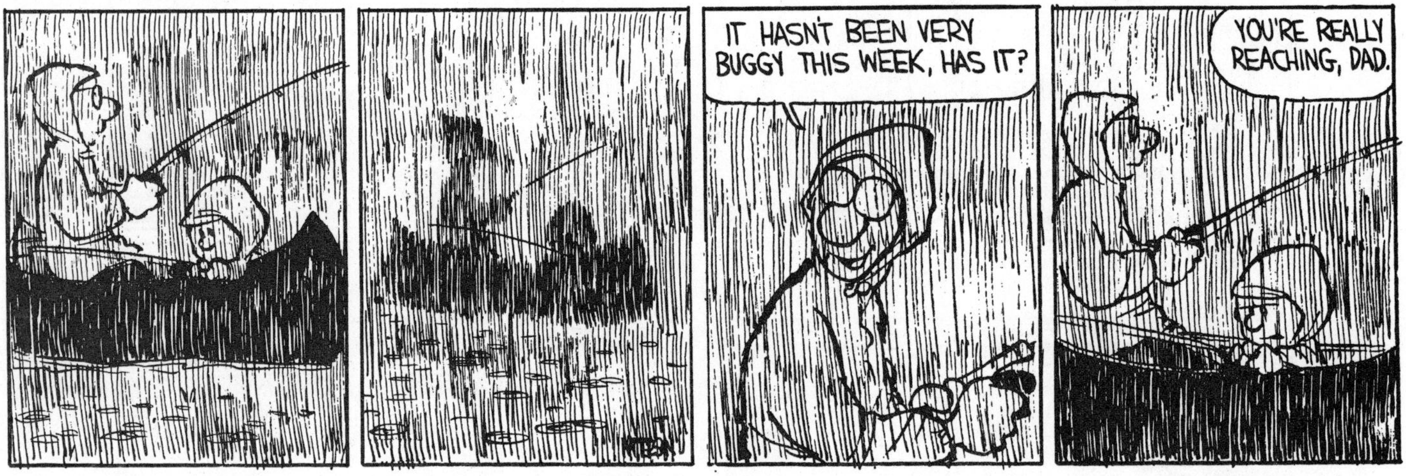
IT HASN'T BEEN VERY BUGGY THIS WEEK, HAS IT?
YOU'RE REALLY REACHING, DAD.

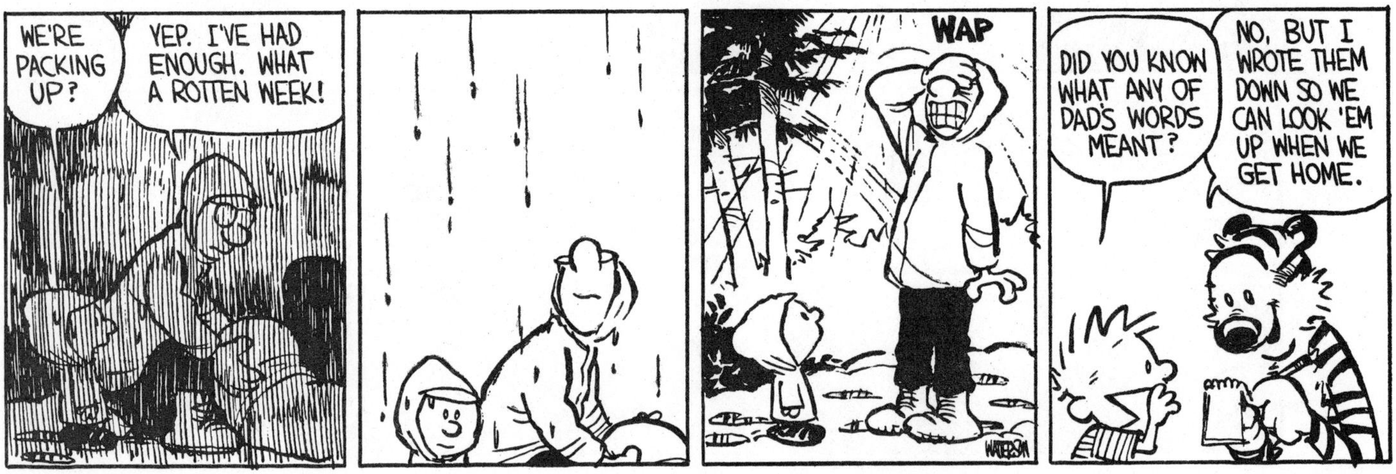
WE'RE PACKING UP?
YEP. I'VE HAD ENOUGH. WHAT A ROTTEN WEEK!
WAP
DID YOU KNOW WHAT ANY OF DAD'S WORDS MEANT?
NO, BUT I WROTE THEM DOWN SO WE CAN LOOK 'EM UP WHEN WE GET HOME.

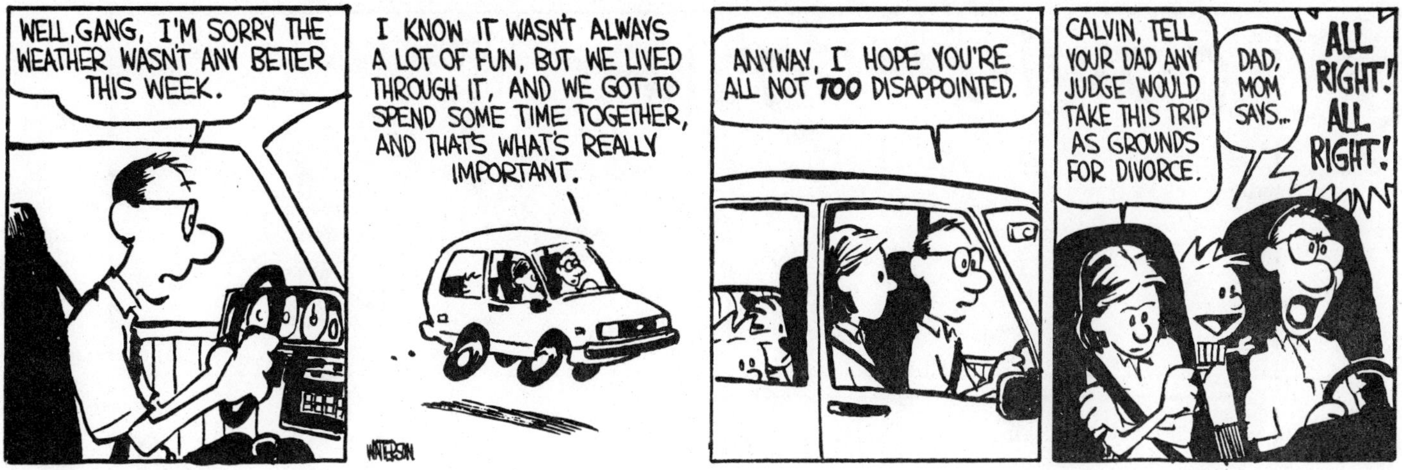
WELL, GANG, I'M SORRY THE WEATHER WASN'T ANY BETTER THIS WEEK.
I KNOW IT WASN'T ALWAYS A LOT OF FUN, BUT WE LIVED THROUGH IT, AND WE GOT TO SPEND SOME TIME TOGETHER, AND THAT'S WHAT'S REALLY IMPORTANT.
WATTERSON
ANYWAY, I HOPE YOU'RE ALL NOT TOO DISAPPOINTED.
CALVIN, TELL YOUR DAD ANY JUDGE WOULD TAKE THIS TRIP AS GROUNDS FOR DIVORCE.
DAD, MOM SAYS...
ALL RIGHT! ALL RIGHT!

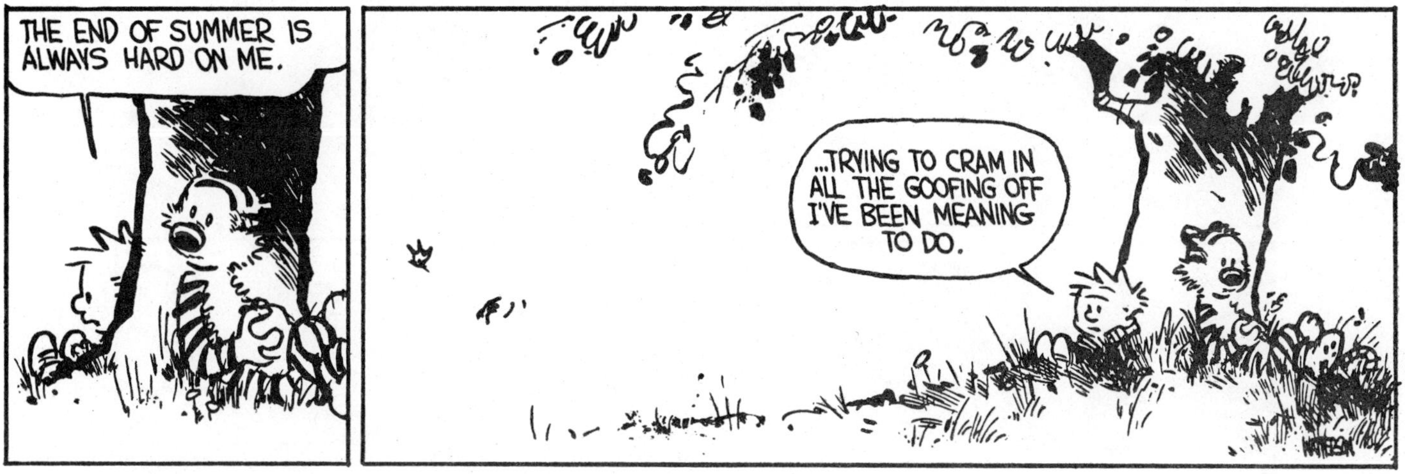
THE END OF SUMMER IS ALWAYS HARD ON ME.
...TRYING TO CRAM IN ALL THE GOOFING OFF I'VE BEEN MEANING TO DO.
WATTERSON

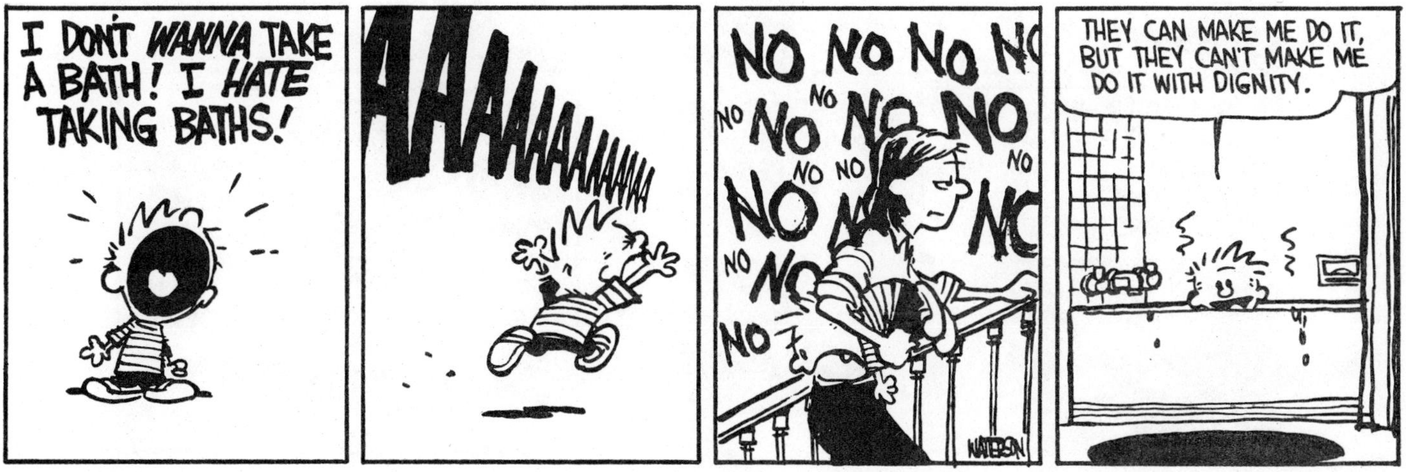
I DON'T WANNA TAKE A BATH! I HATE TAKING BATHS!
AAAAAAAAAAAAAA
NO NO NO NO
NO NO NO NO
NO NO NO
NO NO NO
NO NO
NO
WATTERSON
THEY CAN MAKE ME DO IT, BUT THEY CAN'T MAKE ME DO IT WITH DIGNITY.

Calvin and Hobbes by WATERSON

AH-CHOO!

WHEN ... NO BRAINS.

AH.. AH.. AH.. **AH**

CHOOO!

THE FORCE OF THE NASAL EXPLOSION SENDS CALVIN REELING THROUGH THE STRATOSPHERE!

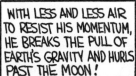

WITH LESS AND LESS AIR TO RESIST HIS MOMENTUM, HE BREAKS THE PULL OF EARTH'S GRAVITY AND HURLS PAST THE MOON!

AS HE PASSES OUT OF THE GALAXY, CALVIN REFLECTS ON THE WISDOM OF COVERING ONE'S MOUTH WHEN SNEEZING TO DEFLECT THE PROPULSION.

ALAS, IT IS KNOWLEDGE GAINED TOO LATE FOR POOR CALVIN, THE HUMAN SATELLITE! ...BUT WAIT! ANOTHER SNEEZE IS BREWING! CALVIN TURNS HIMSELF AROUND!

THE SECOND SNEEZE ROCKETS HIM BACK TO EARTH! HE'S SAVED! IT'S A MIRACLE!

AH CHOO!

GOD BLESS YOU.

OH, HE *DOES*, MOM. HE *DOES*.

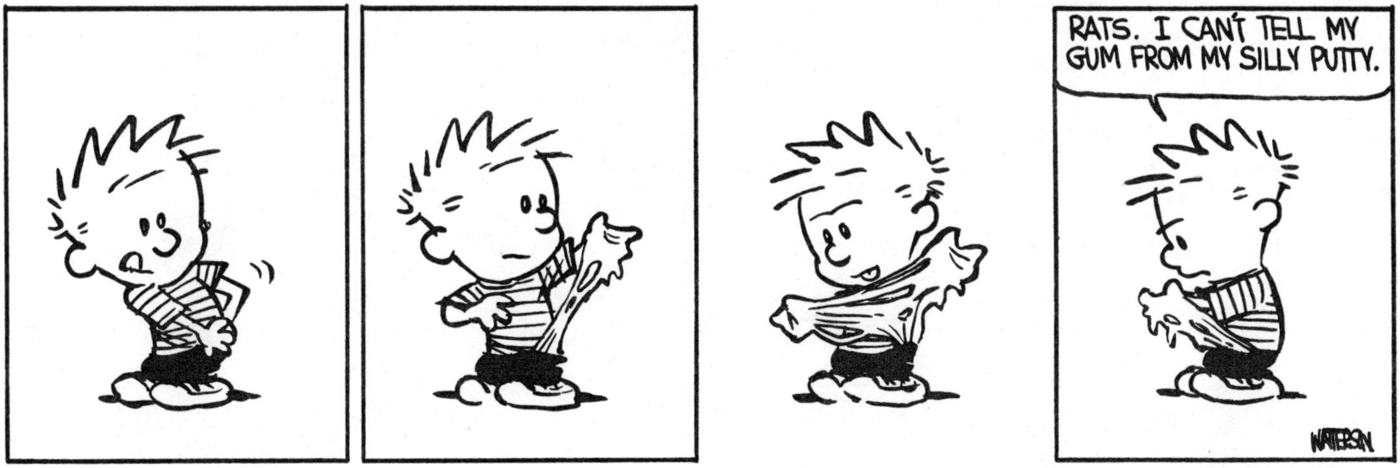
RATS. I CAN'T TELL MY GUM FROM MY SILLY PUTTY.

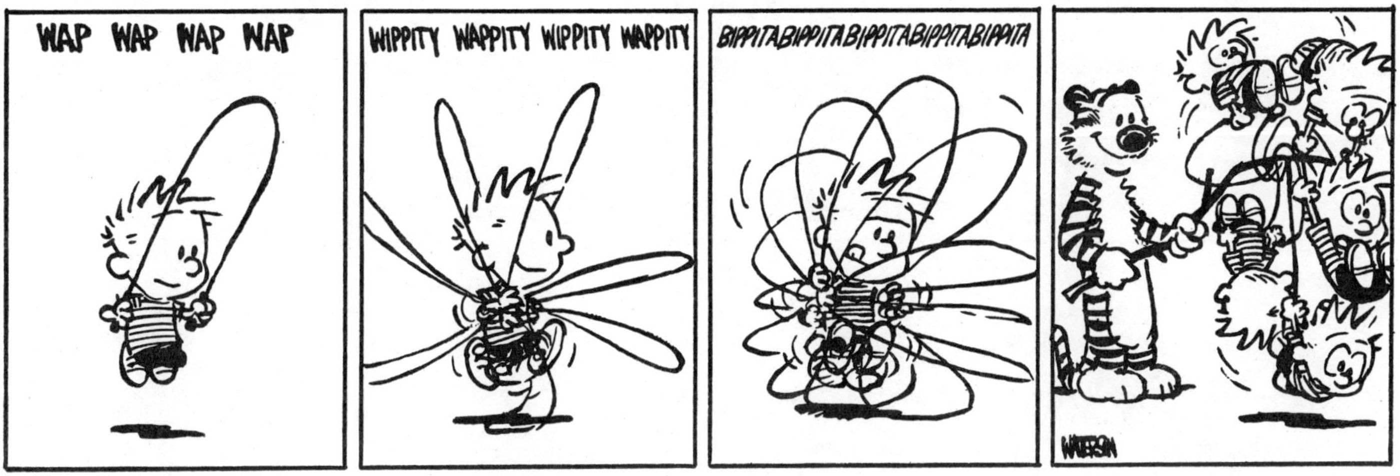
WAP WAP WAP WAP
WIPPITY WAPPITY WIPPITY WAPPITY
BIPPITABIPPITABIPPITABIPPITABIPPITA

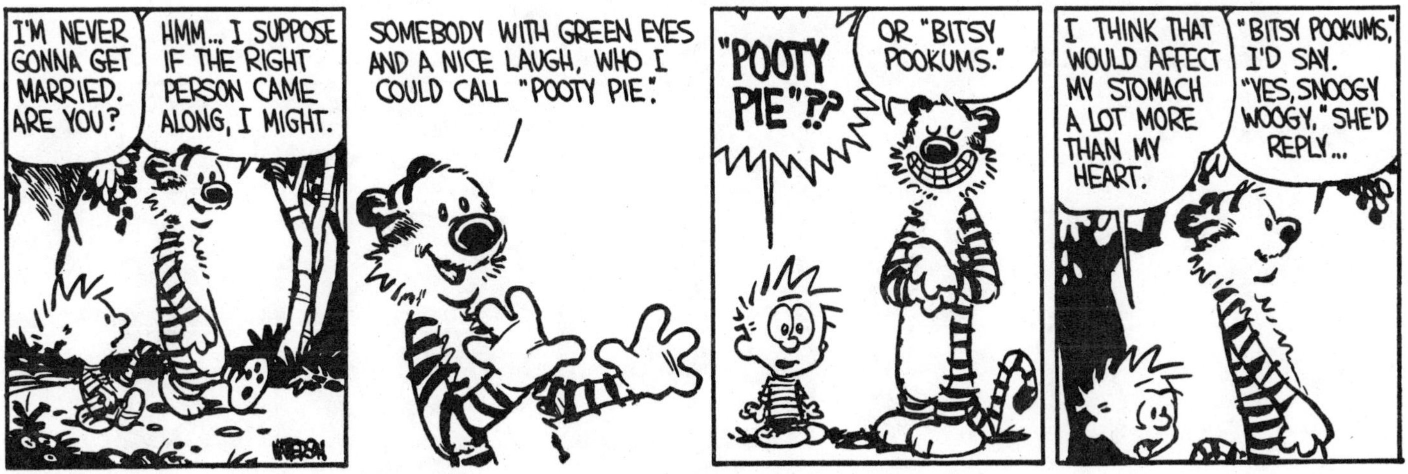
I'M NEVER GONNA GET MARRIED. ARE YOU?
HMM... I SUPPOSE IF THE RIGHT PERSON CAME ALONG, I MIGHT.
SOMEBODY WITH GREEN EYES AND A NICE LAUGH, WHO I COULD CALL "POOTY PIE."
"POOTY PIE"?!?
OR "BITSY POOKUMS."
I THINK THAT WOULD AFFECT MY STOMACH A LOT MORE THAN MY HEART.
"BITSY POOKUMS," I'D SAY. "YES, SNOOGY WOOGY," SHE'D REPLY...

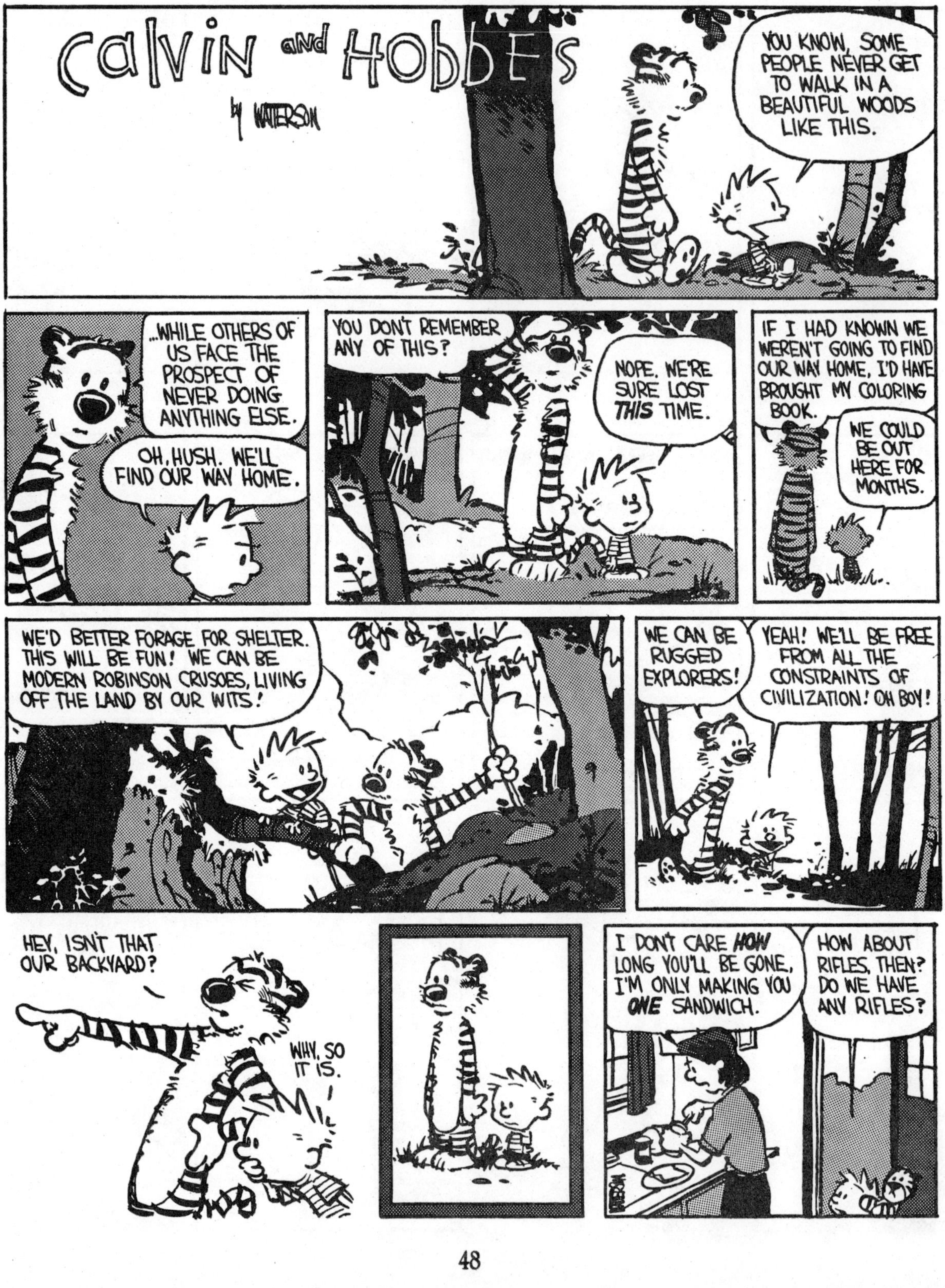
Calvin and HOBBES
by WATTERSON
YOU KNOW, SOME PEOPLE NEVER GET TO WALK IN A BEAUTIFUL WOODS LIKE THIS.
...WHILE OTHERS OF US FACE THE PROSPECT OF NEVER DOING ANYTHING ELSE.
OH, HUSH. WE'LL FIND OUR WAY HOME.
YOU DON'T REMEMBER ANY OF THIS?
NOPE. WE'RE SURE LOST THIS TIME.
IF I HAD KNOWN WE WEREN'T GOING TO FIND OUR WAY HOME, I'D HAVE BROUGHT MY COLORING BOOK.
WE COULD BE OUT HERE FOR MONTHS.
WE'D BETTER FORAGE FOR SHELTER. THIS WILL BE FUN! WE CAN BE MODERN ROBINSON CRUSOES, LIVING OFF THE LAND BY OUR WITS!
WE CAN BE RUGGED EXPLORERS!
YEAH! WE'LL BE FREE FROM ALL THE CONSTRAINTS OF CIVILIZATION! OH BOY!
HEY, ISN'T THAT OUR BACKYARD?
WHY, SO IT IS.
I DON'T CARE HOW LONG YOU'LL BE GONE, I'M ONLY MAKING YOU ONE SANDWICH.
HOW ABOUT RIFLES, THEN? DO WE HAVE ANY RIFLES?

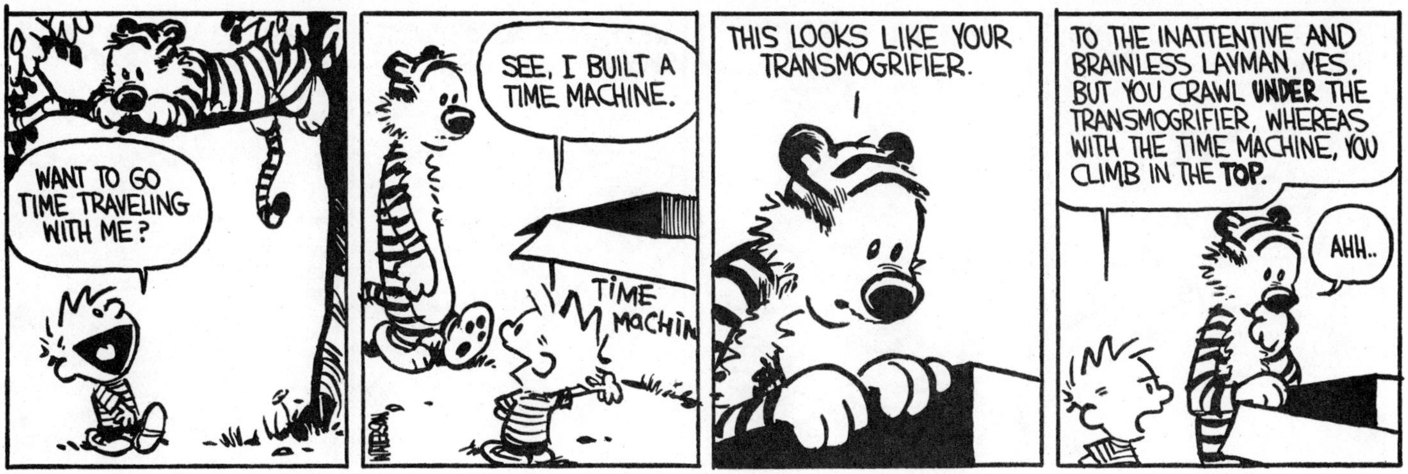
WANT TO GO TIME TRAVELING WITH ME?
SEE, I BUILT A TIME MACHINE.
TIME MACHIN
THIS LOOKS LIKE YOUR TRANSMOGRIFIER.
TO THE INATTENTIVE AND BRAINLESS LAYMAN, YES. BUT YOU CRAWL **UNDER** THE TRANSMOGRIFIER, WHEREAS WITH THE TIME MACHINE, YOU CLIMB IN THE **TOP**.
AHH..
WATTERSON

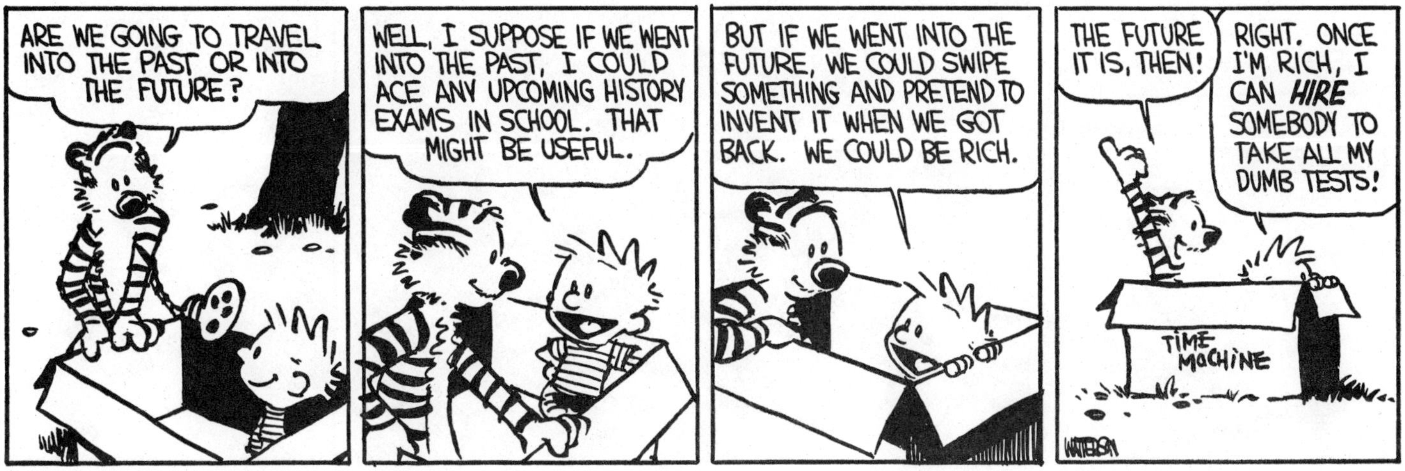
ARE WE GOING TO TRAVEL INTO THE PAST OR INTO THE FUTURE?
WELL, I SUPPOSE IF WE WENT INTO THE PAST, I COULD ACE ANY UPCOMING HISTORY EXAMS IN SCHOOL. THAT MIGHT BE USEFUL.
BUT IF WE WENT INTO THE FUTURE, WE COULD SWIPE SOMETHING AND PRETEND TO INVENT IT WHEN WE GOT BACK. WE COULD BE RICH.
THE FUTURE IT IS, THEN!
RIGHT. ONCE I'M RICH, I CAN *HIRE* SOMEBODY TO TAKE ALL MY DUMB TESTS!
TIME MACHINE
WATTERSON

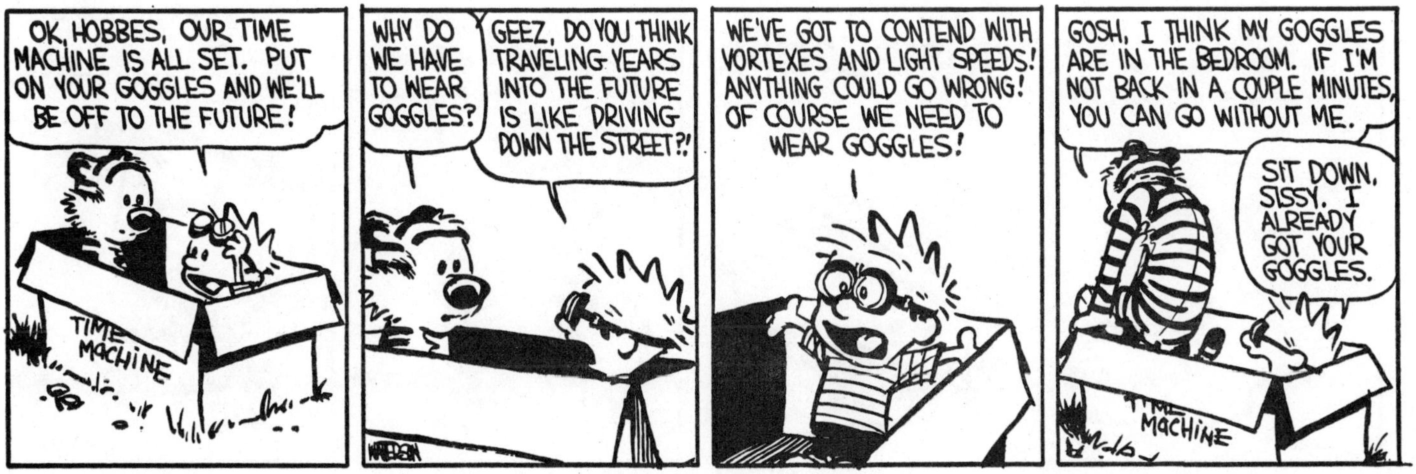
OK, HOBBES, OUR TIME MACHINE IS ALL SET. PUT ON YOUR GOGGLES AND WE'LL BE OFF TO THE FUTURE!
TIME MACHINE
WHY DO WE HAVE TO WEAR GOGGLES?
GEEZ, DO YOU THINK TRAVELING YEARS INTO THE FUTURE IS LIKE DRIVING DOWN THE STREET?!
WATTERSON
WE'VE GOT TO CONTEND WITH VORTEXES AND LIGHT SPEEDS! ANYTHING COULD GO WRONG! OF COURSE WE NEED TO WEAR GOGGLES!
GOSH, I THINK MY GOGGLES ARE IN THE BEDROOM. IF I'M NOT BACK IN A COUPLE MINUTES, YOU CAN GO WITHOUT ME.
SIT DOWN, SISSY. I ALREADY GOT YOUR GOGGLES.
MACHINE

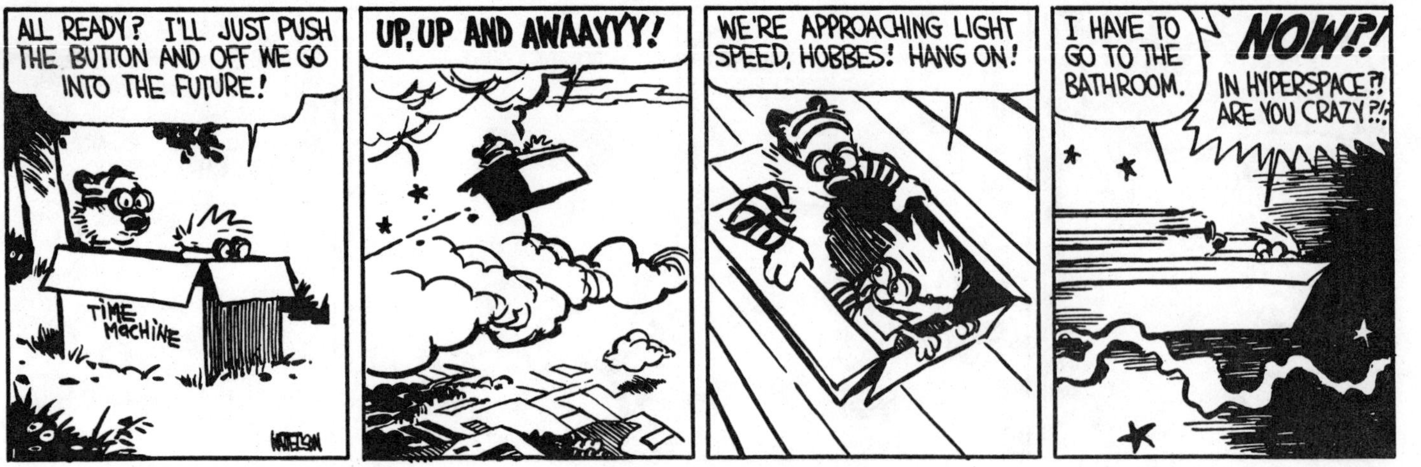
ALL READY? I'LL JUST PUSH THE BUTTON AND OFF WE GO INTO THE FUTURE!
TIME MACHINE
UP, UP AND AWAAYYY!
WE'RE APPROACHING LIGHT SPEED, HOBBES! HANG ON!
I HAVE TO GO TO THE BATHROOM.
NOW?! IN HYPERSPACE?! ARE YOU CRAZY?!

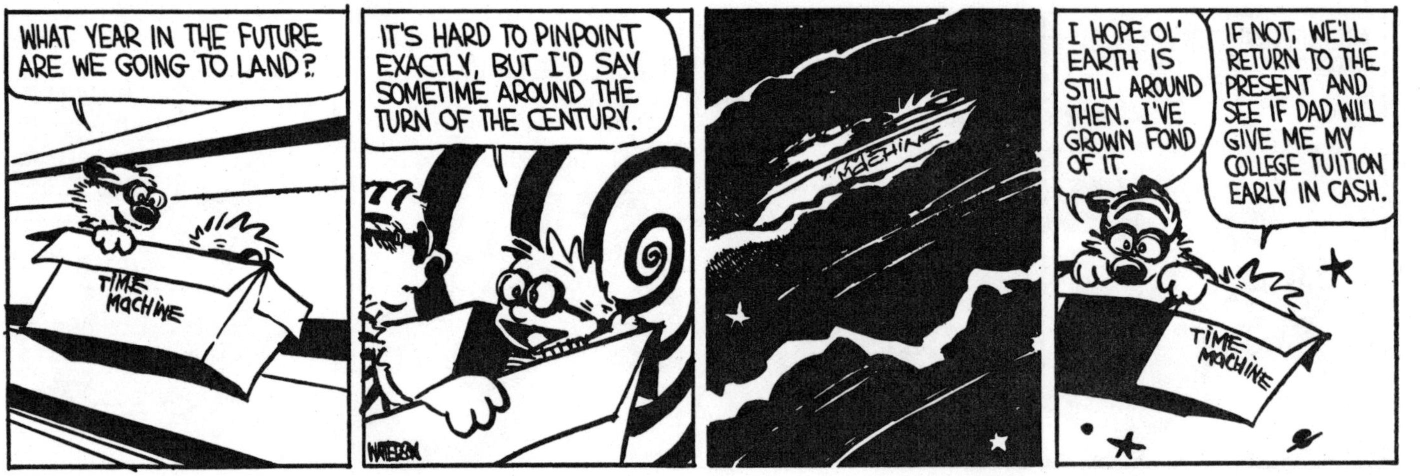
WHAT YEAR IN THE FUTURE ARE WE GOING TO LAND?
TIME MACHINE
IT'S HARD TO PINPOINT EXACTLY, BUT I'D SAY SOMETIME AROUND THE TURN OF THE CENTURY.
TIME MACHINE
I HOPE OL' EARTH IS STILL AROUND THEN. I'VE GROWN FOND OF IT.
IF NOT, WE'LL RETURN TO THE PRESENT AND SEE IF DAD WILL GIVE ME MY COLLEGE TUITION EARLY IN CASH.
TIME MACHINE

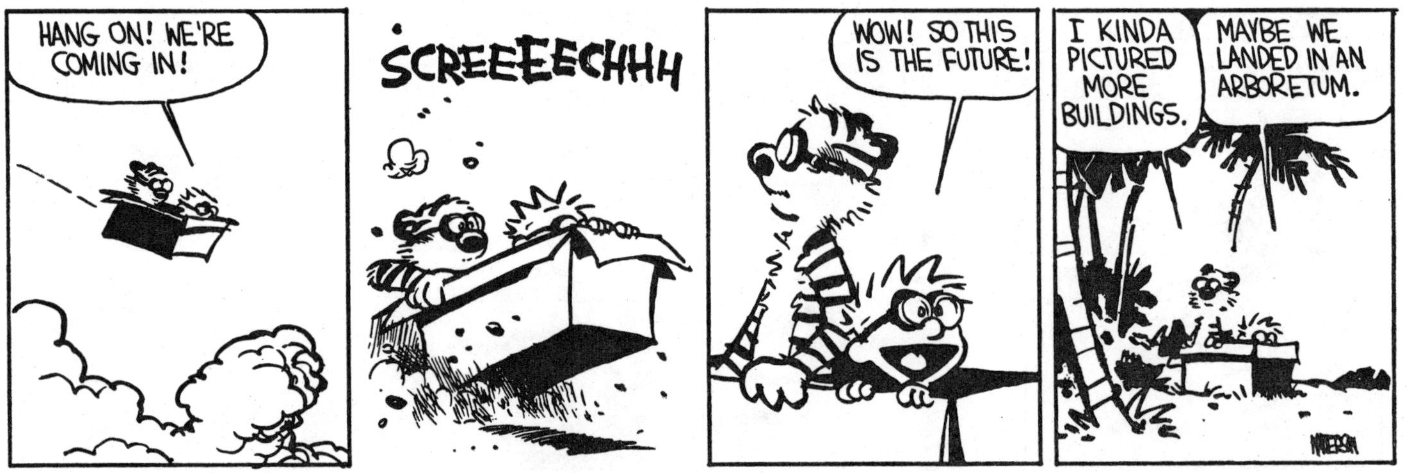
HANG ON! WE'RE COMING IN!
SCREEEECHHH
WOW! SO THIS IS THE FUTURE!
I KINDA PICTURED MORE BUILDINGS.
MAYBE WE LANDED IN AN ARBORETUM.

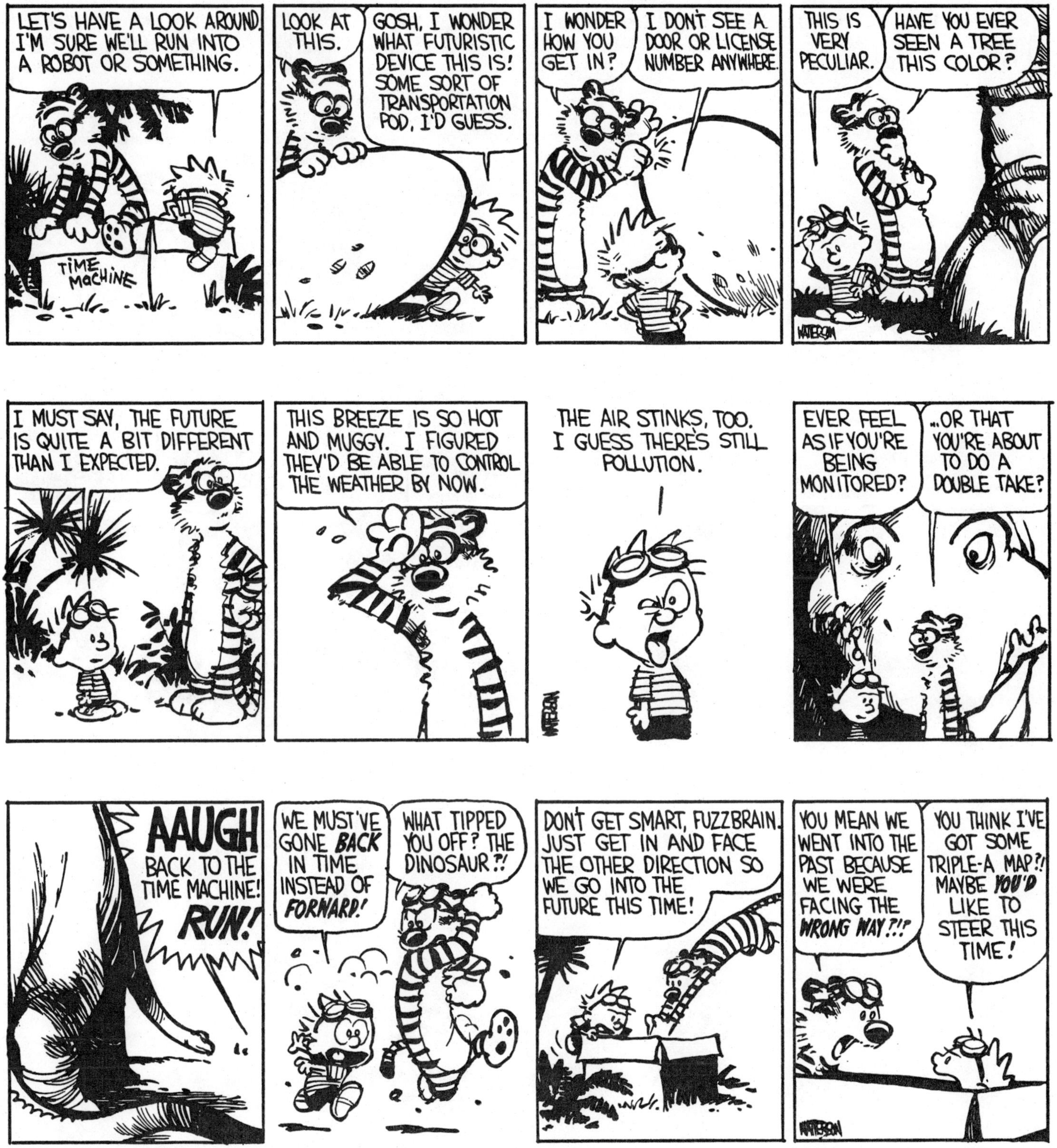

LET'S HAVE A LOOK AROUND. I'M SURE WE'LL RUN INTO A ROBOT OR SOMETHING.
TIME MACHINE
LOOK AT THIS.
GOSH, I WONDER WHAT FUTURISTIC DEVICE THIS IS! SOME SORT OF TRANSPORTATION POD, I'D GUESS.
I WONDER HOW YOU GET IN?
I DON'T SEE A DOOR OR LICENSE NUMBER ANYWHERE.
THIS IS VERY PECULIAR.
HAVE YOU EVER SEEN A TREE THIS COLOR?
WATTERSON
I MUST SAY, THE FUTURE IS QUITE A BIT DIFFERENT THAN I EXPECTED.
THIS BREEZE IS SO HOT AND MUGGY. I FIGURED THEY'D BE ABLE TO CONTROL THE WEATHER BY NOW.
THE AIR STINKS, TOO. I GUESS THERE'S STILL POLLUTION.
WATTERSON
EVER FEEL AS IF YOU'RE BEING MONITORED?
...OR THAT YOU'RE ABOUT TO DO A DOUBLE TAKE?
AAUGH
BACK TO THE TIME MACHINE! RUN!
WE MUST'VE GONE BACK IN TIME INSTEAD OF FORWARD!
WHAT TIPPED YOU OFF? THE DINOSAUR?!
DON'T GET SMART, FUZZBRAIN. JUST GET IN AND FACE THE OTHER DIRECTION SO WE GO INTO THE FUTURE THIS TIME!
YOU MEAN WE WENT INTO THE PAST BECAUSE WE WERE FACING THE WRONG WAY?!?
YOU THINK I'VE GOT SOME TRIPLE-A MAP?! MAYBE YOU'D LIKE TO STEER THIS TIME!
WATTERSON

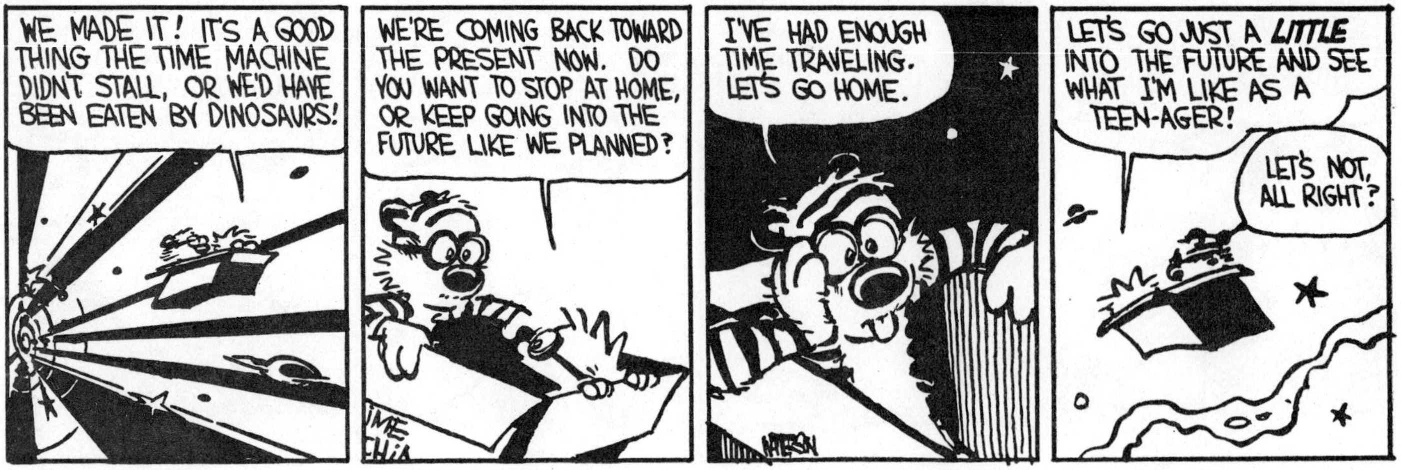
WE MADE IT! IT'S A GOOD THING THE TIME MACHINE DIDN'T STALL, OR WE'D HAVE BEEN EATEN BY DINOSAURS!
WE'RE COMING BACK TOWARD THE PRESENT NOW. DO YOU WANT TO STOP AT HOME, OR KEEP GOING INTO THE FUTURE LIKE WE PLANNED?
I'VE HAD ENOUGH TIME TRAVELING. LET'S GO HOME.
LET'S GO JUST A *LITTLE* INTO THE FUTURE AND SEE WHAT I'M LIKE AS A TEEN-AGER!
LET'S NOT, ALL RIGHT?

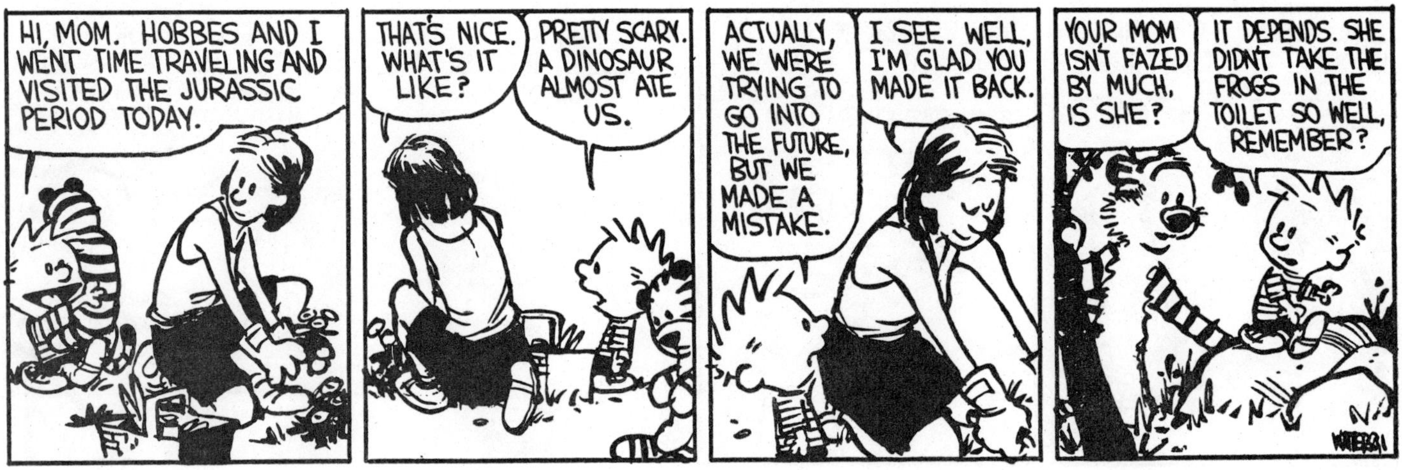
HI, MOM. HOBBES AND I WENT TIME TRAVELING AND VISITED THE JURASSIC PERIOD TODAY.
THAT'S NICE. WHAT'S IT LIKE?
PRETTY SCARY. A DINOSAUR ALMOST ATE US.
ACTUALLY, WE WERE TRYING TO GO INTO THE FUTURE, BUT WE MADE A MISTAKE.
I SEE. WELL, I'M GLAD YOU MADE IT BACK.
YOUR MOM ISN'T FAZED BY MUCH, IS SHE?
IT DEPENDS. SHE DIDN'T TAKE THE FROGS IN THE TOILET SO WELL, REMEMBER?

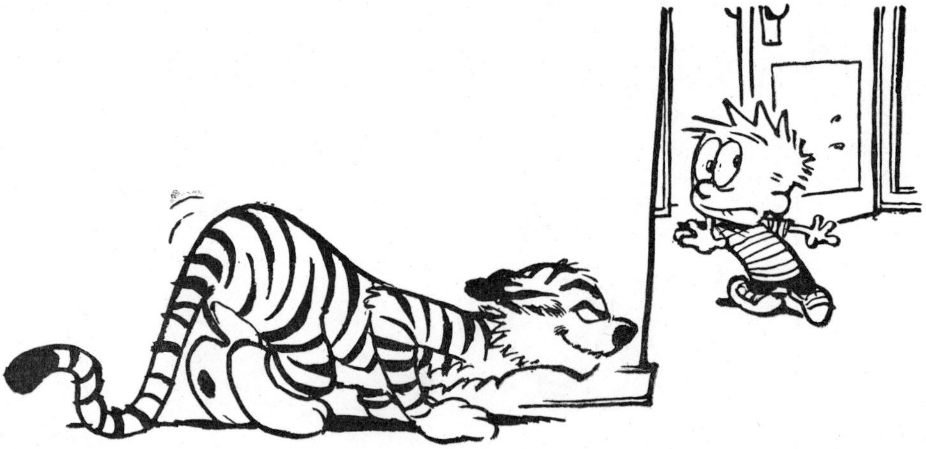

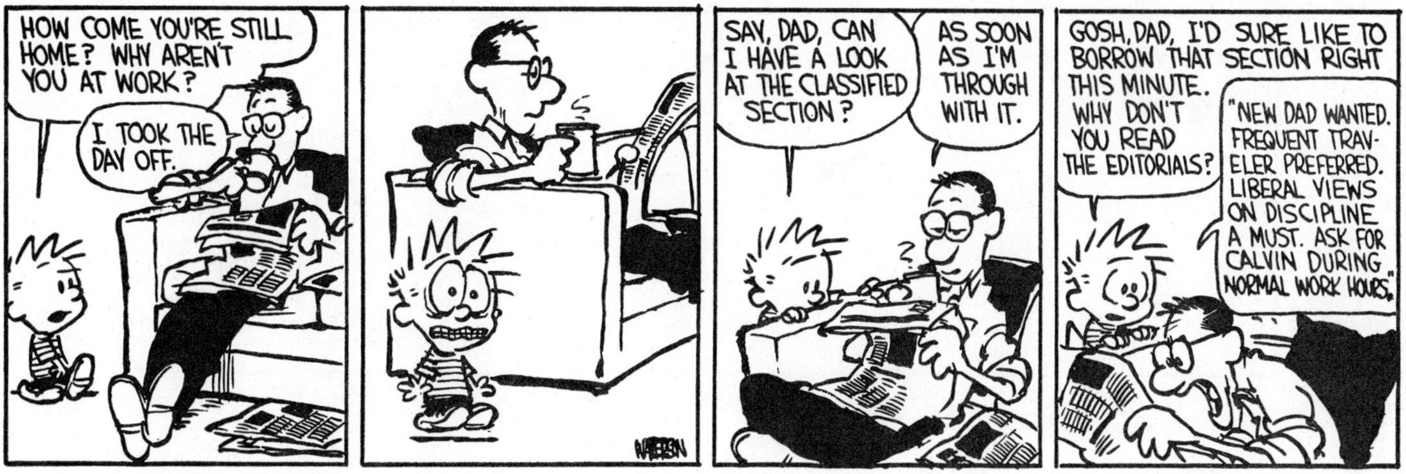
HOW COME YOU'RE STILL HOME? WHY AREN'T YOU AT WORK?
I TOOK THE DAY OFF.
SAY, DAD, CAN I HAVE A LOOK AT THE CLASSIFIED SECTION?
AS SOON AS I'M THROUGH WITH IT.
GOSH, DAD, I'D SURE LIKE TO BORROW THAT SECTION RIGHT THIS MINUTE.
WHY DON'T YOU READ THE EDITORIALS?
"NEW DAD WANTED. FREQUENT TRAVELER PREFERRED. LIBERAL VIEWS ON DISCIPLINE A MUST. ASK FOR CALVIN DURING NORMAL WORK HOURS."
WATTERSON

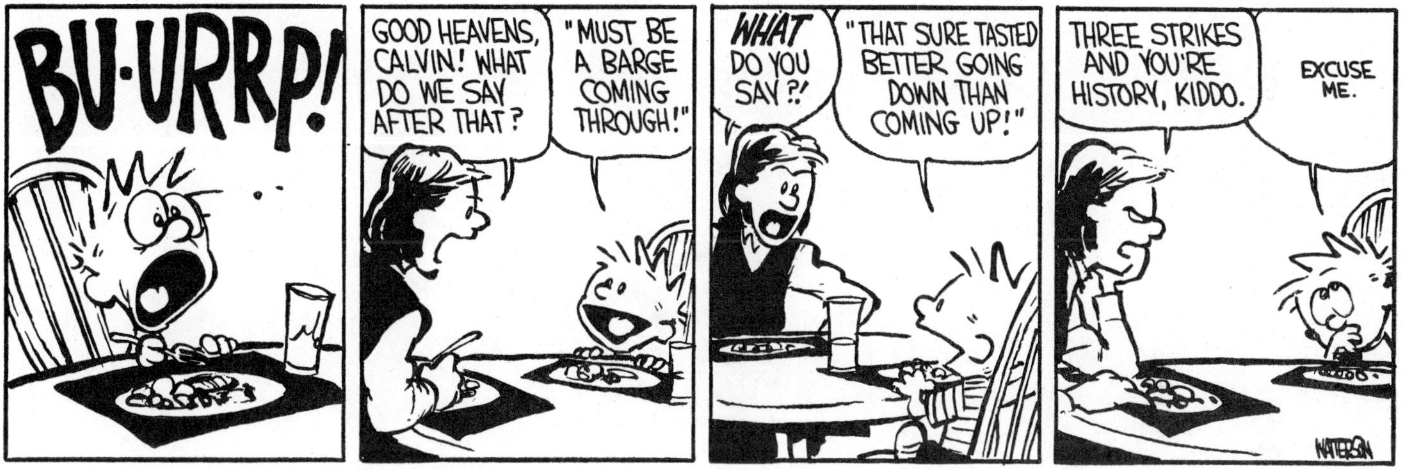
BU-URRP!
GOOD HEAVENS, CALVIN! WHAT DO WE SAY AFTER THAT?
"MUST BE A BARGE COMING THROUGH!"
WHAT DO YOU SAY?!
"THAT SURE TASTED BETTER GOING DOWN THAN COMING UP!"
THREE STRIKES AND YOU'RE HISTORY, KIDDO.
EXCUSE ME.
WATTERSON

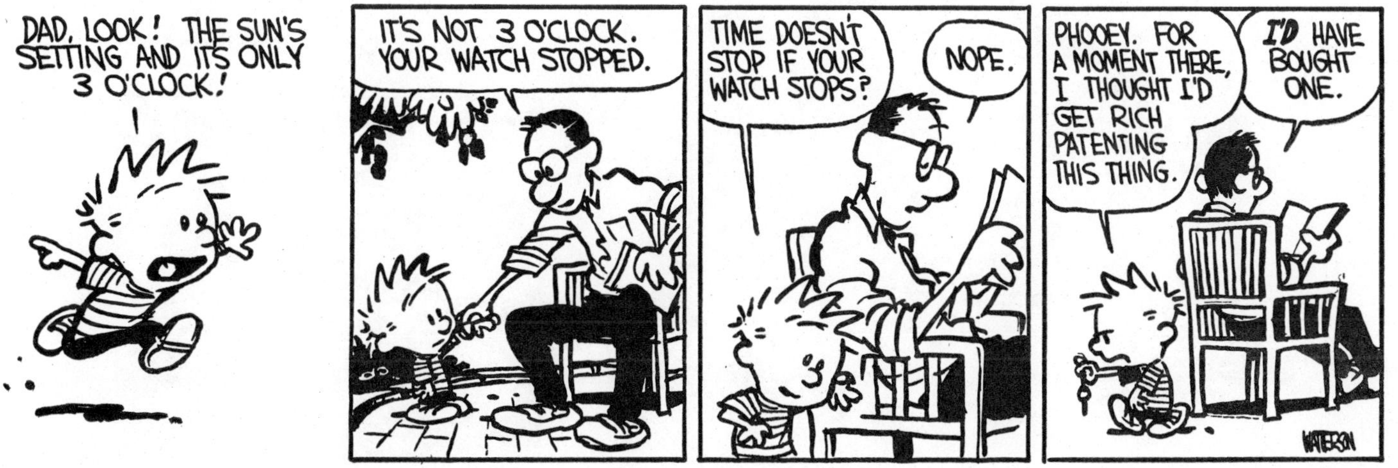
DAD, LOOK! THE SUN'S SETTING AND IT'S ONLY 3 O'CLOCK!
IT'S NOT 3 O'CLOCK. YOUR WATCH STOPPED.
TIME DOESN'T STOP IF YOUR WATCH STOPS?
NOPE.
PHOOEY. FOR A MOMENT THERE, I THOUGHT I'D GET RICH PATENTING THIS THING.
I'D HAVE BOUGHT ONE.
WATTERSON

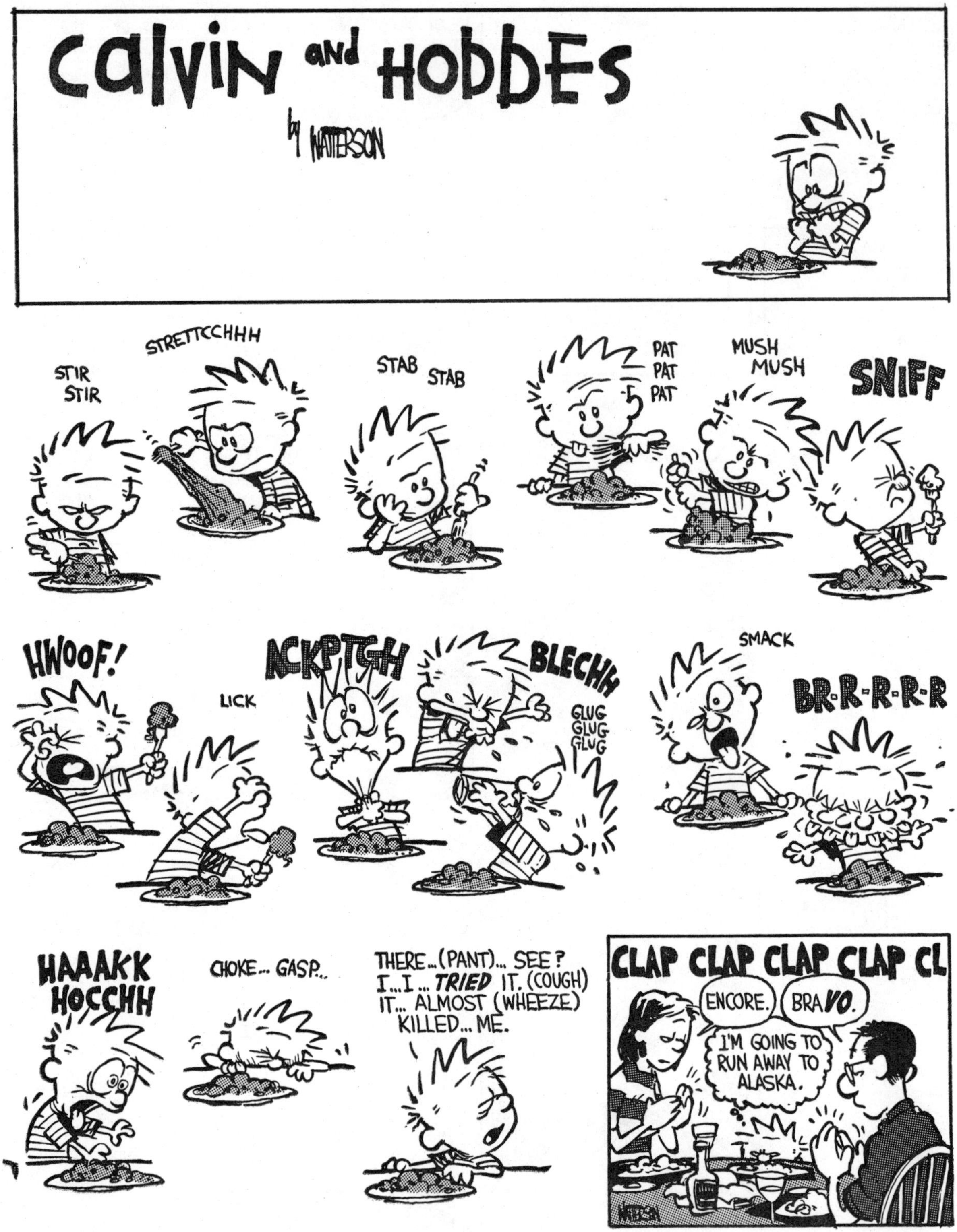

Calvin and HOBBES
by WATTERSON
STIR STIR
STRETTCCHHH
STAB STAB
PAT PAT PAT
MUSH MUSH
SNIFF
HWOOF!
LICK
ACKPTGH
BLECHH
GLUG GLUG GLUG
SMACK
BR-R-R-R-R
HAAAKK HOCCHH
CHOKE... GASP...
THERE...(PANT)... SEE? I...I... TRIED IT. (COUGH) IT... ALMOST (WHEEZE) KILLED... ME.
CLAP CLAP CLAP CLAP CL
ENCORE.
BRAVO.
I'M GOING TO RUN AWAY TO ALASKA.

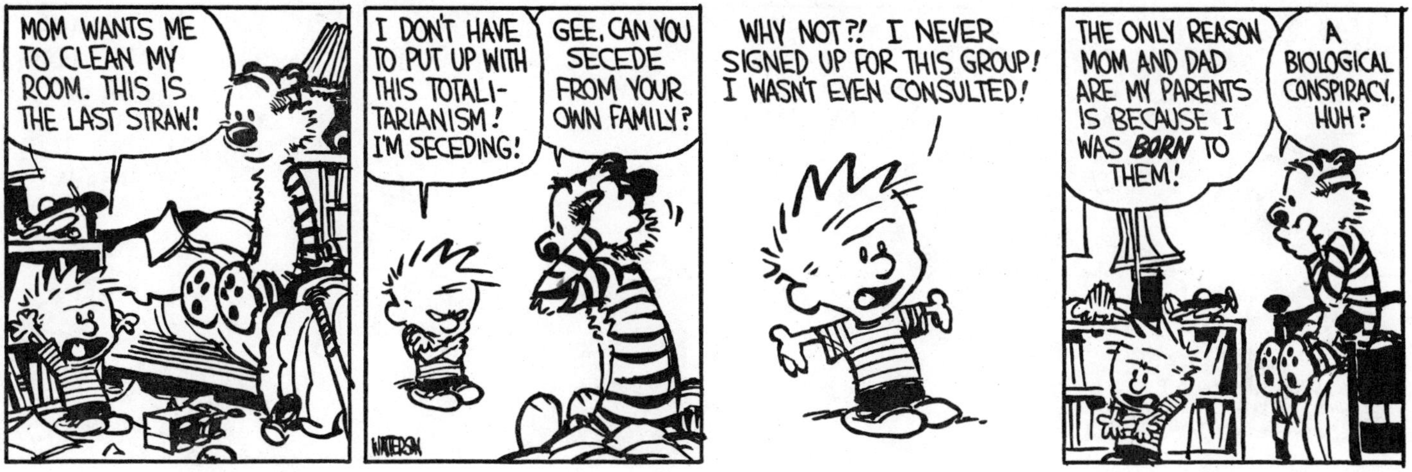
MOM WANTS ME TO CLEAN MY ROOM. THIS IS THE LAST STRAW!
I DON'T HAVE TO PUT UP WITH THIS TOTALITARIANISM! I'M SECEDING!
GEE, CAN YOU SECEDE FROM YOUR OWN FAMILY?
WATTERSON
WHY NOT?! I NEVER SIGNED UP FOR THIS GROUP! I WASN'T EVEN CONSULTED!
THE ONLY REASON MOM AND DAD ARE MY PARENTS IS BECAUSE I WAS BORN TO THEM!
A BIOLOGICAL CONSPIRACY, HUH?

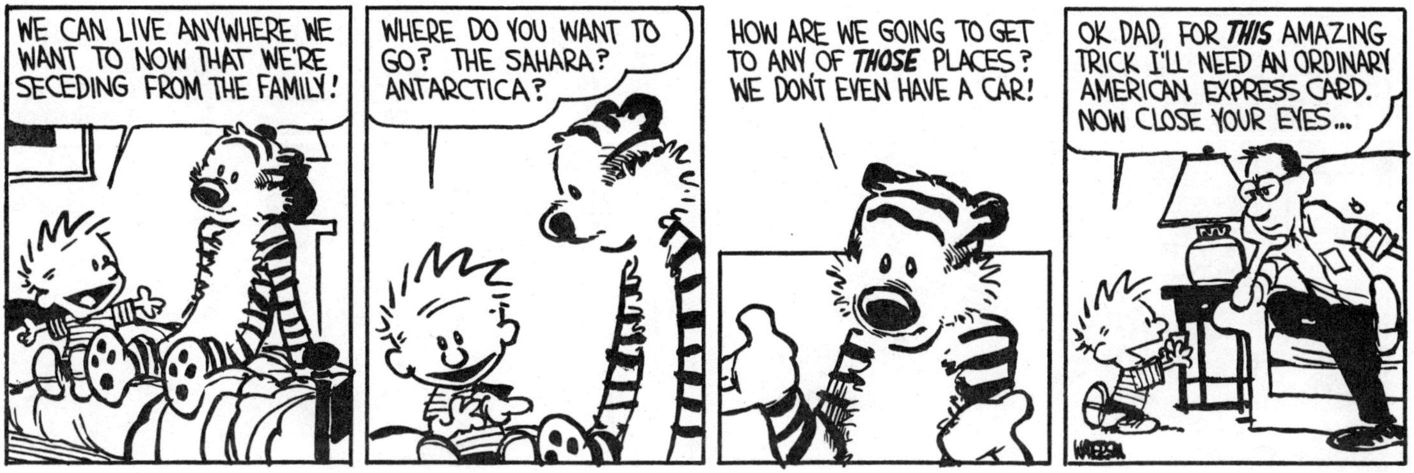
WE CAN LIVE ANYWHERE WE WANT TO NOW THAT WE'RE SECEDING FROM THE FAMILY!
WHERE DO YOU WANT TO GO? THE SAHARA? ANTARCTICA?
HOW ARE WE GOING TO GET TO ANY OF THOSE PLACES? WE DON'T EVEN HAVE A CAR!
OK DAD, FOR THIS AMAZING TRICK I'LL NEED AN ORDINARY AMERICAN EXPRESS CARD. NOW CLOSE YOUR EYES...
WATTERSON

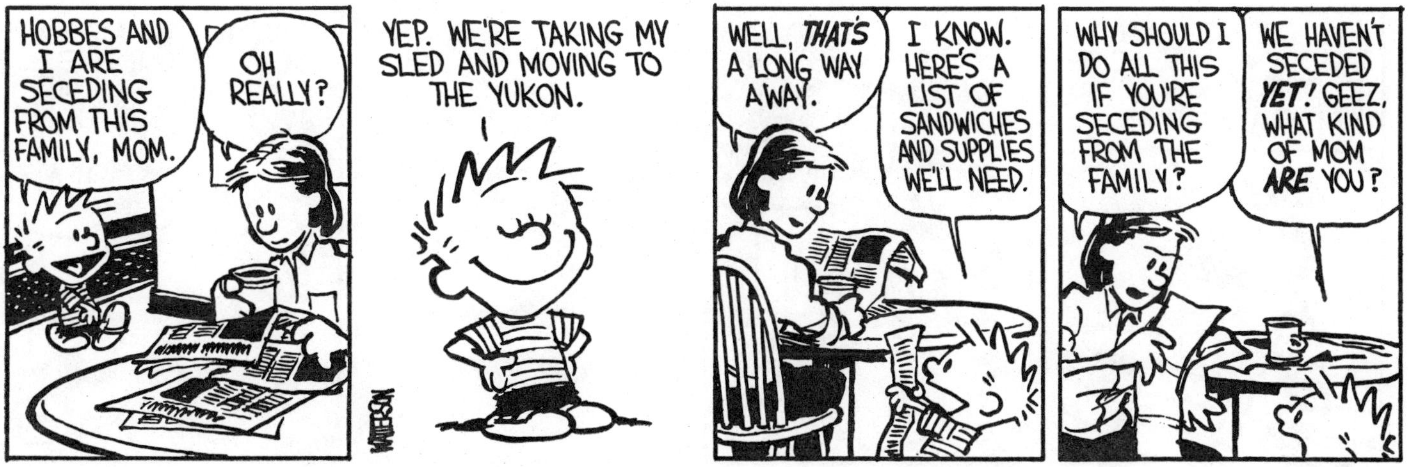
HOBBES AND I ARE SECEDING FROM THIS FAMILY, MOM.
OH REALLY?
WATTERSON
YEP. WE'RE TAKING MY SLED AND MOVING TO THE YUKON.
WELL, THAT'S A LONG WAY AWAY.
I KNOW. HERE'S A LIST OF SANDWICHES AND SUPPLIES WE'LL NEED.
WHY SHOULD I DO ALL THIS IF YOU'RE SECEDING FROM THE FAMILY?
WE HAVEN'T SECEDED YET! GEEZ, WHAT KIND OF MOM ARE YOU?

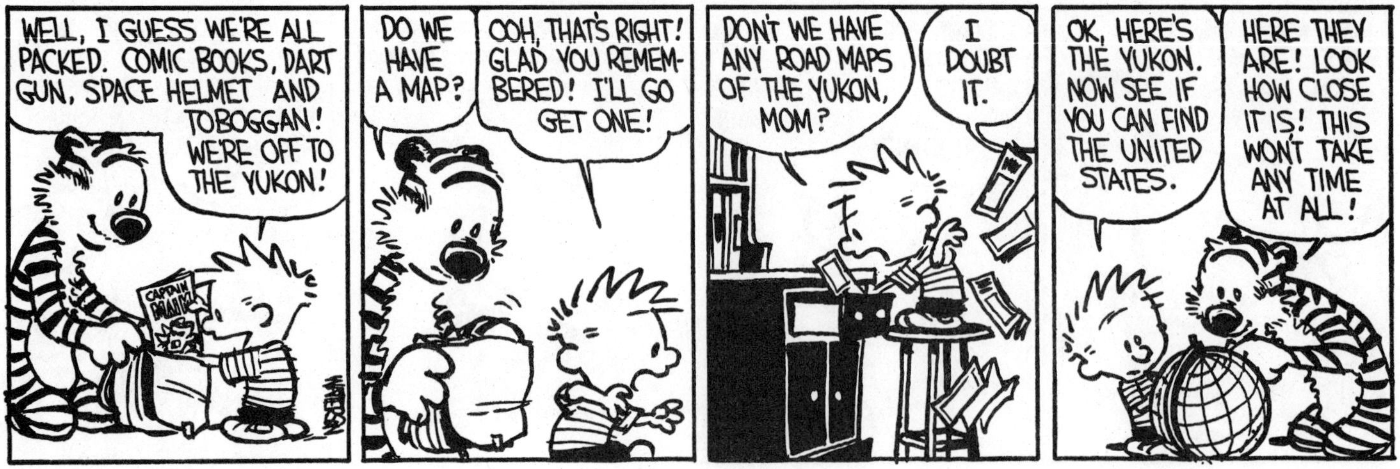
WELL, I GUESS WE'RE ALL PACKED. COMIC BOOKS, DART GUN, SPACE HELMET AND TOBOGGAN! WE'RE OFF TO THE YUKON!
DO WE HAVE A MAP?
OOH, THAT'S RIGHT! GLAD YOU REMEMBERED! I'LL GO GET ONE!
DON'T WE HAVE ANY ROAD MAPS OF THE YUKON, MOM?
I DOUBT IT.
OK, HERE'S THE YUKON. NOW SEE IF YOU CAN FIND THE UNITED STATES.
HERE THEY ARE! LOOK HOW CLOSE IT IS! THIS WON'T TAKE ANY TIME AT ALL!

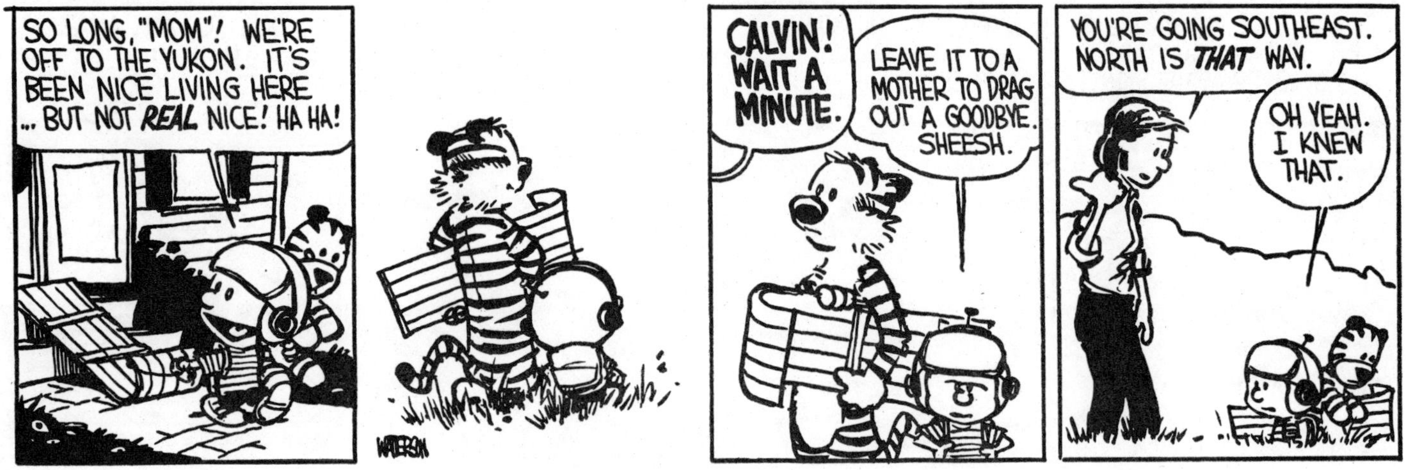
SO LONG, "MOM"! WE'RE OFF TO THE YUKON. IT'S BEEN NICE LIVING HERE ... BUT NOT *REAL* NICE! HA HA!
CALVIN! WAIT A MINUTE.
LEAVE IT TO A MOTHER TO DRAG OUT A GOODBYE. SHEESH.
YOU'RE GOING SOUTHEAST. NORTH IS *THAT* WAY.
OH YEAH. I KNEW THAT.

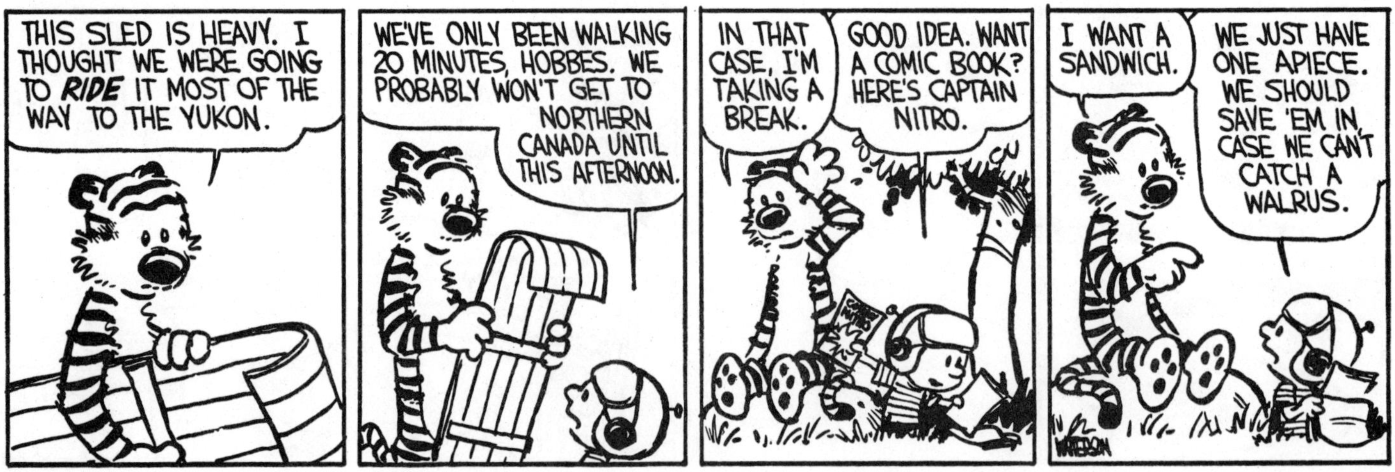
THIS SLED IS HEAVY. I THOUGHT WE WERE GOING TO *RIDE* IT MOST OF THE WAY TO THE YUKON.
WE'VE ONLY BEEN WALKING 20 MINUTES, HOBBES. WE PROBABLY WON'T GET TO NORTHERN CANADA UNTIL THIS AFTERNOON.
IN THAT CASE, I'M TAKING A BREAK.
GOOD IDEA. WANT A COMIC BOOK? HERE'S CAPTAIN NITRO.
I WANT A SANDWICH.
WE JUST HAVE ONE APIECE. WE SHOULD SAVE 'EM IN CASE WE CAN'T CATCH A WALRUS.

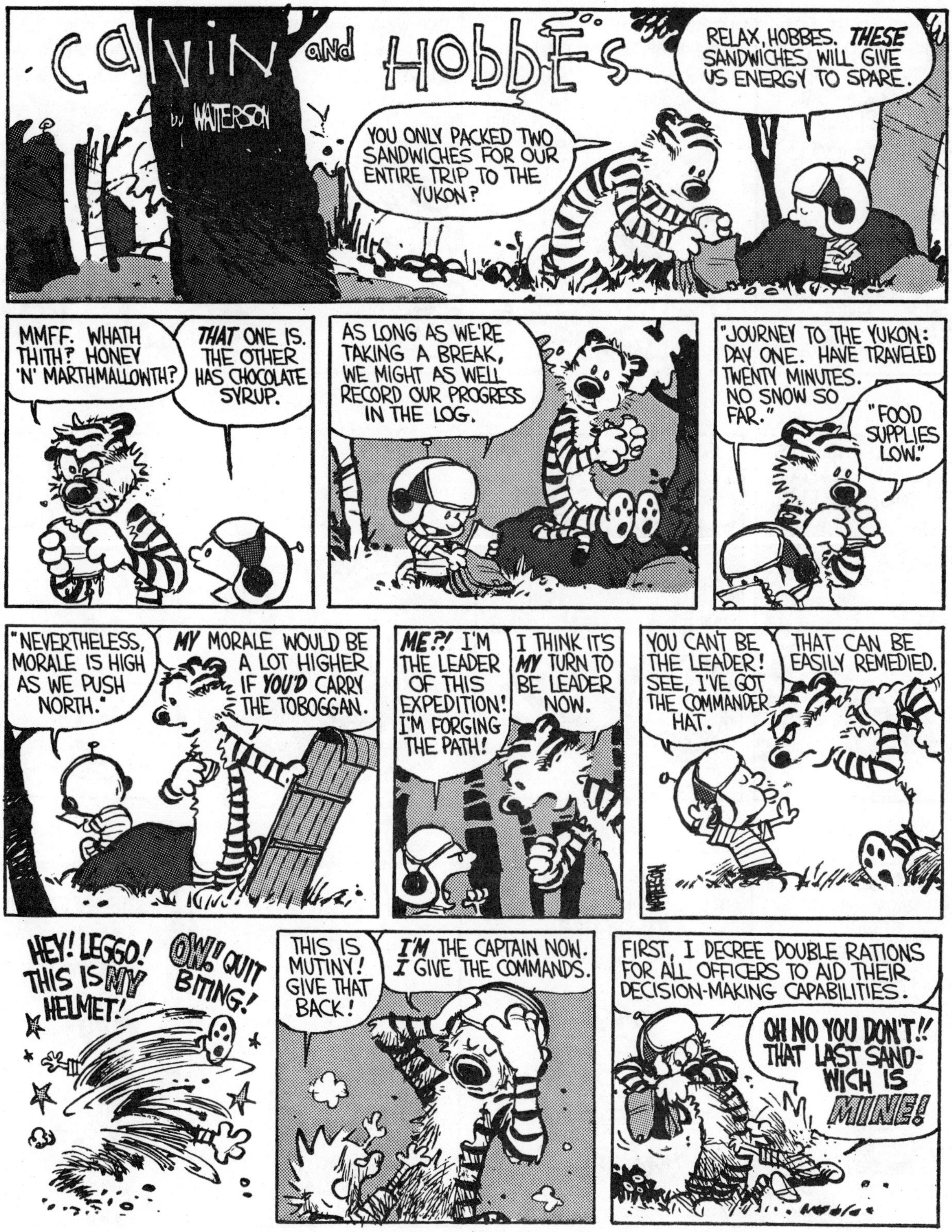
Calvin and HOBBES
by WATTERSON
YOU ONLY PACKED TWO SANDWICHES FOR OUR ENTIRE TRIP TO THE YUKON?
RELAX, HOBBES. THESE SANDWICHES WILL GIVE US ENERGY TO SPARE.
MMFF. WHATH THITH? HONEY 'N' MARTHMALLOWTH?
THAT ONE IS. THE OTHER HAS CHOCOLATE SYRUP.
AS LONG AS WE'RE TAKING A BREAK, WE MIGHT AS WELL RECORD OUR PROGRESS IN THE LOG.
"JOURNEY TO THE YUKON: DAY ONE. HAVE TRAVELED TWENTY MINUTES. NO SNOW SO FAR."
"FOOD SUPPLIES LOW."
"NEVERTHELESS, MORALE IS HIGH AS WE PUSH NORTH."
MY MORALE WOULD BE A LOT HIGHER IF YOU'D CARRY THE TOBOGGAN.
ME?! I'M THE LEADER OF THIS EXPEDITION! I'M FORGING THE PATH!
I THINK IT'S MY TURN TO BE LEADER NOW.
YOU CAN'T BE THE LEADER! SEE, I'VE GOT THE COMMANDER HAT.
THAT CAN BE EASILY REMEDIED.
WATTERSON
HEY! LEGGO! THIS IS MY HELMET!
OW! QUIT BITING!
THIS IS MUTINY! GIVE THAT BACK!
I'M THE CAPTAIN NOW. I GIVE THE COMMANDS.
FIRST, I DECREE DOUBLE RATIONS FOR ALL OFFICERS TO AID THEIR DECISION-MAKING CAPABILITIES.
OH NO YOU DON'T!! THAT LAST SANDWICH IS MINE!

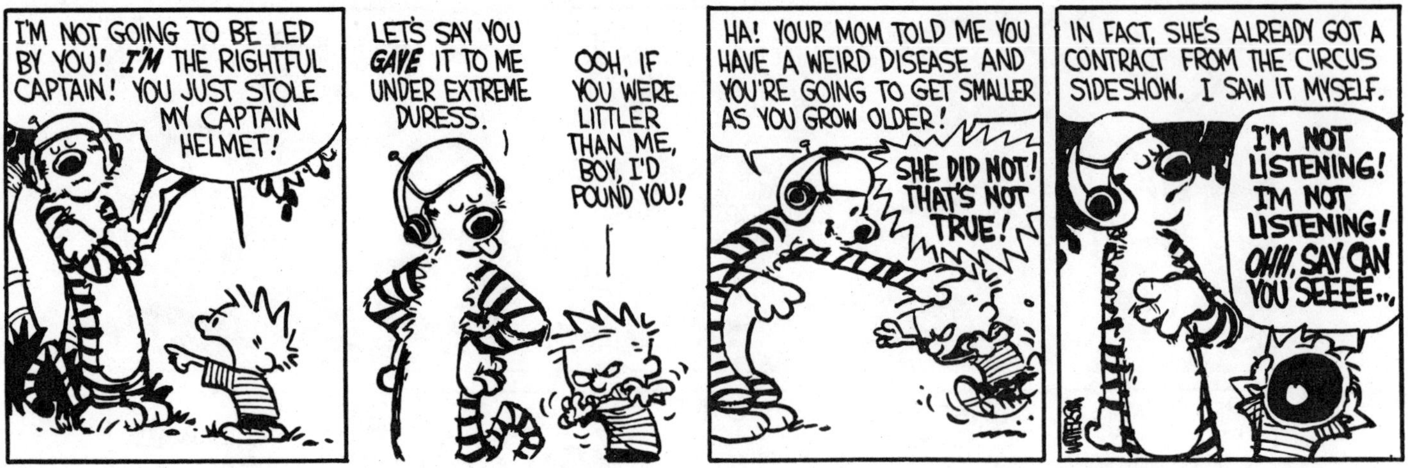
I'M NOT GOING TO BE LED BY YOU! I'M THE RIGHTFUL CAPTAIN! YOU JUST STOLE MY CAPTAIN HELMET!
LET'S SAY YOU GAVE IT TO ME UNDER EXTREME DURESS.
OOH, IF YOU WERE LITTLER THAN ME, BOY, I'D POUND YOU!
HA! YOUR MOM TOLD ME YOU HAVE A WEIRD DISEASE AND YOU'RE GOING TO GET SMALLER AS YOU GROW OLDER!
SHE DID NOT! THAT'S NOT TRUE!
IN FACT, SHE'S ALREADY GOT A CONTRACT FROM THE CIRCUS SIDESHOW. I SAW IT MYSELF.
I'M NOT LISTENING! I'M NOT LISTENING! OHH, SAY CAN YOU SEEEE...

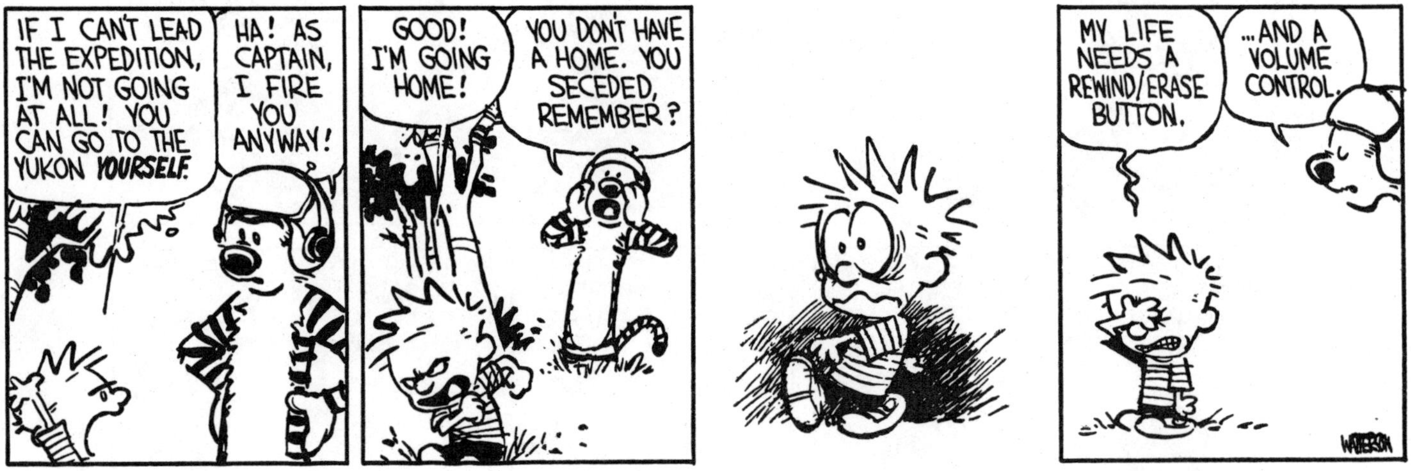
IF I CAN'T LEAD THE EXPEDITION, I'M NOT GOING AT ALL! YOU CAN GO TO THE YUKON YOURSELF.
HA! AS CAPTAIN, I FIRE YOU ANYWAY!
GOOD! I'M GOING HOME!
YOU DON'T HAVE A HOME. YOU SECEDED, REMEMBER?
MY LIFE NEEDS A REWIND/ERASE BUTTON.
...AND A VOLUME CONTROL.

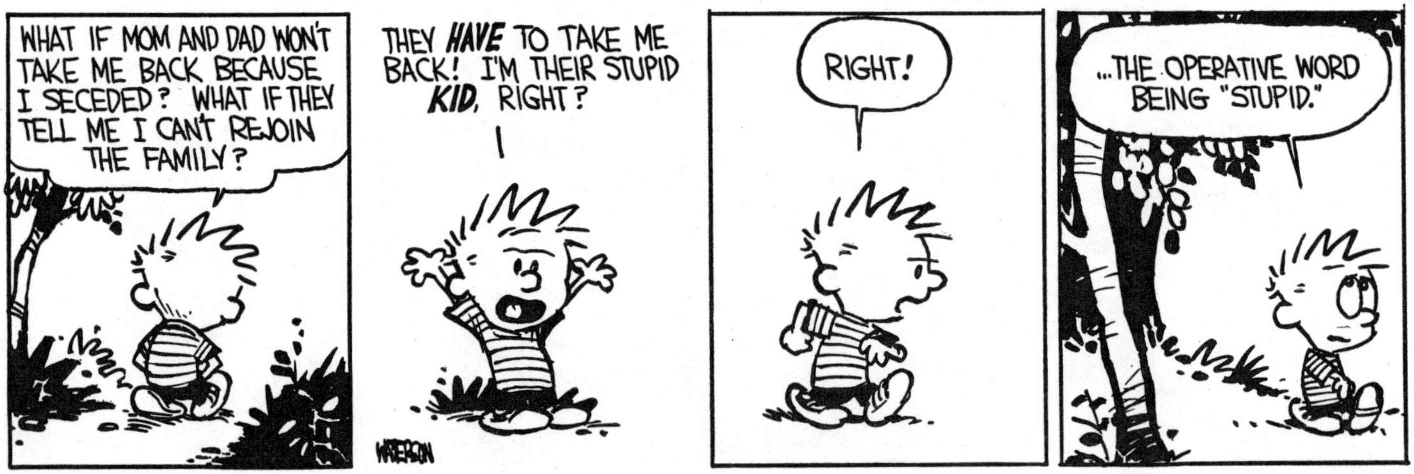
WHAT IF MOM AND DAD WON'T TAKE ME BACK BECAUSE I SECEDED? WHAT IF THEY TELL ME I CAN'T REJOIN THE FAMILY?
THEY HAVE TO TAKE ME BACK! I'M THEIR STUPID KID, RIGHT?
RIGHT!
...THE OPERATIVE WORD BEING "STUPID."

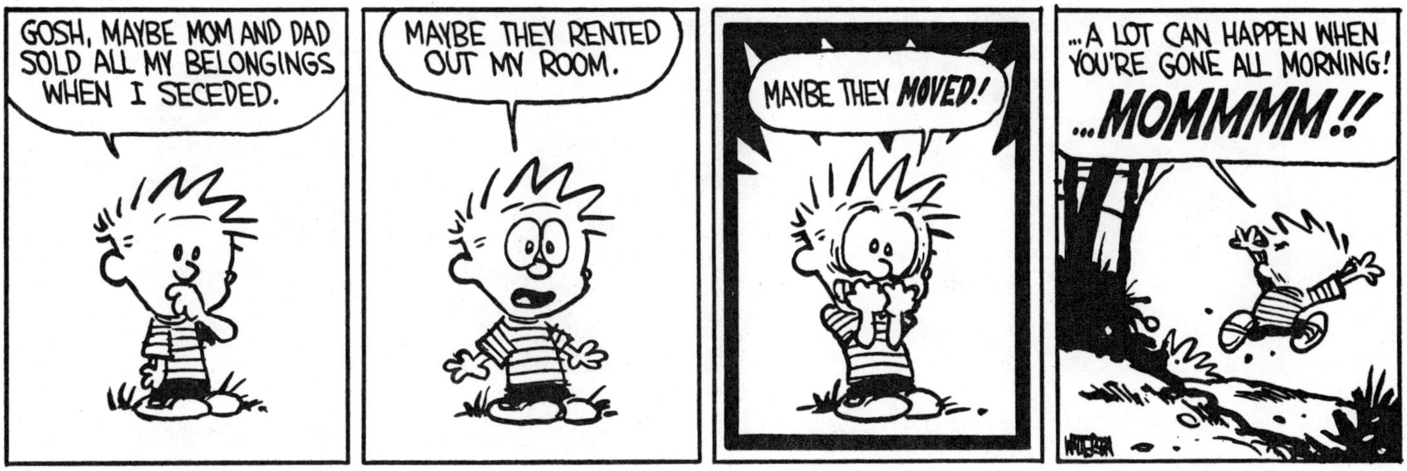
GOSH, MAYBE MOM AND DAD SOLD ALL MY BELONGINGS WHEN I SECEDED.
MAYBE THEY RENTED OUT MY ROOM.
MAYBE THEY *MOVED!*
...A LOT CAN HAPPEN WHEN YOU'RE GONE ALL MORNING! ...**MOMMMM!!**
WATTERSON

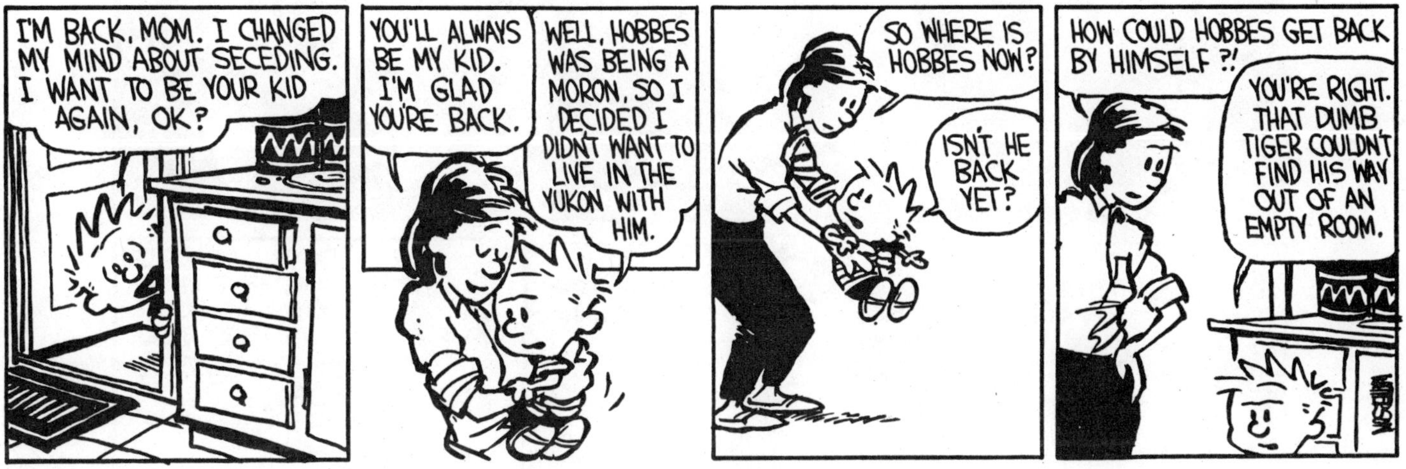
I'M BACK, MOM. I CHANGED MY MIND ABOUT SECEDING. I WANT TO BE YOUR KID AGAIN, OK?
YOU'LL ALWAYS BE MY KID. I'M GLAD YOU'RE BACK.
WELL, HOBBES WAS BEING A MORON, SO I DECIDED I DIDN'T WANT TO LIVE IN THE YUKON WITH HIM.
SO WHERE IS HOBBES NOW?
ISN'T HE BACK YET?
HOW COULD HOBBES GET BACK BY HIMSELF ?!
YOU'RE RIGHT. THAT DUMB TIGER COULDN'T FIND HIS WAY OUT OF AN EMPTY ROOM.
WATTERSON

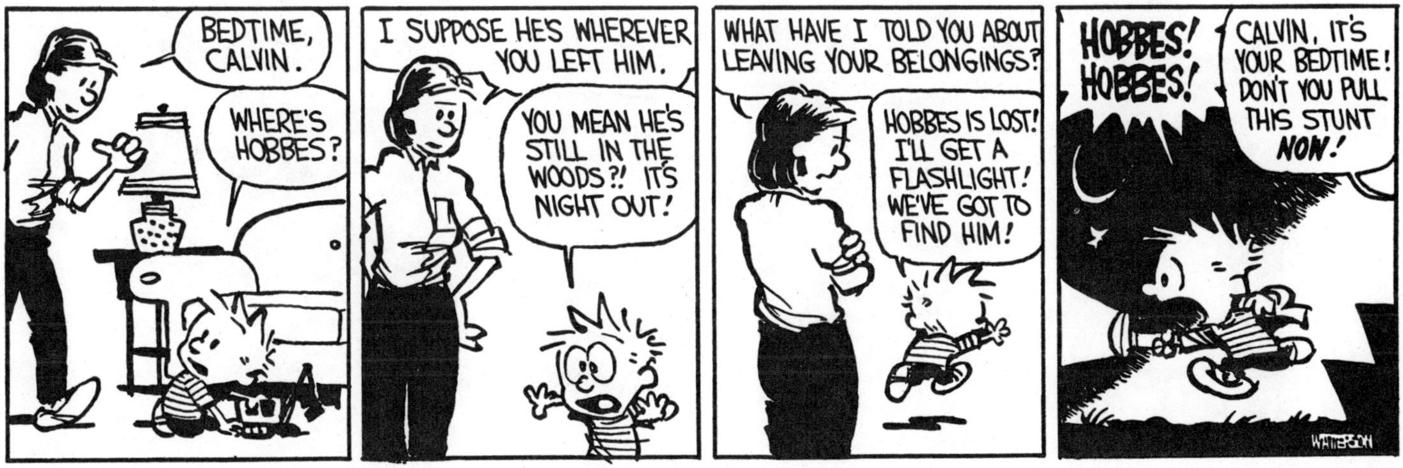
BEDTIME, CALVIN.
WHERE'S HOBBES?
I SUPPOSE HE'S WHEREVER YOU LEFT HIM.
YOU MEAN HE'S STILL IN THE WOODS?! IT'S NIGHT OUT!
WHAT HAVE I TOLD YOU ABOUT LEAVING YOUR BELONGINGS?
HOBBES IS LOST! I'LL GET A FLASHLIGHT! WE'VE GOT TO FIND HIM!
HOBBES! HOBBES!
CALVIN, IT'S YOUR BEDTIME! DON'T YOU PULL THIS STUNT *NOW!*
WATTERSON

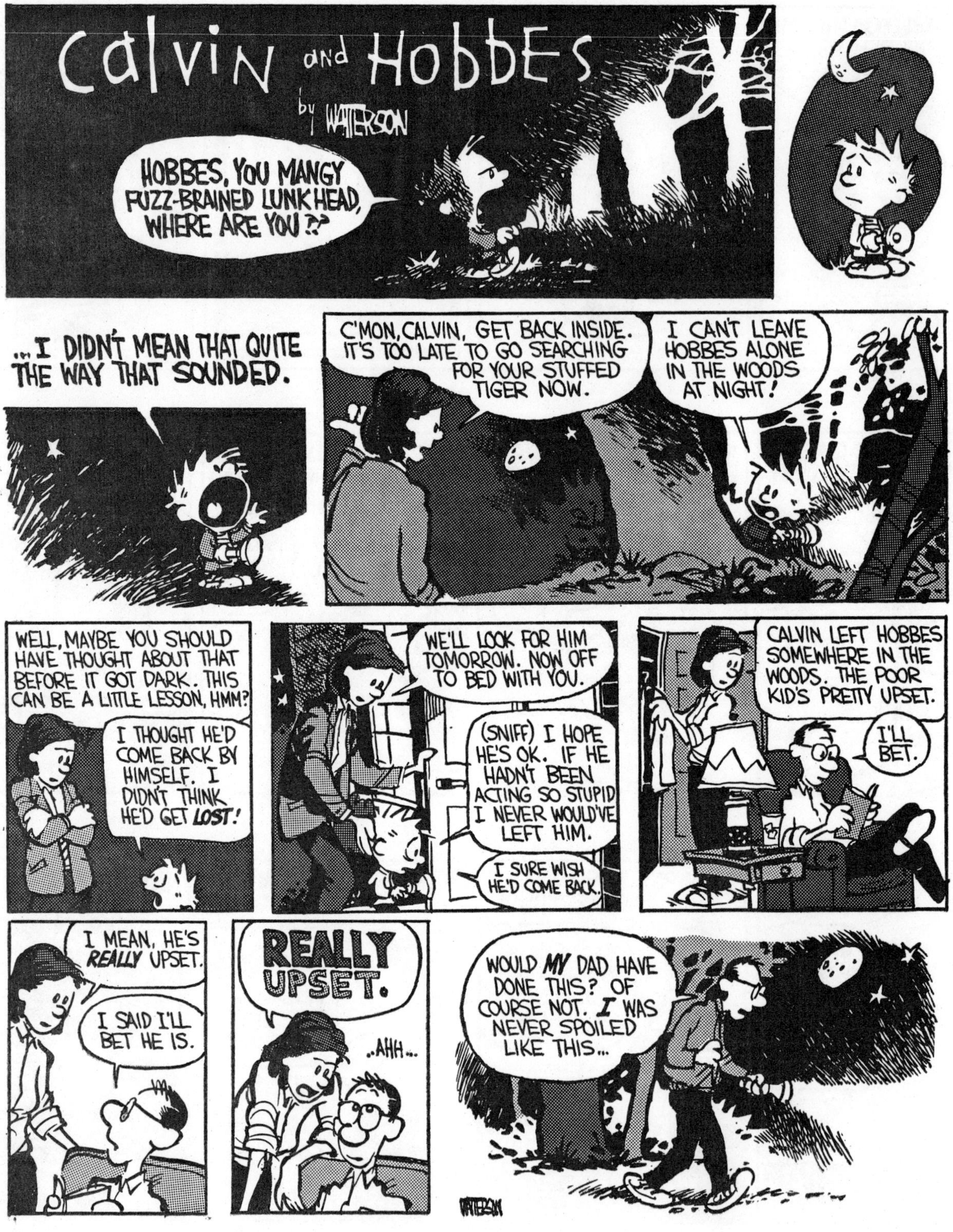
Calvin and HOBBES
by WATTERSON
HOBBES, YOU MANGY FUZZ-BRAINED LUNKHEAD, WHERE ARE YOU ?!?
...I DIDN'T MEAN THAT QUITE THE WAY THAT SOUNDED.
C'MON, CALVIN, GET BACK INSIDE. IT'S TOO LATE TO GO SEARCHING FOR YOUR STUFFED TIGER NOW.
I CAN'T LEAVE HOBBES ALONE IN THE WOODS AT NIGHT!
WELL, MAYBE YOU SHOULD HAVE THOUGHT ABOUT THAT BEFORE IT GOT DARK. THIS CAN BE A LITTLE LESSON, HMM?
I THOUGHT HE'D COME BACK BY HIMSELF. I DIDN'T THINK HE'D GET LOST!
WE'LL LOOK FOR HIM TOMORROW. NOW OFF TO BED WITH YOU.
(SNIFF) I HOPE HE'S OK. IF HE HADN'T BEEN ACTING SO STUPID I NEVER WOULD'VE LEFT HIM.
I SURE WISH HE'D COME BACK.
CALVIN LEFT HOBBES SOMEWHERE IN THE WOODS. THE POOR KID'S PRETTY UPSET.
I'LL BET.
I MEAN, HE'S REALLY UPSET.
I SAID I'LL BET HE IS.
REALLY UPSET.
..AHH...
WOULD MY DAD HAVE DONE THIS? OF COURSE NOT. I WAS NEVER SPOILED LIKE THIS...
WATTERSON

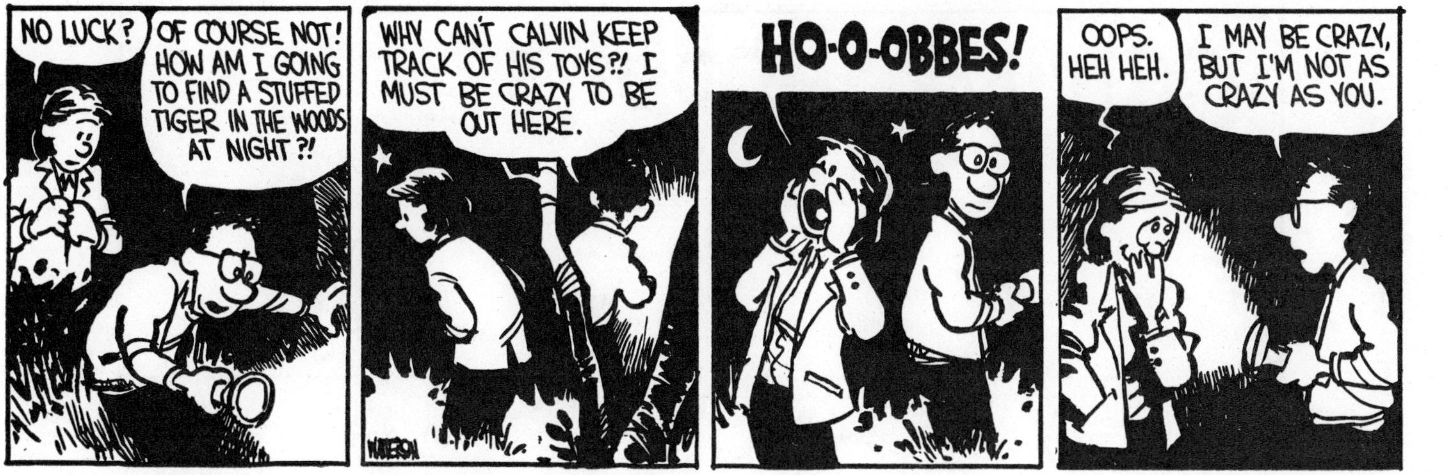
NO LUCK?
OF COURSE NOT! HOW AM I GOING TO FIND A STUFFED TIGER IN THE WOODS AT NIGHT?!
WHY CAN'T CALVIN KEEP TRACK OF HIS TOYS?! I MUST BE CRAZY TO BE OUT HERE.
HO-O-OBBES!
OOPS. HEH HEH.
I MAY BE CRAZY, BUT I'M NOT AS CRAZY AS YOU.

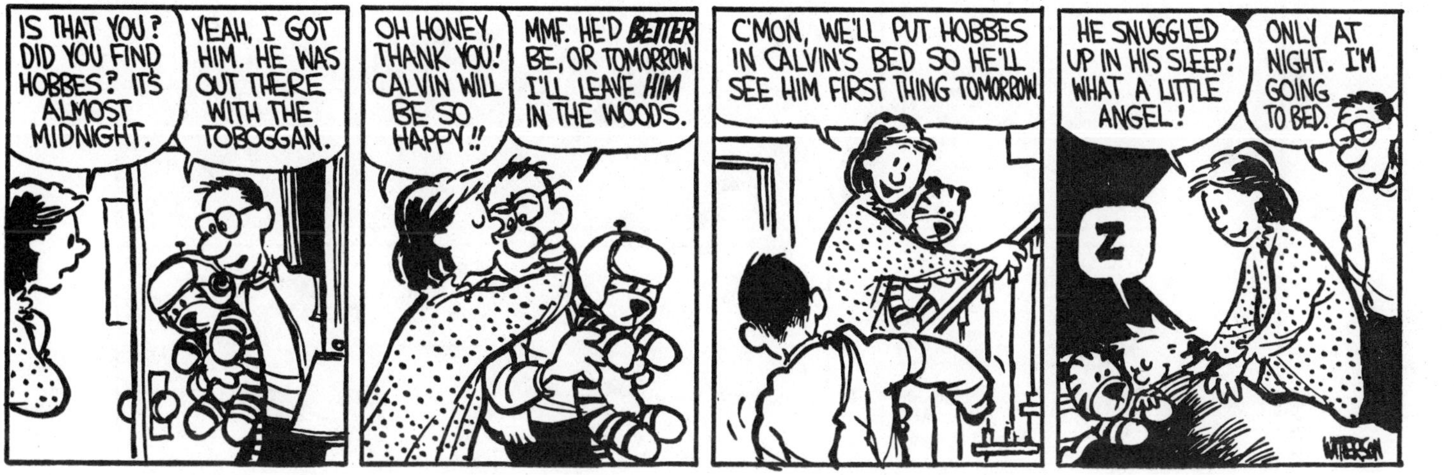
IS THAT YOU? DID YOU FIND HOBBES? IT'S ALMOST MIDNIGHT.
YEAH, I GOT HIM. HE WAS OUT THERE WITH THE TOBOGGAN.
OH HONEY, THANK YOU! CALVIN WILL BE SO HAPPY!!
MMF. HE'D BETTER BE, OR TOMORROW I'LL LEAVE HIM IN THE WOODS.
C'MON, WE'LL PUT HOBBES IN CALVIN'S BED SO HE'LL SEE HIM FIRST THING TOMORROW.
HE SNUGGLED UP IN HIS SLEEP! WHAT A LITTLE ANGEL!
ONLY AT NIGHT. I'M GOING TO BED.
Z

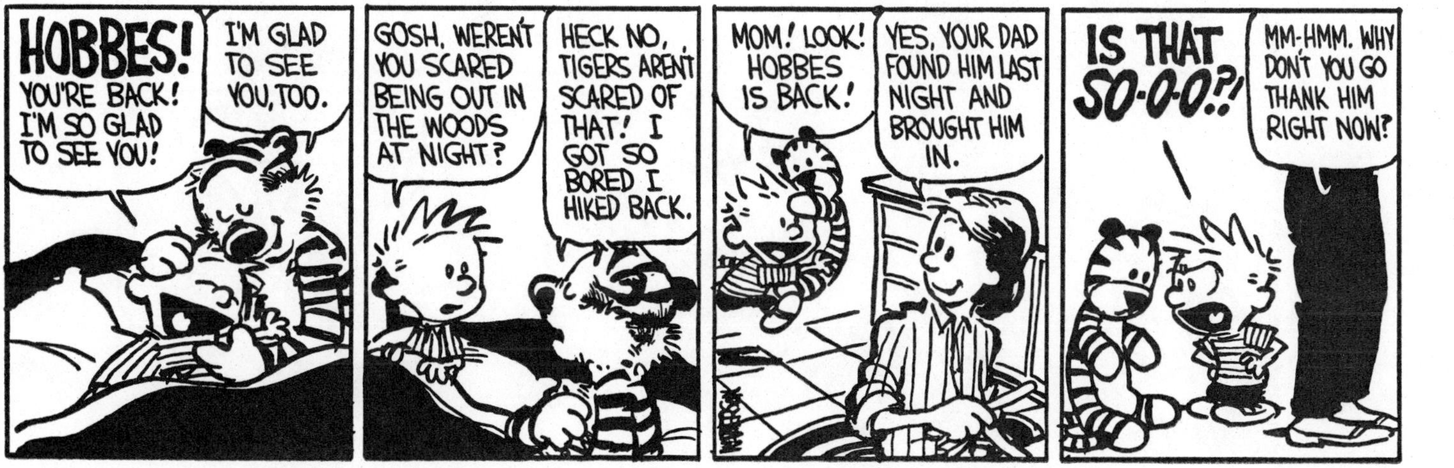
HOBBES! YOU'RE BACK! I'M SO GLAD TO SEE YOU!
I'M GLAD TO SEE YOU, TOO.
GOSH, WEREN'T YOU SCARED BEING OUT IN THE WOODS AT NIGHT?
HECK NO, TIGERS AREN'T SCARED OF THAT! I GOT SO BORED I HIKED BACK.
MOM! LOOK! HOBBES IS BACK!
YES, YOUR DAD FOUND HIM LAST NIGHT AND BROUGHT HIM IN.
IS THAT SO-O-O?!
MM-HMM. WHY DON'T YOU GO THANK HIM RIGHT NOW?

Calvin and Hobbes

by WATTERSON

WIPE THAT GRIN OFF YOUR FACE!

WELL, HOBBES, HOW DO I LOOK?

I'M DOING MY BEST TO BITE MY TONGUE.

I CUT OUT CONSTRUCTION PAPER FEATHERS AND TAPED THEM ON MY ARMS SO I CAN FLY! PRETTY NEAT, HUH?

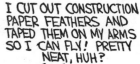

IF PAPER FEATHERS ARE ALL IT TAKES TO FLY, DON'T YOU THINK WE'D HAVE HEARD ABOUT IT BEFORE?

IT TAKES AN UNCOMMON MIND TO THINK OF THESE THINGS, HOBBES.

I'D AGREE WITH THAT.

HERE'S A GORGE. THIS IS A GOOD SPOT.

YOU'RE GOING TO JUMP OFF THIS LEDGE?

HECK NO! I NEED MOMENTUM! I WANT YOU TO TOSS ME OVER.

YOU UNDERSTAND I ASSUME NO RESPONSIBILITY FOR THIS?

RIGHT. I GET THE PATENT.

HEAVE!

I'M FLYING! I'M FLYING!

I'M..... UH OH...

DON'T SELL THE BIKE SHOP, ORVILLE.

SHUT UP AND GO GET ME SOME ANTISEPTIC.

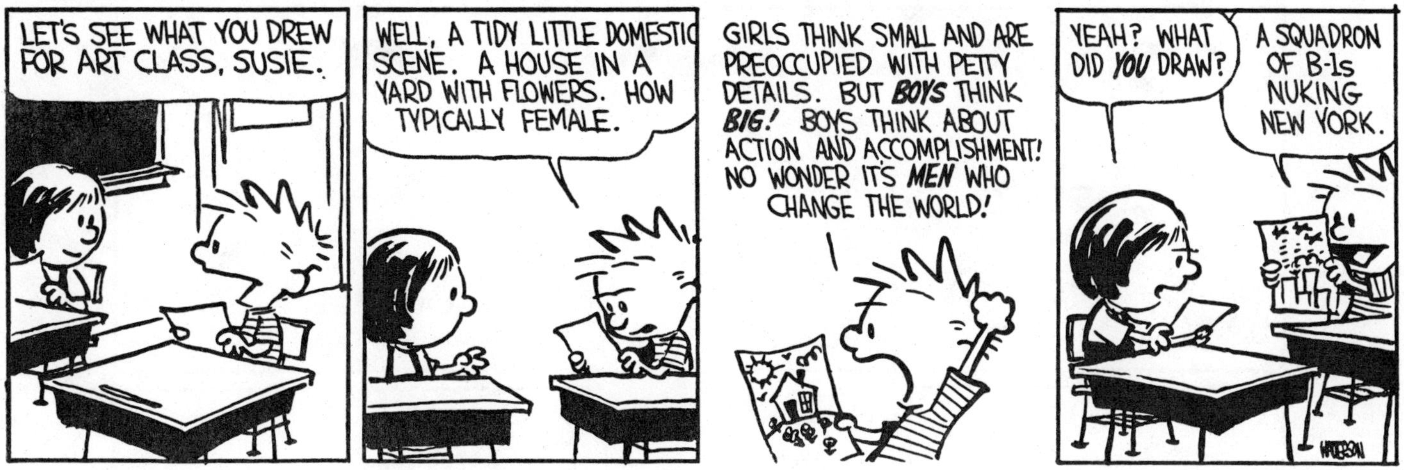
LET'S SEE WHAT YOU DREW FOR ART CLASS, SUSIE.
WELL, A TIDY LITTLE DOMESTIC SCENE. A HOUSE IN A YARD WITH FLOWERS. HOW TYPICALLY FEMALE.
GIRLS THINK SMALL AND ARE PREOCCUPIED WITH PETTY DETAILS. BUT **BOYS** THINK **BIG!** BOYS THINK ABOUT ACTION AND ACCOMPLISHMENT! NO WONDER IT'S **MEN** WHO CHANGE THE WORLD!
YEAH? WHAT DID **YOU** DRAW?
A SQUADRON OF B-1s NUKING NEW YORK.

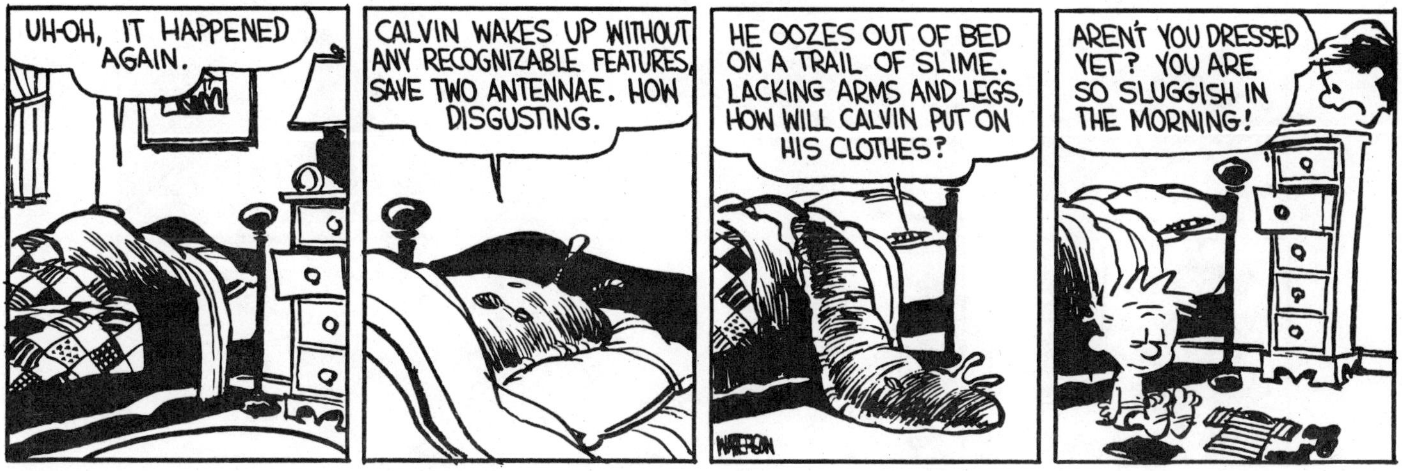
UH-OH, IT HAPPENED AGAIN.
CALVIN WAKES UP WITHOUT ANY RECOGNIZABLE FEATURES, SAVE TWO ANTENNAE. HOW DISGUSTING.
HE OOZES OUT OF BED ON A TRAIL OF SLIME. LACKING ARMS AND LEGS, HOW WILL CALVIN PUT ON HIS CLOTHES?
AREN'T YOU DRESSED YET? YOU ARE SO SLUGGISH IN THE MORNING!

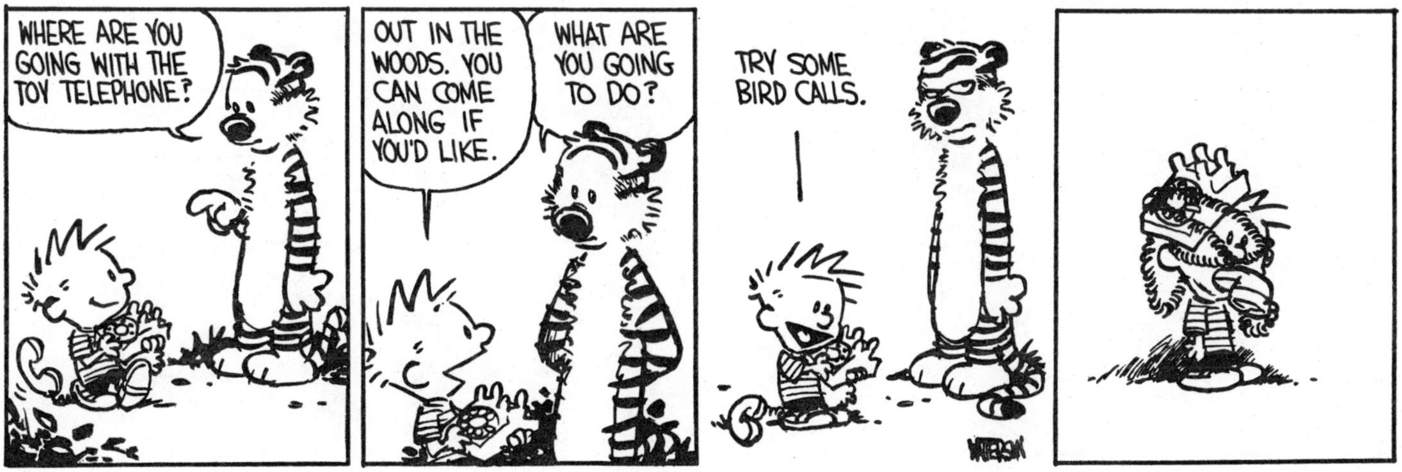
WHERE ARE YOU GOING WITH THE TOY TELEPHONE?
OUT IN THE WOODS. YOU CAN COME ALONG IF YOU'D LIKE.
WHAT ARE YOU GOING TO DO?
TRY SOME BIRD CALLS.

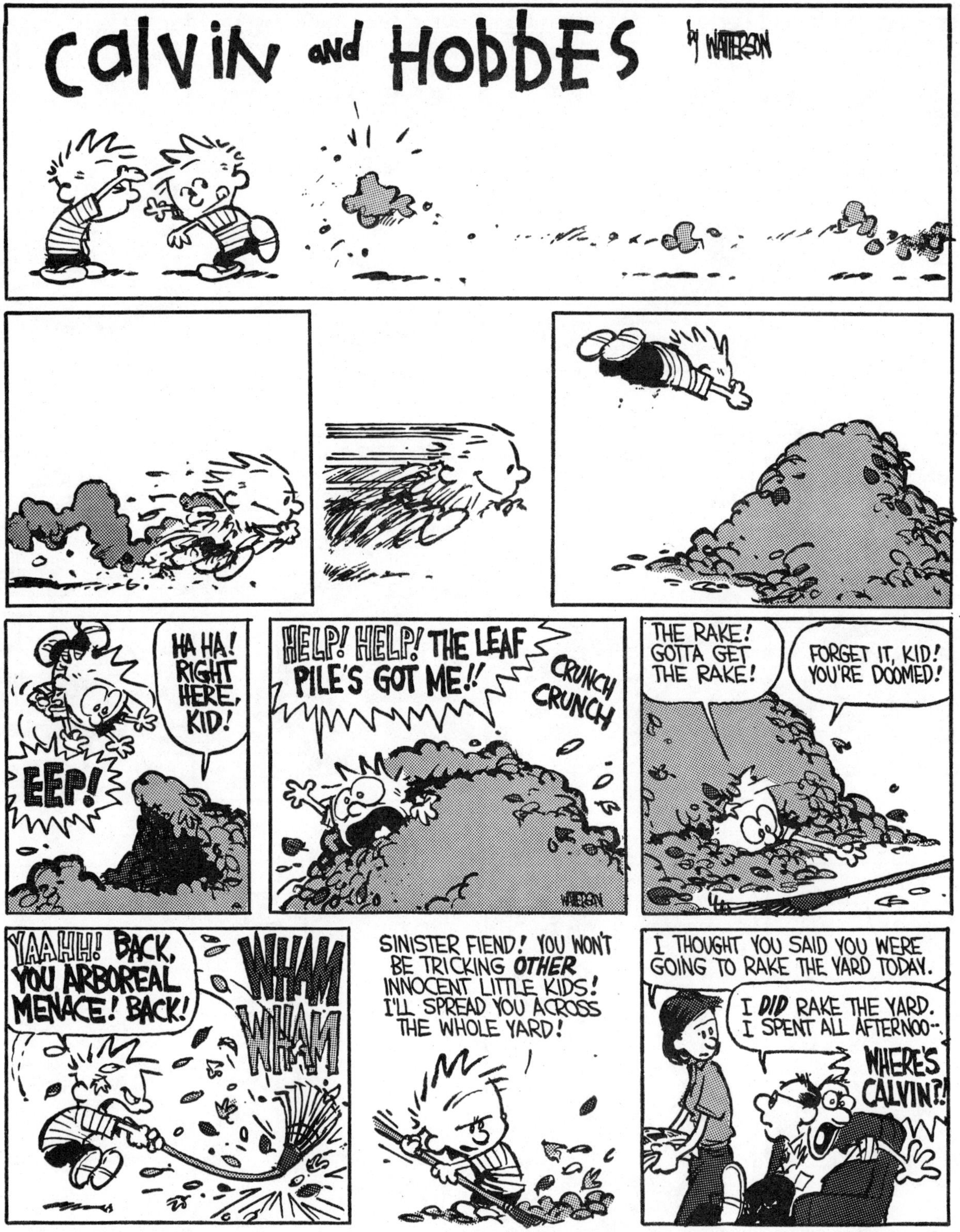
Calvin and HOBBES
by WATTERSON
EEP!
HA HA! RIGHT HERE, KID!
HELP! HELP! THE LEAF PILE'S GOT ME!!
CRUNCH CRUNCH
THE RAKE! GOTTA GET THE RAKE!
FORGET IT, KID! YOU'RE DOOMED!
YAAHH! BACK, YOU ARBOREAL MENACE! BACK!
WHAM WHAM WHAM
SINISTER FIEND! YOU WON'T BE TRICKING OTHER INNOCENT LITTLE KIDS! I'LL SPREAD YOU ACROSS THE WHOLE YARD!
I THOUGHT YOU SAID YOU WERE GOING TO RAKE THE YARD TODAY.
I DID RAKE THE YARD. I SPENT ALL AFTERNOO--
WHERE'S CALVIN?!

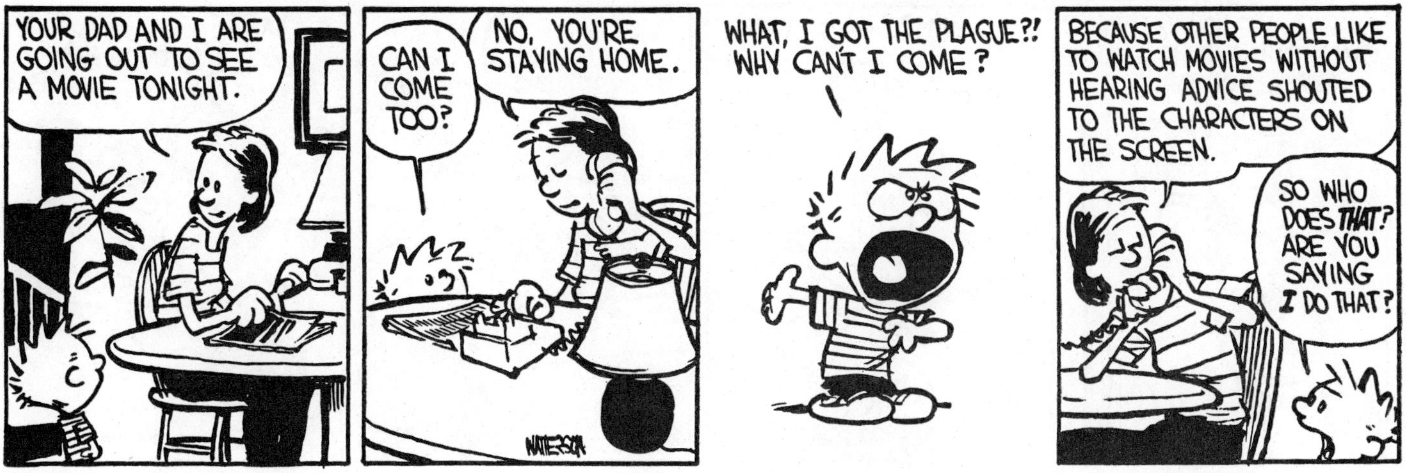
YOUR DAD AND I ARE GOING OUT TO SEE A MOVIE TONIGHT.
CAN I COME TOO?
NO, YOU'RE STAYING HOME.
WHAT, I GOT THE PLAGUE?! WHY CAN'T I COME?
BECAUSE OTHER PEOPLE LIKE TO WATCH MOVIES WITHOUT HEARING ADVICE SHOUTED TO THE CHARACTERS ON THE SCREEN.
SO WHO DOES THAT? ARE YOU SAYING I DO THAT?

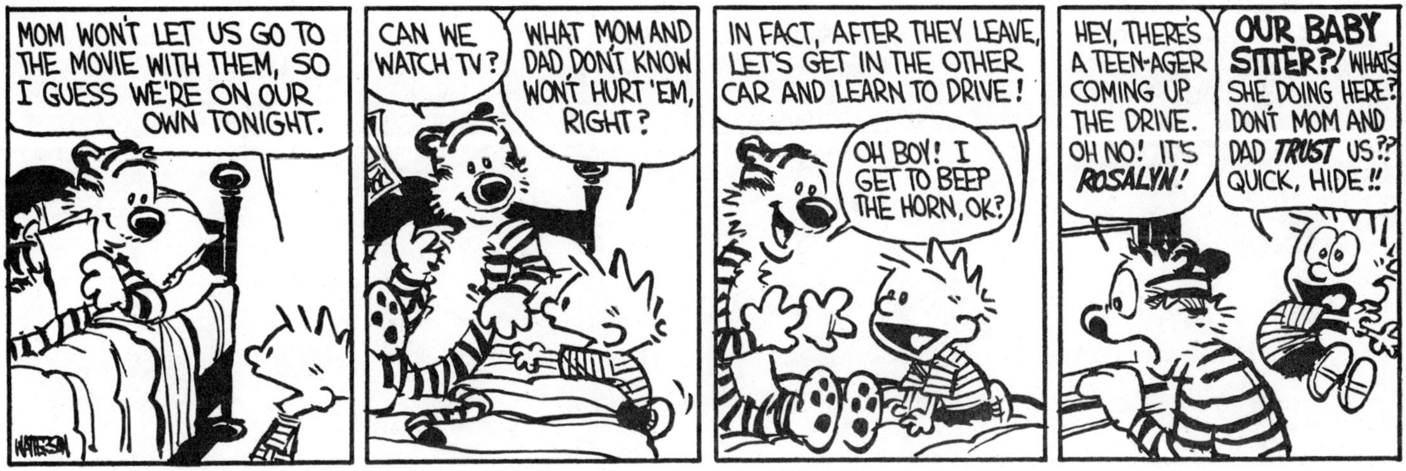
MOM WON'T LET US GO TO THE MOVIE WITH THEM, SO I GUESS WE'RE ON OUR OWN TONIGHT.
CAN WE WATCH TV?
WHAT MOM AND DAD DON'T KNOW WON'T HURT 'EM, RIGHT?
IN FACT, AFTER THEY LEAVE, LET'S GET IN THE OTHER CAR AND LEARN TO DRIVE!
OH BOY! I GET TO BEEP THE HORN, OK?
HEY, THERE'S A TEEN-AGER COMING UP THE DRIVE. OH NO! IT'S ROSALYN!
OUR BABY SITTER?! WHAT'S SHE DOING HERE? DON'T MOM AND DAD TRUST US?? QUICK, HIDE!!

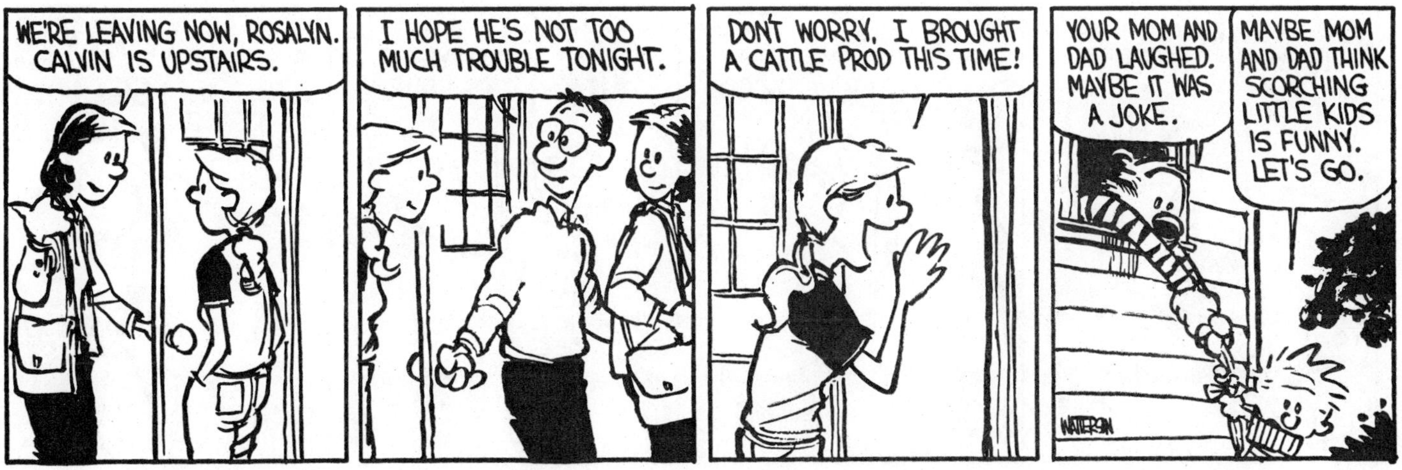
WE'RE LEAVING NOW, ROSALYN. CALVIN IS UPSTAIRS.
I HOPE HE'S NOT TOO MUCH TROUBLE TONIGHT.
DON'T WORRY. I BROUGHT A CATTLE PROD THIS TIME!
YOUR MOM AND DAD LAUGHED. MAYBE IT WAS A JOKE.
MAYBE MOM AND DAD THINK SCORCHING LITTLE KIDS IS FUNNY. LET'S GO.

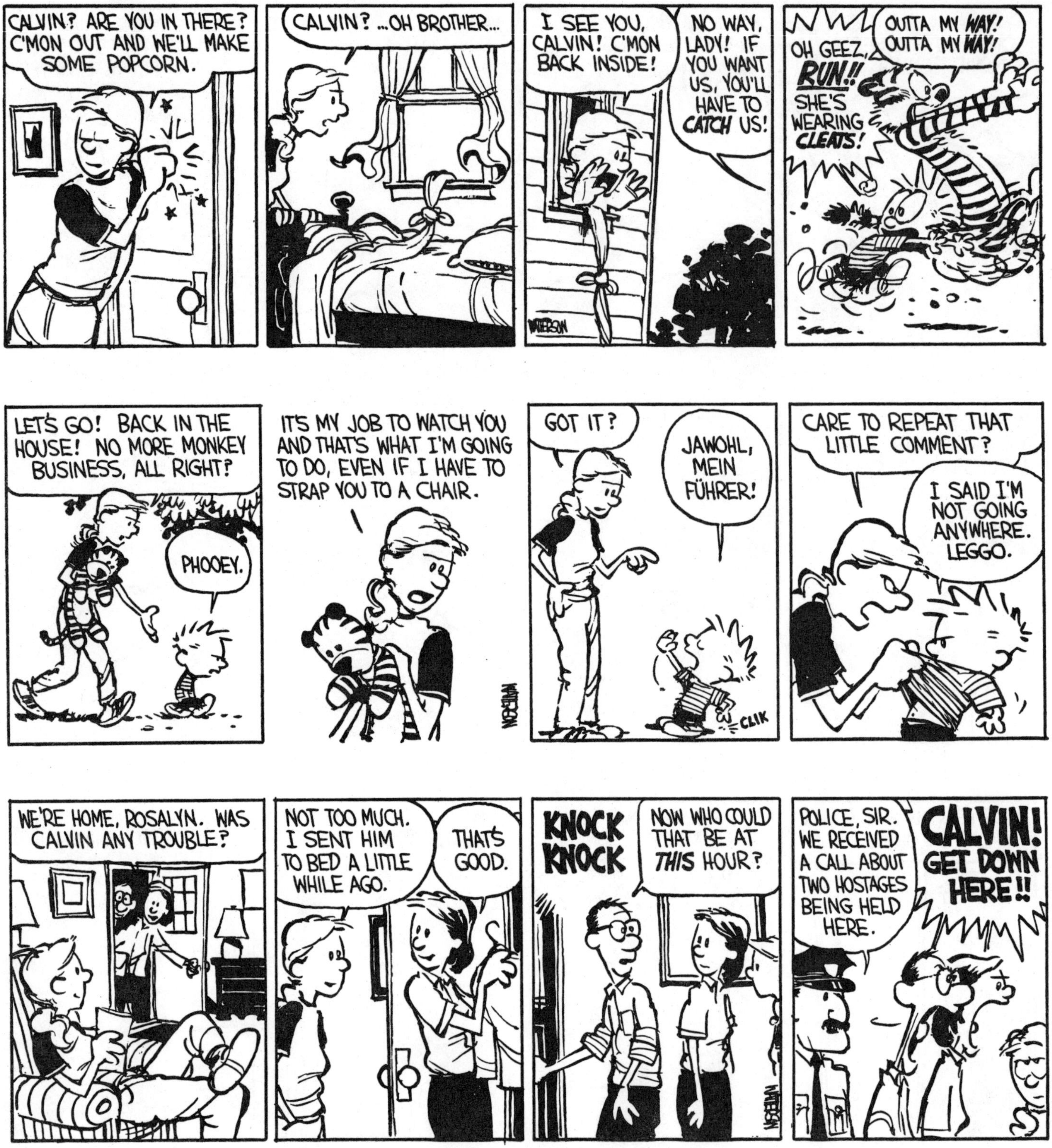
CALVIN? ARE YOU IN THERE? C'MON OUT AND WE'LL MAKE SOME POPCORN.
CALVIN? ...OH BROTHER...
I SEE YOU, CALVIN! C'MON BACK INSIDE!
NO WAY, LADY! IF YOU WANT US, YOU'LL HAVE TO CATCH US!
OH GEEZ, RUN!! SHE'S WEARING CLEATS!
OUTTA MY WAY! OUTTA MY WAY!
LET'S GO! BACK IN THE HOUSE! NO MORE MONKEY BUSINESS, ALL RIGHT?
PHOOEY.
IT'S MY JOB TO WATCH YOU AND THAT'S WHAT I'M GOING TO DO, EVEN IF I HAVE TO STRAP YOU TO A CHAIR.
GOT IT?
JAWOHL, MEIN FÜHRER!
CLIK
CARE TO REPEAT THAT LITTLE COMMENT?
I SAID I'M NOT GOING ANYWHERE. LEGGO.
WE'RE HOME, ROSALYN. WAS CALVIN ANY TROUBLE?
NOT TOO MUCH. I SENT HIM TO BED A LITTLE WHILE AGO.
THAT'S GOOD.
KNOCK KNOCK
NOW WHO COULD THAT BE AT THIS HOUR?
POLICE, SIR. WE RECEIVED A CALL ABOUT TWO HOSTAGES BEING HELD HERE.
CALVIN! GET DOWN HERE!!

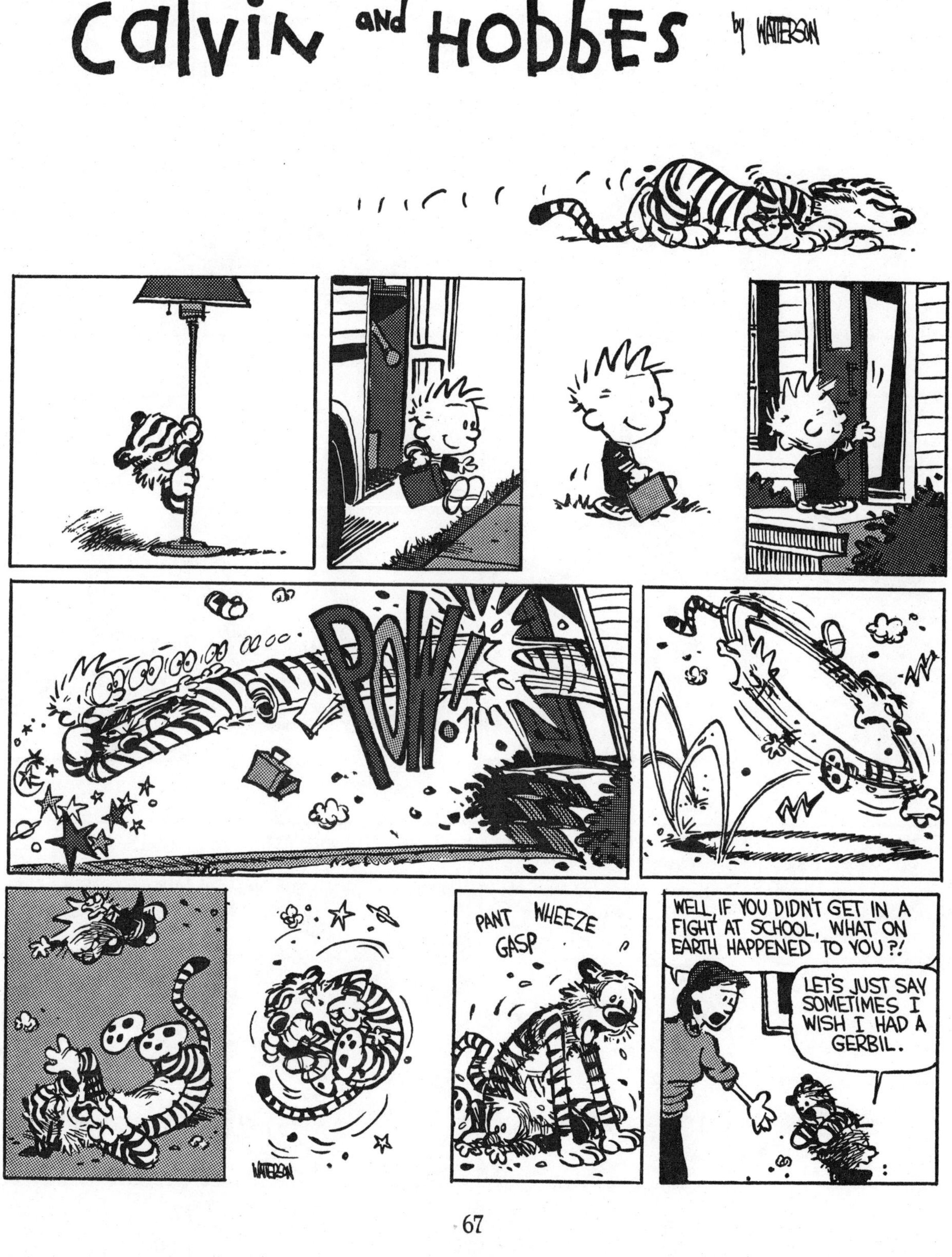
Calvin and HOBBES
by WATTERSON
POW!
PANT
WHEEZE
GASP
WELL, IF YOU DIDN'T GET IN A FIGHT AT SCHOOL, WHAT ON EARTH HAPPENED TO YOU?!
LET'S JUST SAY SOMETIMES I WISH I HAD A GERBIL.
WATTERSON

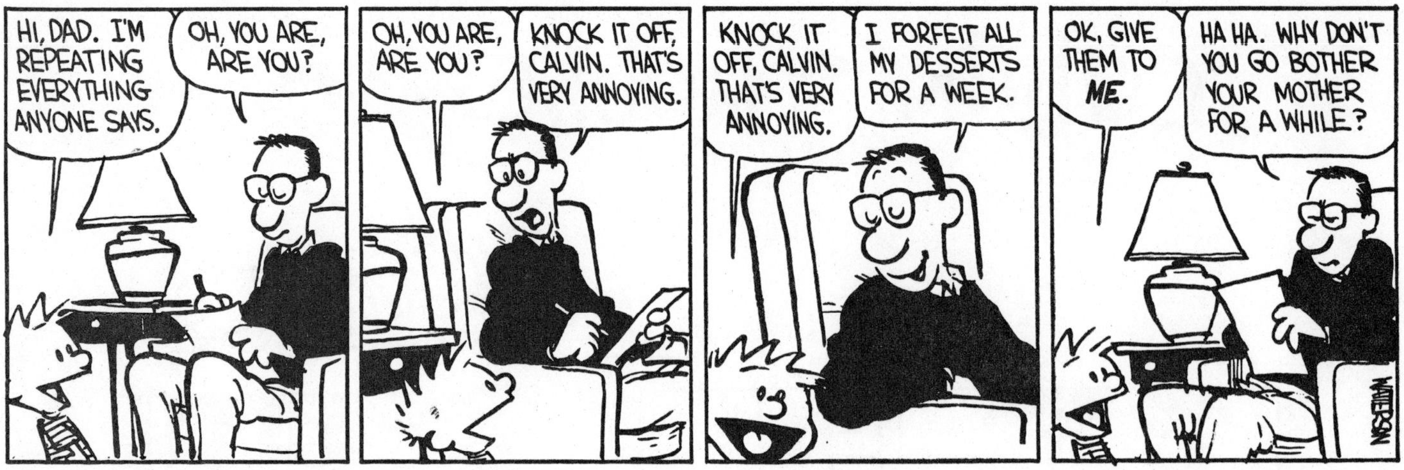
HI, DAD. I'M REPEATING EVERYTHING ANYONE SAYS.
OH, YOU ARE, ARE YOU?
OH, YOU ARE, ARE YOU?
KNOCK IT OFF, CALVIN. THAT'S VERY ANNOYING.
KNOCK IT OFF, CALVIN. THAT'S VERY ANNOYING.
I FORFEIT ALL MY DESSERTS FOR A WEEK.
OK, GIVE THEM TO *ME*.
HA HA. WHY DON'T YOU GO BOTHER YOUR MOTHER FOR A WHILE?

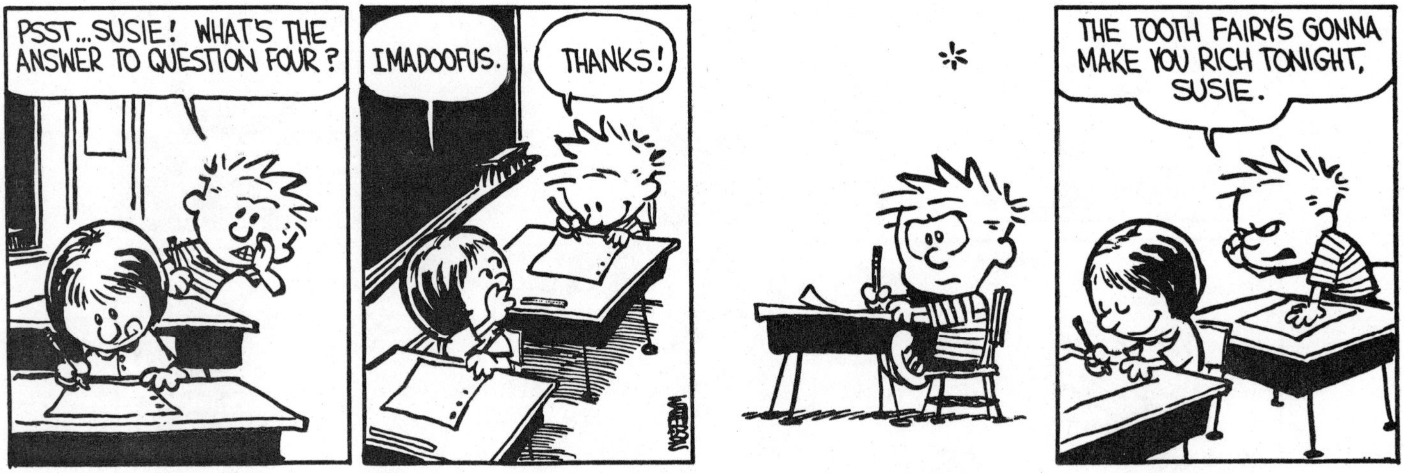
PSST...SUSIE! WHAT'S THE ANSWER TO QUESTION FOUR?
IMADOOFUS.
THANKS!
THE TOOTH FAIRY'S GONNA MAKE YOU RICH TONIGHT, SUSIE.

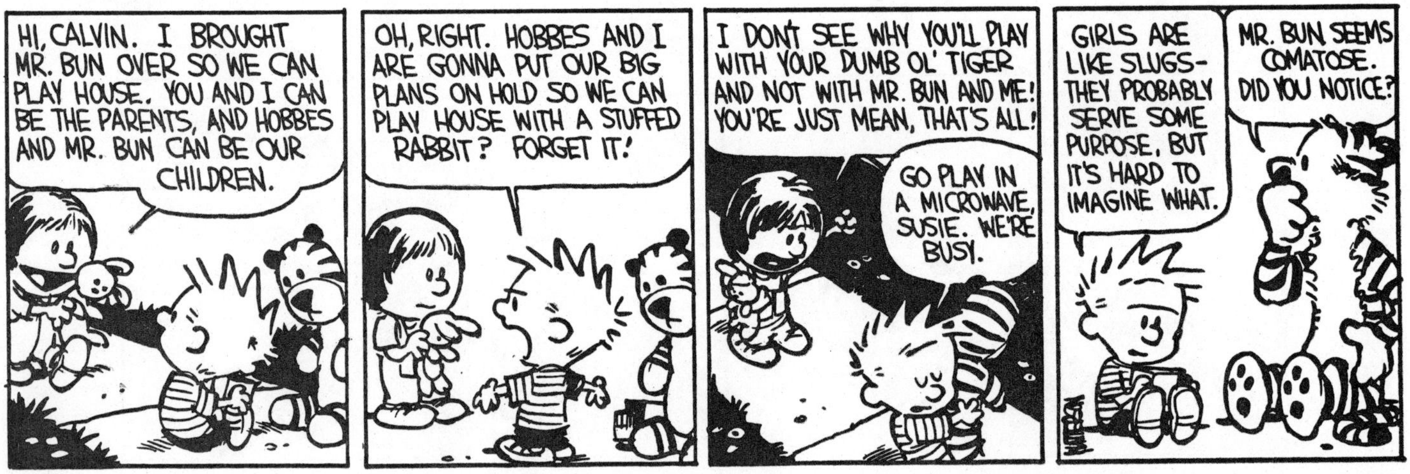
HI, CALVIN. I BROUGHT MR. BUN OVER SO WE CAN PLAY HOUSE. YOU AND I CAN BE THE PARENTS, AND HOBBES AND MR. BUN CAN BE OUR CHILDREN.
OH, RIGHT. HOBBES AND I ARE GONNA PUT OUR BIG PLANS ON HOLD SO WE CAN PLAY HOUSE WITH A STUFFED RABBIT? FORGET IT!
I DON'T SEE WHY YOU'LL PLAY WITH YOUR DUMB OL' TIGER AND NOT WITH MR. BUN AND ME! YOU'RE JUST MEAN, THAT'S ALL!
GO PLAY IN A MICROWAVE, SUSIE. WE'RE BUSY.
GIRLS ARE LIKE SLUGS- THEY PROBABLY SERVE SOME PURPOSE, BUT IT'S HARD TO IMAGINE WHAT.
MR. BUN SEEMS COMATOSE. DID YOU NOTICE?

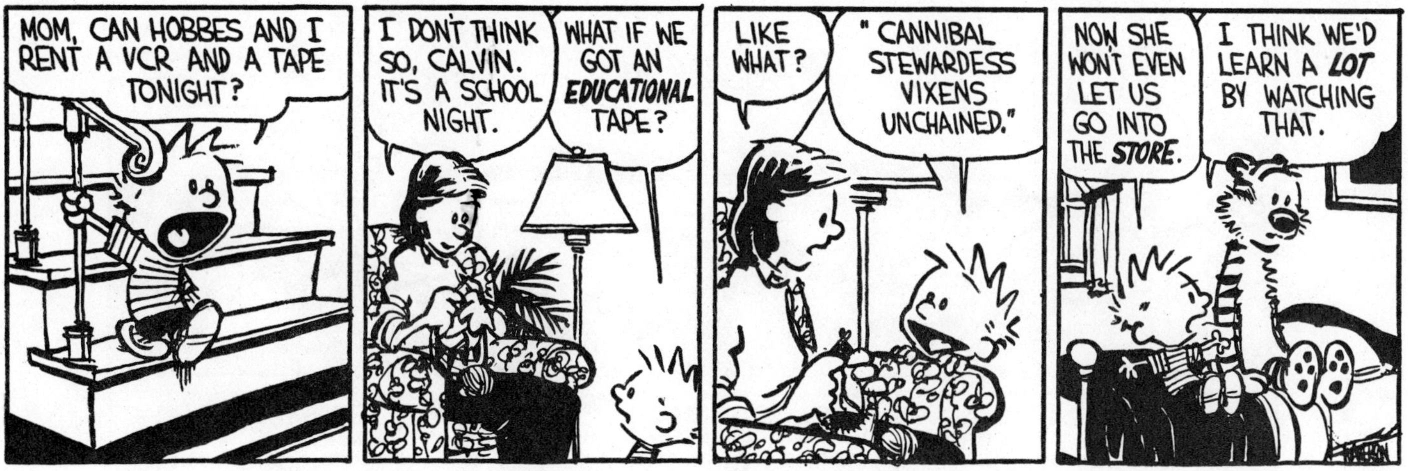
MOM, CAN HOBBES AND I RENT A VCR AND A TAPE TONIGHT?
I DON'T THINK SO, CALVIN. IT'S A SCHOOL NIGHT.
WHAT IF WE GOT AN *EDUCATIONAL* TAPE?
LIKE WHAT?
"CANNIBAL STEWARDESS VIXENS UNCHAINED."
NOW SHE WON'T EVEN LET US GO INTO THE *STORE*.
I THINK WE'D LEARN A *LOT* BY WATCHING THAT.

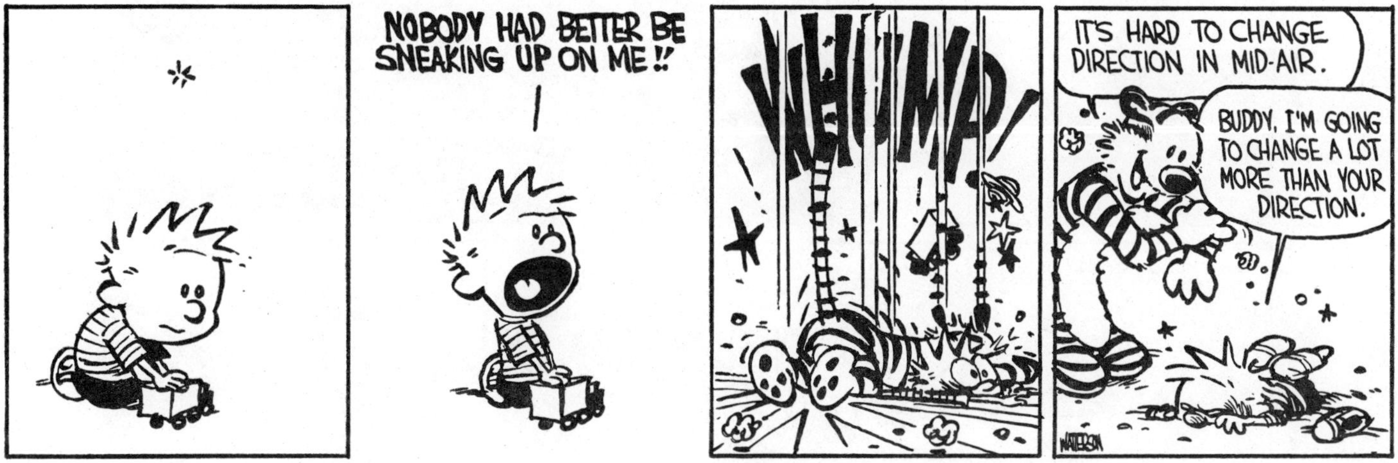
NOBODY HAD BETTER BE SNEAKING UP ON ME!!
WHUMP!
IT'S HARD TO CHANGE DIRECTION IN MID-AIR.
BUDDY, I'M GOING TO CHANGE A LOT MORE THAN YOUR DIRECTION.

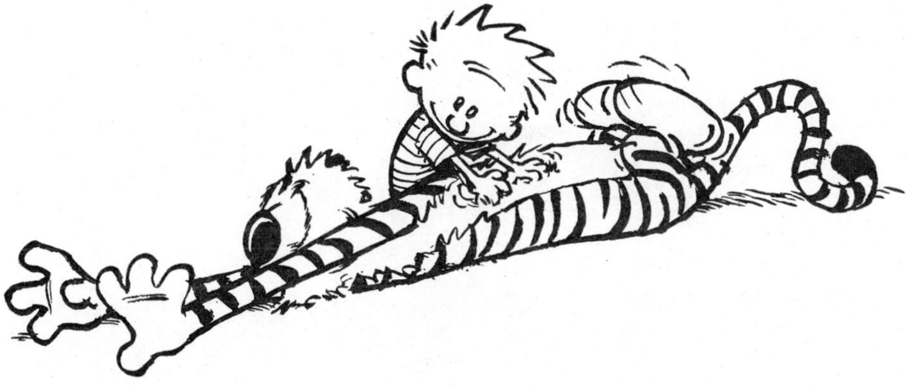

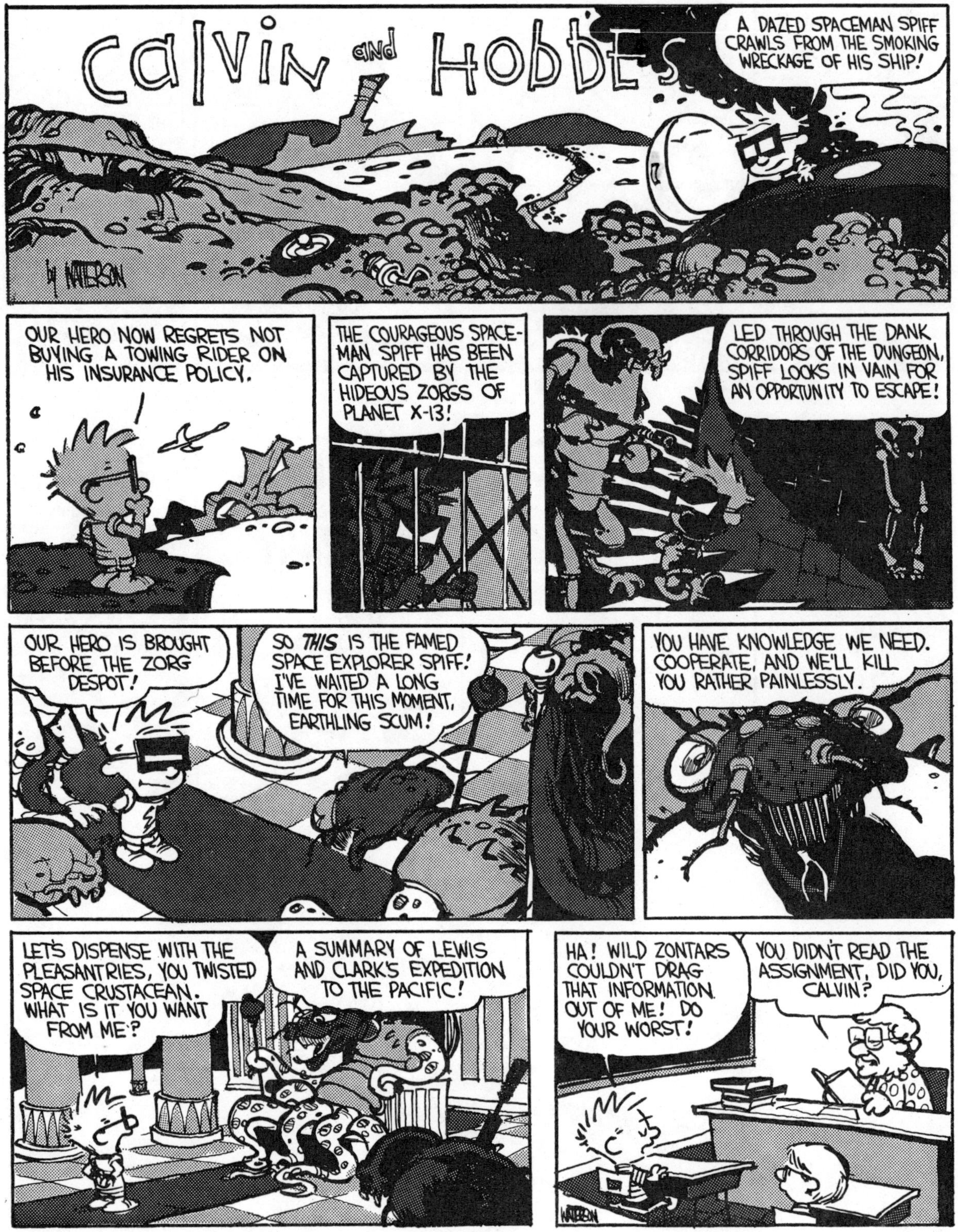
Calvin and Hobbes
by WATTERSON
A DAZED SPACEMAN SPIFF CRAWLS FROM THE SMOKING WRECKAGE OF HIS SHIP!
OUR HERO NOW REGRETS NOT BUYING A TOWING RIDER ON HIS INSURANCE POLICY.
THE COURAGEOUS SPACEMAN SPIFF HAS BEEN CAPTURED BY THE HIDEOUS ZORGS OF PLANET X-13!
LED THROUGH THE DANK CORRIDORS OF THE DUNGEON, SPIFF LOOKS IN VAIN FOR AN OPPORTUNITY TO ESCAPE!
OUR HERO IS BROUGHT BEFORE THE ZORG DESPOT!
SO THIS IS THE FAMED SPACE EXPLORER SPIFF! I'VE WAITED A LONG TIME FOR THIS MOMENT, EARTHLING SCUM!
YOU HAVE KNOWLEDGE WE NEED. COOPERATE, AND WE'LL KILL YOU RATHER PAINLESSLY.
LET'S DISPENSE WITH THE PLEASANTRIES, YOU TWISTED SPACE CRUSTACEAN. WHAT IS IT YOU WANT FROM ME?
A SUMMARY OF LEWIS AND CLARK'S EXPEDITION TO THE PACIFIC!
HA! WILD ZONTARS COULDN'T DRAG THAT INFORMATION OUT OF ME! DO YOUR WORST!
YOU DIDN'T READ THE ASSIGNMENT, DID YOU, CALVIN?
WATTERSON

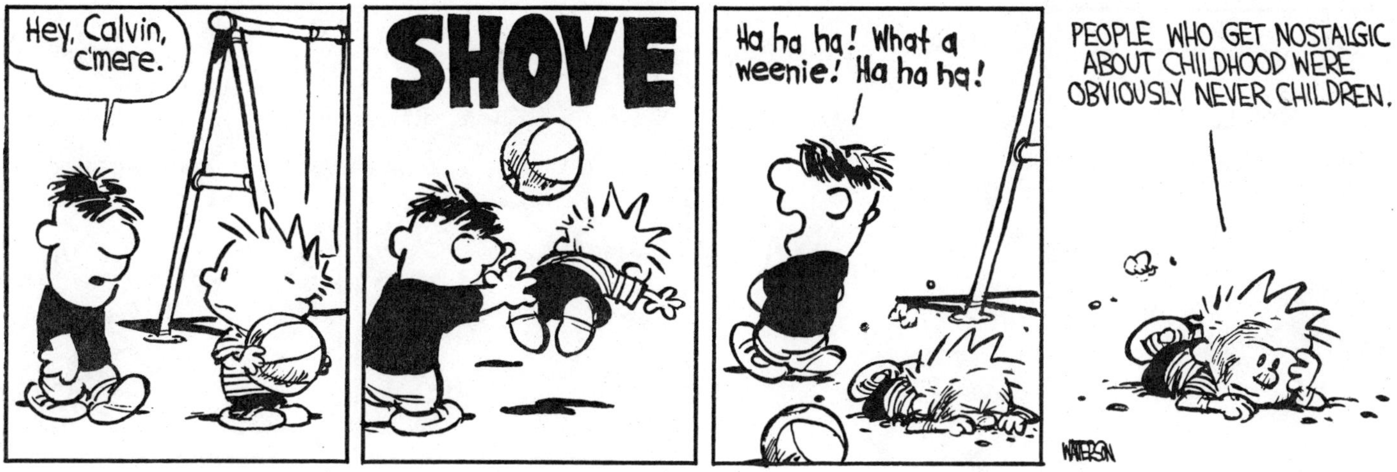
Hey, Calvin, c'mere.
SHOVE
Ha ha ha! What a weenie! Ha ha ha!
PEOPLE WHO GET NOSTALGIC ABOUT CHILDHOOD WERE OBVIOUSLY NEVER CHILDREN.

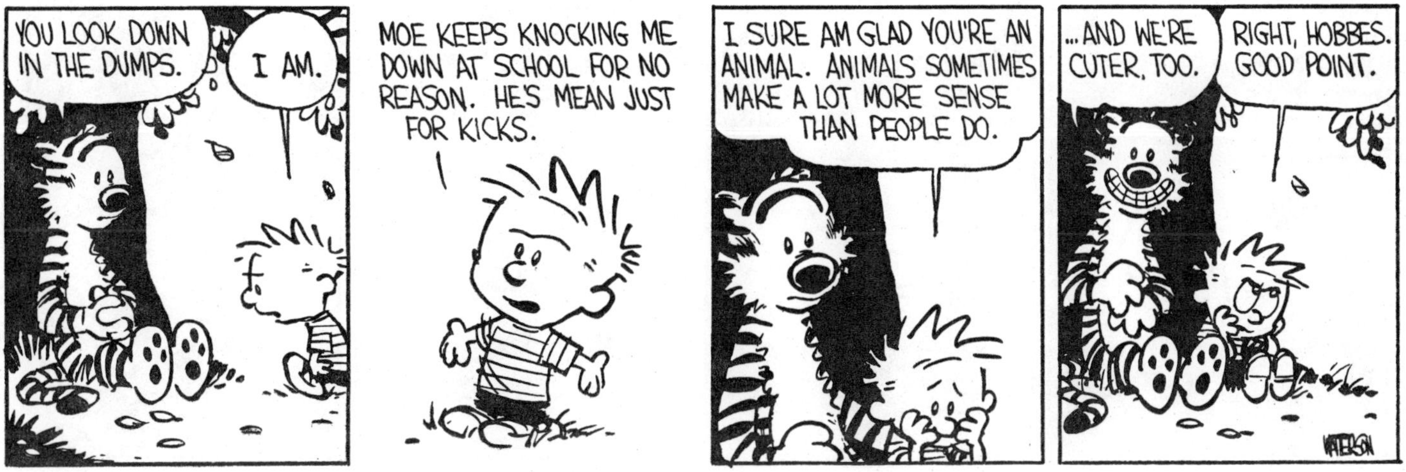
YOU LOOK DOWN IN THE DUMPS.
I AM.
MOE KEEPS KNOCKING ME DOWN AT SCHOOL FOR NO REASON. HE'S MEAN JUST FOR KICKS.
I SURE AM GLAD YOU'RE AN ANIMAL. ANIMALS SOMETIMES MAKE A LOT MORE SENSE THAN PEOPLE DO.
...AND WE'RE CUTER, TOO.
RIGHT, HOBBES. GOOD POINT.

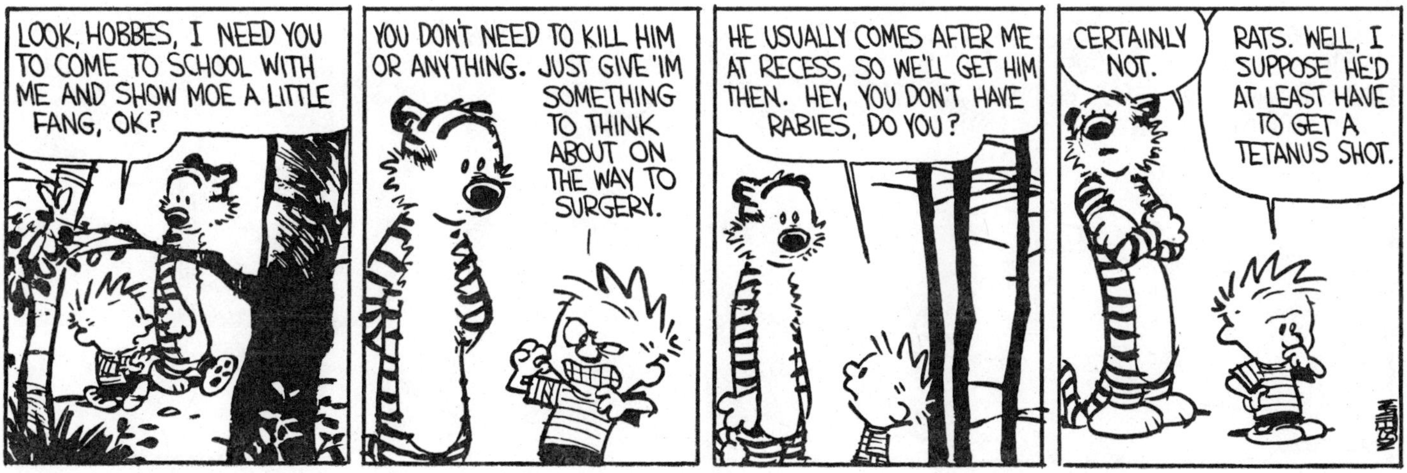
LOOK, HOBBES, I NEED YOU TO COME TO SCHOOL WITH ME AND SHOW MOE A LITTLE FANG, OK?
YOU DON'T NEED TO KILL HIM OR ANYTHING. JUST GIVE 'IM SOMETHING TO THINK ABOUT ON THE WAY TO SURGERY.
HE USUALLY COMES AFTER ME AT RECESS, SO WE'LL GET HIM THEN. HEY, YOU DON'T HAVE RABIES, DO YOU?
CERTAINLY NOT.
RATS. WELL, I SUPPOSE HE'D AT LEAST HAVE TO GET A TETANUS SHOT.

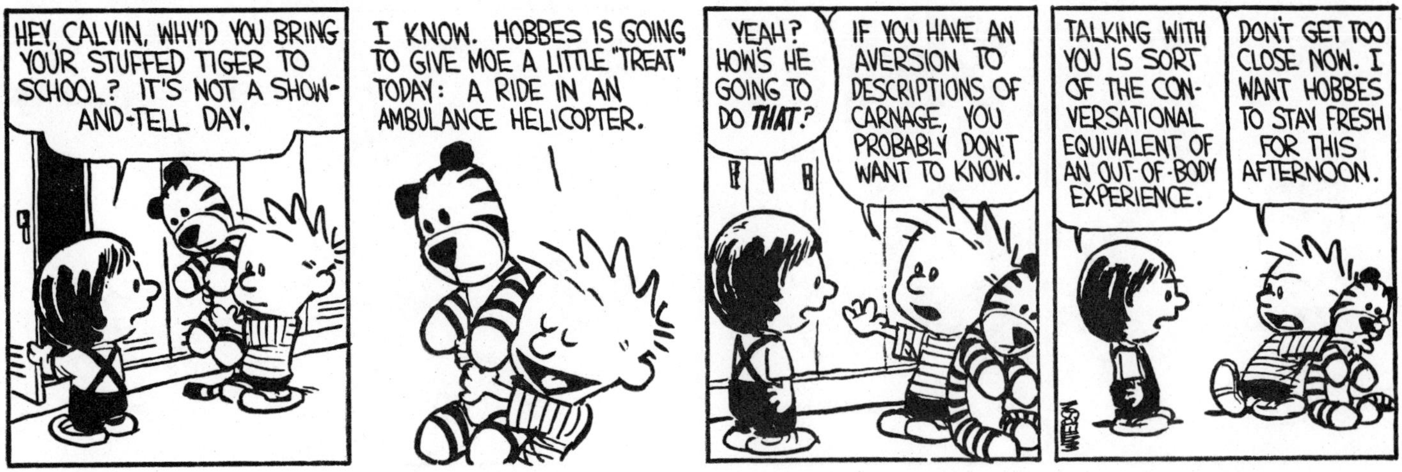
HEY, CALVIN, WHY'D YOU BRING YOUR STUFFED TIGER TO SCHOOL? IT'S NOT A SHOW-AND-TELL DAY.
I KNOW. HOBBES IS GOING TO GIVE MOE A LITTLE "TREAT" TODAY: A RIDE IN AN AMBULANCE HELICOPTER.
YEAH? HOW'S HE GOING TO DO *THAT*?
IF YOU HAVE AN AVERSION TO DESCRIPTIONS OF CARNAGE, YOU PROBABLY DON'T WANT TO KNOW.
TALKING WITH YOU IS SORT OF THE CONVERSATIONAL EQUIVALENT OF AN OUT-OF-BODY EXPERIENCE.
DON'T GET TOO CLOSE NOW. I WANT HOBBES TO STAY FRESH FOR THIS AFTERNOON.

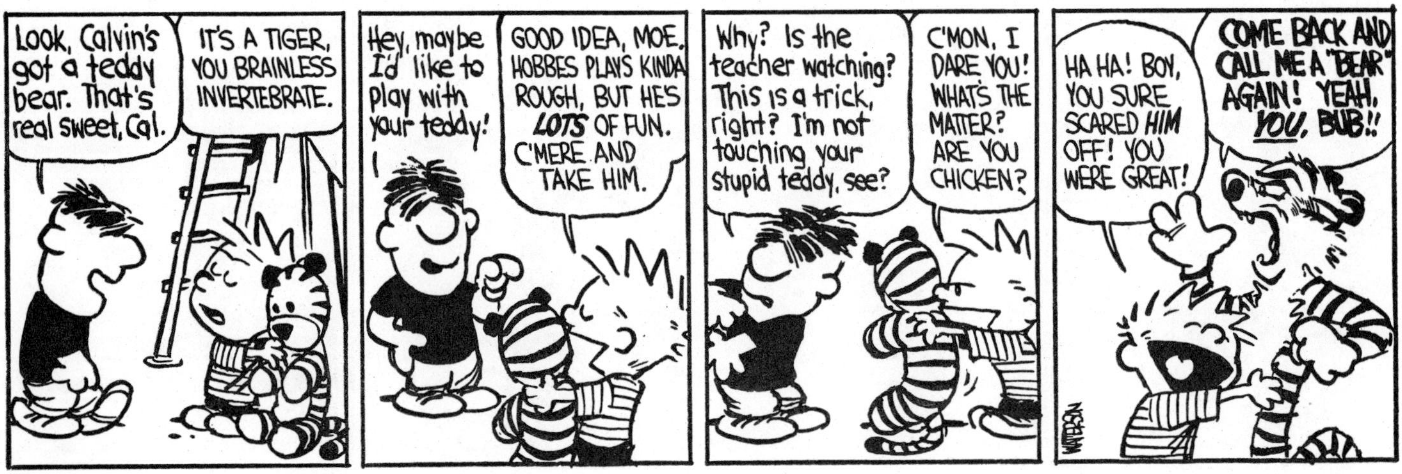
Look, Calvin's got a teddy bear. That's real sweet, Cal.
IT'S A TIGER, YOU BRAINLESS INVERTEBRATE.
Hey, maybe I'd like to play with your teddy!
GOOD IDEA, MOE. HOBBES PLAYS KINDA ROUGH, BUT HE'S *LOTS* OF FUN. C'MERE AND TAKE HIM.
Why? Is the teacher watching? This is a trick, right? I'm not touching your stupid teddy, see?
C'MON, I DARE YOU! WHAT'S THE MATTER? ARE YOU CHICKEN?
HA HA! BOY, YOU SURE SCARED *HIM* OFF! YOU WERE GREAT!
COME BACK AND CALL ME A "BEAR" AGAIN! YEAH, *YOU*, BUB!!

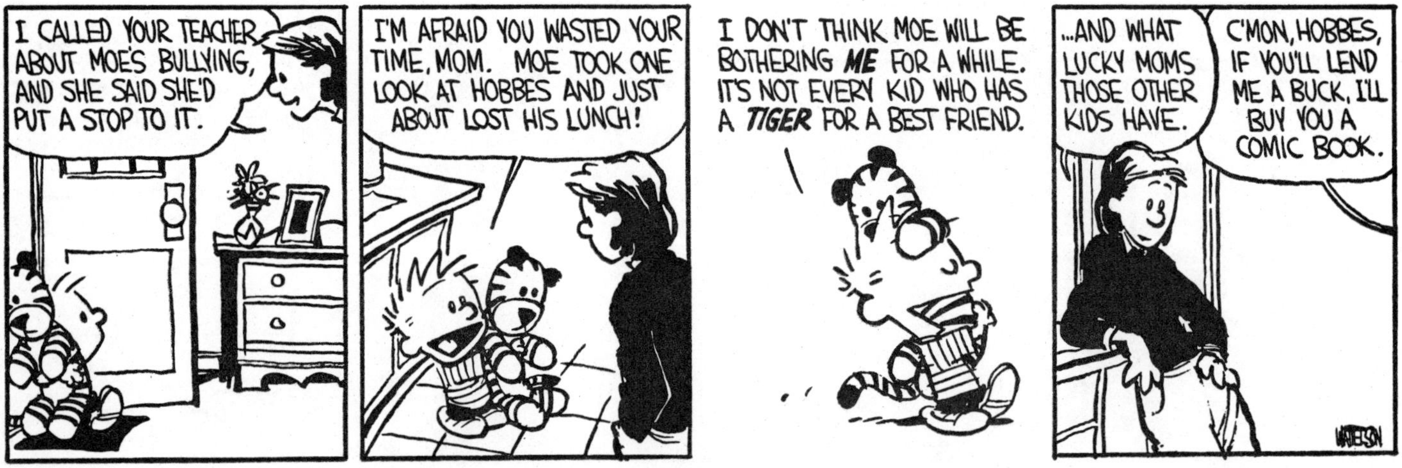
I CALLED YOUR TEACHER ABOUT MOE'S BULLYING, AND SHE SAID SHE'D PUT A STOP TO IT.
I'M AFRAID YOU WASTED YOUR TIME, MOM. MOE TOOK ONE LOOK AT HOBBES AND JUST ABOUT LOST HIS LUNCH!
I DON'T THINK MOE WILL BE BOTHERING *ME* FOR A WHILE. IT'S NOT EVERY KID WHO HAS A *TIGER* FOR A BEST FRIEND.
...AND WHAT LUCKY MOMS THOSE OTHER KIDS HAVE.
C'MON, HOBBES, IF YOU'LL LEND ME A BUCK, I'LL BUY YOU A COMIC BOOK.

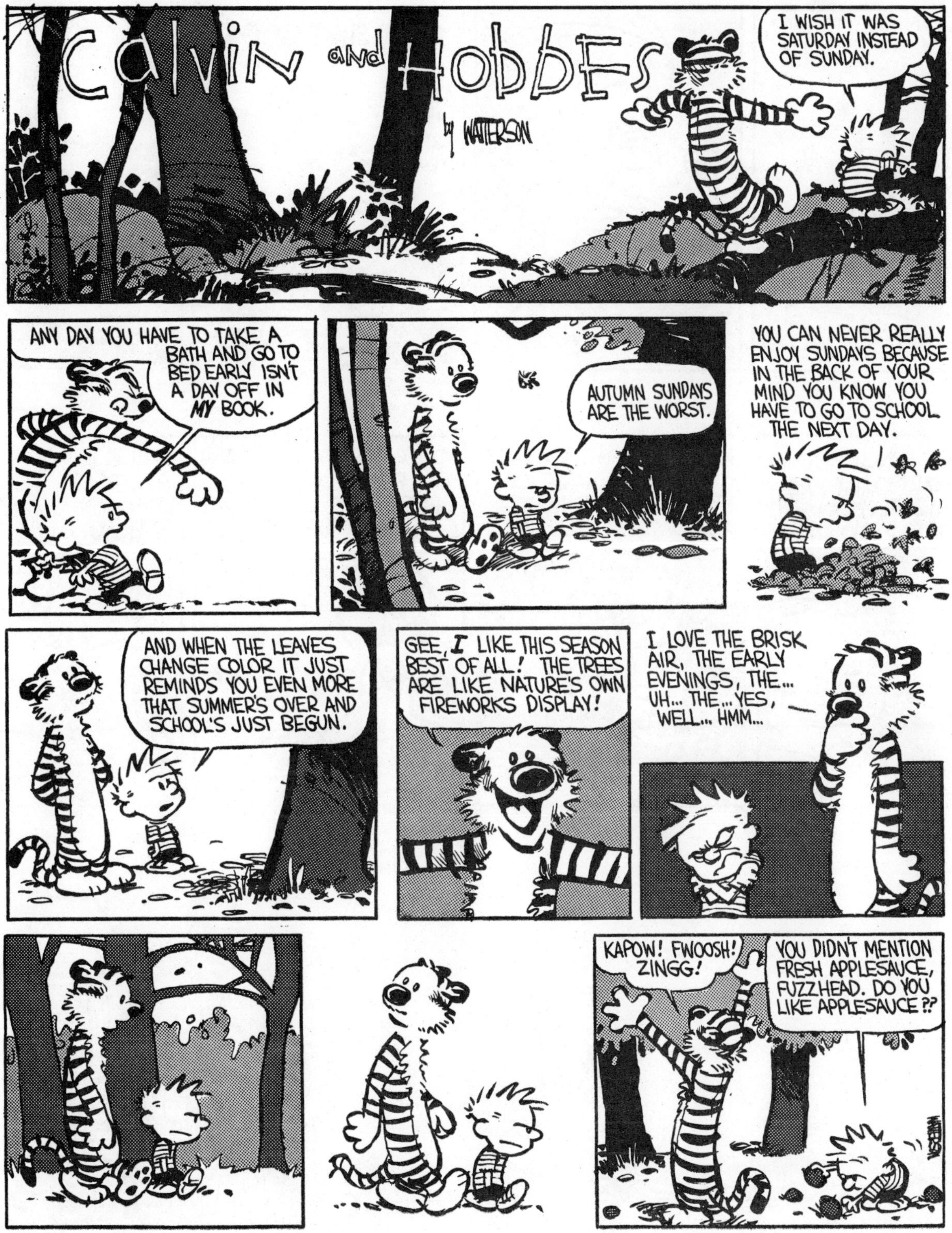
Calvin and Hobbes
by WATTERSON
I WISH IT WAS SATURDAY INSTEAD OF SUNDAY.
ANY DAY YOU HAVE TO TAKE A BATH AND GO TO BED EARLY ISN'T A DAY OFF IN MY BOOK.
AUTUMN SUNDAYS ARE THE WORST.
YOU CAN NEVER REALLY ENJOY SUNDAYS BECAUSE IN THE BACK OF YOUR MIND YOU KNOW YOU HAVE TO GO TO SCHOOL THE NEXT DAY.
AND WHEN THE LEAVES CHANGE COLOR IT JUST REMINDS YOU EVEN MORE THAT SUMMER'S OVER AND SCHOOL'S JUST BEGUN.
GEE, I LIKE THIS SEASON BEST OF ALL! THE TREES ARE LIKE NATURE'S OWN FIREWORKS DISPLAY!
I LOVE THE BRISK AIR, THE EARLY EVENINGS, THE... UH... THE... YES, WELL... HMM...
KAPOW! FWOOSH! ZINGG!
YOU DIDN'T MENTION FRESH APPLESAUCE, FUZZHEAD. DO YOU LIKE APPLESAUCE ??
WATTERSON

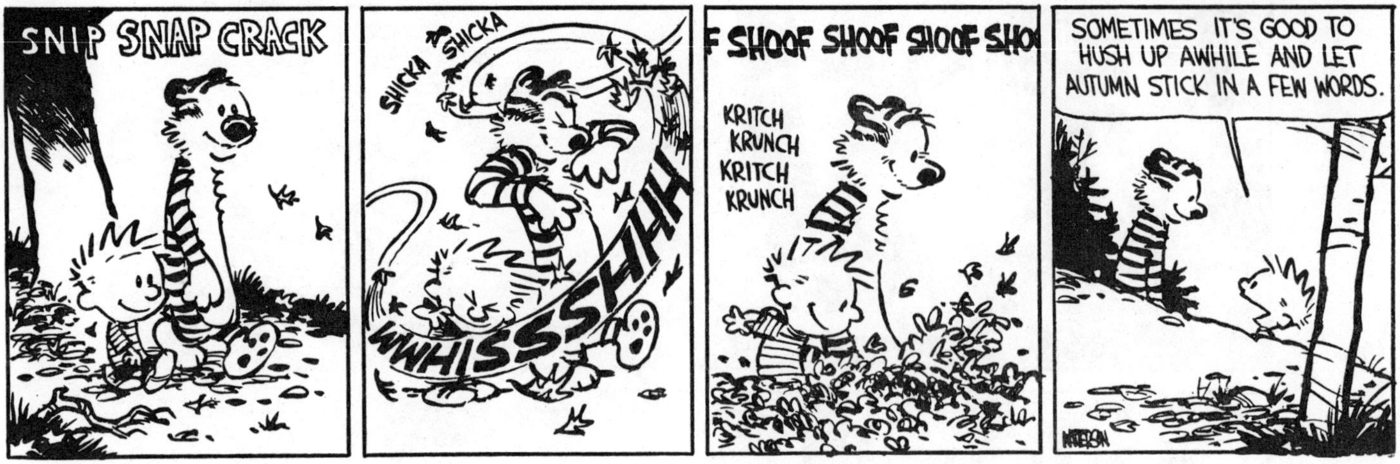
SNIP SNAP CRACK
SHICKA SHICKA
WWHISSSSHHH
SHOOF SHOOF SHOOF
KRITCH KRUNCH KRITCH KRUNCH
SOMETIMES IT'S GOOD TO HUSH UP AWHILE AND LET AUTUMN STICK IN A FEW WORDS.
WATTERSON

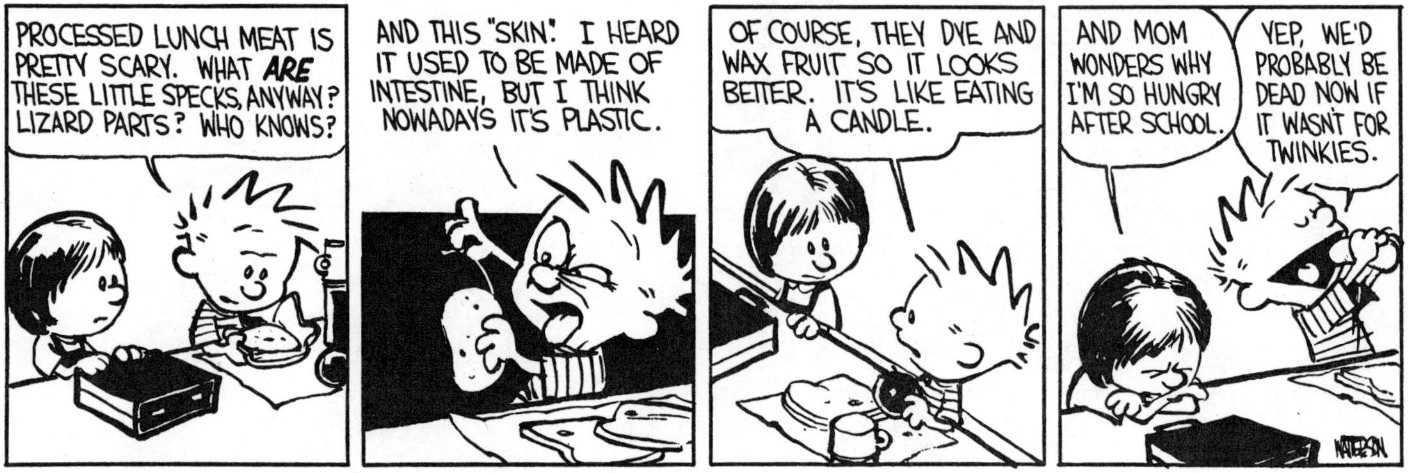
PROCESSED LUNCH MEAT IS PRETTY SCARY. WHAT ***ARE*** THESE LITTLE SPECKS, ANYWAY? LIZARD PARTS? WHO KNOWS?
AND THIS "SKIN." I HEARD IT USED TO BE MADE OF INTESTINE, BUT I THINK NOWADAYS IT'S PLASTIC.
OF COURSE, THEY DYE AND WAX FRUIT SO IT LOOKS BETTER. IT'S LIKE EATING A CANDLE.
AND MOM WONDERS WHY I'M SO HUNGRY AFTER SCHOOL.
YEP, WE'D PROBABLY BE DEAD NOW IF IT WASN'T FOR TWINKIES.
WATTERSON

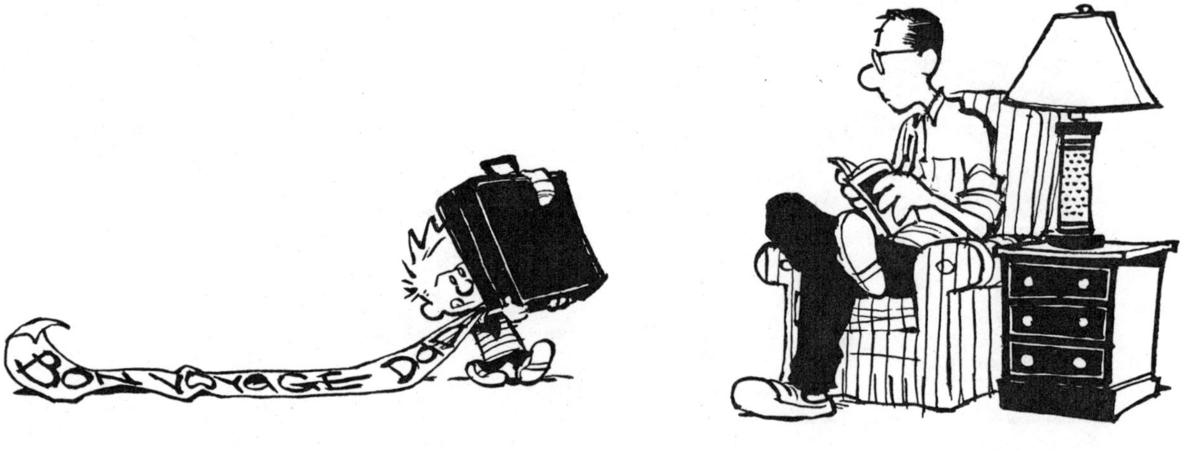
BON VOYAGE

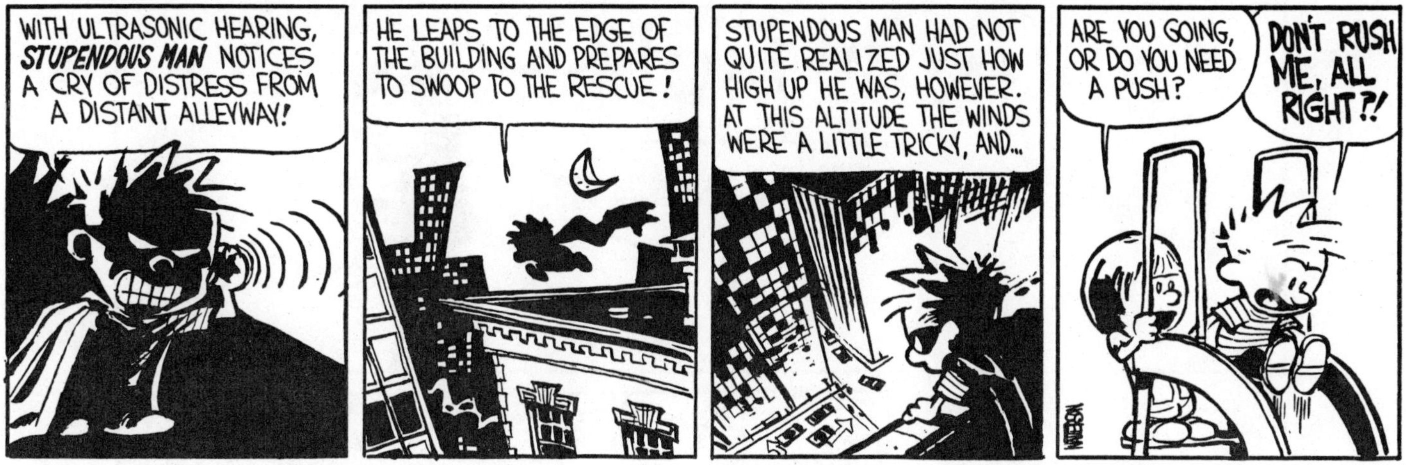
WITH ULTRASONIC HEARING, STUPENDOUS MAN NOTICES A CRY OF DISTRESS FROM A DISTANT ALLEYWAY!
HE LEAPS TO THE EDGE OF THE BUILDING AND PREPARES TO SWOOP TO THE RESCUE!
STUPENDOUS MAN HAD NOT QUITE REALIZED JUST HOW HIGH UP HE WAS, HOWEVER. AT THIS ALTITUDE THE WINDS WERE A LITTLE TRICKY, AND...
ARE YOU GOING, OR DO YOU NEED A PUSH?
DON'T RUSH ME, ALL RIGHT?!
WATTERSON

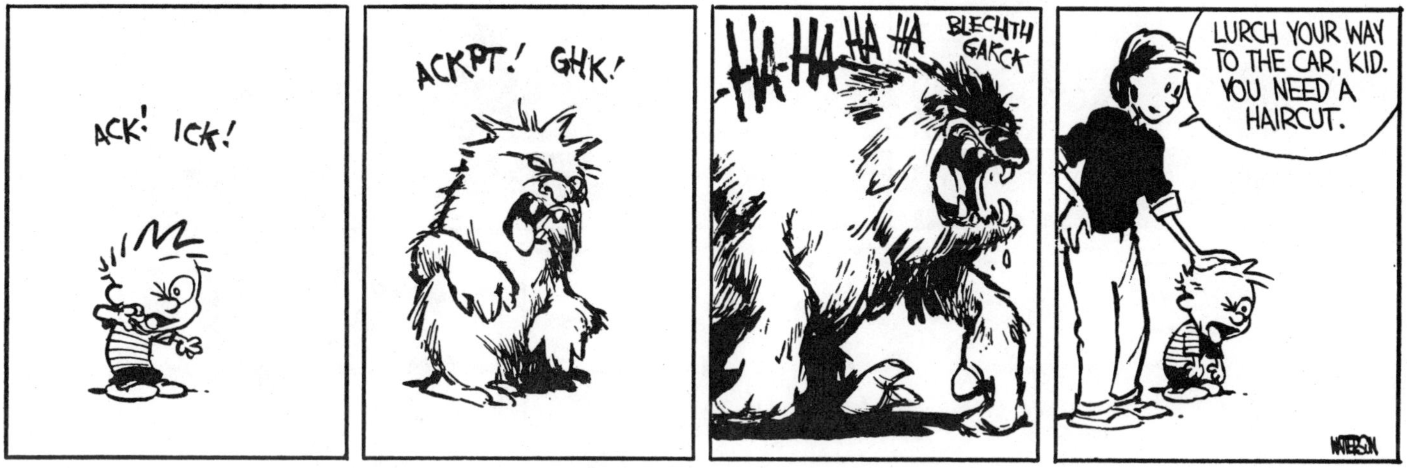
ACK! ICK!
ACKPT! GHK!
HA-HA-HA HA
BLECHTH GARCK
LURCH YOUR WAY TO THE CAR, KID. YOU NEED A HAIRCUT.
WATTERSON

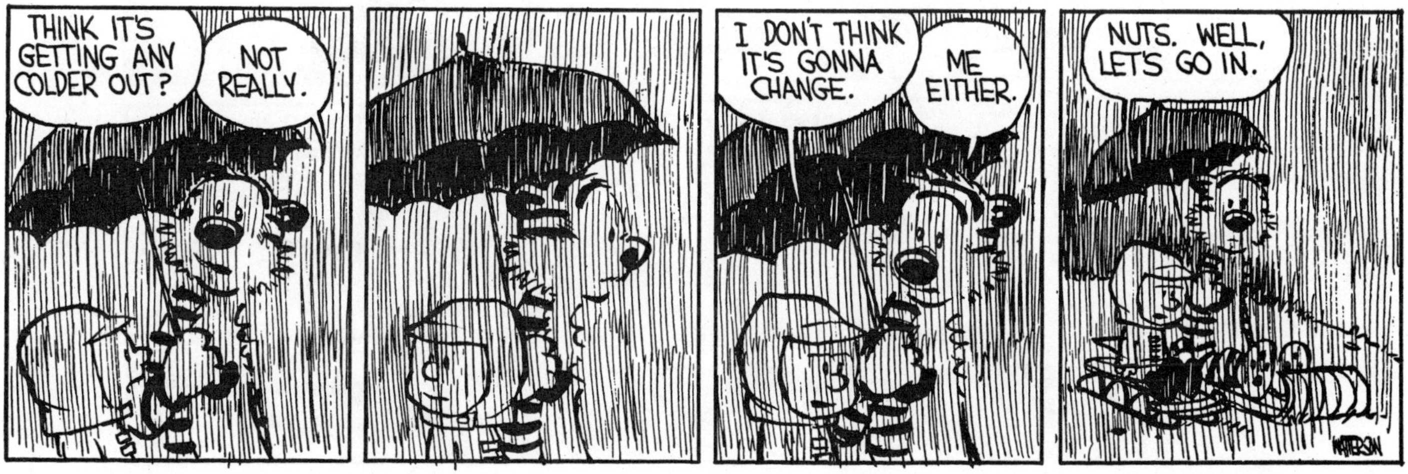
THINK IT'S GETTING ANY COLDER OUT?
NOT REALLY.
I DON'T THINK IT'S GONNA CHANGE.
ME EITHER.
NUTS. WELL, LET'S GO IN.
WATTERSON

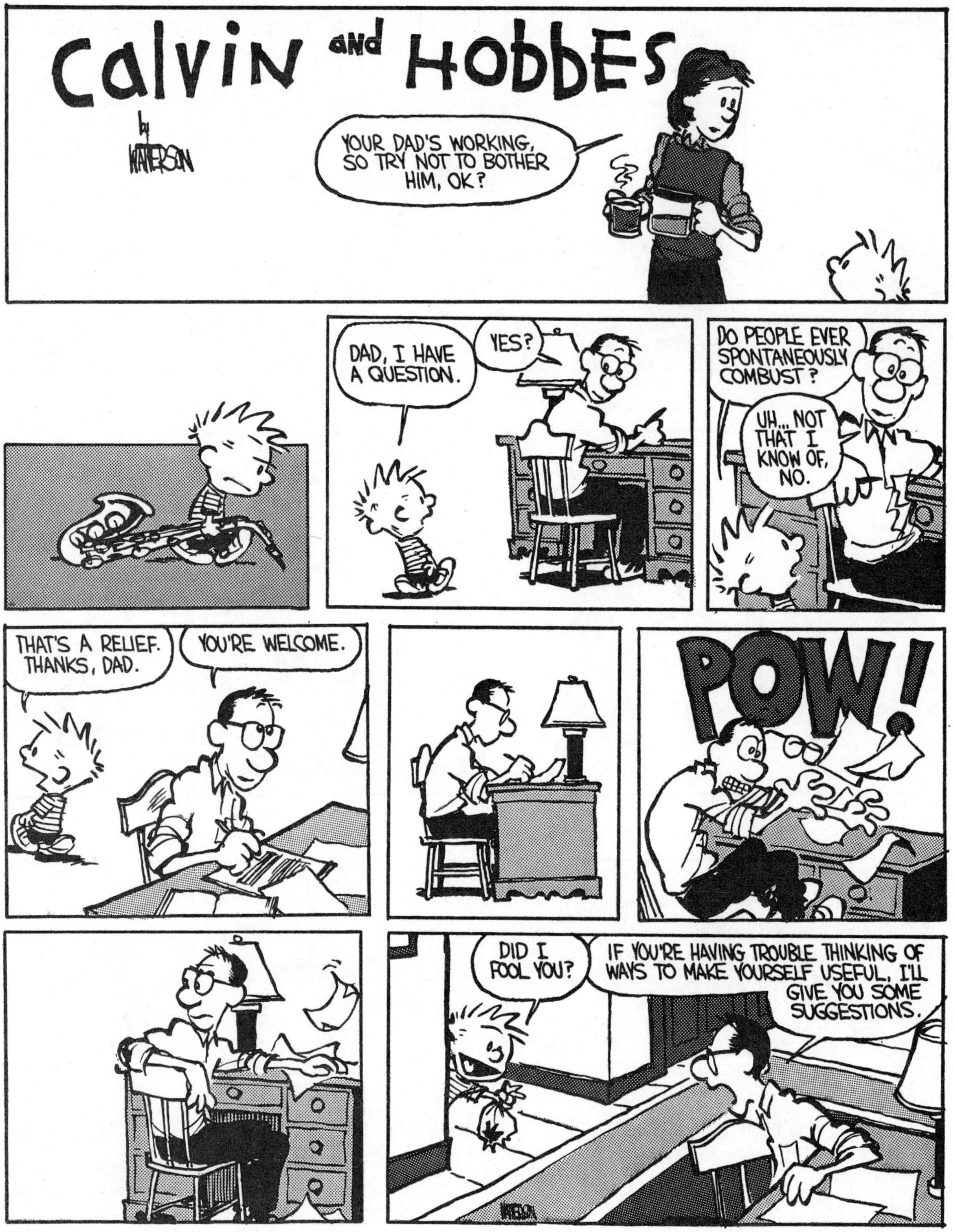
Calvin and HOBBES
by WATTERSON
YOUR DAD'S WORKING, SO TRY NOT TO BOTHER HIM, OK?
DAD, I HAVE A QUESTION.
YES?
DO PEOPLE EVER SPONTANEOUSLY COMBUST?
UH... NOT THAT I KNOW OF, NO.
THAT'S A RELIEF. THANKS, DAD.
YOU'RE WELCOME.
POW!
DID I FOOL YOU?
IF YOU'RE HAVING TROUBLE THINKING OF WAYS TO MAKE YOURSELF USEFUL, I'LL GIVE YOU SOME SUGGESTIONS.
WATTERSON

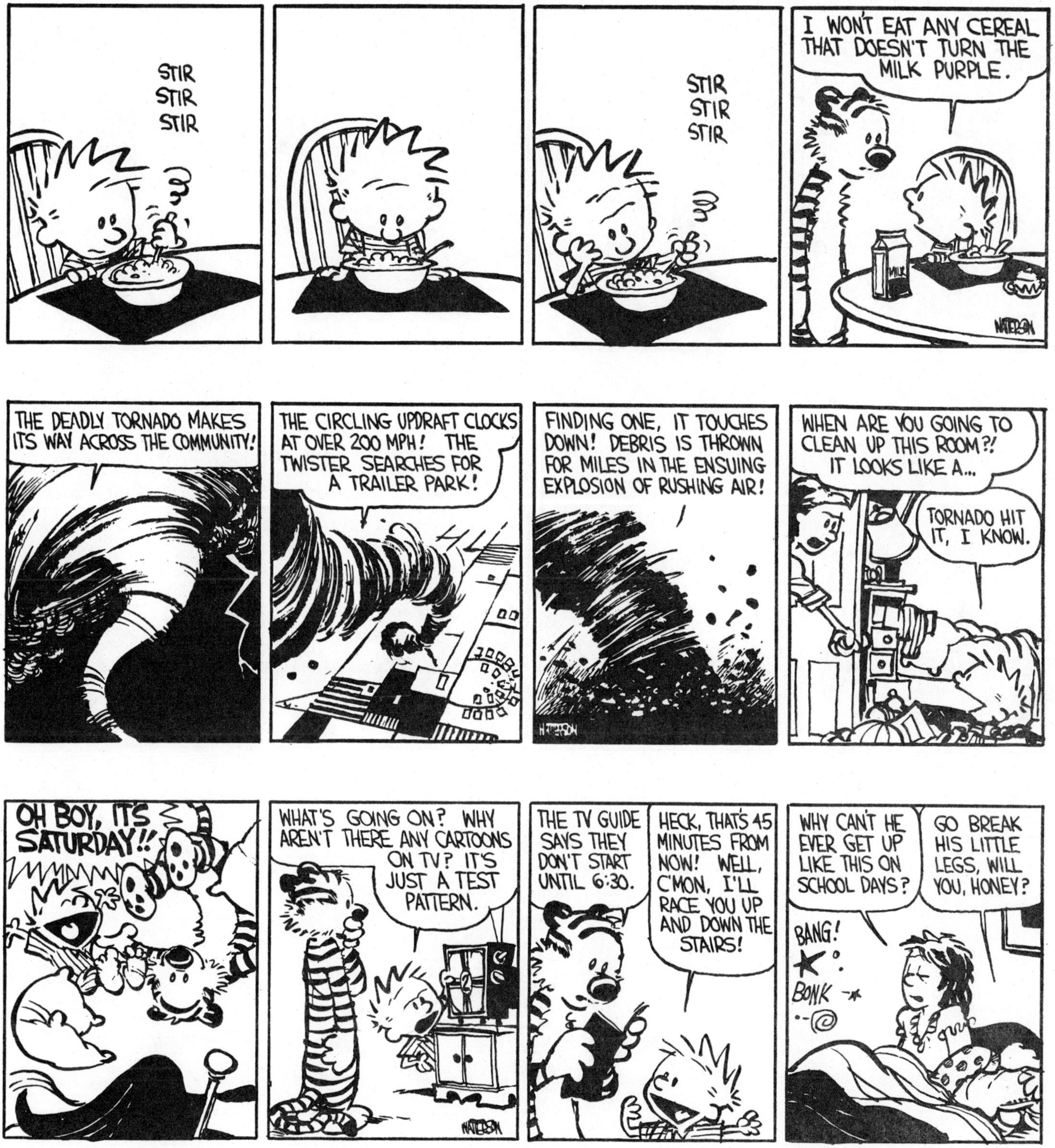
STIR STIR STIR
STIR STIR STIR
I WON'T EAT ANY CEREAL THAT DOESN'T TURN THE MILK PURPLE.
MILK
THE DEADLY TORNADO MAKES ITS WAY ACROSS THE COMMUNITY!
THE CIRCLING UPDRAFT CLOCKS AT OVER 200 MPH! THE TWISTER SEARCHES FOR A TRAILER PARK!
FINDING ONE, IT TOUCHES DOWN! DEBRIS IS THROWN FOR MILES IN THE ENSUING EXPLOSION OF RUSHING AIR!
WHEN ARE YOU GOING TO CLEAN UP THIS ROOM?! IT LOOKS LIKE A...
TORNADO HIT IT, I KNOW.
OH BOY, IT'S SATURDAY!!
WHAT'S GOING ON? WHY AREN'T THERE ANY CARTOONS ON TV? IT'S JUST A TEST PATTERN.
THE TV GUIDE SAYS THEY DON'T START UNTIL 6:30.
HECK, THAT'S 45 MINUTES FROM NOW! WELL, C'MON, I'LL RACE YOU UP AND DOWN THE STAIRS!
WHY CAN'T HE EVER GET UP LIKE THIS ON SCHOOL DAYS?
GO BREAK HIS LITTLE LEGS, WILL YOU, HONEY?
BANG!
BONK

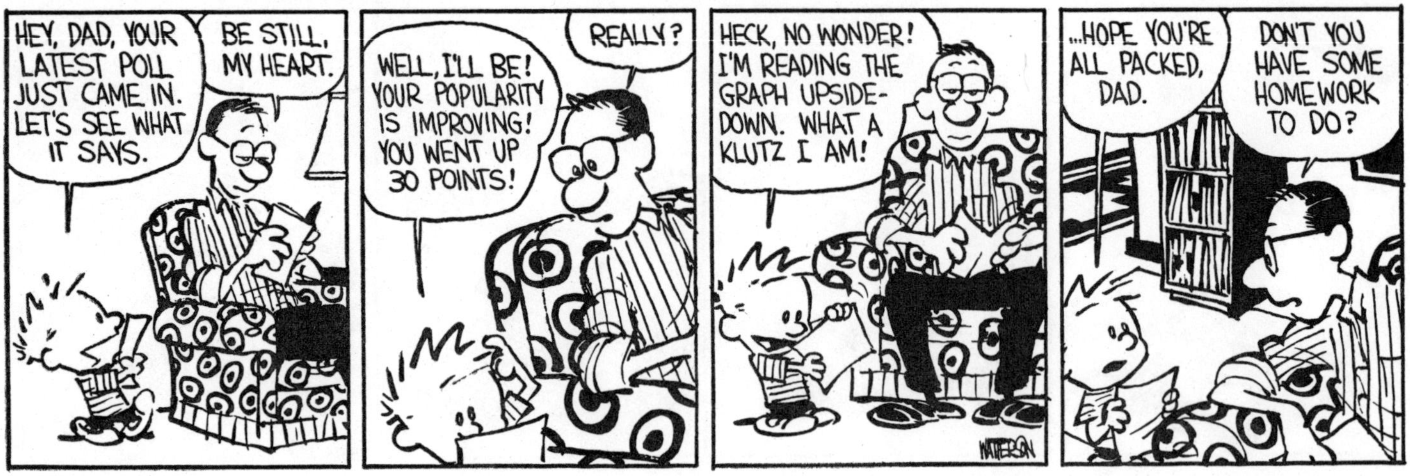
HEY, DAD, YOUR LATEST POLL JUST CAME IN. LET'S SEE WHAT IT SAYS.
BE STILL, MY HEART.
WELL, I'LL BE! YOUR POPULARITY IS IMPROVING! YOU WENT UP 30 POINTS!
REALLY?
HECK, NO WONDER! I'M READING THE GRAPH UPSIDE-DOWN. WHAT A KLUTZ I AM!
...HOPE YOU'RE ALL PACKED, DAD.
DON'T YOU HAVE SOME HOMEWORK TO DO?
WATTERSON

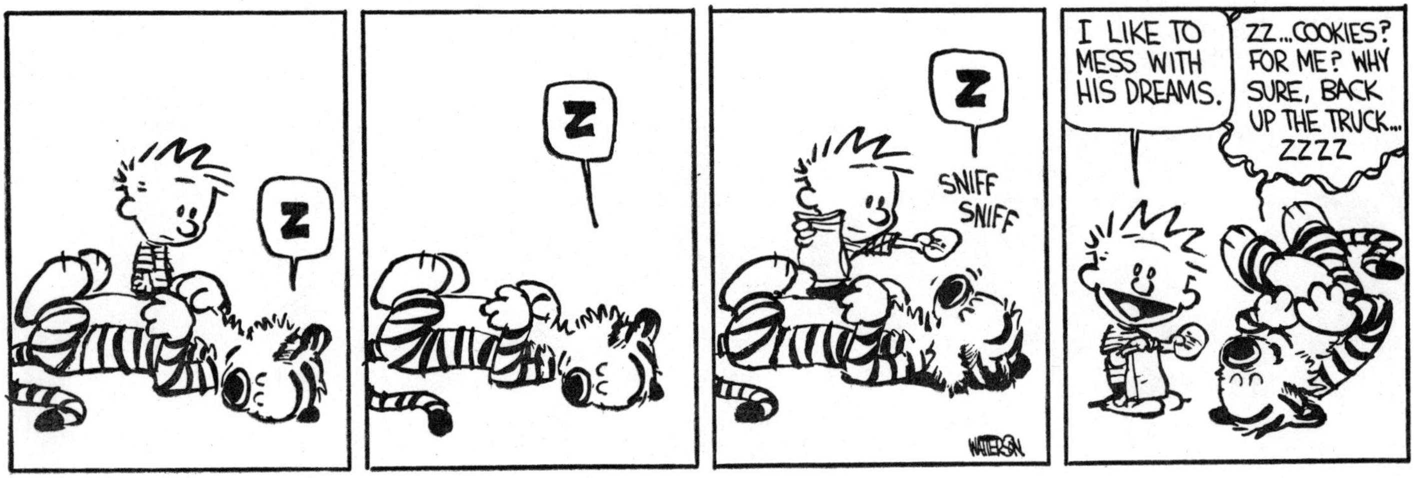
Z
Z
Z
SNIFF SNIFF
I LIKE TO MESS WITH HIS DREAMS.
ZZ...COOKIES? FOR ME? WHY SURE, BACK UP THE TRUCK... ZZZZ
WATTERSON

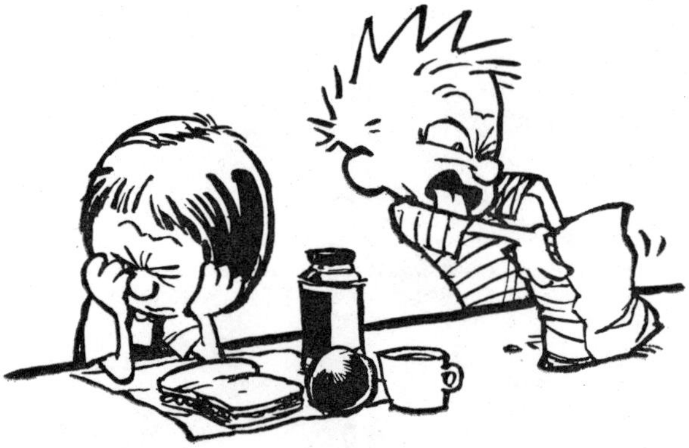

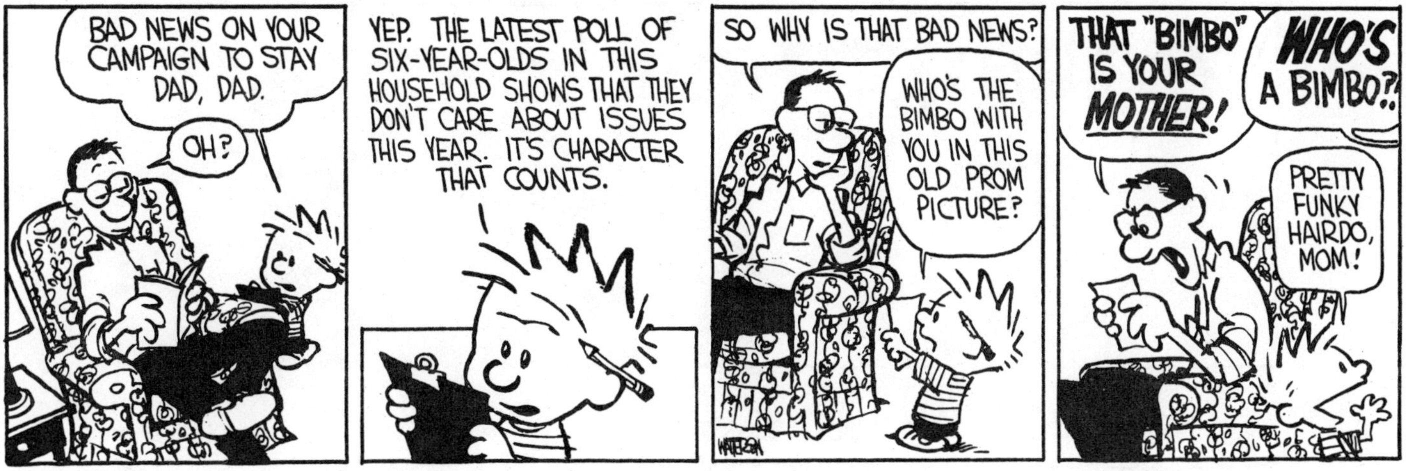
BAD NEWS ON YOUR CAMPAIGN TO STAY DAD, DAD.
OH?
YEP. THE LATEST POLL OF SIX-YEAR-OLDS IN THIS HOUSEHOLD SHOWS THAT THEY DON'T CARE ABOUT ISSUES THIS YEAR. IT'S CHARACTER THAT COUNTS.
SO WHY IS THAT BAD NEWS?
WHO'S THE BIMBO WITH YOU IN THIS OLD PROM PICTURE?
THAT "BIMBO" IS YOUR MOTHER!
WHO'S A BIMBO?!
PRETTY FUNKY HAIRDO, MOM!

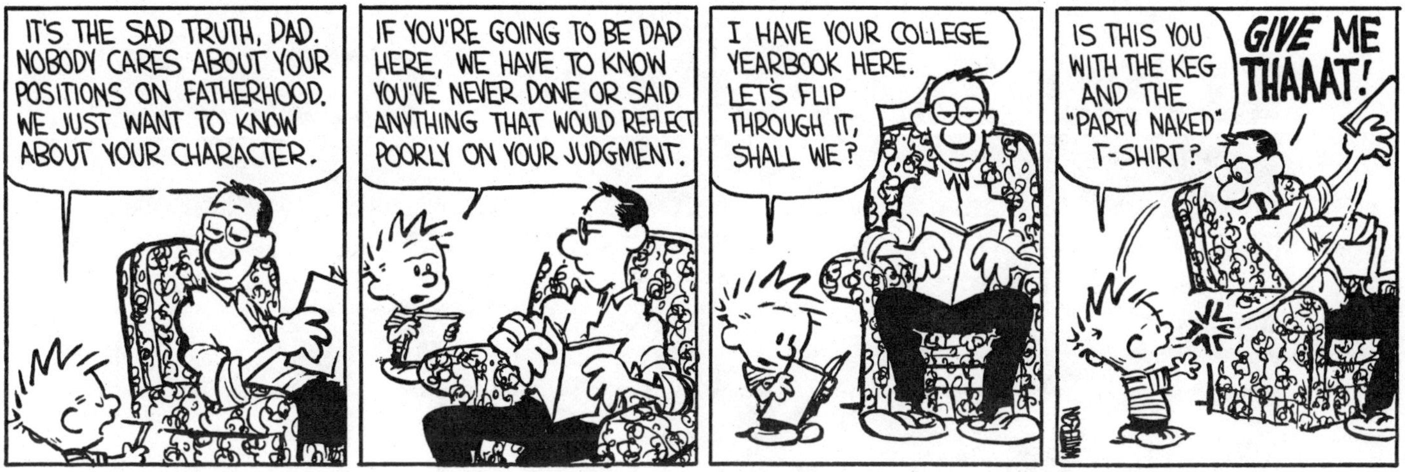
IT'S THE SAD TRUTH, DAD. NOBODY CARES ABOUT YOUR POSITIONS ON FATHERHOOD. WE JUST WANT TO KNOW ABOUT YOUR CHARACTER.
IF YOU'RE GOING TO BE DAD HERE, WE HAVE TO KNOW YOU'VE NEVER DONE OR SAID ANYTHING THAT WOULD REFLECT POORLY ON YOUR JUDGMENT.
I HAVE YOUR COLLEGE YEARBOOK HERE. LET'S FLIP THROUGH IT, SHALL WE?
IS THIS YOU WITH THE KEG AND THE "PARTY NAKED" T-SHIRT?
GIVE ME THAAAT!

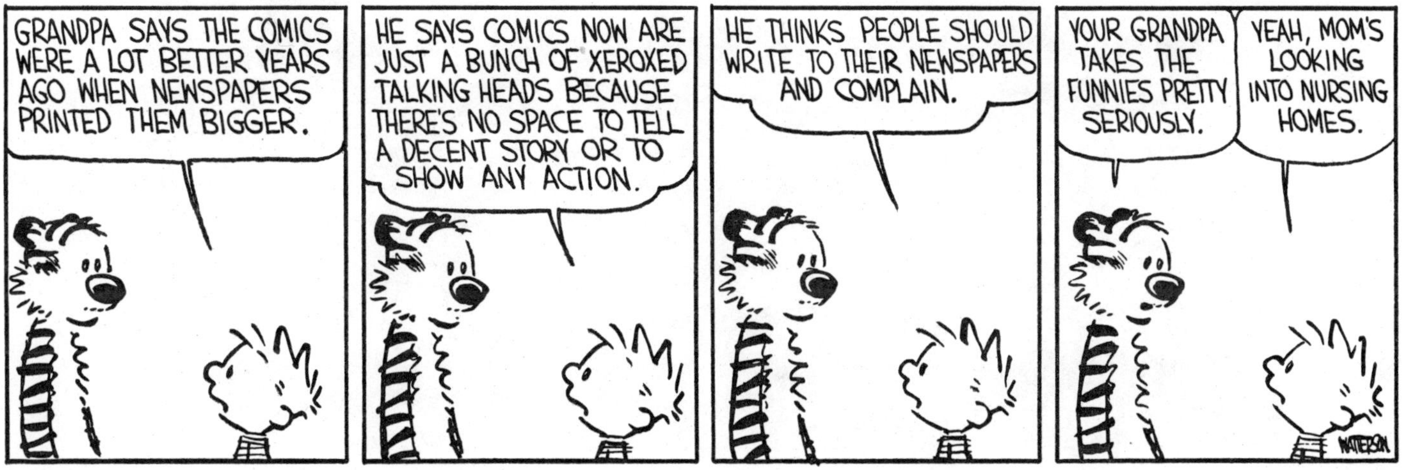
GRANDPA SAYS THE COMICS WERE A LOT BETTER YEARS AGO WHEN NEWSPAPERS PRINTED THEM BIGGER.
HE SAYS COMICS NOW ARE JUST A BUNCH OF XEROXED TALKING HEADS BECAUSE THERE'S NO SPACE TO TELL A DECENT STORY OR TO SHOW ANY ACTION.
HE THINKS PEOPLE SHOULD WRITE TO THEIR NEWSPAPERS AND COMPLAIN.
YOUR GRANDPA TAKES THE FUNNIES PRETTY SERIOUSLY.
YEAH, MOM'S LOOKING INTO NURSING HOMES.

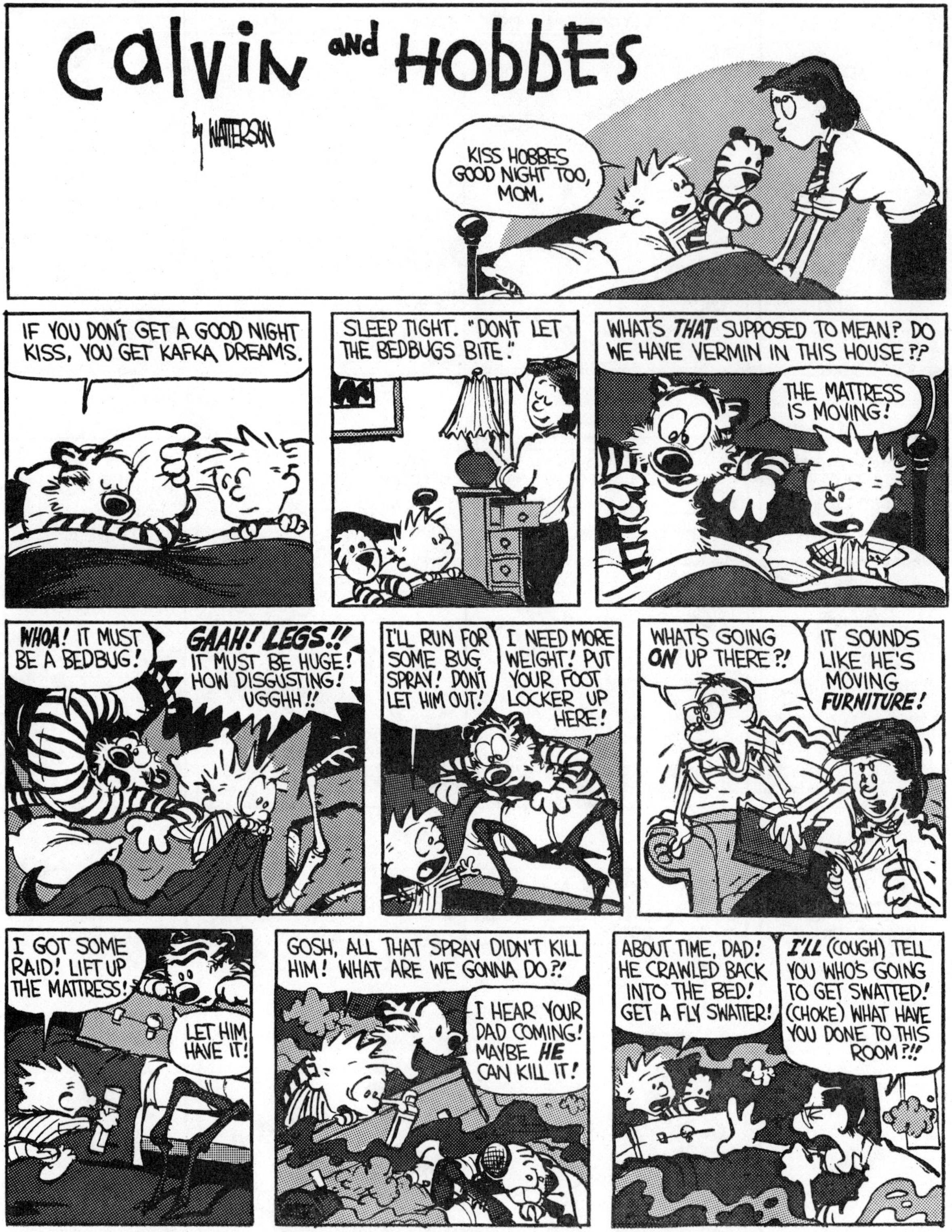
Calvin and HOBBES
by WATTERSON
KISS HOBBES GOOD NIGHT TOO, MOM.
IF YOU DON'T GET A GOOD NIGHT KISS, YOU GET KAFKA DREAMS.
SLEEP TIGHT. "DON'T LET THE BEDBUGS BITE."
WHAT'S THAT SUPPOSED TO MEAN? DO WE HAVE VERMIN IN THIS HOUSE?!?
THE MATTRESS IS MOVING!
WHOA! IT MUST BE A BEDBUG!
GAAH! LEGS!! IT MUST BE HUGE! HOW DISGUSTING! UGGHH!!
I'LL RUN FOR SOME BUG SPRAY! DON'T LET HIM OUT!
I NEED MORE WEIGHT! PUT YOUR FOOT LOCKER UP HERE!
WHAT'S GOING ON UP THERE?!
IT SOUNDS LIKE HE'S MOVING FURNITURE!
I GOT SOME RAID! LIFT UP THE MATTRESS!
LET HIM HAVE IT!
GOSH, ALL THAT SPRAY DIDN'T KILL HIM! WHAT ARE WE GONNA DO?!
I HEAR YOUR DAD COMING! MAYBE HE CAN KILL IT!
ABOUT TIME, DAD! HE CRAWLED BACK INTO THE BED! GET A FLY SWATTER!
I'LL (COUGH) TELL YOU WHO'S GOING TO GET SWATTED! (CHOKE) WHAT HAVE YOU DONE TO THIS ROOM?!!

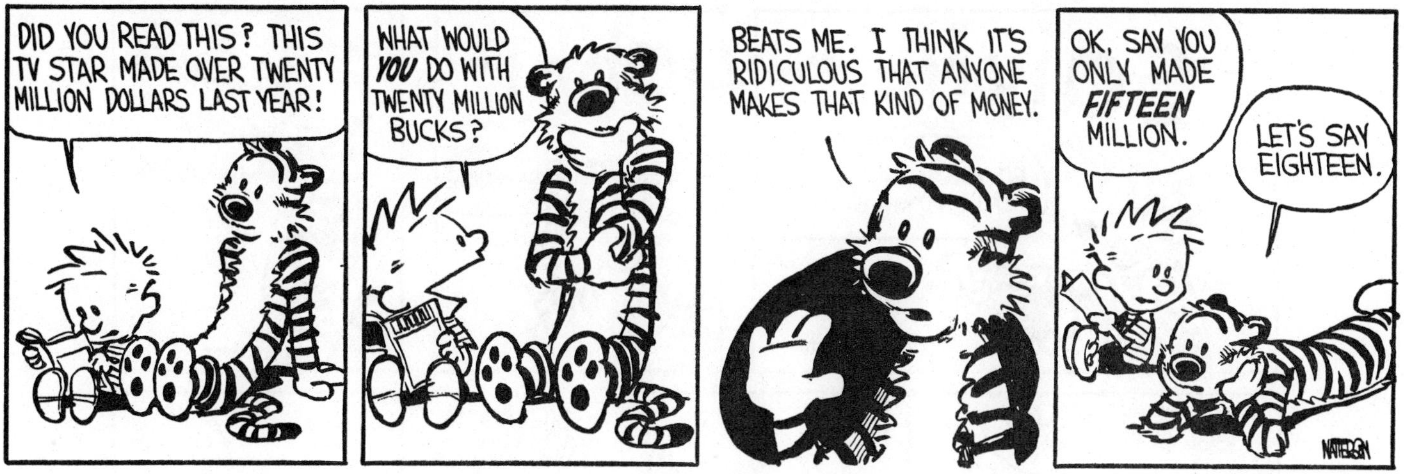
DID YOU READ THIS? THIS TV STAR MADE OVER TWENTY MILLION DOLLARS LAST YEAR!
WHAT WOULD ***YOU*** DO WITH TWENTY MILLION BUCKS?
BEATS ME. I THINK IT'S RIDICULOUS THAT ANYONE MAKES THAT KIND OF MONEY.
OK, SAY YOU ONLY MADE ***FIFTEEN*** MILLION.
LET'S SAY EIGHTEEN.

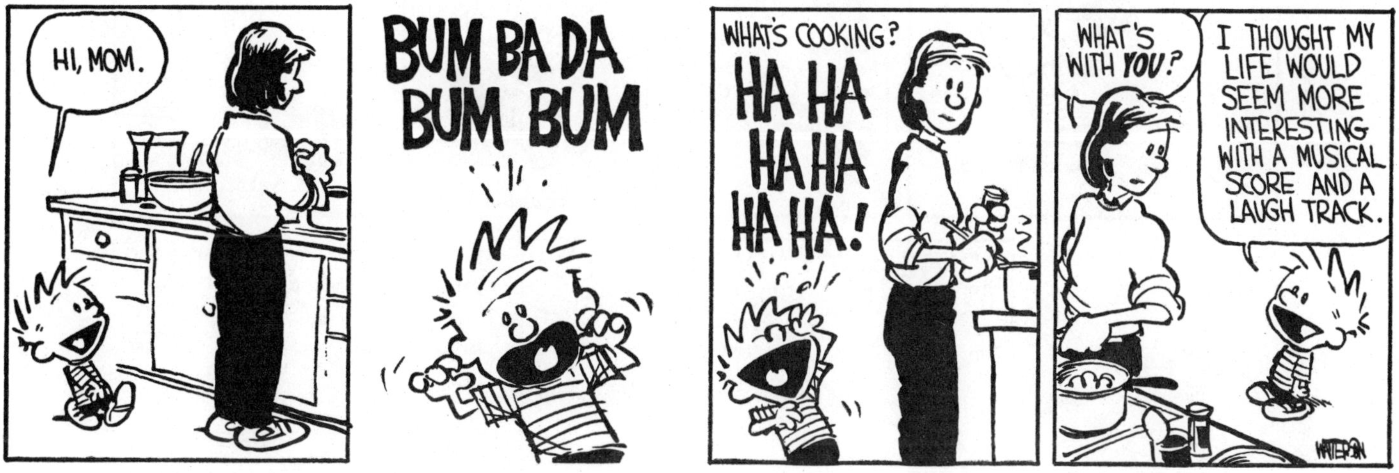
HI, MOM.
BUM BA DA BUM BUM
WHAT'S COOKING?
HA HA HA HA HA HA!
WHAT'S WITH ***YOU***?
I THOUGHT MY LIFE WOULD SEEM MORE INTERESTING WITH A MUSICAL SCORE AND A LAUGH TRACK.

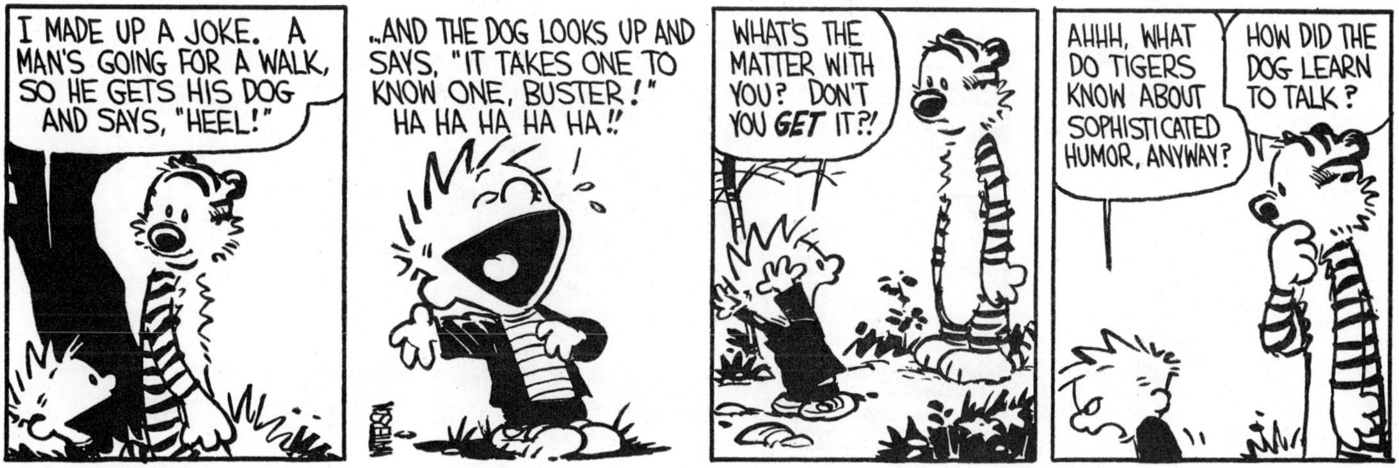
I MADE UP A JOKE. A MAN'S GOING FOR A WALK, SO HE GETS HIS DOG AND SAYS, "HEEL!"
..AND THE DOG LOOKS UP AND SAYS, "IT TAKES ONE TO KNOW ONE, BUSTER!" HA HA HA HA HA!!
WHAT'S THE MATTER WITH YOU? DON'T YOU ***GET*** IT?!
AHHH, WHAT DO TIGERS KNOW ABOUT SOPHISTICATED HUMOR, ANYWAY?
HOW DID THE DOG LEARN TO TALK?

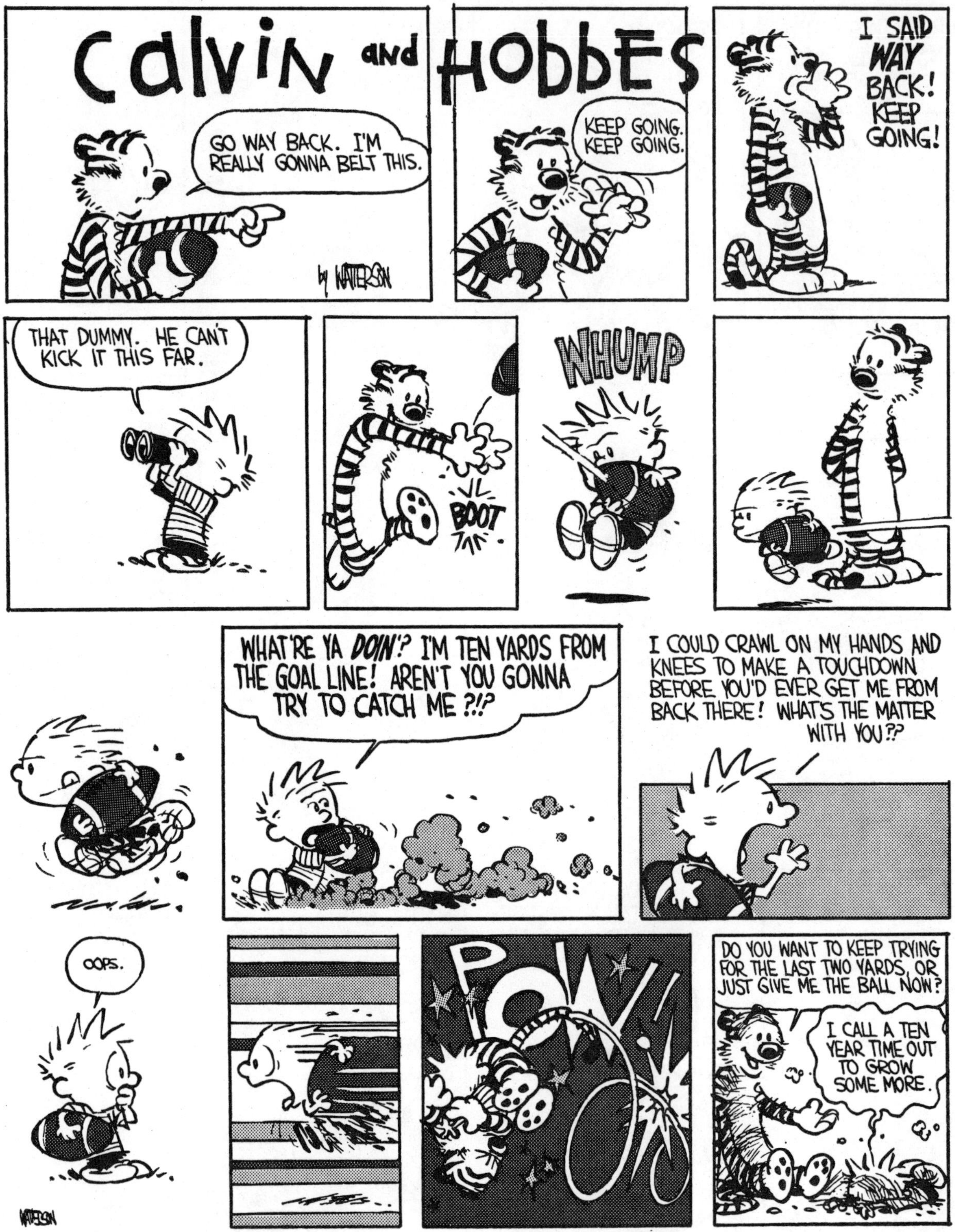
Calvin and HOBBES
GO WAY BACK. I'M REALLY GONNA BELT THIS.
by WATTERSON
KEEP GOING. KEEP GOING.
I SAID WAY BACK! KEEP GOING!
THAT DUMMY. HE CAN'T KICK IT THIS FAR.
BOOT
WHUMP
WHAT'RE YA DOIN'? I'M TEN YARDS FROM THE GOAL LINE! AREN'T YOU GONNA TRY TO CATCH ME ?!?
I COULD CRAWL ON MY HANDS AND KNEES TO MAKE A TOUCHDOWN BEFORE YOU'D EVER GET ME FROM BACK THERE! WHAT'S THE MATTER WITH YOU ?!?
OOPS.
WATTERSON
POW!
DO YOU WANT TO KEEP TRYING FOR THE LAST TWO YARDS, OR JUST GIVE ME THE BALL NOW?
I CALL A TEN YEAR TIME OUT TO GROW SOME MORE.

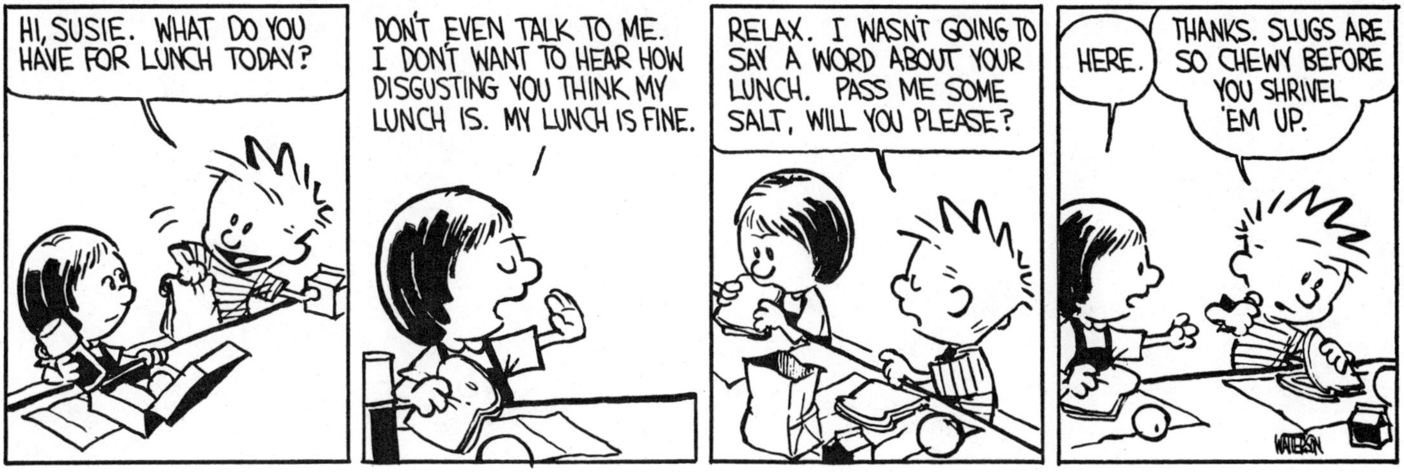
HI, SUSIE. WHAT DO YOU HAVE FOR LUNCH TODAY?
DON'T EVEN TALK TO ME. I DON'T WANT TO HEAR HOW DISGUSTING YOU THINK MY LUNCH IS. MY LUNCH IS FINE.
RELAX. I WASN'T GOING TO SAY A WORD ABOUT YOUR LUNCH. PASS ME SOME SALT, WILL YOU PLEASE?
HERE.
THANKS. SLUGS ARE SO CHEWY BEFORE YOU SHRIVEL 'EM UP.
WATERSON

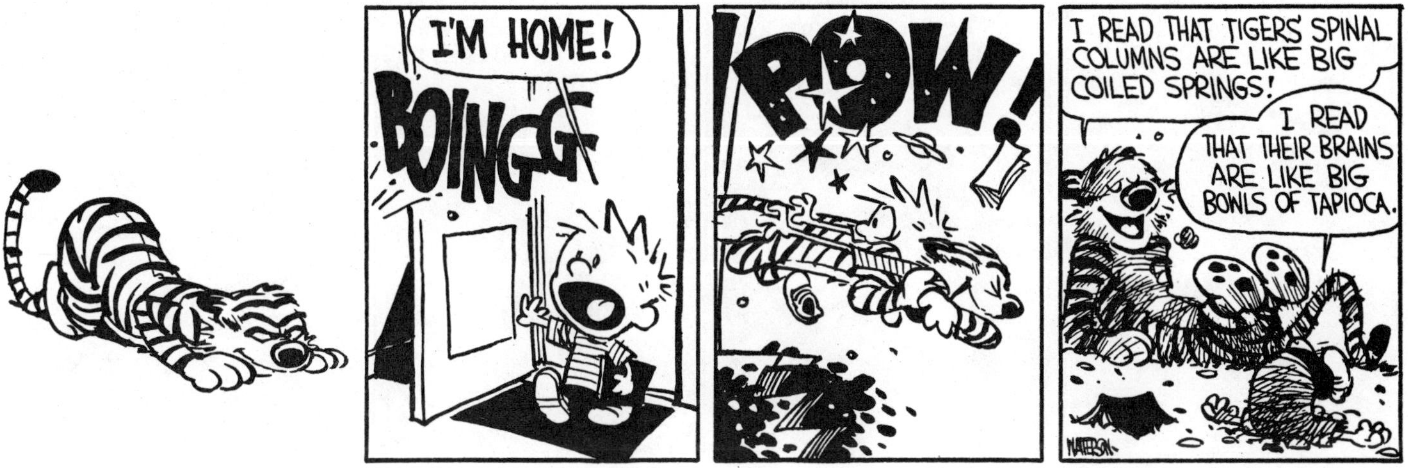
I'M HOME!
BOINGG
POW!
I READ THAT TIGERS' SPINAL COLUMNS ARE LIKE BIG COILED SPRINGS!
I READ THAT THEIR BRAINS ARE LIKE BIG BOWLS OF TAPIOCA.
WATERSON

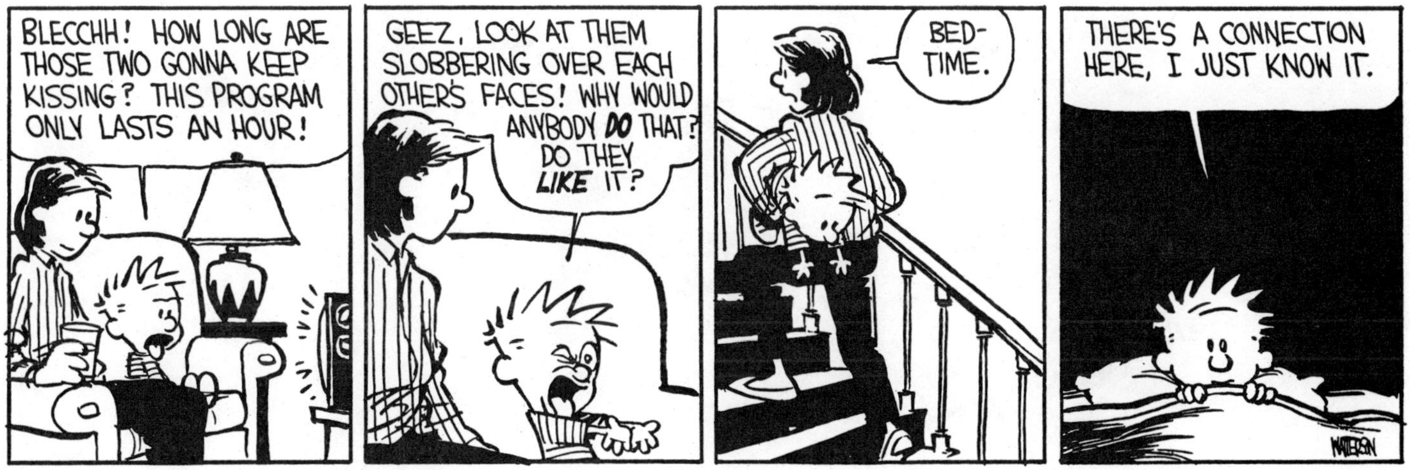
BLECCHH! HOW LONG ARE THOSE TWO GONNA KEEP KISSING? THIS PROGRAM ONLY LASTS AN HOUR!
GEEZ, LOOK AT THEM SLOBBERING OVER EACH OTHER'S FACES! WHY WOULD ANYBODY DO THAT? DO THEY LIKE IT?
BED-TIME.
THERE'S A CONNECTION HERE, I JUST KNOW IT.
WATERSON

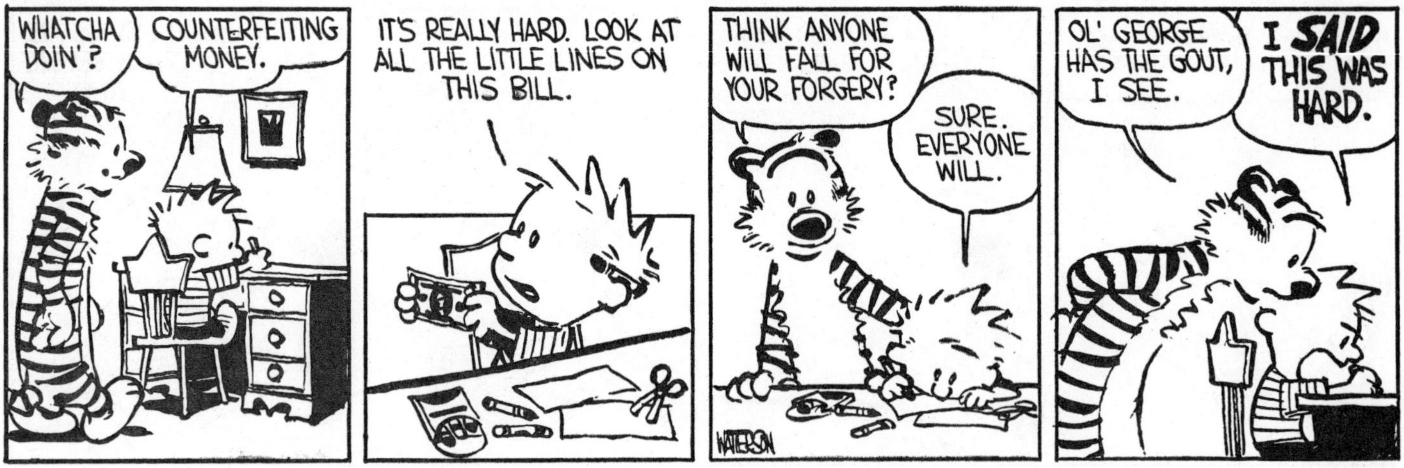
WHATCHA DOIN'?
COUNTERFEITING MONEY.
IT'S REALLY HARD. LOOK AT ALL THE LITTLE LINES ON THIS BILL.
THINK ANYONE WILL FALL FOR YOUR FORGERY?
SURE. EVERYONE WILL.
OL' GEORGE HAS THE GOUT, I SEE.
I SAID THIS WAS HARD.
WATTERSON

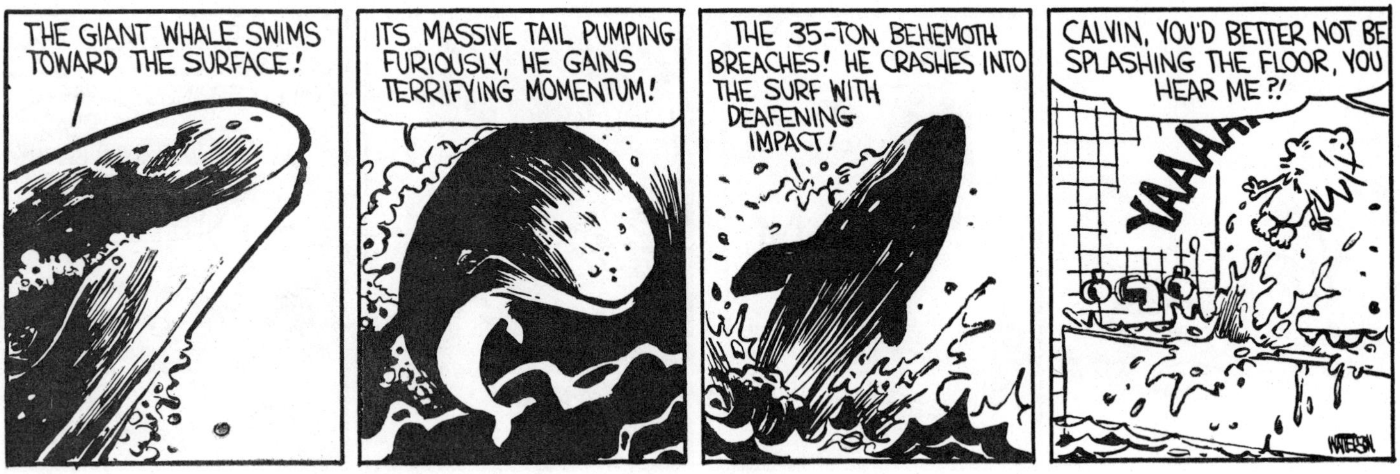
THE GIANT WHALE SWIMS TOWARD THE SURFACE!
ITS MASSIVE TAIL PUMPING FURIOUSLY, HE GAINS TERRIFYING MOMENTUM!
THE 35-TON BEHEMOTH BREACHES! HE CRASHES INTO THE SURF WITH DEAFENING IMPACT!
CALVIN, YOU'D BETTER NOT BE SPLASHING THE FLOOR, YOU HEAR ME?!
WATTERSON

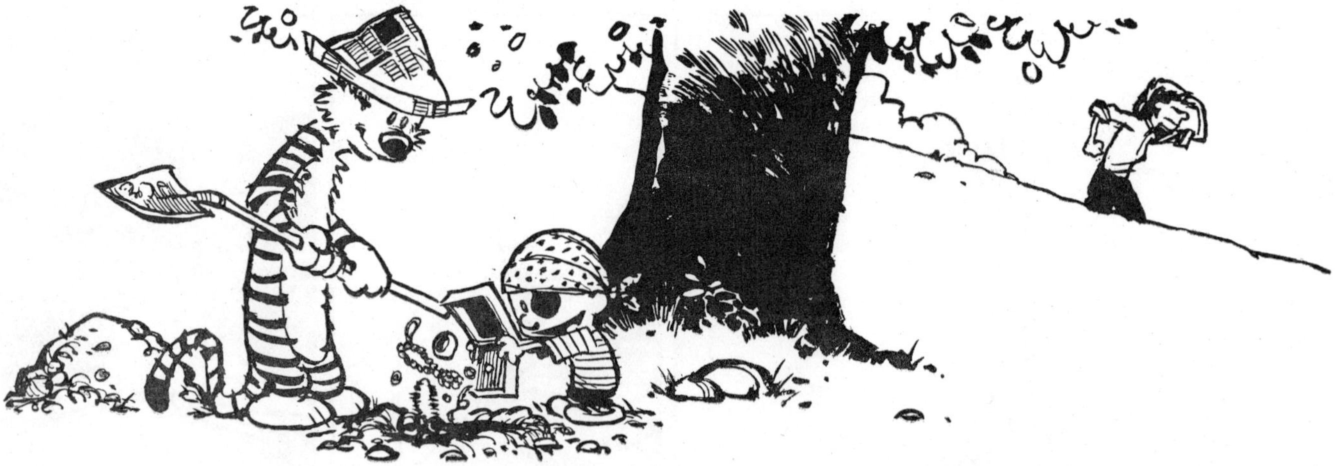

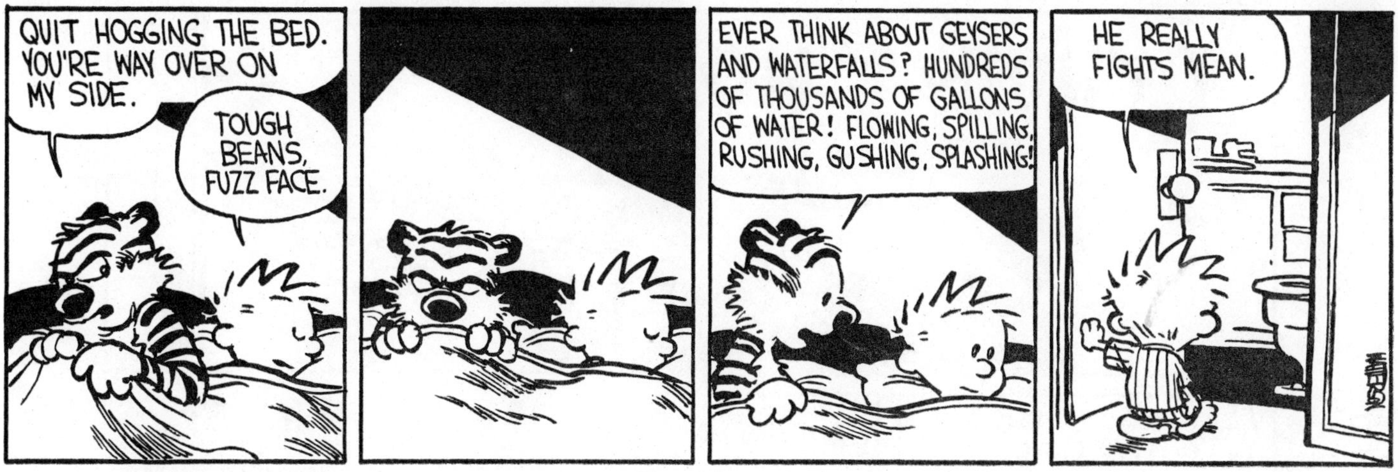
QUIT HOGGING THE BED. YOU'RE WAY OVER ON MY SIDE.
TOUGH BEANS, FUZZ FACE.
EVER THINK ABOUT GEYSERS AND WATERFALLS? HUNDREDS OF THOUSANDS OF GALLONS OF WATER! FLOWING, SPILLING, RUSHING, GUSHING, SPLASHING!
HE REALLY FIGHTS MEAN.
WATTERSON

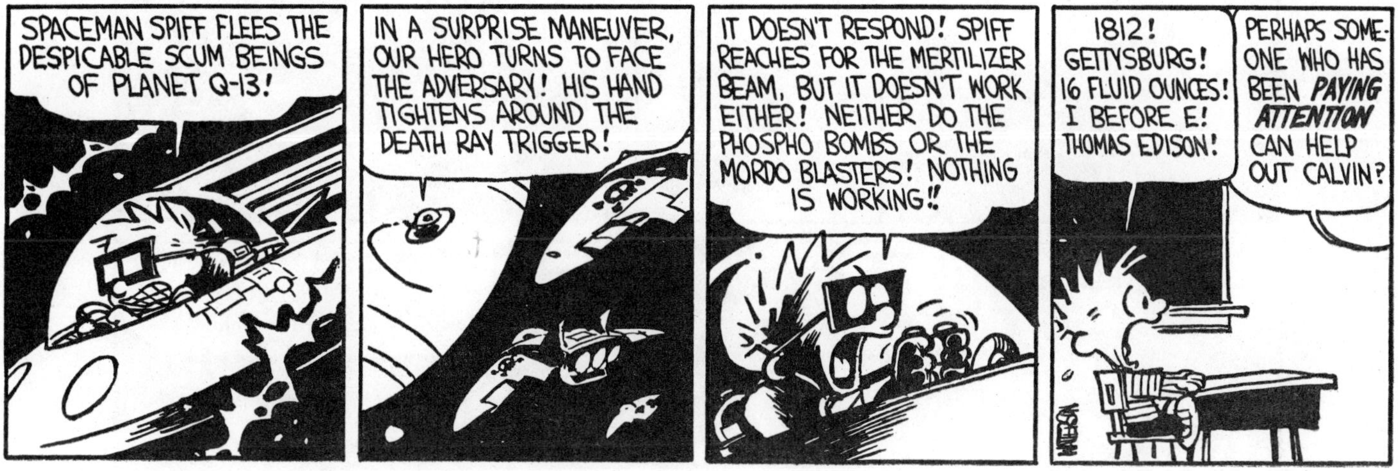
SPACEMAN SPIFF FLEES THE DESPICABLE SCUM BEINGS OF PLANET Q-13!
IN A SURPRISE MANEUVER, OUR HERO TURNS TO FACE THE ADVERSARY! HIS HAND TIGHTENS AROUND THE DEATH RAY TRIGGER!
IT DOESN'T RESPOND! SPIFF REACHES FOR THE MERTILIZER BEAM, BUT IT DOESN'T WORK EITHER! NEITHER DO THE PHOSPHO BOMBS OR THE MORDO BLASTERS! NOTHING IS WORKING!!
1812! GETTYSBURG! 16 FLUID OUNCES! I BEFORE E! THOMAS EDISON!
PERHAPS SOMEONE WHO HAS BEEN *PAYING ATTENTION* CAN HELP OUT CALVIN?
WATTERSON

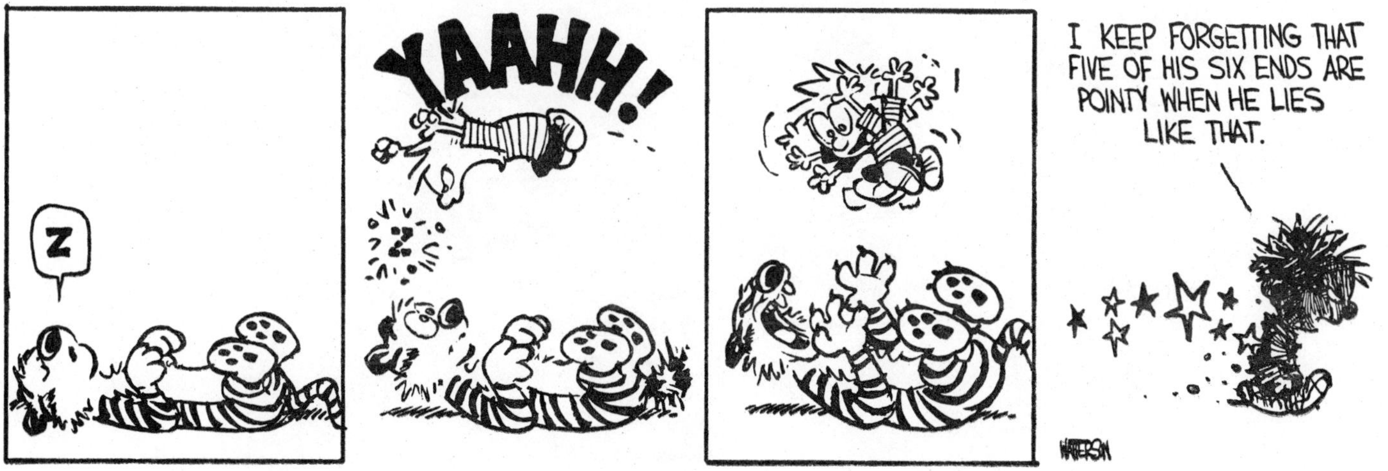
Z
YAAHH!
I KEEP FORGETTING THAT FIVE OF HIS SIX ENDS ARE POINTY WHEN HE LIES LIKE THAT.
WATTERSON

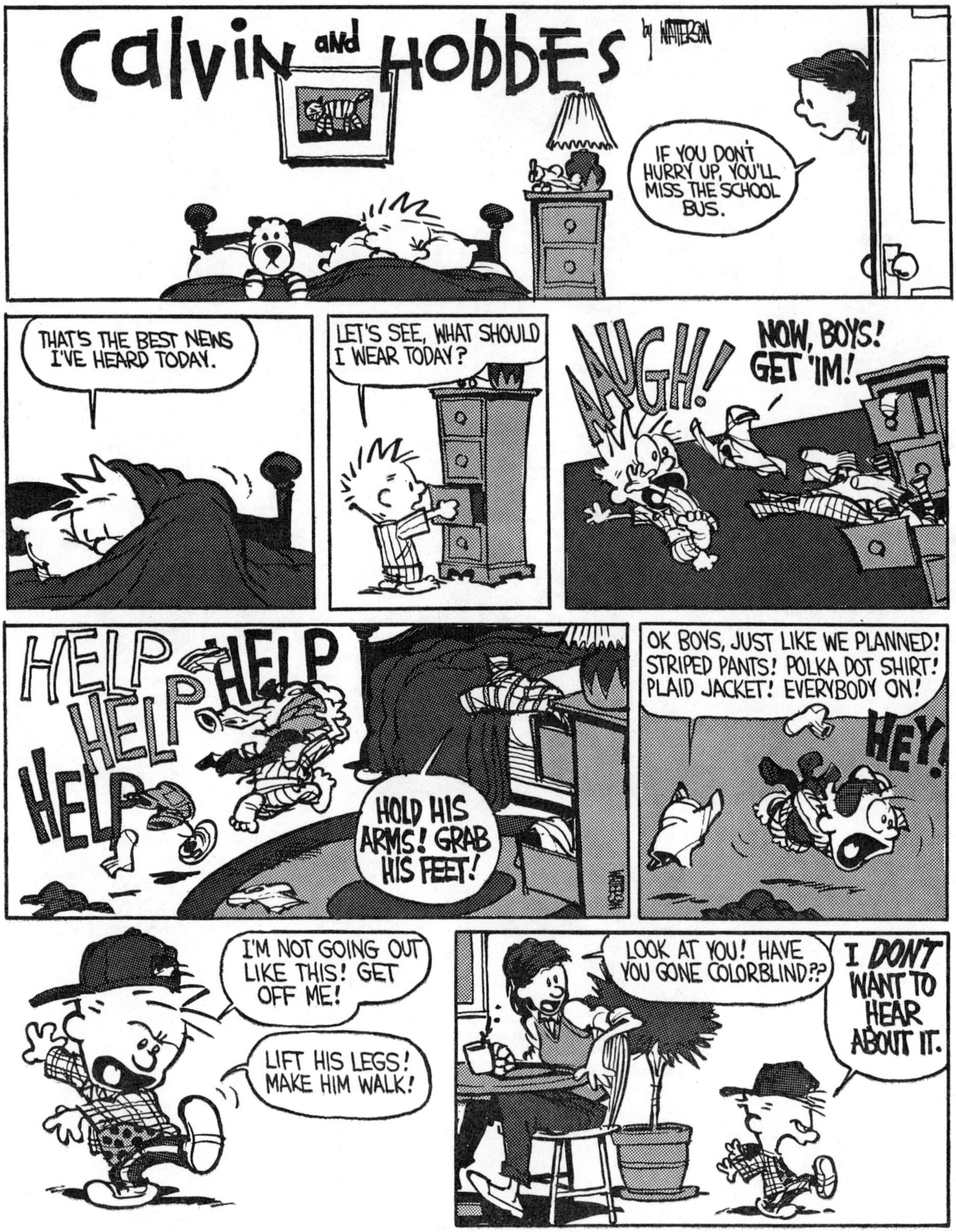
Calvin and HOBBES
by WATTERSON
IF YOU DON'T HURRY UP, YOU'LL MISS THE SCHOOL BUS.
THAT'S THE BEST NEWS I'VE HEARD TODAY.
LET'S SEE, WHAT SHOULD I WEAR TODAY?
AAUGH!!
NOW, BOYS! GET 'IM!
HELP HELP HELP HELP
HOLD HIS ARMS! GRAB HIS FEET!
OK BOYS, JUST LIKE WE PLANNED! STRIPED PANTS! POLKA DOT SHIRT! PLAID JACKET! EVERYBODY ON!
HEY!
I'M NOT GOING OUT LIKE THIS! GET OFF ME!
LIFT HIS LEGS! MAKE HIM WALK!
LOOK AT YOU! HAVE YOU GONE COLORBLIND?!?
I DON'T WANT TO HEAR ABOUT IT.

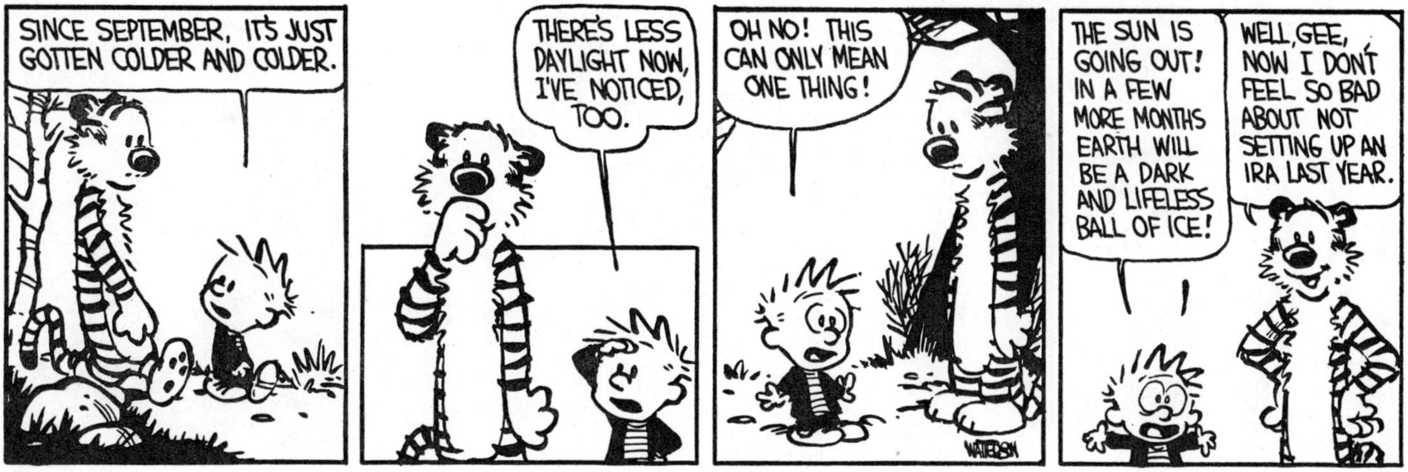
SINCE SEPTEMBER, IT'S JUST GOTTEN COLDER AND COLDER.
THERE'S LESS DAYLIGHT NOW, I'VE NOTICED, TOO.
OH NO! THIS CAN ONLY MEAN ONE THING!
THE SUN IS GOING OUT! IN A FEW MORE MONTHS EARTH WILL BE A DARK AND LIFELESS BALL OF ICE!
WELL, GEE, NOW I DON'T FEEL SO BAD ABOUT NOT SETTING UP AN IRA LAST YEAR.
WATERSON

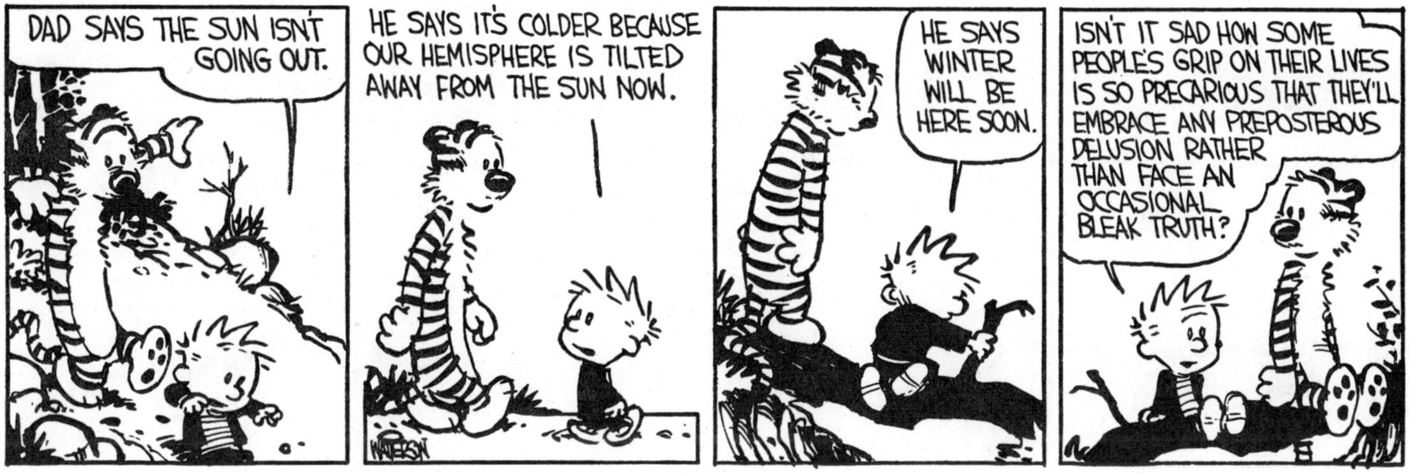
DAD SAYS THE SUN ISN'T GOING OUT.
HE SAYS IT'S COLDER BECAUSE OUR HEMISPHERE IS TILTED AWAY FROM THE SUN NOW.
HE SAYS WINTER WILL BE HERE SOON.
ISN'T IT SAD HOW SOME PEOPLE'S GRIP ON THEIR LIVES IS SO PRECARIOUS THAT THEY'LL EMBRACE ANY PREPOSTEROUS DELUSION RATHER THAN FACE AN OCCASIONAL BLEAK TRUTH?
WATERSON

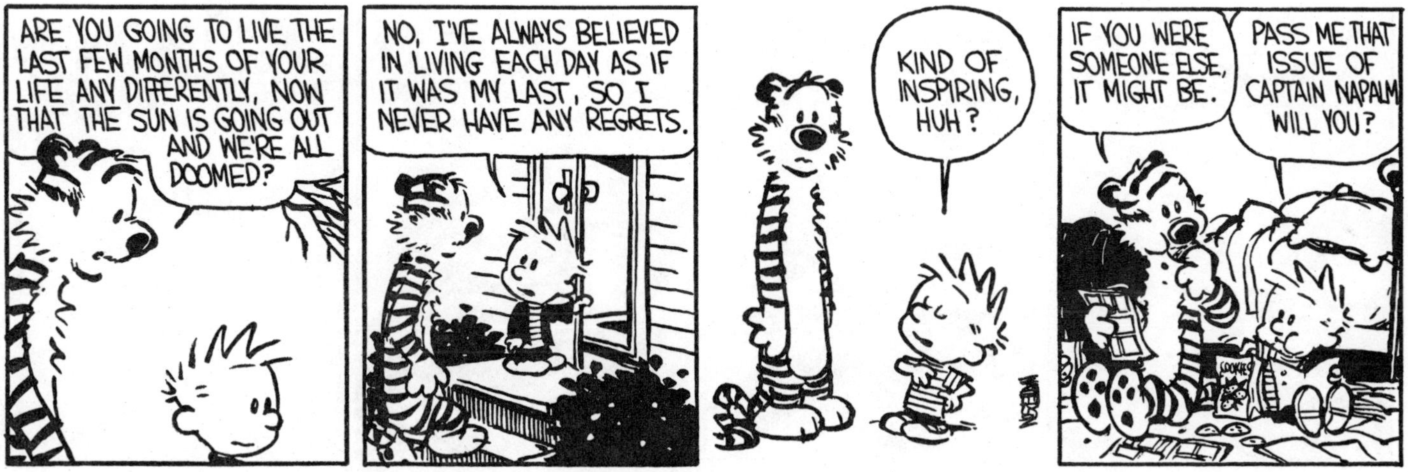
ARE YOU GOING TO LIVE THE LAST FEW MONTHS OF YOUR LIFE ANY DIFFERENTLY, NOW THAT THE SUN IS GOING OUT AND WE'RE ALL DOOMED?
NO, I'VE ALWAYS BELIEVED IN LIVING EACH DAY AS IF IT WAS MY LAST, SO I NEVER HAVE ANY REGRETS.
KIND OF INSPIRING, HUH?
IF YOU WERE SOMEONE ELSE, IT MIGHT BE.
PASS ME THAT ISSUE OF CAPTAIN NAPALM WILL YOU?
COOKIES

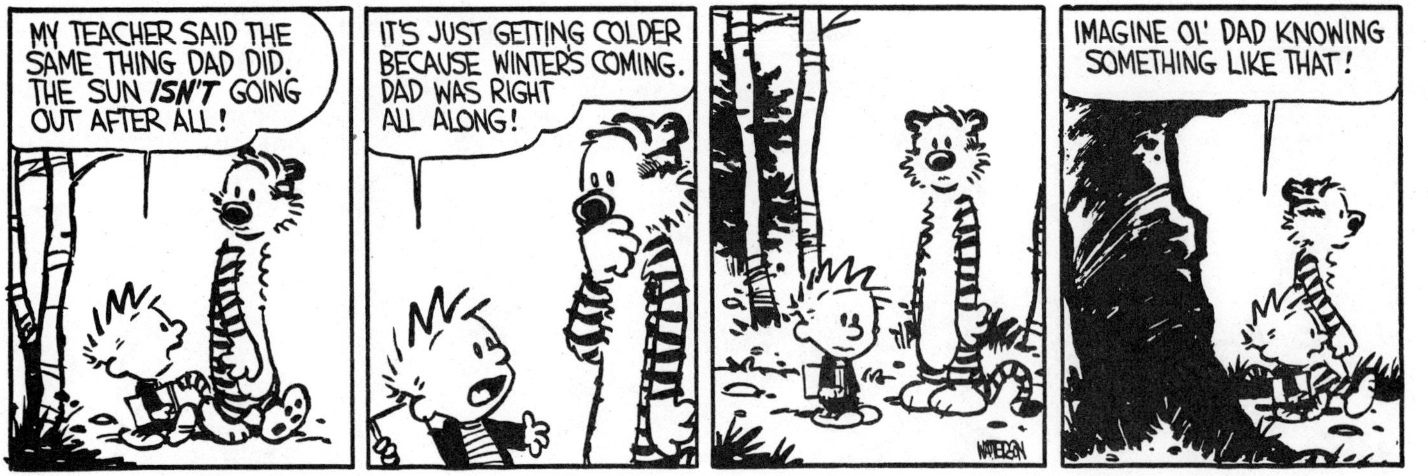
MY TEACHER SAID THE SAME THING DAD DID. THE SUN *ISN'T* GOING OUT AFTER ALL!
IT'S JUST GETTING COLDER BECAUSE WINTER'S COMING. DAD WAS RIGHT ALL ALONG!
IMAGINE OL' DAD KNOWING SOMETHING LIKE THAT!
WATTERSON

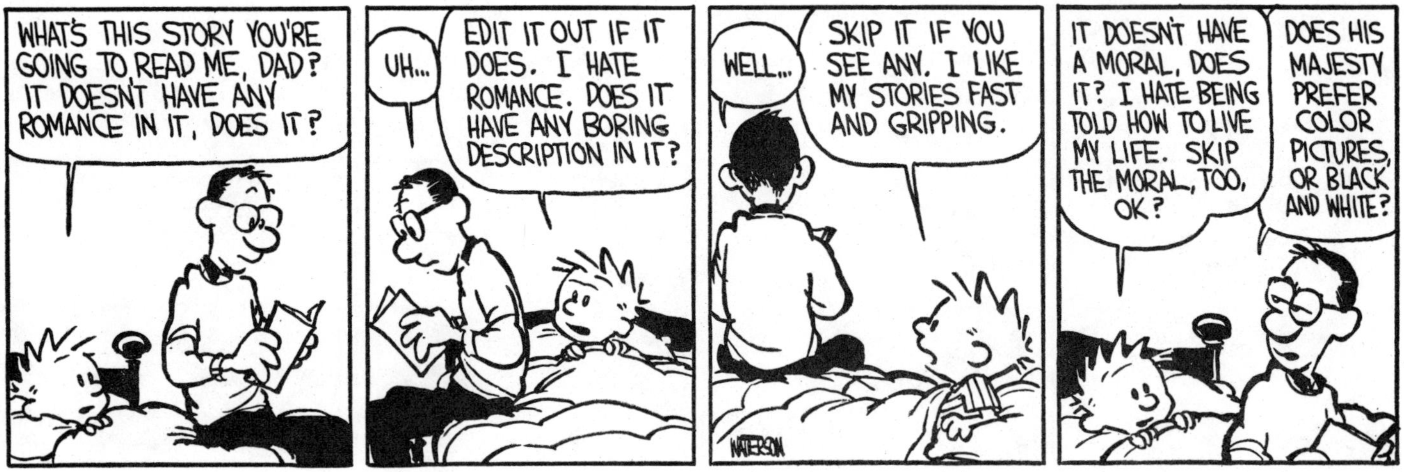
WHAT'S THIS STORY YOU'RE GOING TO READ ME, DAD? IT DOESN'T HAVE ANY ROMANCE IN IT, DOES IT?
UH...
EDIT IT OUT IF IT DOES. I HATE ROMANCE. DOES IT HAVE ANY BORING DESCRIPTION IN IT?
WELL...
SKIP IT IF YOU SEE ANY. I LIKE MY STORIES FAST AND GRIPPING.
WATTERSON
IT DOESN'T HAVE A MORAL, DOES IT? I HATE BEING TOLD HOW TO LIVE MY LIFE. SKIP THE MORAL, TOO, OK?
DOES HIS MAJESTY PREFER COLOR PICTURES, OR BLACK AND WHITE?

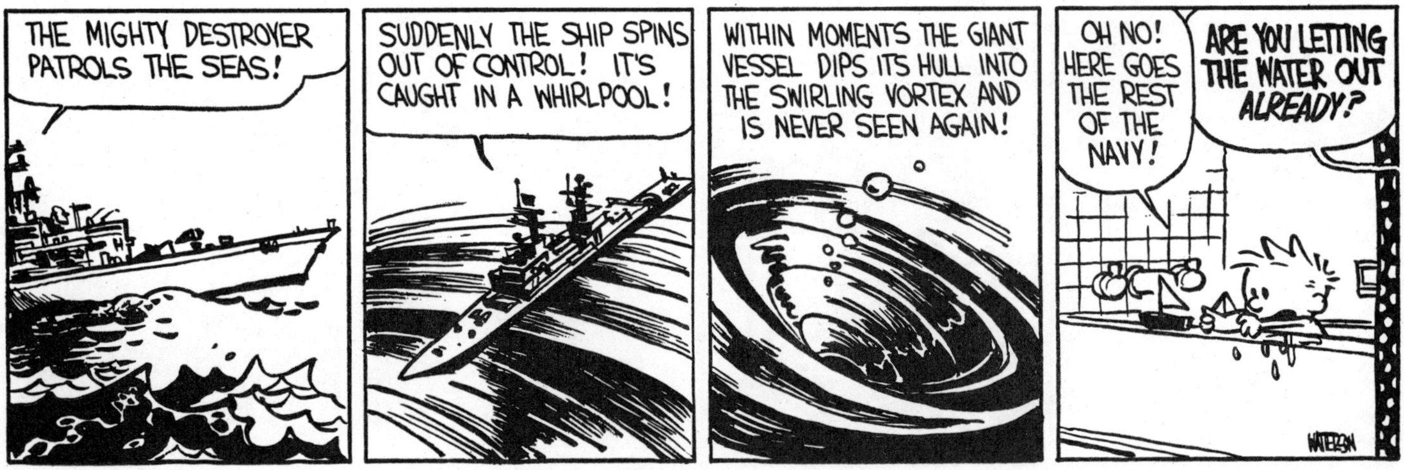
THE MIGHTY DESTROYER PATROLS THE SEAS!
SUDDENLY THE SHIP SPINS OUT OF CONTROL! IT'S CAUGHT IN A WHIRLPOOL!
WITHIN MOMENTS THE GIANT VESSEL DIPS ITS HULL INTO THE SWIRLING VORTEX AND IS NEVER SEEN AGAIN!
OH NO! HERE GOES THE REST OF THE NAVY!
ARE YOU LETTING THE WATER OUT *ALREADY?*
WATTERSON

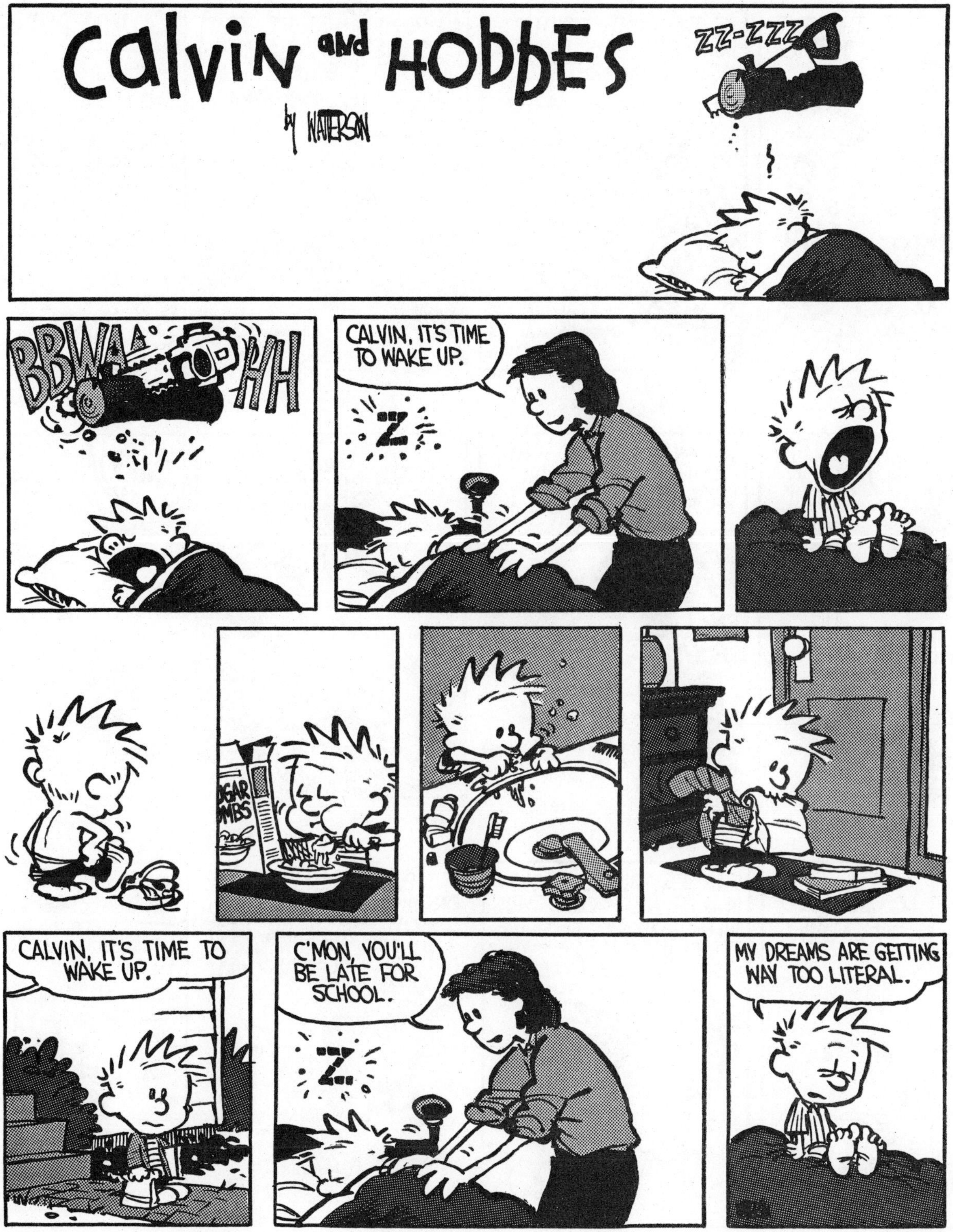
Calvin and HOBBES
by WATTERSON
ZZ-ZZZ
BBWAAAHH
CALVIN, IT'S TIME TO WAKE UP.
Z
CALVIN, IT'S TIME TO WAKE UP.
C'MON, YOU'LL BE LATE FOR SCHOOL.
Z
MY DREAMS ARE GETTING WAY TOO LITERAL.

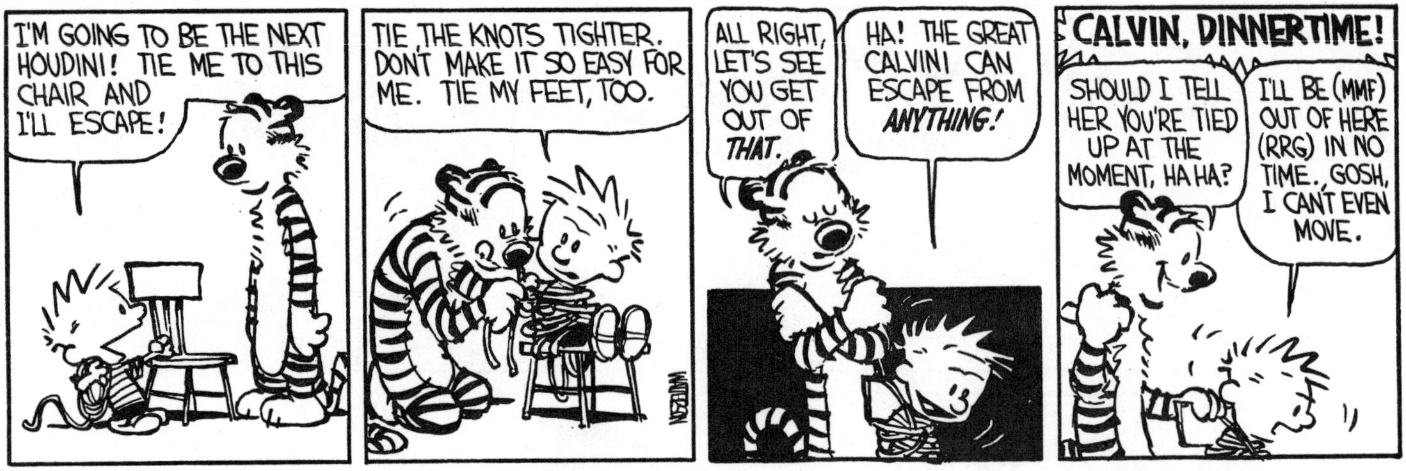
I'M GOING TO BE THE NEXT HOUDINI! TIE ME TO THIS CHAIR AND I'LL ESCAPE!
TIE THE KNOTS TIGHTER. DON'T MAKE IT SO EASY FOR ME. TIE MY FEET, TOO.
ALL RIGHT, LET'S SEE YOU GET OUT OF THAT.
HA! THE GREAT CALVINI CAN ESCAPE FROM ANYTHING!
CALVIN, DINNERTIME!
SHOULD I TELL HER YOU'RE TIED UP AT THE MOMENT, HA HA?
I'LL BE (MMF) OUT OF HERE (RRG) IN NO TIME. GOSH, I CAN'T EVEN MOVE.

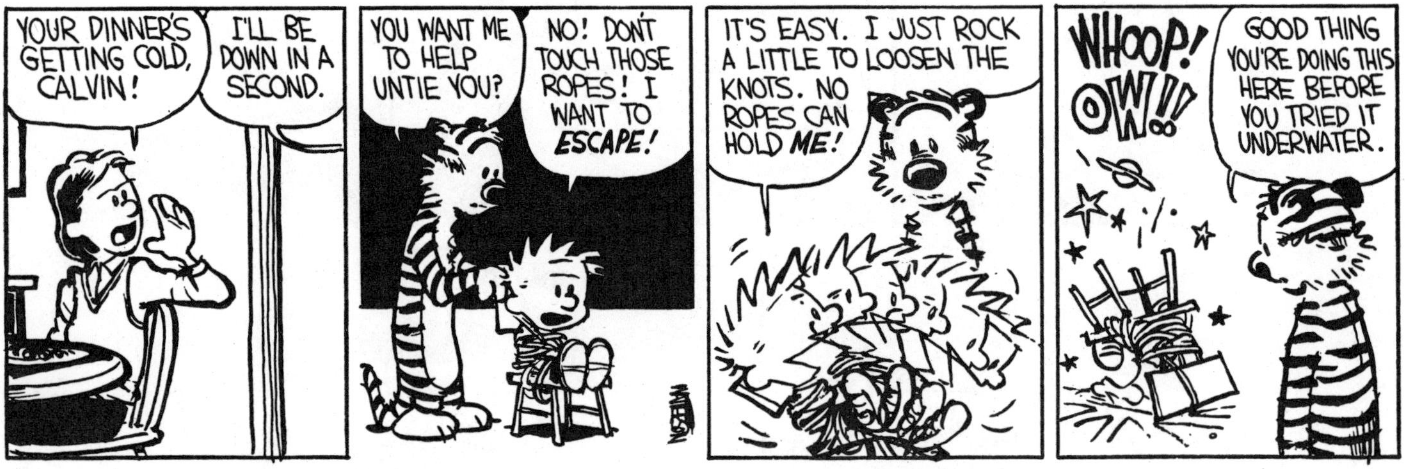
YOUR DINNER'S GETTING COLD, CALVIN!
I'LL BE DOWN IN A SECOND.
YOU WANT ME TO HELP UNTIE YOU?
NO! DON'T TOUCH THOSE ROPES! I WANT TO ESCAPE!
IT'S EASY. I JUST ROCK A LITTLE TO LOOSEN THE KNOTS. NO ROPES CAN HOLD ME!
WHOOP! OW!!
GOOD THING YOU'RE DOING THIS HERE BEFORE YOU TRIED IT UNDERWATER.

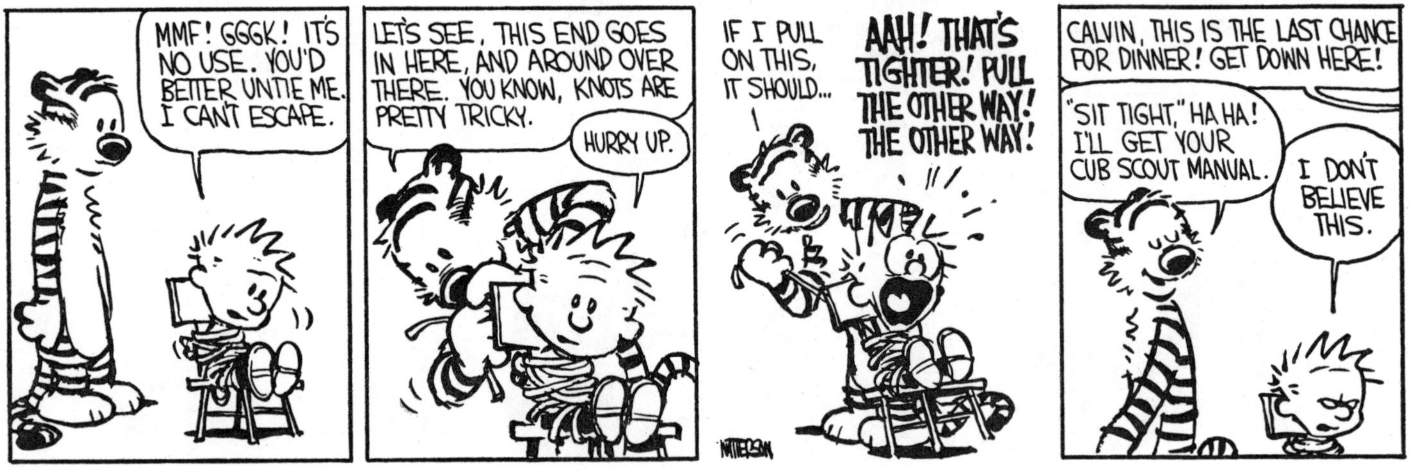
MMF! GGGK! IT'S NO USE. YOU'D BETTER UNTIE ME. I CAN'T ESCAPE.
LET'S SEE, THIS END GOES IN HERE, AND AROUND OVER THERE. YOU KNOW, KNOTS ARE PRETTY TRICKY.
HURRY UP.
IF I PULL ON THIS, IT SHOULD...
AAH! THAT'S TIGHTER! PULL THE OTHER WAY! THE OTHER WAY!
CALVIN, THIS IS THE LAST CHANCE FOR DINNER! GET DOWN HERE!
"SIT TIGHT," HA HA! I'LL GET YOUR CUB SCOUT MANUAL.
I DON'T BELIEVE THIS.

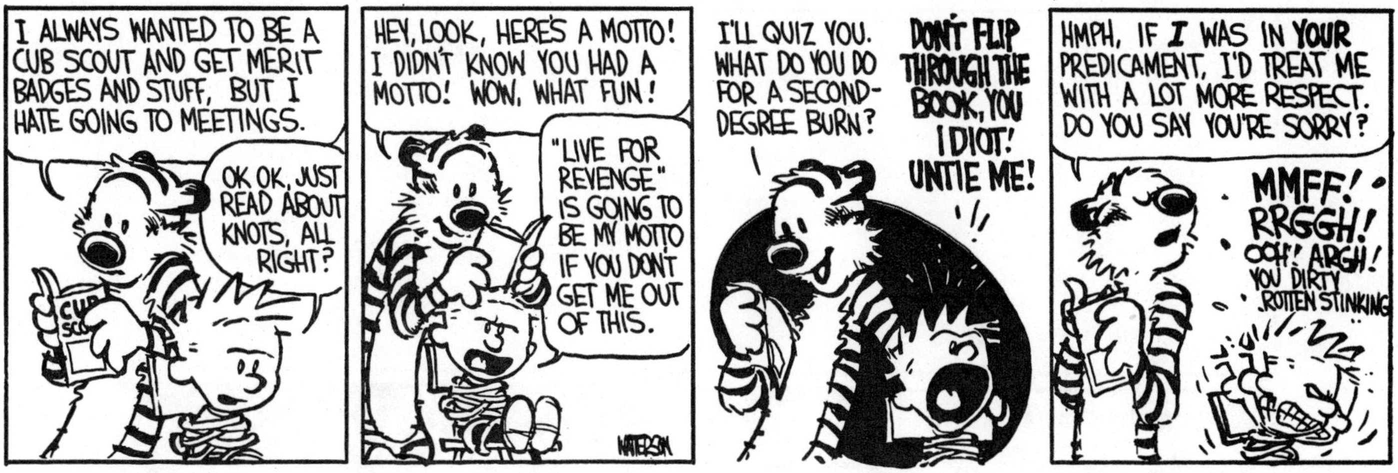
I ALWAYS WANTED TO BE A CUB SCOUT AND GET MERIT BADGES AND STUFF, BUT I HATE GOING TO MEETINGS.
OK OK, JUST READ ABOUT KNOTS, ALL RIGHT?
HEY, LOOK, HERE'S A MOTTO! I DIDN'T KNOW YOU HAD A MOTTO! WOW, WHAT FUN!
"LIVE FOR REVENGE" IS GOING TO BE MY MOTTO IF YOU DON'T GET ME OUT OF THIS.
I'LL QUIZ YOU. WHAT DO YOU DO FOR A SECOND-DEGREE BURN?
DON'T FLIP THROUGH THE BOOK, YOU IDIOT! UNTIE ME!
HMPH, IF I WAS IN YOUR PREDICAMENT, I'D TREAT ME WITH A LOT MORE RESPECT. DO YOU SAY YOU'RE SORRY?
MMFF! RRGGH! OOH! ARGH! YOU DIRTY ROTTEN STINKING

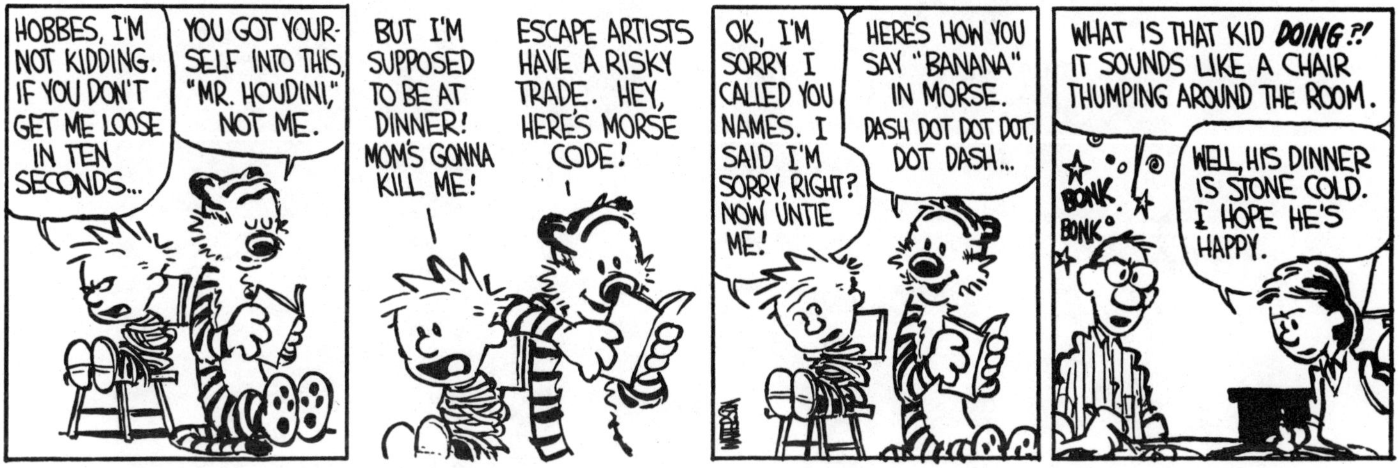
HOBBES, I'M NOT KIDDING. IF YOU DON'T GET ME LOOSE IN TEN SECONDS...
YOU GOT YOURSELF INTO THIS, "MR. HOUDINI," NOT ME.
BUT I'M SUPPOSED TO BE AT DINNER! MOM'S GONNA KILL ME!
ESCAPE ARTISTS HAVE A RISKY TRADE. HEY, HERE'S MORSE CODE!
OK, I'M SORRY I CALLED YOU NAMES. I SAID I'M SORRY, RIGHT? NOW UNTIE ME!
HERE'S HOW YOU SAY "BANANA" IN MORSE. DASH DOT DOT DOT, DOT DASH...
WHAT IS THAT KID DOING?! IT SOUNDS LIKE A CHAIR THUMPING AROUND THE ROOM.
BONK
BONK
WELL, HIS DINNER IS STONE COLD. I HOPE HE'S HAPPY.

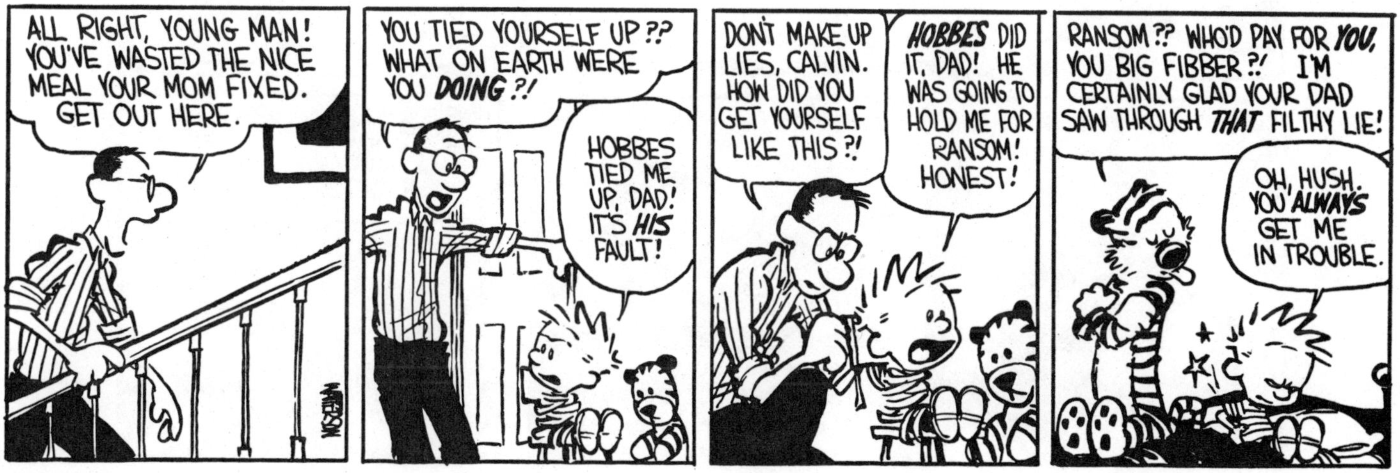
ALL RIGHT, YOUNG MAN! YOU'VE WASTED THE NICE MEAL YOUR MOM FIXED. GET OUT HERE.
YOU TIED YOURSELF UP?? WHAT ON EARTH WERE YOU DOING?!
HOBBES TIED ME UP, DAD! IT'S HIS FAULT!
DON'T MAKE UP LIES, CALVIN. HOW DID YOU GET YOURSELF LIKE THIS?!
HOBBES DID IT, DAD! HE WAS GOING TO HOLD ME FOR RANSOM! HONEST!
RANSOM?? WHO'D PAY FOR YOU, YOU BIG FIBBER?! I'M CERTAINLY GLAD YOUR DAD SAW THROUGH THAT FILTHY LIE!
OH, HUSH. YOU ALWAYS GET ME IN TROUBLE.

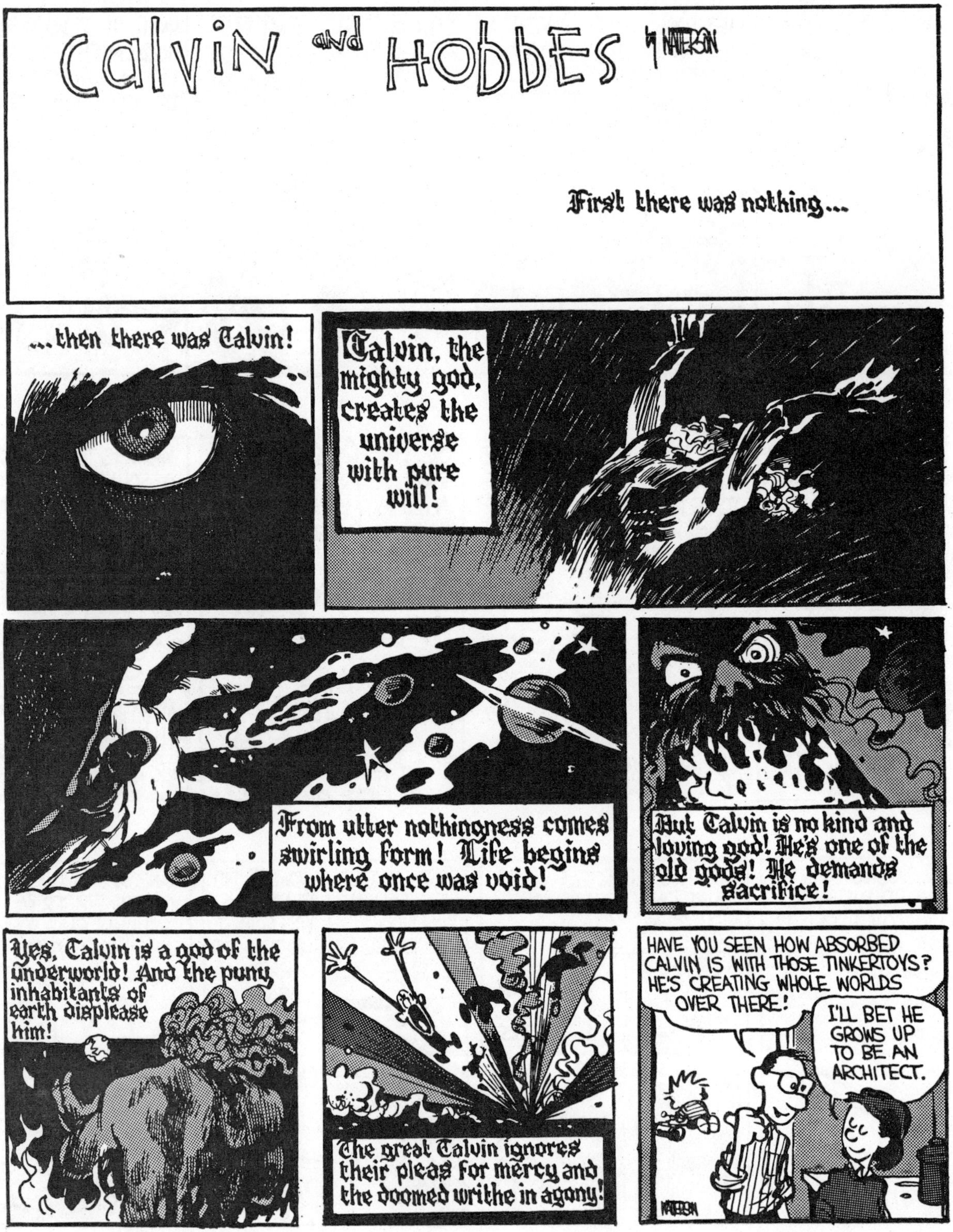

Calvin and Hobbes by Watterson
First there was nothing...
...then there was Calvin!
Calvin, the mighty god, creates the universe with pure will!
From utter nothingness comes swirling form! Life begins where once was void!
But Calvin is no kind and loving god! He's one of the old gods! He demands sacrifice!
Yes, Calvin is a god of the underworld! And the puny inhabitants of earth displease him!
The great Calvin ignores their pleas for mercy and the doomed writhe in agony!
HAVE YOU SEEN HOW ABSORBED CALVIN IS WITH THOSE TINKERTOYS? HE'S CREATING WHOLE WORLDS OVER THERE!
I'LL BET HE GROWS UP TO BE AN ARCHITECT.
WATTERSON

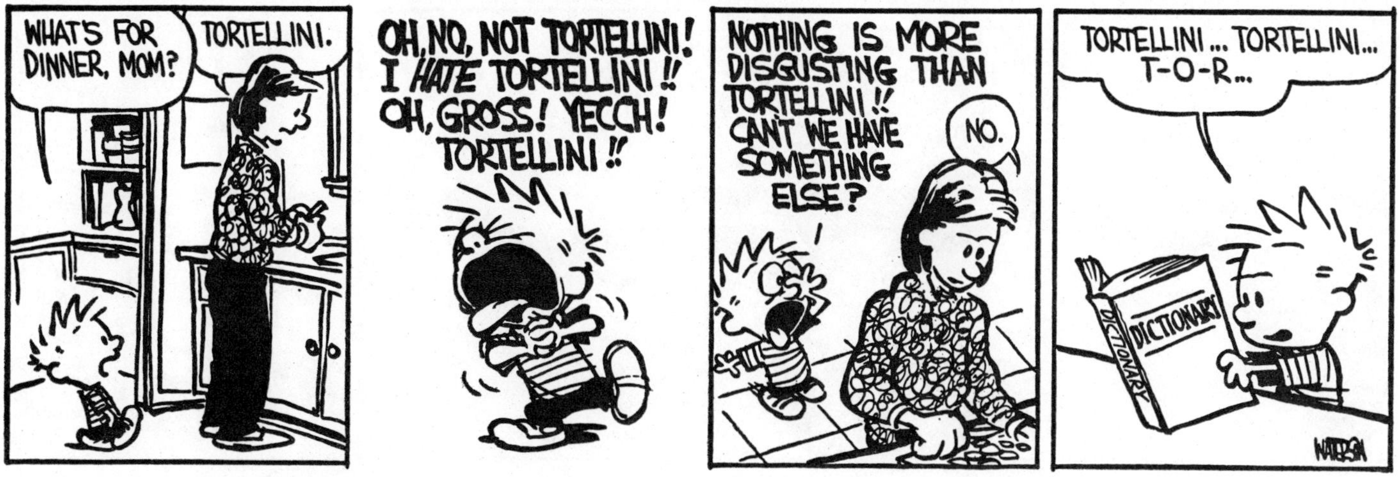
WHAT'S FOR DINNER, MOM?
TORTELLINI.
OH, NO, NOT TORTELLINI! I HATE TORTELLINI!! OH, GROSS! YECCH! TORTELLINI!!
NOTHING IS MORE DISGUSTING THAN TORTELLINI!! CAN'T WE HAVE SOMETHING ELSE?
NO.
TORTELLINI... TORTELLINI... T-O-R...
DICTIONARY
DICTIONARY
WATTERSON

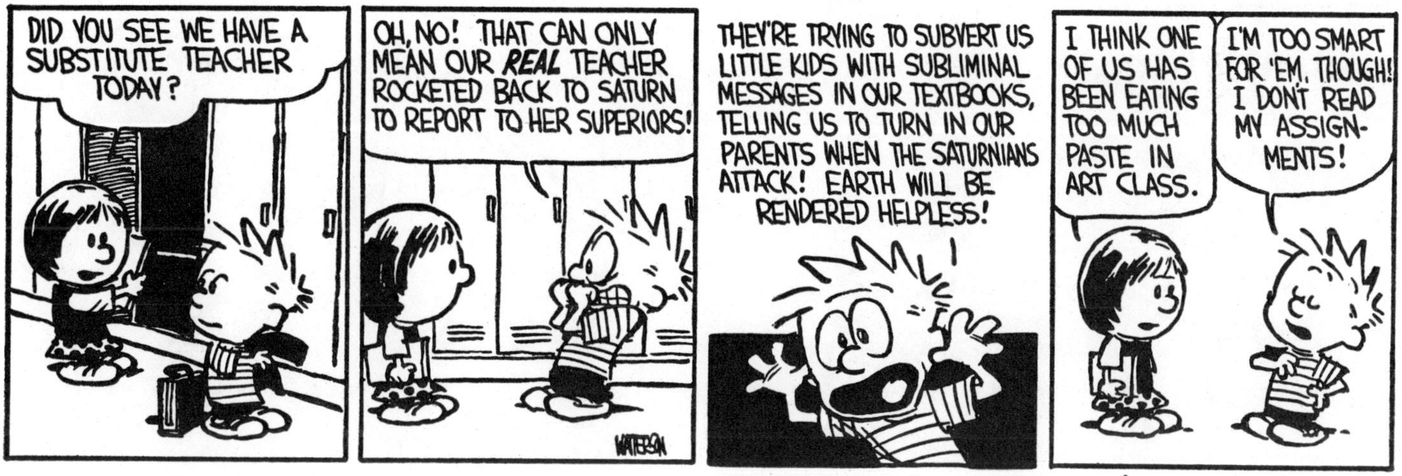
DID YOU SEE WE HAVE A SUBSTITUTE TEACHER TODAY?
OH, NO! THAT CAN ONLY MEAN OUR REAL TEACHER ROCKETED BACK TO SATURN TO REPORT TO HER SUPERIORS!
WATTERSON
THEY'RE TRYING TO SUBVERT US LITTLE KIDS WITH SUBLIMINAL MESSAGES IN OUR TEXTBOOKS, TELLING US TO TURN IN OUR PARENTS WHEN THE SATURNIANS ATTACK! EARTH WILL BE RENDERED HELPLESS!
I THINK ONE OF US HAS BEEN EATING TOO MUCH PASTE IN ART CLASS.
I'M TOO SMART FOR 'EM, THOUGH! I DON'T READ MY ASSIGNMENTS!

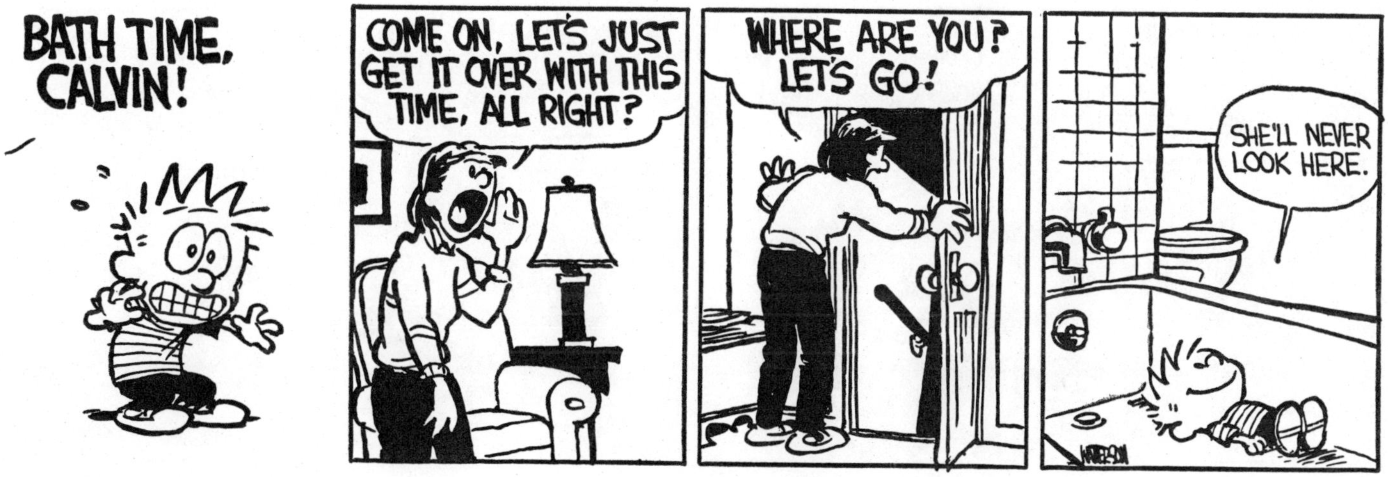
BATH TIME, CALVIN!
COME ON, LET'S JUST GET IT OVER WITH THIS TIME, ALL RIGHT?
WHERE ARE YOU? LET'S GO!
SHE'LL NEVER LOOK HERE.
WATTERSON

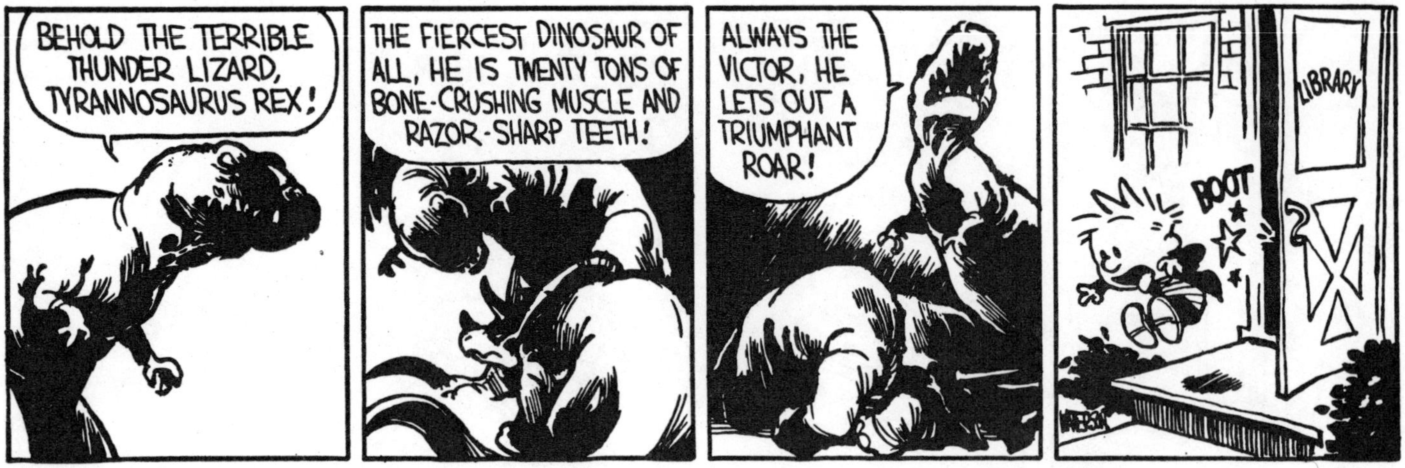
BEHOLD THE TERRIBLE THUNDER LIZARD, TYRANNOSAURUS REX!
THE FIERCEST DINOSAUR OF ALL, HE IS TWENTY TONS OF BONE-CRUSHING MUSCLE AND RAZOR-SHARP TEETH!
ALWAYS THE VICTOR, HE LETS OUT A TRIUMPHANT ROAR!
LIBRARY
BOOT

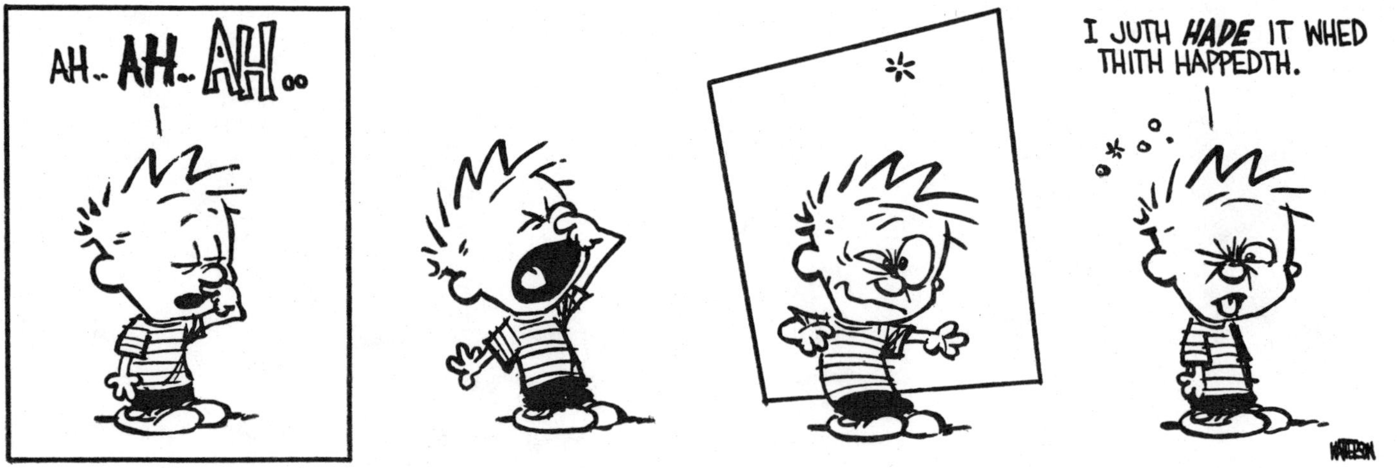
AH.. AH.. AH..
I JUTH *HADE* IT WHED THITH HAPPEDTH.

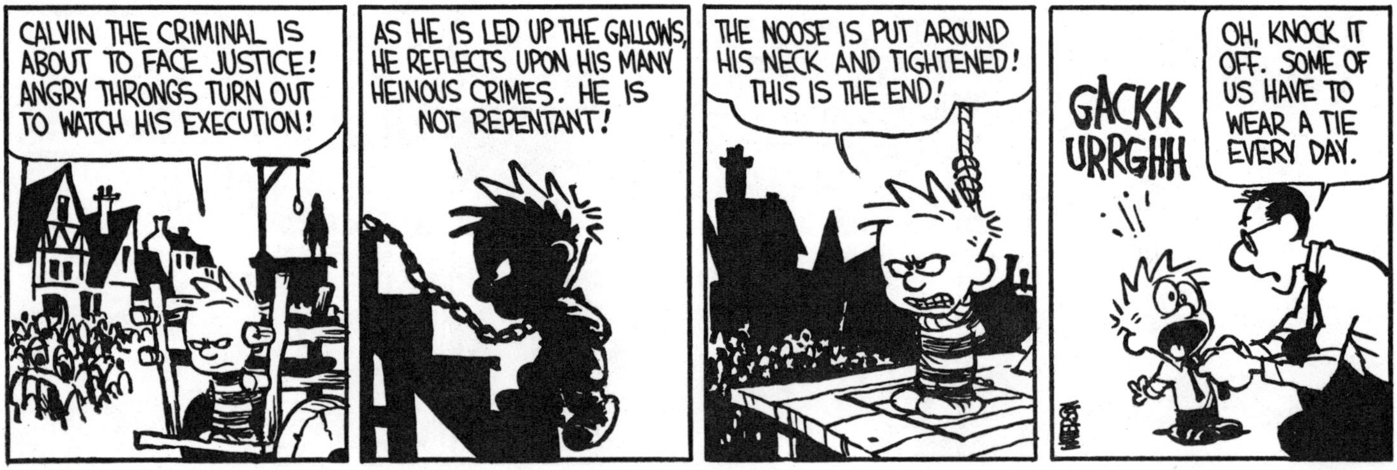
CALVIN THE CRIMINAL IS ABOUT TO FACE JUSTICE! ANGRY THRONGS TURN OUT TO WATCH HIS EXECUTION!
AS HE IS LED UP THE GALLOWS, HE REFLECTS UPON HIS MANY HEINOUS CRIMES. HE IS NOT REPENTANT!
THE NOOSE IS PUT AROUND HIS NECK AND TIGHTENED! THIS IS THE END!
GACKK URRGHH
OH, KNOCK IT OFF. SOME OF US HAVE TO WEAR A TIE EVERY DAY.

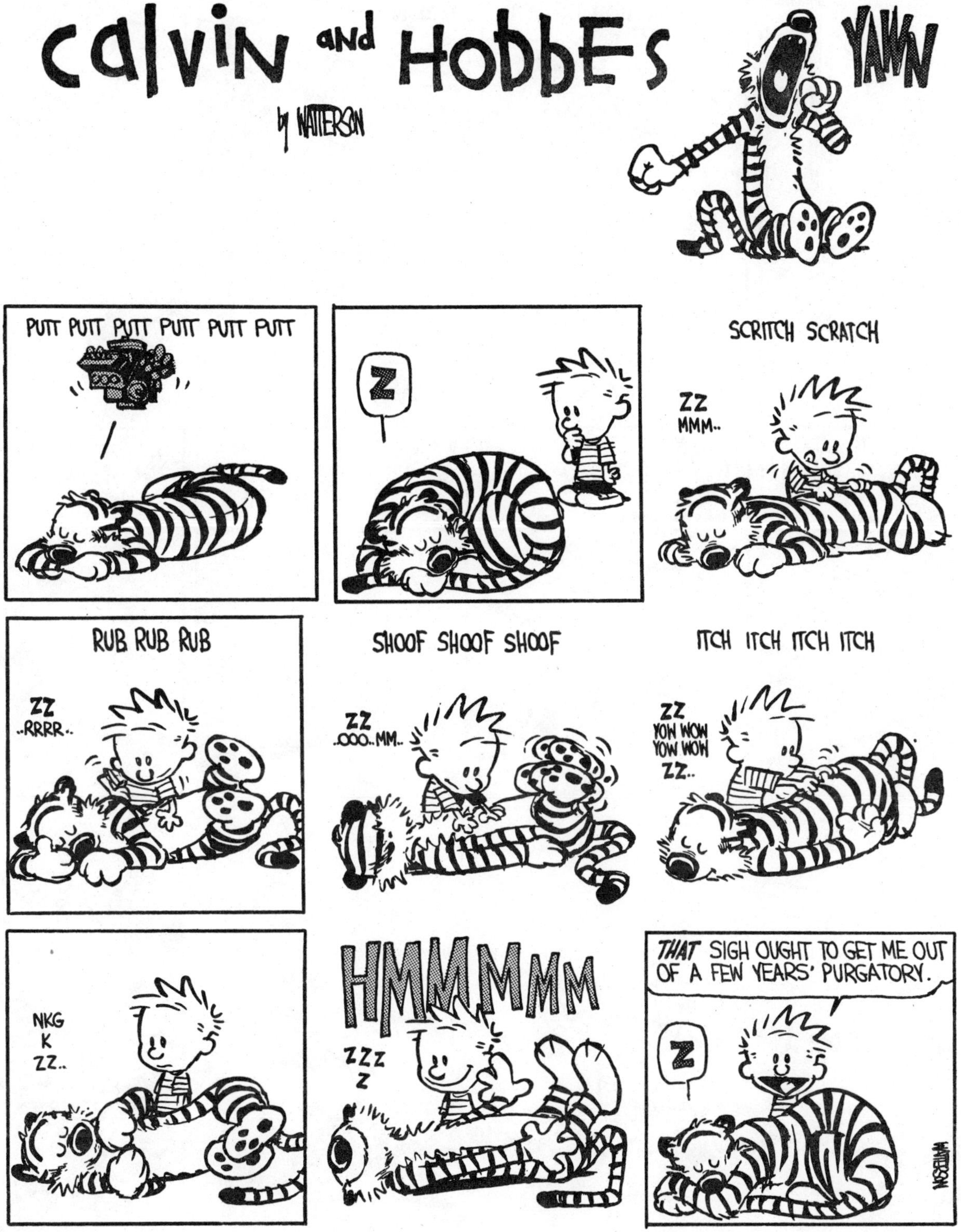
Calvin and HOBBES
by WATTERSON
YAWN
PUTT PUTT PUTT PUTT PUTT PUTT
Z
SCRITCH SCRATCH
ZZ MMM..
RUB RUB RUB
ZZ ..RRRR..
SHOOF SHOOF SHOOF
ZZ .OOO..MM..
ITCH ITCH ITCH ITCH
ZZ YOW WOW YOW WOW ZZ..
NKG K ZZ..
HMMMMMM
ZZZ Z
THAT SIGH OUGHT TO GET ME OUT OF A FEW YEARS' PURGATORY.
Z
WATTERSON

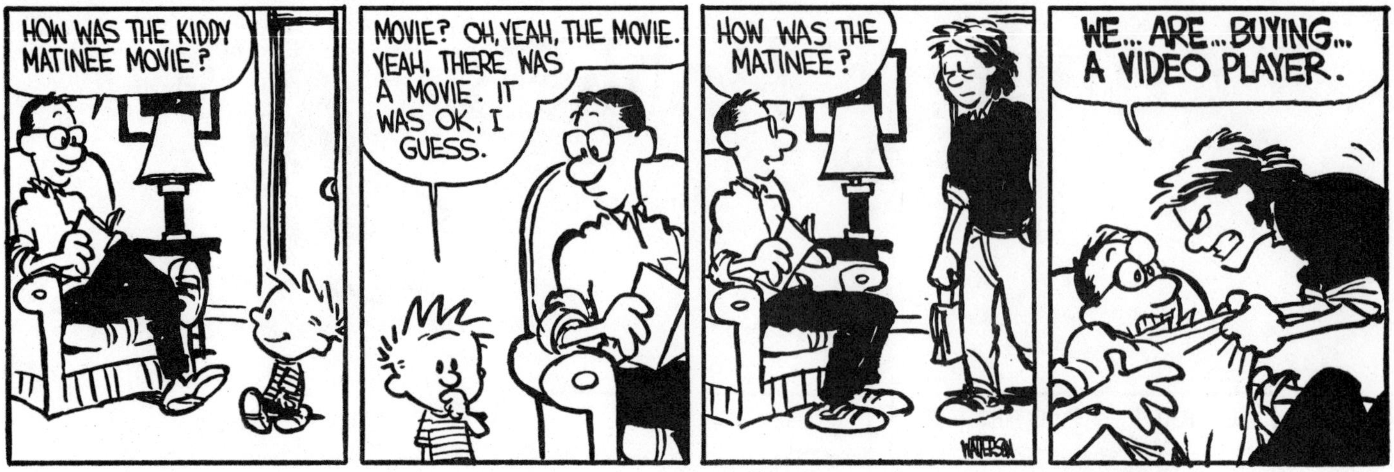
HOW WAS THE KIDDY MATINEE MOVIE?
MOVIE? OH, YEAH, THE MOVIE. YEAH, THERE WAS A MOVIE. IT WAS OK, I GUESS.
HOW WAS THE MATINEE?
WE... ARE... BUYING... A VIDEO PLAYER.

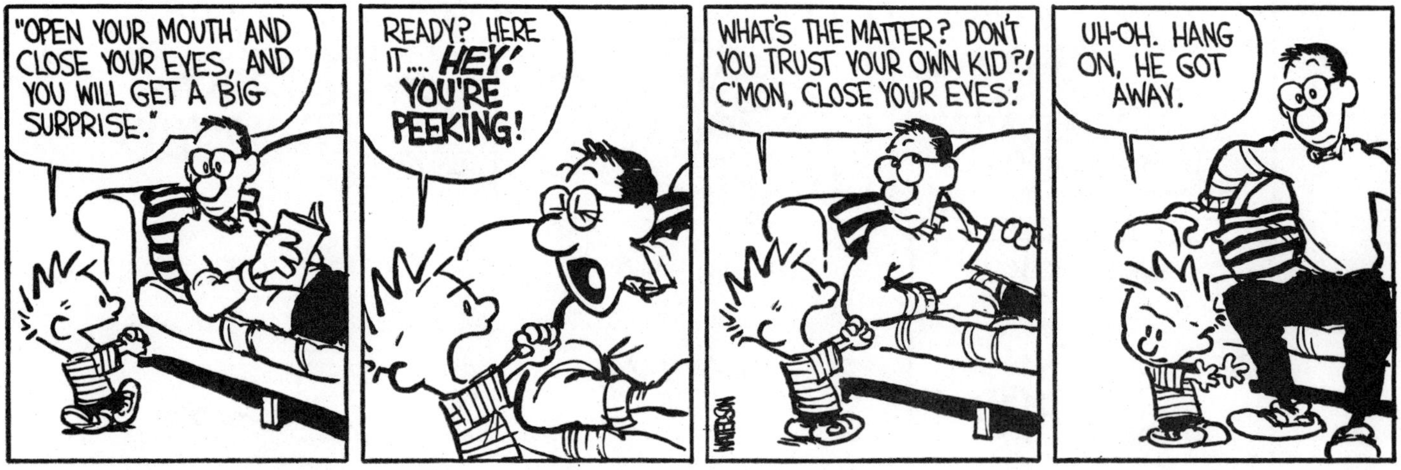
"OPEN YOUR MOUTH AND CLOSE YOUR EYES, AND YOU WILL GET A BIG SURPRISE."
READY? HERE IT.... HEY! YOU'RE PEEKING!
WHAT'S THE MATTER? DON'T YOU TRUST YOUR OWN KID?! C'MON, CLOSE YOUR EYES!
UH-OH. HANG ON, HE GOT AWAY.

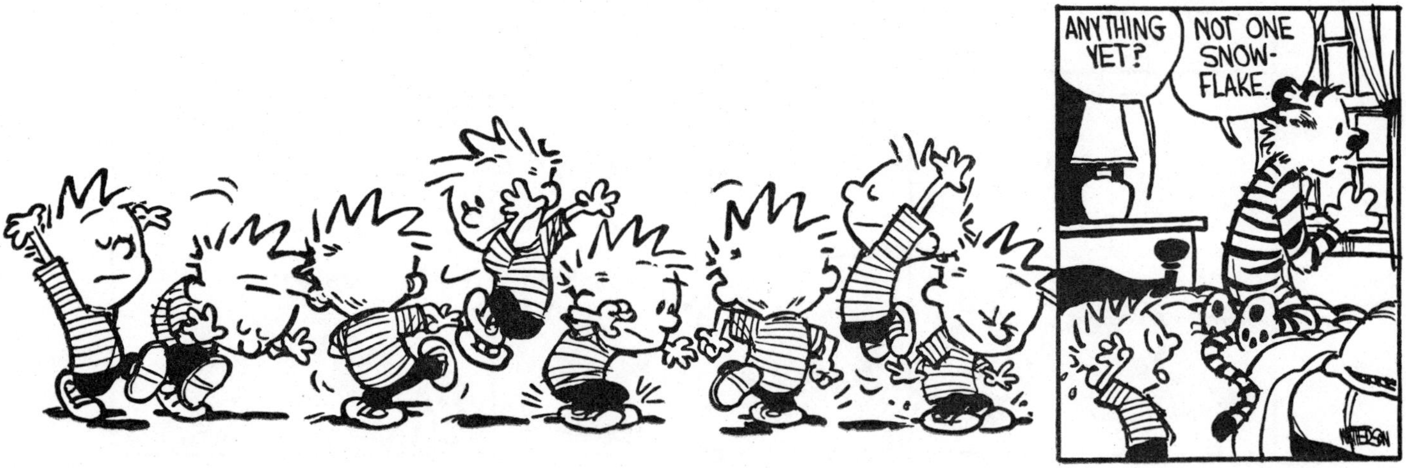
ANYTHING YET?
NOT ONE SNOW-FLAKE.

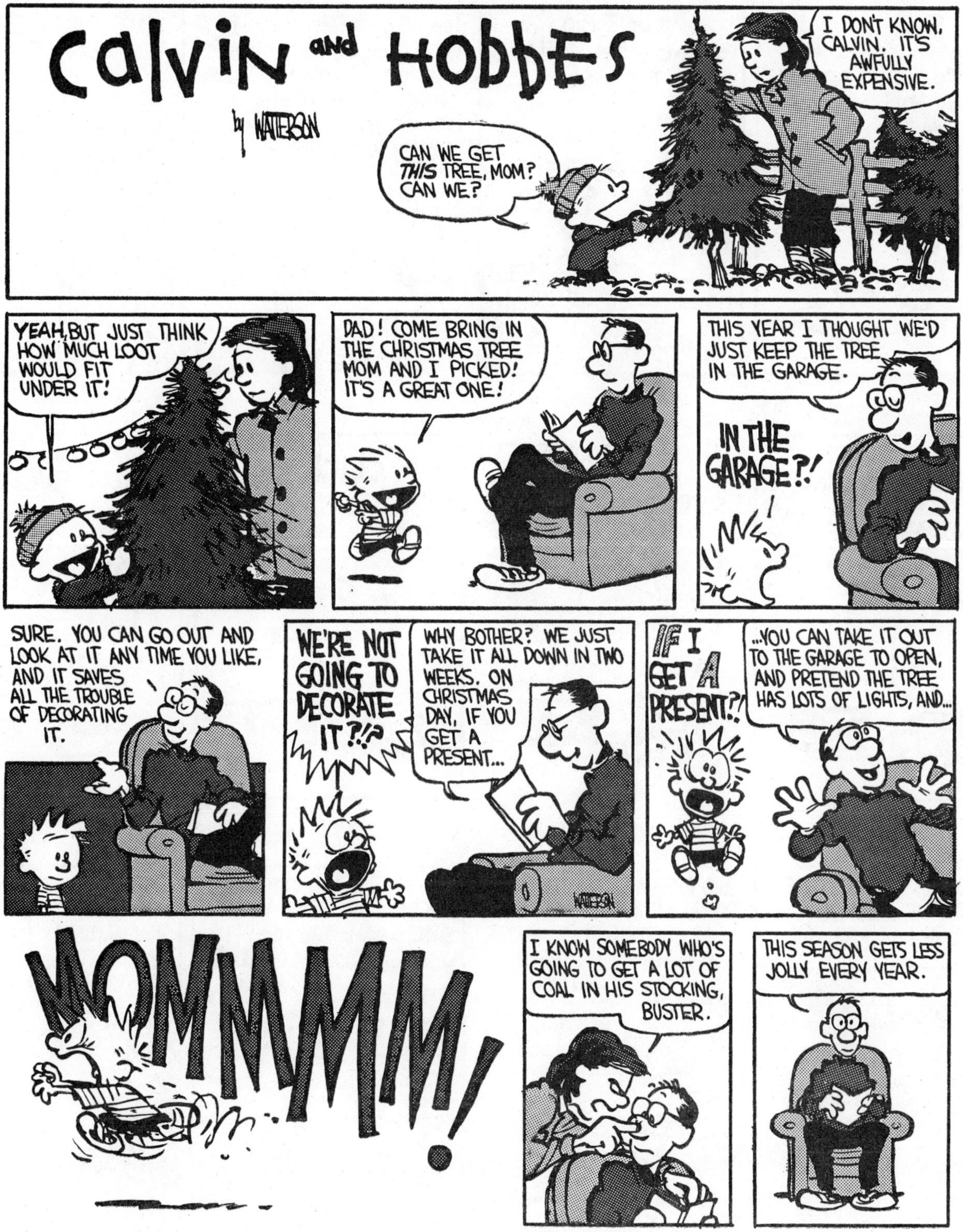
Calvin and Hobbes
by WATTERSON
CAN WE GET THIS TREE, MOM? CAN WE?
I DON'T KNOW, CALVIN. IT'S AWFULLY EXPENSIVE.
YEAH, BUT JUST THINK HOW MUCH LOOT WOULD FIT UNDER IT!
DAD! COME BRING IN THE CHRISTMAS TREE MOM AND I PICKED! IT'S A GREAT ONE!
THIS YEAR I THOUGHT WE'D JUST KEEP THE TREE IN THE GARAGE.
IN THE GARAGE?!
SURE. YOU CAN GO OUT AND LOOK AT IT ANY TIME YOU LIKE, AND IT SAVES ALL THE TROUBLE OF DECORATING IT.
WE'RE NOT GOING TO DECORATE IT?!?
WHY BOTHER? WE JUST TAKE IT ALL DOWN IN TWO WEEKS. ON CHRISTMAS DAY, IF YOU GET A PRESENT...
IF I GET A PRESENT?!
...YOU CAN TAKE IT OUT TO THE GARAGE TO OPEN, AND PRETEND THE TREE HAS LOTS OF LIGHTS, AND...
WATTERSON
MOMMMM!
I KNOW SOMEBODY WHO'S GOING TO GET A LOT OF COAL IN HIS STOCKING, BUSTER.
THIS SEASON GETS LESS JOLLY EVERY YEAR.

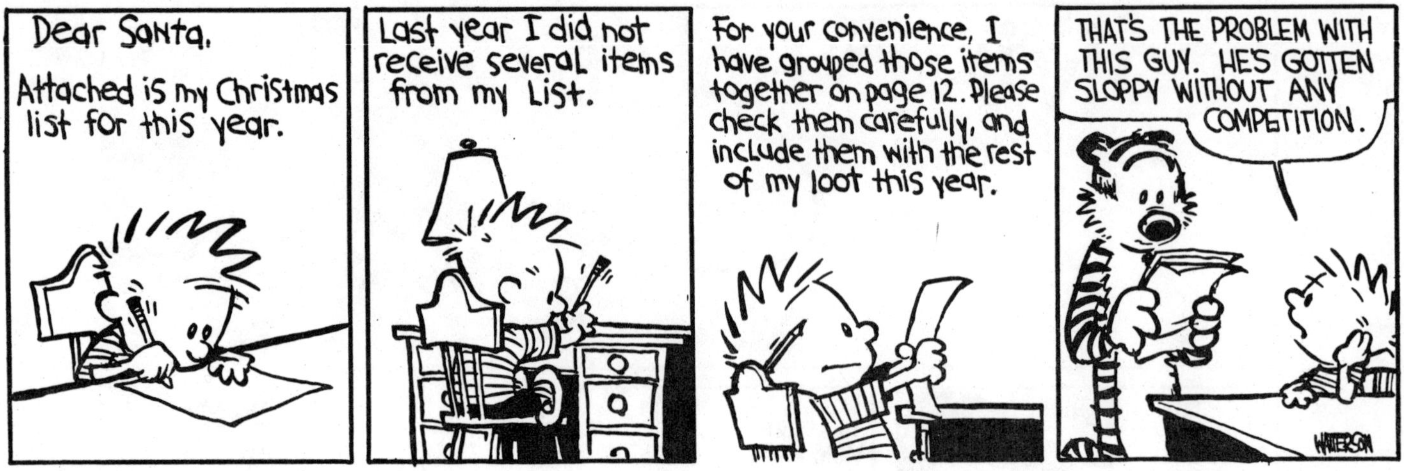
Dear Santa,
Attached is my Christmas list for this year.
Last year I did not receive several items from my List.
For your convenience, I have grouped those items together on page 12. Please check them carefully, and include them with the rest of my loot this year.
THAT'S THE PROBLEM WITH THIS GUY. HE'S GOTTEN SLOPPY WITHOUT ANY COMPETITION.

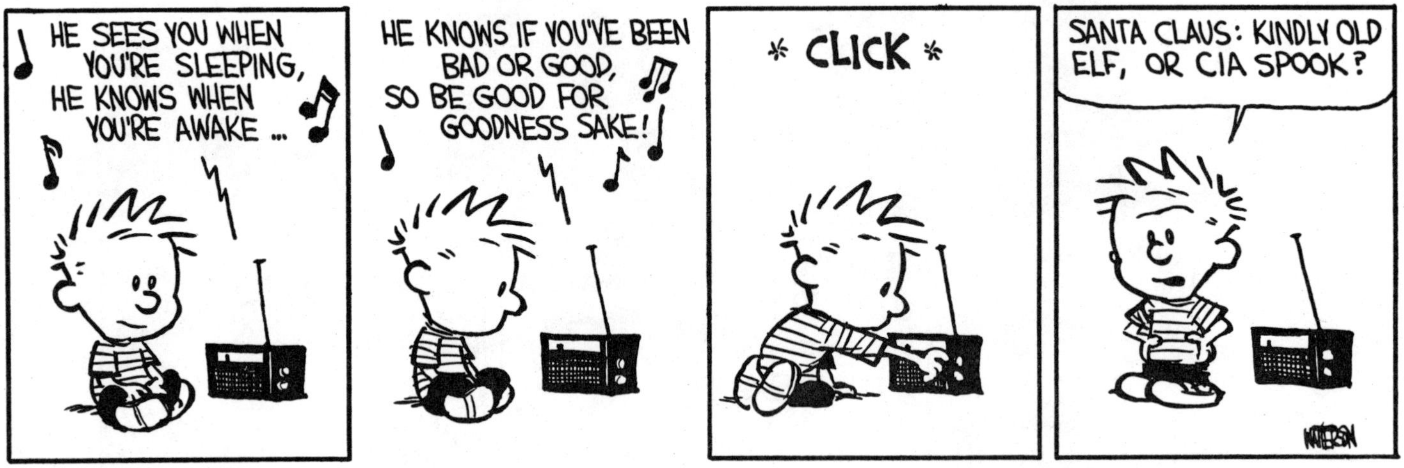
HE SEES YOU WHEN YOU'RE SLEEPING, HE KNOWS WHEN YOU'RE AWAKE ...
HE KNOWS IF YOU'VE BEEN BAD OR GOOD, SO BE GOOD FOR GOODNESS SAKE!
* CLICK *
SANTA CLAUS: KINDLY OLD ELF, OR CIA SPOOK?

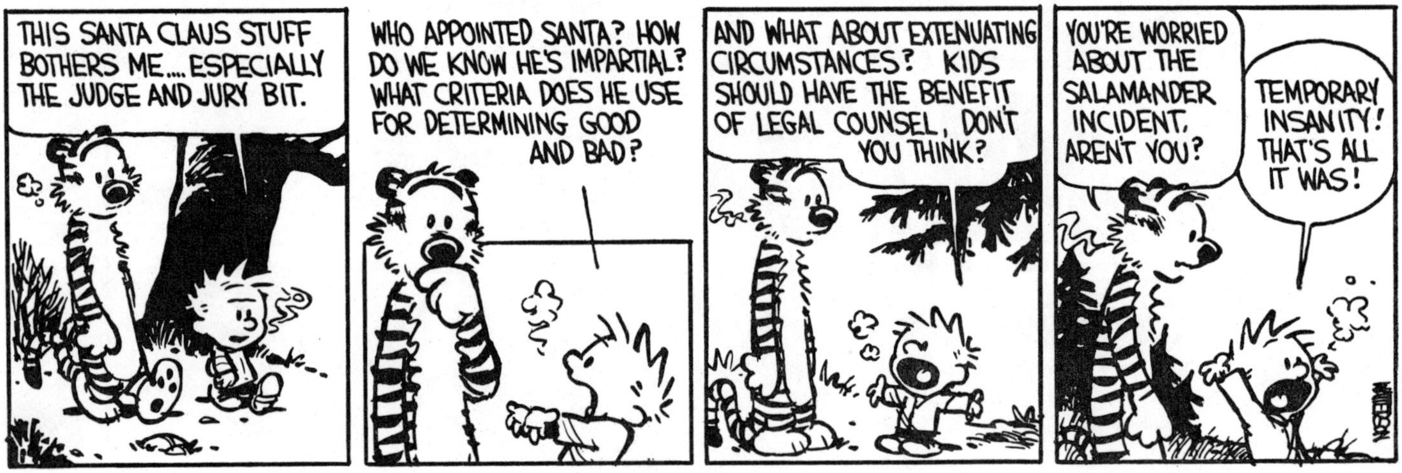
THIS SANTA CLAUS STUFF BOTHERS ME.... ESPECIALLY THE JUDGE AND JURY BIT.
WHO APPOINTED SANTA? HOW DO WE KNOW HE'S IMPARTIAL? WHAT CRITERIA DOES HE USE FOR DETERMINING GOOD AND BAD?
AND WHAT ABOUT EXTENUATING CIRCUMSTANCES? KIDS SHOULD HAVE THE BENEFIT OF LEGAL COUNSEL, DON'T YOU THINK?
YOU'RE WORRIED ABOUT THE SALAMANDER INCIDENT, AREN'T YOU?
TEMPORARY INSANITY! THAT'S ALL IT WAS!

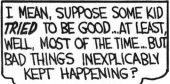

Panel 1: THEY SAY SANTA KNOWS IF YOU'VE BEEN GOOD OR BAD, BUT WHAT IF SOMEONE HAD BEEN SORT OF *BOTH*?

Panel 2: I MEAN, SUPPOSE SOME KID *TRIED* TO BE GOOD...AT LEAST, WELL, MOST OF THE TIME...BUT BAD THINGS INEXPLICABLY KEPT HAPPENING?

Panel 3: SUPPOSE SOME KID JUST HAD TERRIBLE LUCK, AND HE GOT BLAMED FOR A LOT OF THINGS HE DID ONLY *SORT* OF ON PURPOSE?

Panel 4: WHO EXACTLY MIGHT WE BE TALKING ABOUT?

THIS IS A PURELY HYPOTHETICAL CASE, MR. SMARTYPANTS.

Panel 5: THIS WHOLE SANTA CLAUS THING JUST DOESN'T MAKE SENSE.

Panel 6: WHY ALL THE SECRECY? WHY ALL THE MYSTERY? IF THE GUY EXISTS, WHY DOESN'T HE EVER SHOW HIMSELF AND PROVE IT?

Panel 7: AND IF HE *DOESN'T* EXIST, WHAT'S THE MEANING OF ALL THIS?

Panel 8: I DUNNO... ISN'T THIS A RELIGIOUS HOLIDAY?

YEAH, BUT ACTUALLY, I'VE GOT THE SAME QUESTIONS ABOUT GOD.

Panel 9: GOSH, HOBBES, WHAT IF I DON'T GET ANY PRESENTS THIS YEAR BECAUSE I DOUBTED THE EXISTENCE OF SANTA?

Panel 10: SUPPOSE HE'S PUTTING MY NAME ON THE "BAD" LIST RIGHT NOW! THAT WOULD BE AWFUL!

Panel 11: PERSONALLY, I'D THINK THAT IF YOU WEREN'T ON THE "BAD" LIST ALL ALONG, THIS WOULDN'T PUSH YOU OVER.

Panel 12: THANKS FOR THE COMFORT, EGGNOG BRAIN.

SEE? *SEE* WHY YOU'RE ON THE "BAD" LIST? INSULTS!

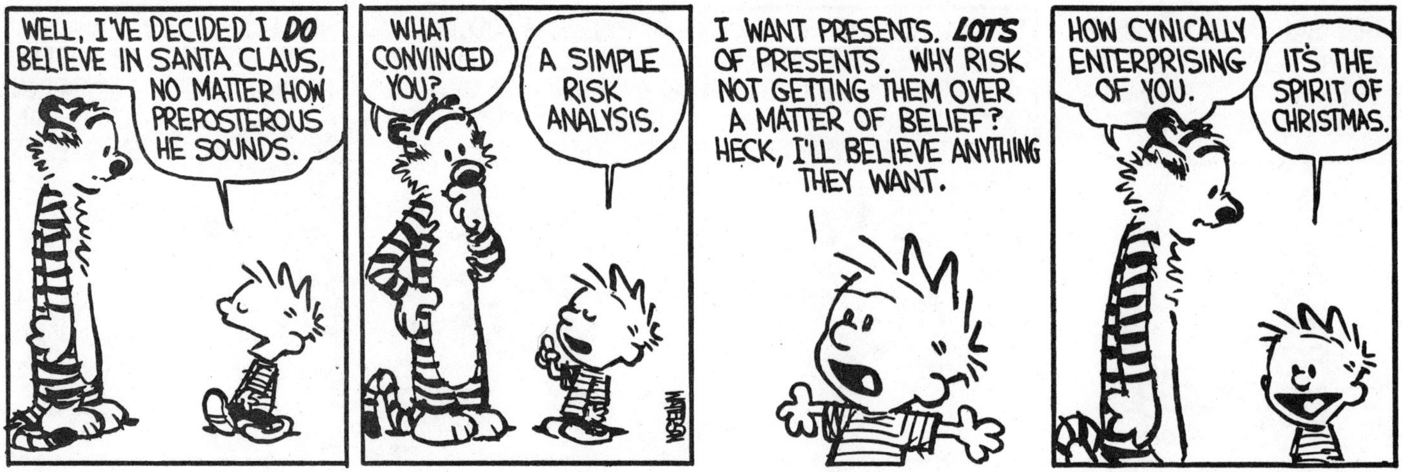
WELL, I'VE DECIDED I **DO** BELIEVE IN SANTA CLAUS, NO MATTER HOW PREPOSTEROUS HE SOUNDS.
WHAT CONVINCED YOU?
A SIMPLE RISK ANALYSIS.
I WANT PRESENTS. **LOTS** OF PRESENTS. WHY RISK NOT GETTING THEM OVER A MATTER OF BELIEF? HECK, I'LL BELIEVE ANYTHING THEY WANT.
HOW CYNICALLY ENTERPRISING OF YOU.
IT'S THE SPIRIT OF CHRISTMAS.

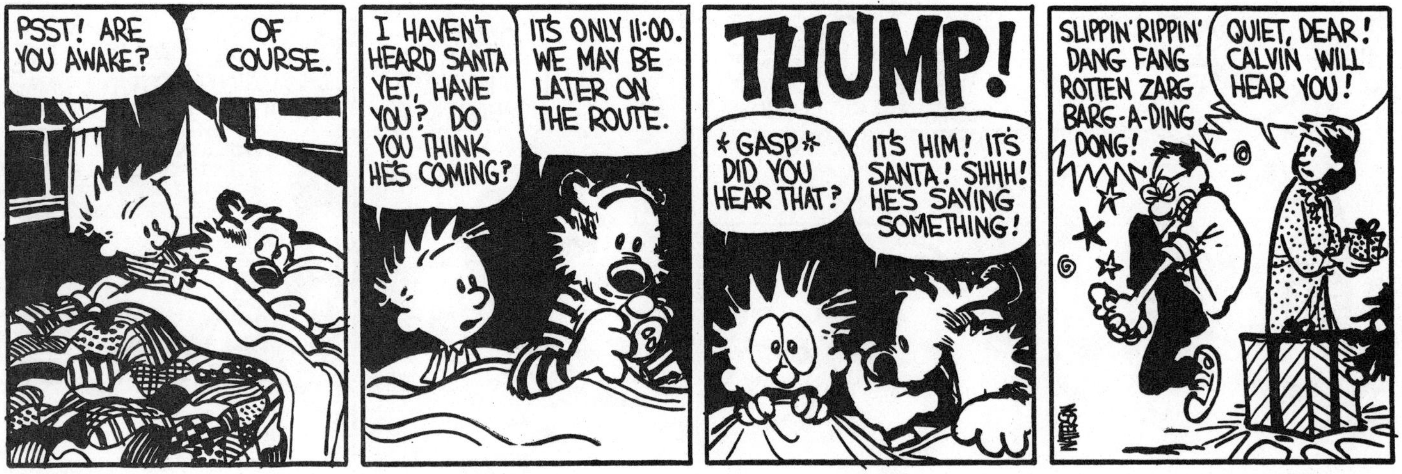
PSST! ARE YOU AWAKE?
OF COURSE.
I HAVEN'T HEARD SANTA YET, HAVE YOU? DO YOU THINK HE'S COMING?
IT'S ONLY 11:00. WE MAY BE LATER ON THE ROUTE.
THUMP!
GASP DID YOU HEAR THAT?
IT'S HIM! IT'S SANTA! SHHH! HE'S SAYING SOMETHING!
SLIPPIN' RIPPIN' DANG FANG ROTTEN ZARG BARG-A-DING DONG!
QUIET, DEAR! CALVIN WILL HEAR YOU!

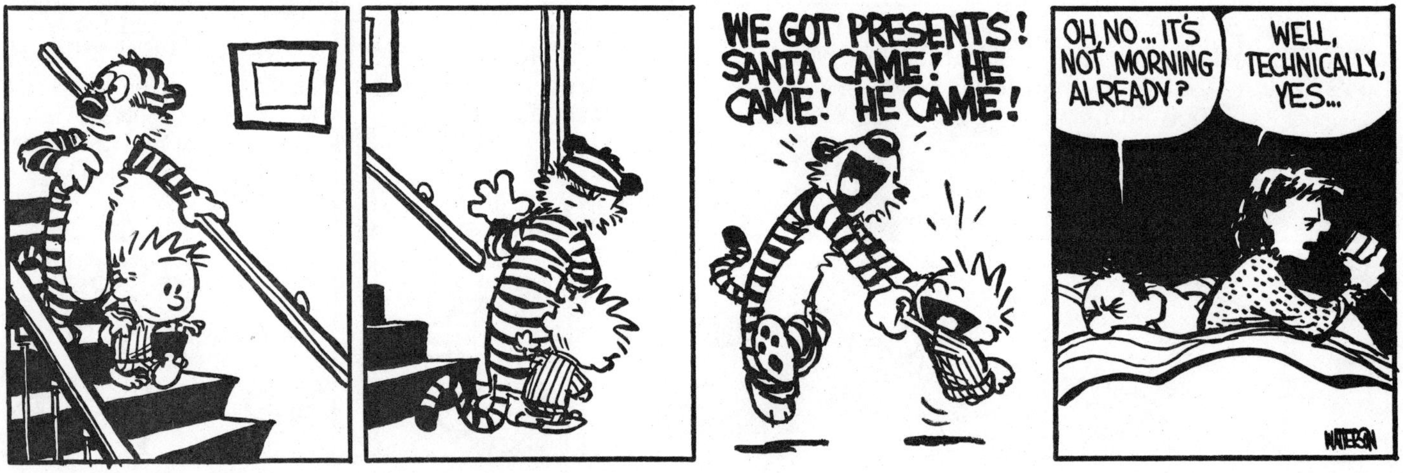
WE GOT PRESENTS! SANTA CAME! HE CAME! HE CAME!
OH, NO... IT'S NOT MORNING ALREADY?
WELL, TECHNICALLY, YES...

CALVIN and HOBBES

HERE'S A BOX OF CRAYONS. I NEED SOME ILLUSTRATIONS FOR A STORY I'M WRITING.

YOU CAN DRAW SOMETHING BESIDES TIGERS, CAN'T YOU?

SURE. LEOPARDS, PUMAS, OCELOTS.. ..YOU NAME IT.

HERE, DAD, READ *THIS* STORY TONIGHT. I WROTE IT AND HOBBES ILLUSTRATED IT.

..UM... OK.

"THE DAD WHO LIVED TO REGRET BEING MEAN TO HIS KID."

WHAT ARE YOU PAUSING FOR? KEEP READING.

Barney's dad was really bad,
So Barney hatched a plan.
When his dad said, "Eat your peas!"
Barney shouted, "NO!" and ran.

peas

Barney

Barney tricked his mean ol' dad,
And locked him in the cellar.
His mom never found out
where he'd gone,
'Cause Barney didn't tell her.

door

key

There his dad spent his life,
Eating mice and gruel.
With every bite for fifty years
He was sorry he'd been cruel.
THE END.

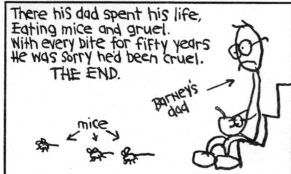

mice

Barney's dad

YOU KNOW HOW A LOT OF STORIES HAVE MORALS TO THEM...?

I *GET* IT, I *GET* IT!

WATTERSON & HOBS

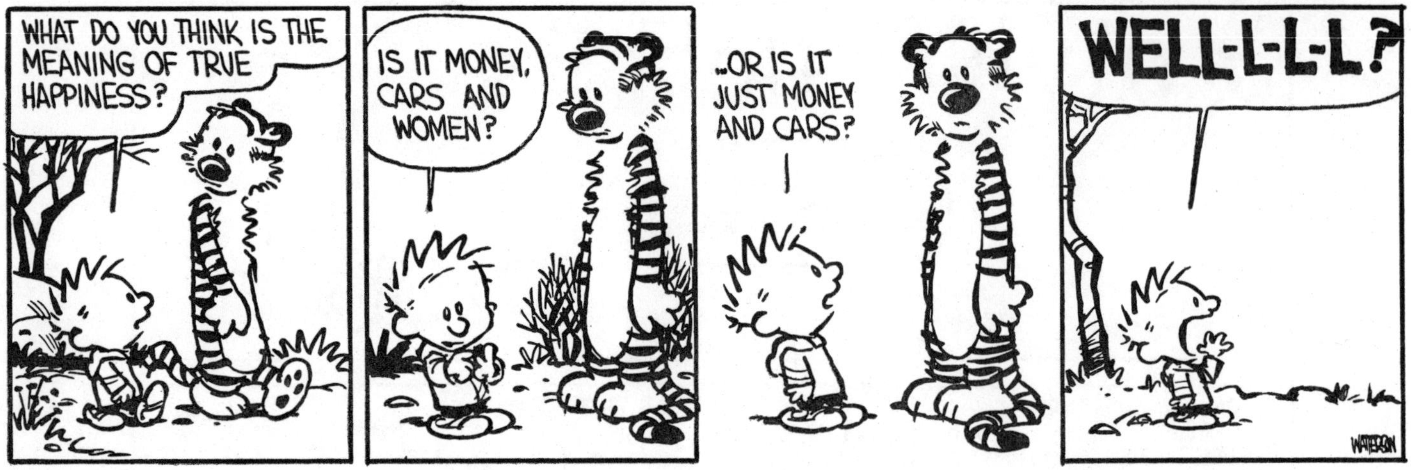
WHAT DO YOU THINK IS THE MEANING OF TRUE HAPPINESS?
IS IT MONEY, CARS AND WOMEN?
..OR IS IT JUST MONEY AND CARS?
WELL-L-L-L?
WATTERSON

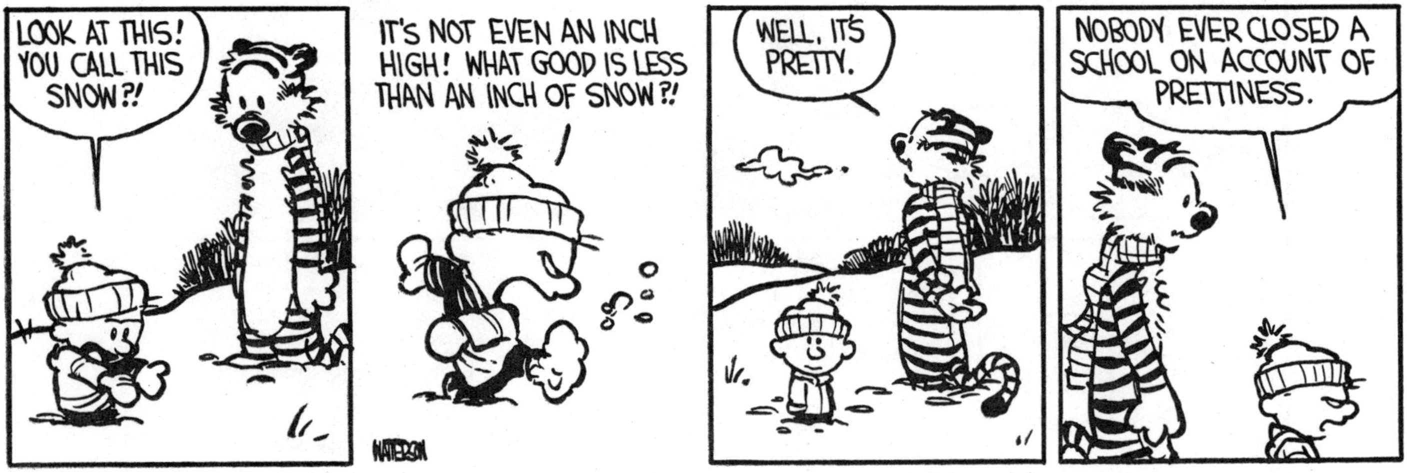
LOOK AT THIS! YOU CALL THIS SNOW?!
IT'S NOT EVEN AN INCH HIGH! WHAT GOOD IS LESS THAN AN INCH OF SNOW?!
WATTERSON
WELL, IT'S PRETTY.
NOBODY EVER CLOSED A SCHOOL ON ACCOUNT OF PRETTINESS.

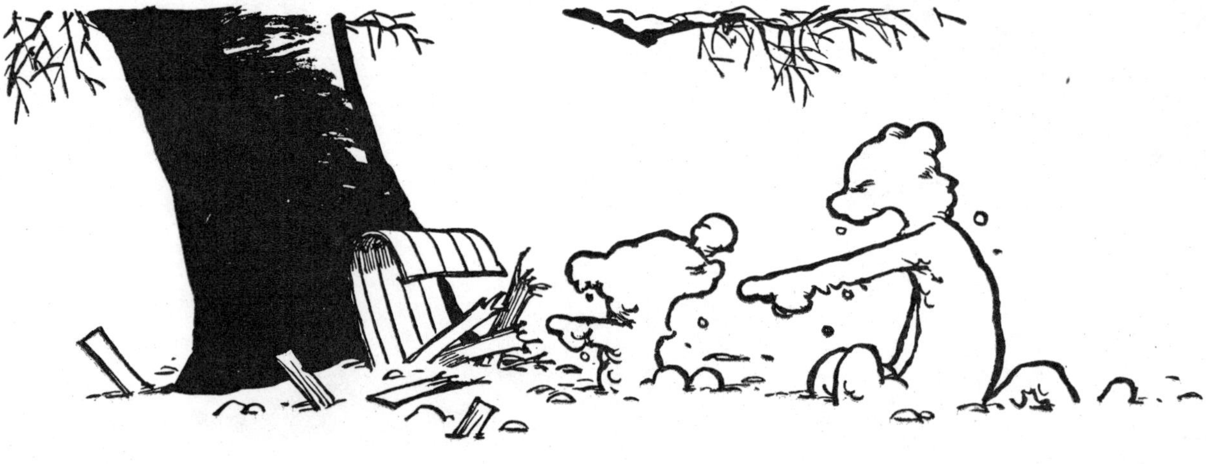

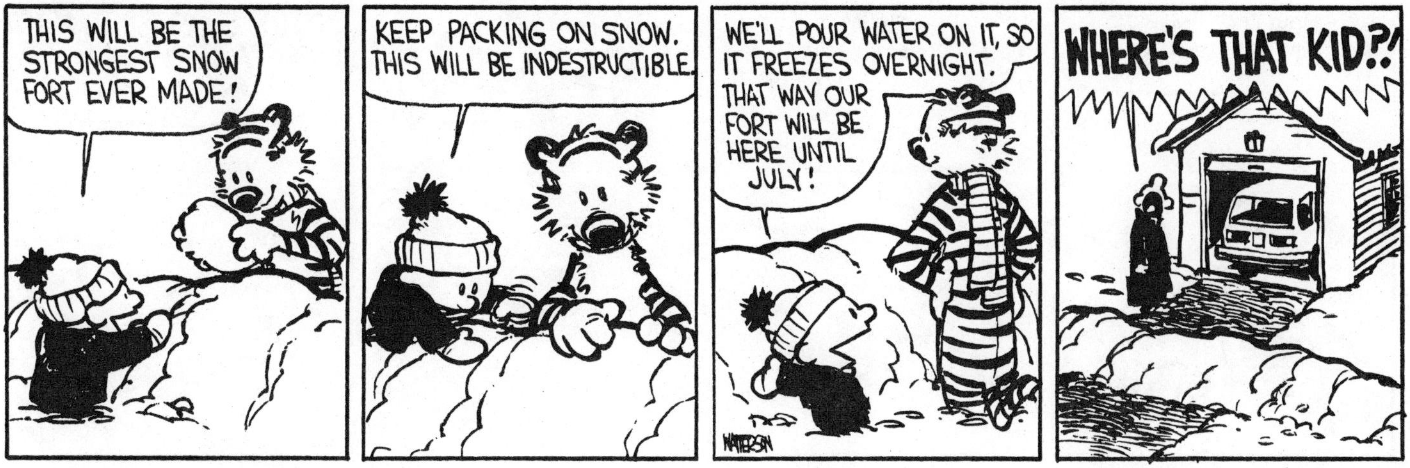
THIS WILL BE THE STRONGEST SNOW FORT EVER MADE!
KEEP PACKING ON SNOW. THIS WILL BE INDESTRUCTIBLE.
WE'LL POUR WATER ON IT, SO IT FREEZES OVERNIGHT.
THAT WAY OUR FORT WILL BE HERE UNTIL JULY!
WATTERSON
WHERE'S THAT KID?!

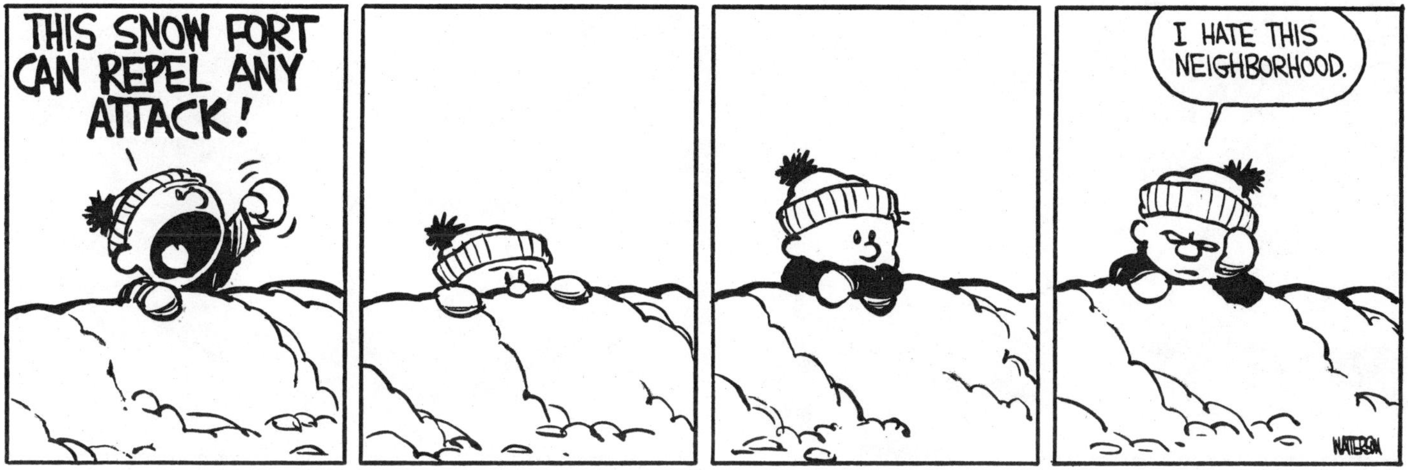
THIS SNOW FORT CAN REPEL ANY ATTACK!
I HATE THIS NEIGHBORHOOD.
WATTERSON

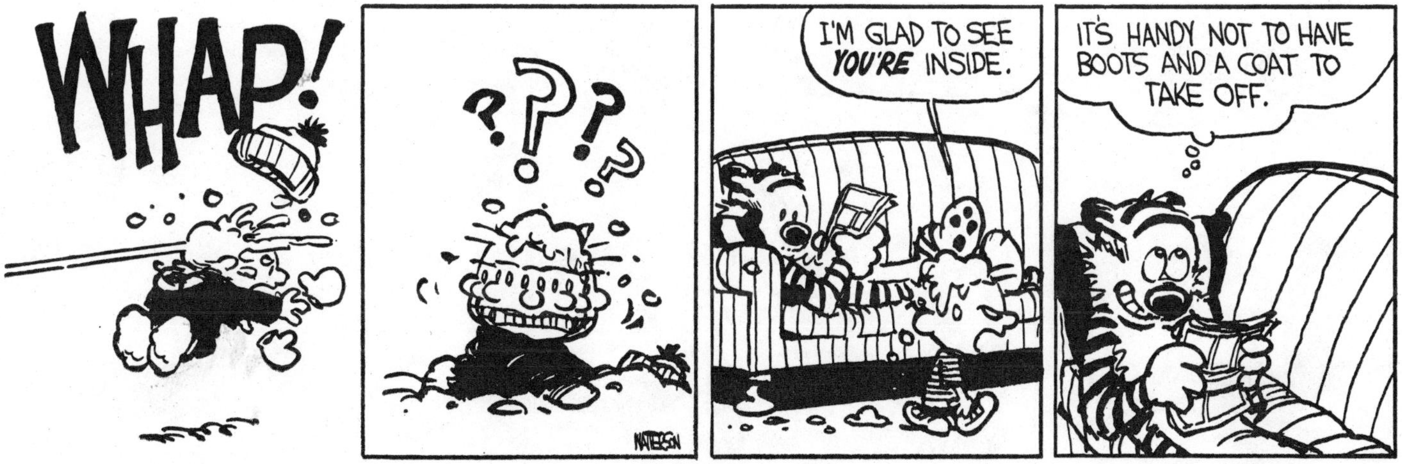
WHAP!
???
WATTERSON
I'M GLAD TO SEE ***YOU'RE*** INSIDE.
IT'S HANDY NOT TO HAVE BOOTS AND A COAT TO TAKE OFF.

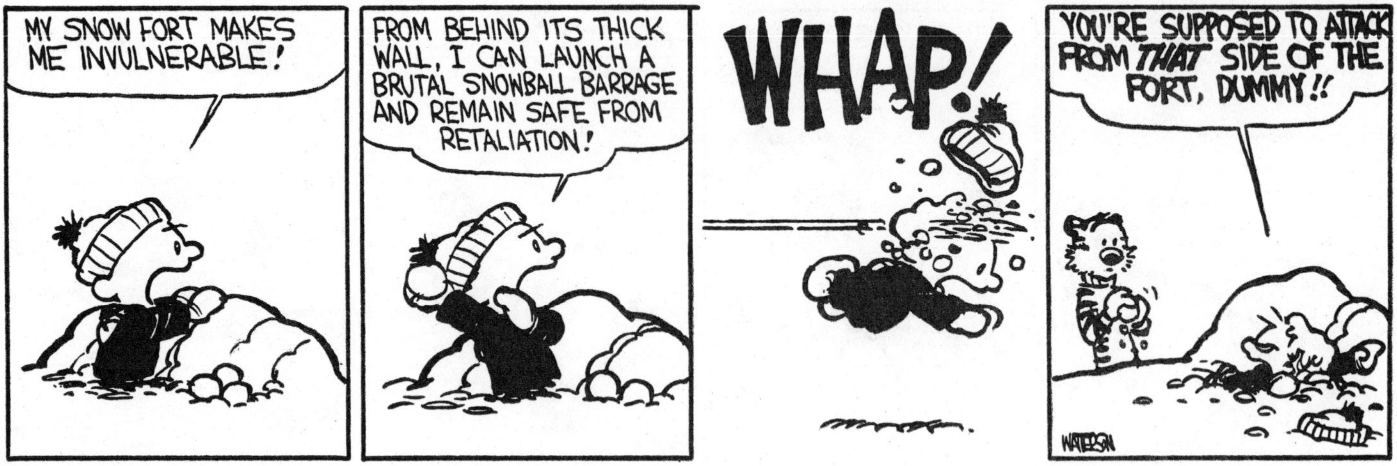
MY SNOW FORT MAKES ME INVULNERABLE!
FROM BEHIND ITS THICK WALL, I CAN LAUNCH A BRUTAL SNOWBALL BARRAGE AND REMAIN SAFE FROM RETALIATION!
WHAP!
YOU'RE SUPPOSED TO ATTACK FROM *THAT* SIDE OF THE FORT, DUMMY!!

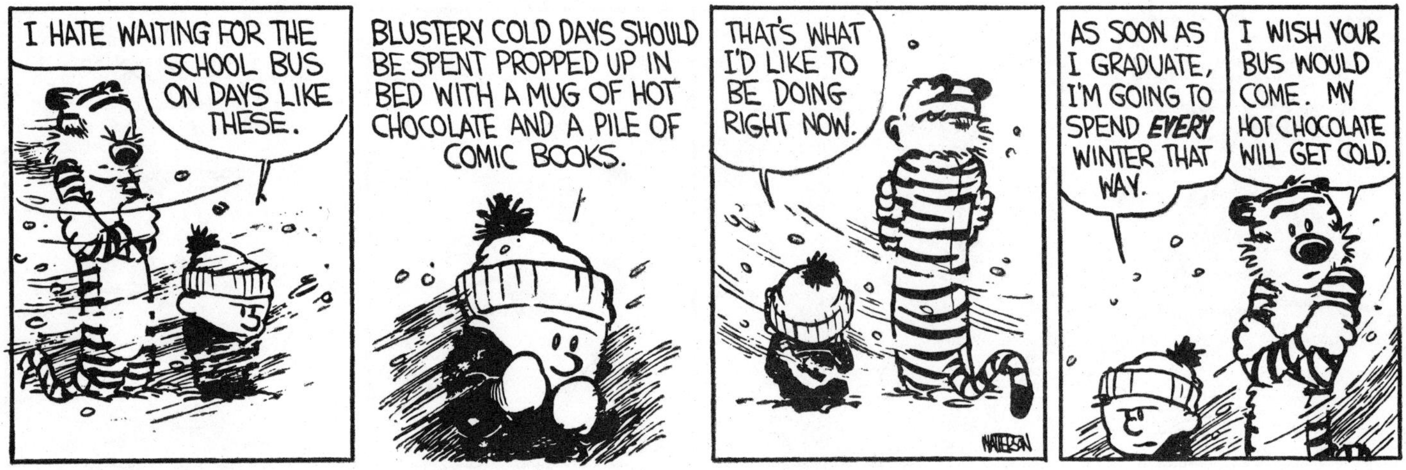
I HATE WAITING FOR THE SCHOOL BUS ON DAYS LIKE THESE.
BLUSTERY COLD DAYS SHOULD BE SPENT PROPPED UP IN BED WITH A MUG OF HOT CHOCOLATE AND A PILE OF COMIC BOOKS.
THAT'S WHAT I'D LIKE TO BE DOING RIGHT NOW.
AS SOON AS I GRADUATE, I'M GOING TO SPEND *EVERY* WINTER THAT WAY.
I WISH YOUR BUS WOULD COME. MY HOT CHOCOLATE WILL GET COLD.

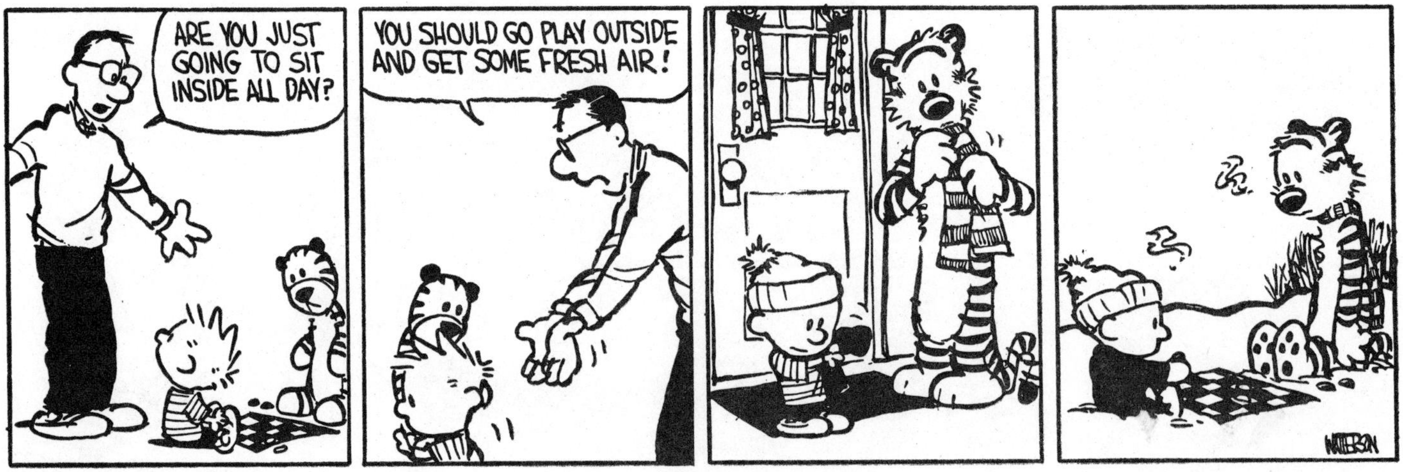
ARE YOU JUST GOING TO SIT INSIDE ALL DAY?
YOU SHOULD GO PLAY OUTSIDE AND GET SOME FRESH AIR!

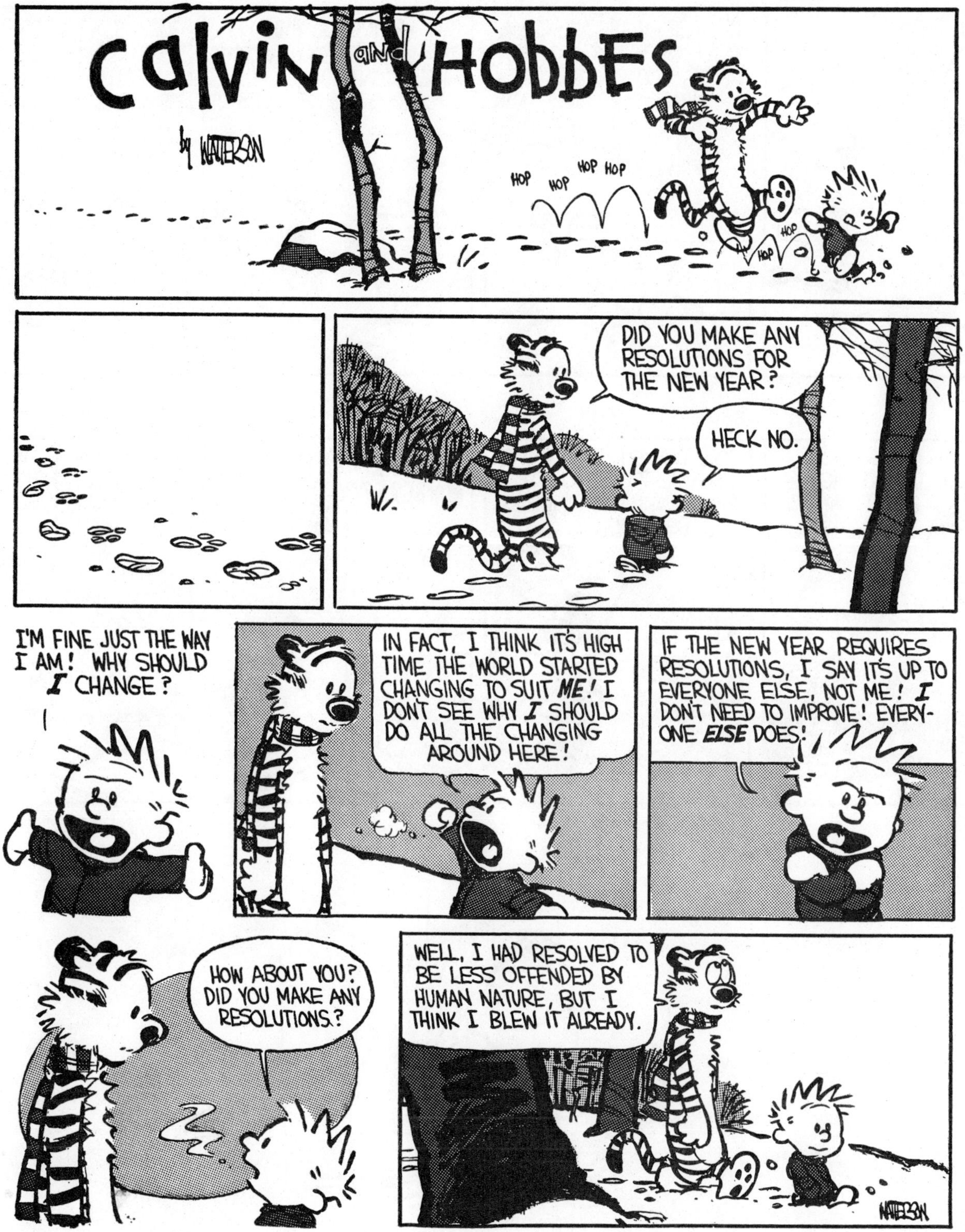
Calvin and HOBBES
by WATTERSON
HOP HOP HOP HOP
HOP HOP
DID YOU MAKE ANY RESOLUTIONS FOR THE NEW YEAR?
HECK NO.
I'M FINE JUST THE WAY I AM! WHY SHOULD *I* CHANGE?
IN FACT, I THINK IT'S HIGH TIME THE WORLD STARTED CHANGING TO SUIT *ME*! I DON'T SEE WHY *I* SHOULD DO ALL THE CHANGING AROUND HERE!
IF THE NEW YEAR REQUIRES RESOLUTIONS, I SAY IT'S UP TO EVERYONE ELSE, NOT ME! *I* DON'T NEED TO IMPROVE! EVERYONE *ELSE* DOES!
HOW ABOUT YOU? DID YOU MAKE ANY RESOLUTIONS?
WELL, I HAD RESOLVED TO BE LESS OFFENDED BY HUMAN NATURE, BUT I THINK I BLEW IT ALREADY.
WATTERSON

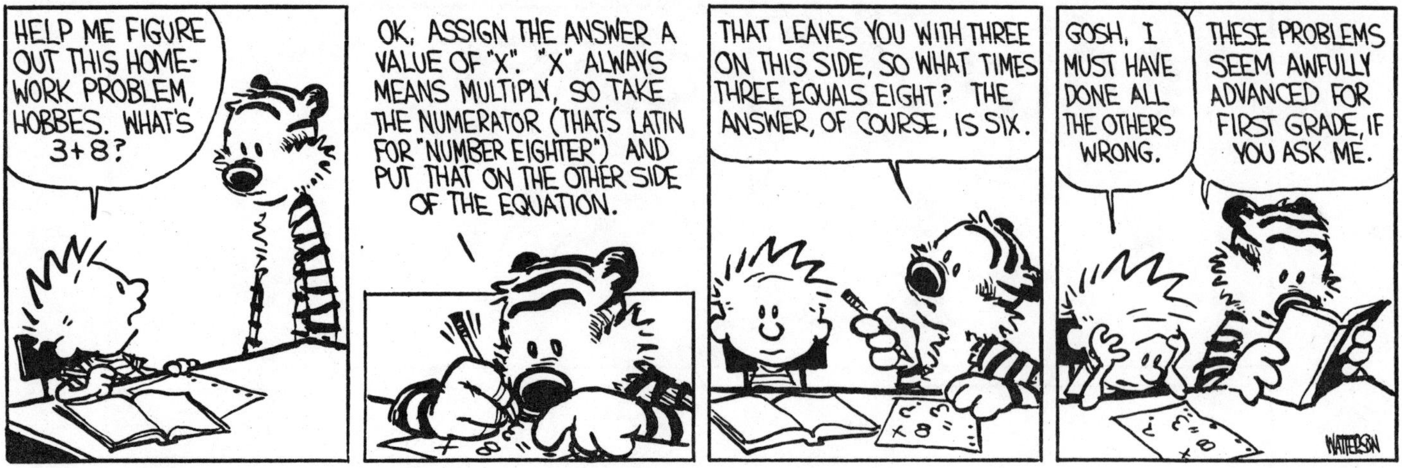
HELP ME FIGURE OUT THIS HOMEWORK PROBLEM, HOBBES. WHAT'S 3+8?
OK, ASSIGN THE ANSWER A VALUE OF "X". "X" ALWAYS MEANS MULTIPLY, SO TAKE THE NUMERATOR (THAT'S LATIN FOR "NUMBER EIGHTER") AND PUT THAT ON THE OTHER SIDE OF THE EQUATION.
THAT LEAVES YOU WITH THREE ON THIS SIDE, SO WHAT TIMES THREE EQUALS EIGHT? THE ANSWER, OF COURSE, IS SIX.
GOSH, I MUST HAVE DONE ALL THE OTHERS WRONG.
THESE PROBLEMS SEEM AWFULLY ADVANCED FOR FIRST GRADE, IF YOU ASK ME.
WATTERSON

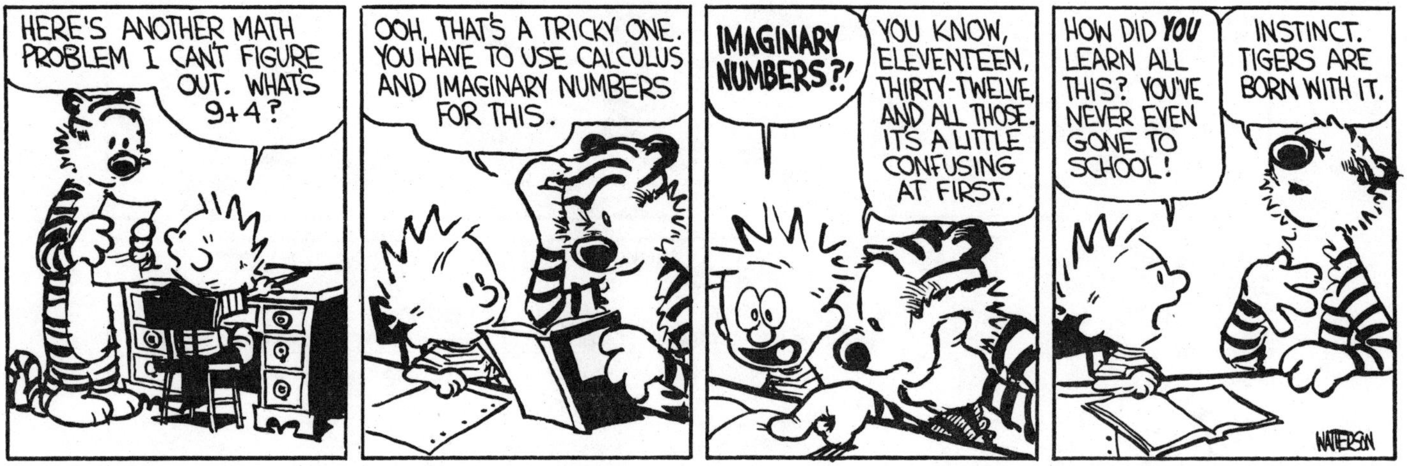
HERE'S ANOTHER MATH PROBLEM I CAN'T FIGURE OUT. WHAT'S 9+4?
OOH, THAT'S A TRICKY ONE. YOU HAVE TO USE CALCULUS AND IMAGINARY NUMBERS FOR THIS.
IMAGINARY NUMBERS?!
YOU KNOW, ELEVENTEEN, THIRTY-TWELVE, AND ALL THOSE. IT'S A LITTLE CONFUSING AT FIRST.
HOW DID YOU LEARN ALL THIS? YOU'VE NEVER EVEN GONE TO SCHOOL!
INSTINCT. TIGERS ARE BORN WITH IT.
WATTERSON

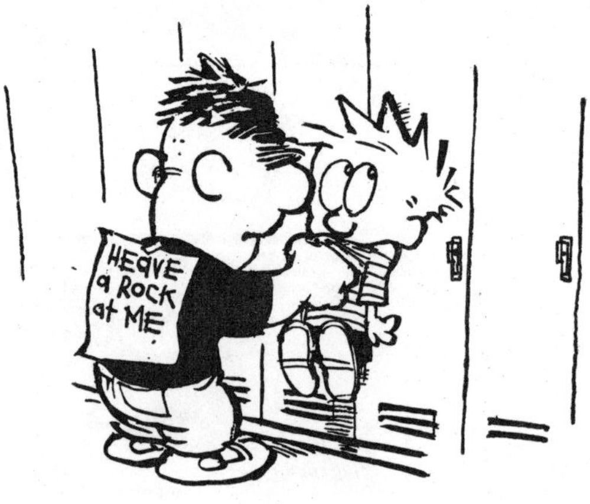
HEAVE a ROCK at ME

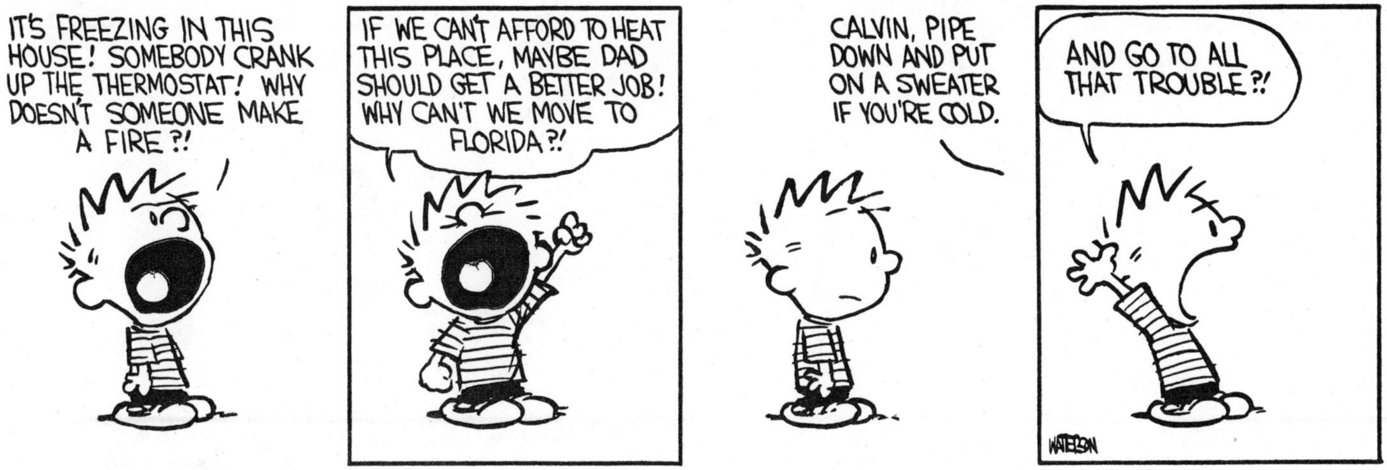
IT'S FREEZING IN THIS HOUSE! SOMEBODY CRANK UP THE THERMOSTAT! WHY DOESN'T SOMEONE MAKE A FIRE?!
IF WE CAN'T AFFORD TO HEAT THIS PLACE, MAYBE DAD SHOULD GET A BETTER JOB! WHY CAN'T WE MOVE TO FLORIDA?!
CALVIN, PIPE DOWN AND PUT ON A SWEATER IF YOU'RE COLD.
AND GO TO ALL THAT TROUBLE?!

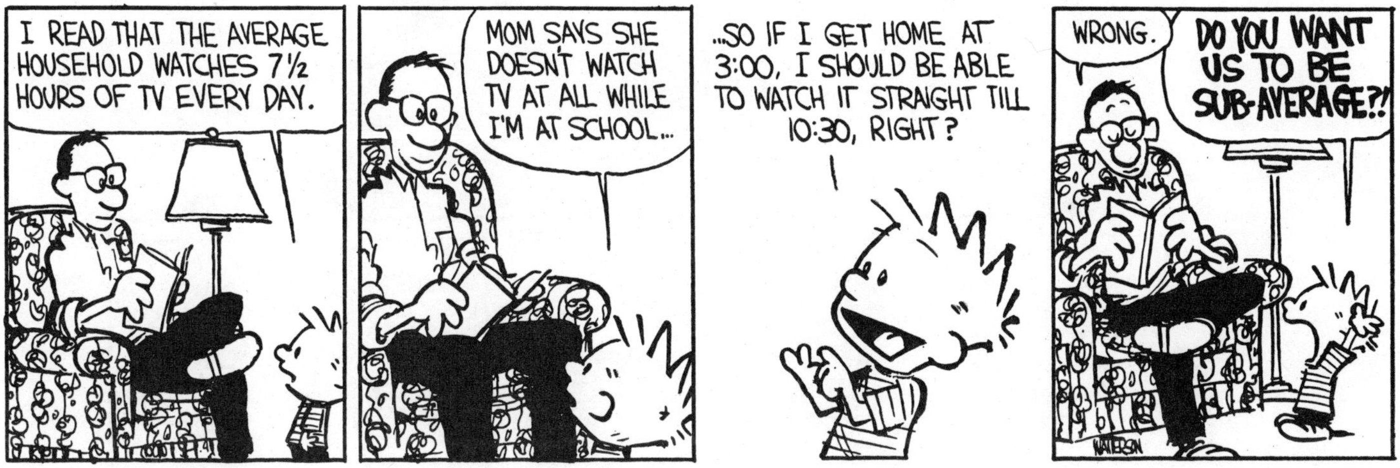
I READ THAT THE AVERAGE HOUSEHOLD WATCHES 7½ HOURS OF TV EVERY DAY.
MOM SAYS SHE DOESN'T WATCH TV AT ALL WHILE I'M AT SCHOOL...
...SO IF I GET HOME AT 3:00, I SHOULD BE ABLE TO WATCH IT STRAIGHT TILL 10:30, RIGHT?
WRONG.
DO YOU WANT US TO BE SUB-AVERAGE?!

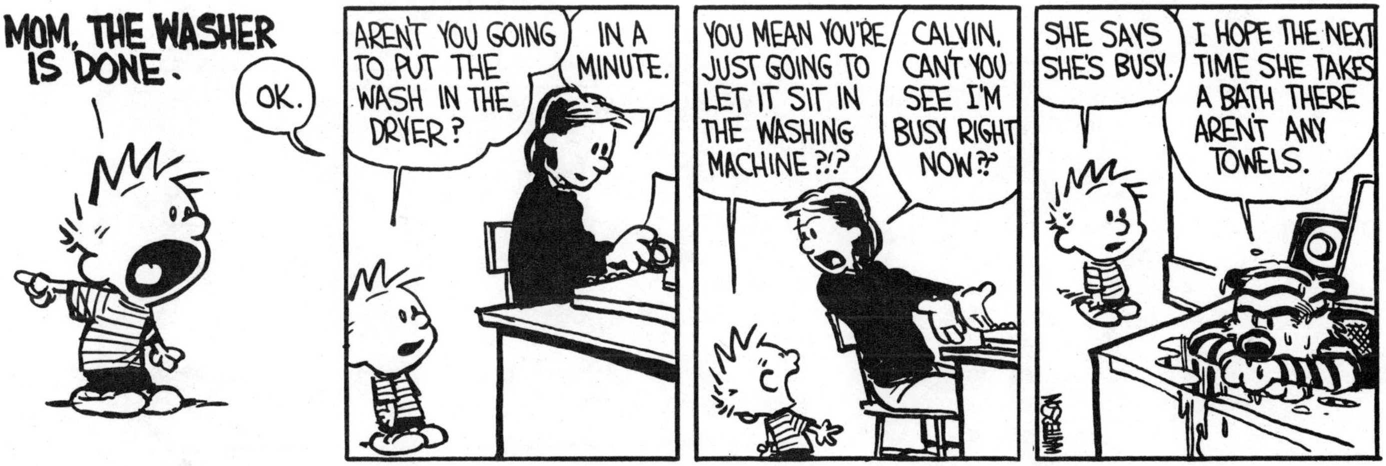
MOM, THE WASHER IS DONE.
OK.
AREN'T YOU GOING TO PUT THE WASH IN THE DRYER?
IN A MINUTE.
YOU MEAN YOU'RE JUST GOING TO LET IT SIT IN THE WASHING MACHINE?!?
CALVIN, CAN'T YOU SEE I'M BUSY RIGHT NOW?!
SHE SAYS SHE'S BUSY.
I HOPE THE NEXT TIME SHE TAKES A BATH THERE AREN'T ANY TOWELS.

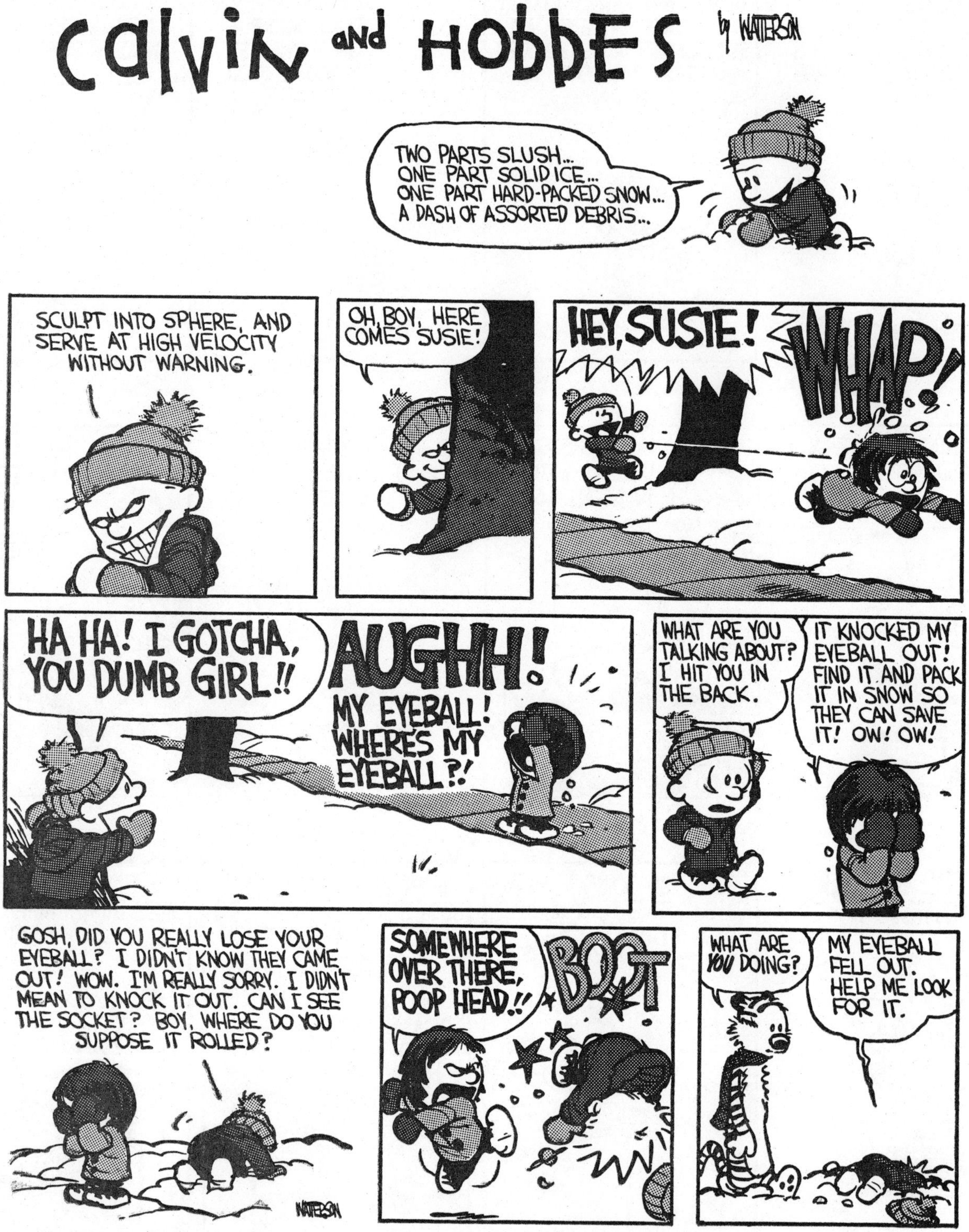
Calvin and HOBBES
by WATTERSON
TWO PARTS SLUSH... ONE PART SOLID ICE... ONE PART HARD-PACKED SNOW... A DASH OF ASSORTED DEBRIS...
SCULPT INTO SPHERE, AND SERVE AT HIGH VELOCITY WITHOUT WARNING.
OH, BOY, HERE COMES SUSIE!
HEY, SUSIE!
WHAP!
HA HA! I GOTCHA, YOU DUMB GIRL!!
AUGHH! MY EYEBALL! WHERE'S MY EYEBALL?!
WHAT ARE YOU TALKING ABOUT? I HIT YOU IN THE BACK.
IT KNOCKED MY EYEBALL OUT! FIND IT AND PACK IT IN SNOW SO THEY CAN SAVE IT! OW! OW!
GOSH, DID YOU REALLY LOSE YOUR EYEBALL? I DIDN'T KNOW THEY CAME OUT! WOW. I'M REALLY SORRY. I DIDN'T MEAN TO KNOCK IT OUT. CAN I SEE THE SOCKET? BOY, WHERE DO YOU SUPPOSE IT ROLLED?
WATTERSON
SOMEWHERE OVER THERE, POOP HEAD!!
BOOT
WHAT ARE YOU DOING?
MY EYEBALL FELL OUT. HELP ME LOOK FOR IT.

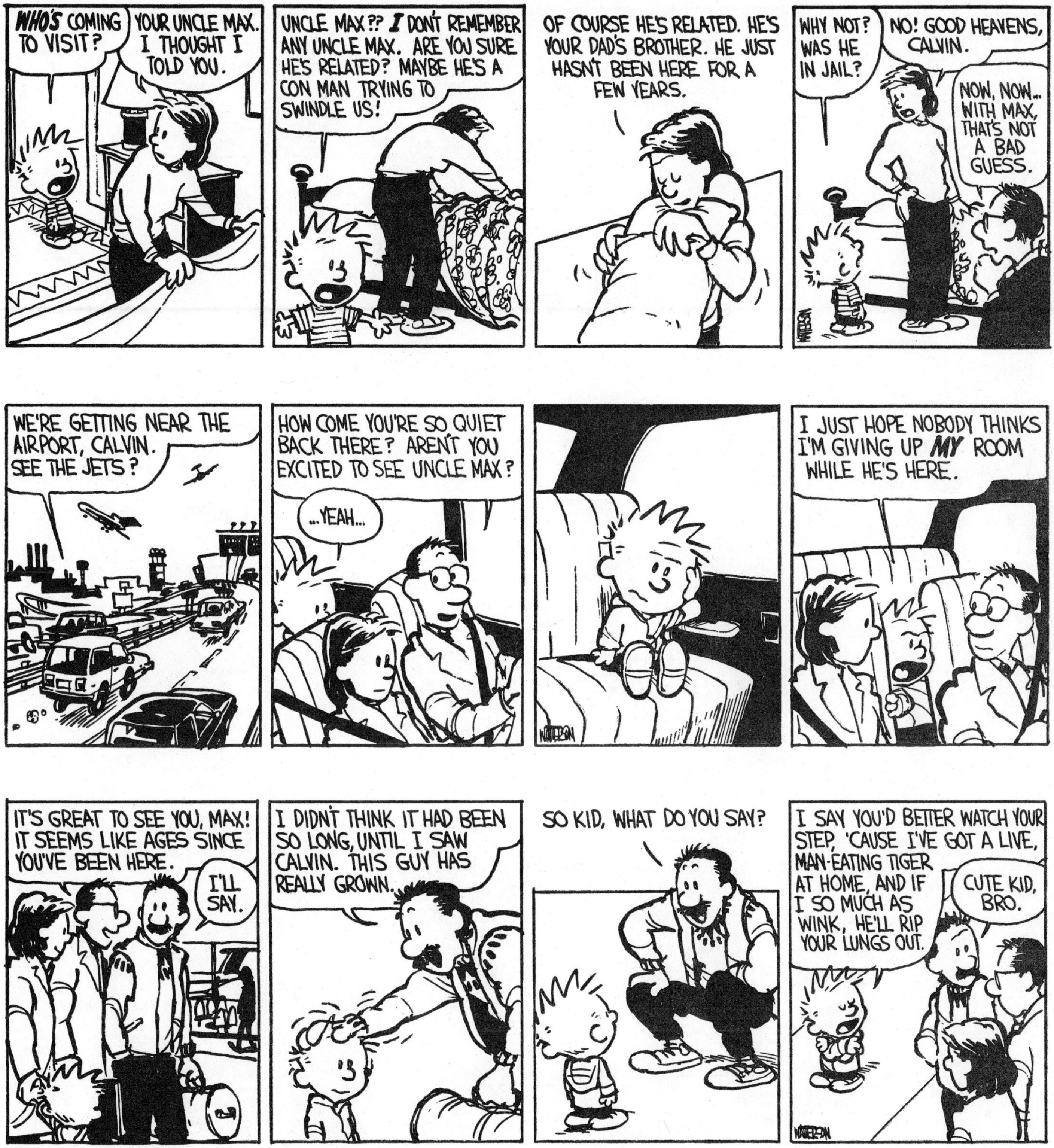
WHO'S COMING TO VISIT?
YOUR UNCLE MAX. I THOUGHT I TOLD YOU.
UNCLE MAX ?? I DON'T REMEMBER ANY UNCLE MAX. ARE YOU SURE HE'S RELATED? MAYBE HE'S A CON MAN TRYING TO SWINDLE US!
OF COURSE HE'S RELATED. HE'S YOUR DAD'S BROTHER. HE JUST HASN'T BEEN HERE FOR A FEW YEARS.
WHY NOT? WAS HE IN JAIL?
NO! GOOD HEAVENS, CALVIN.
NOW, NOW... WITH MAX, THAT'S NOT A BAD GUESS.
WATTERSON
WE'RE GETTING NEAR THE AIRPORT, CALVIN. SEE THE JETS?
HOW COME YOU'RE SO QUIET BACK THERE? AREN'T YOU EXCITED TO SEE UNCLE MAX?
...YEAH...
WATTERSON
I JUST HOPE NOBODY THINKS I'M GIVING UP MY ROOM WHILE HE'S HERE.
IT'S GREAT TO SEE YOU, MAX! IT SEEMS LIKE AGES SINCE YOU'VE BEEN HERE.
I'LL SAY.
I DIDN'T THINK IT HAD BEEN SO LONG, UNTIL I SAW CALVIN. THIS GUY HAS REALLY GROWN.
SO KID, WHAT DO YOU SAY?
I SAY YOU'D BETTER WATCH YOUR STEP, 'CAUSE I'VE GOT A LIVE, MAN-EATING TIGER AT HOME, AND IF I SO MUCH AS WINK, HE'LL RIP YOUR LUNGS OUT.
CUTE KID, BRO.
WATTERSON

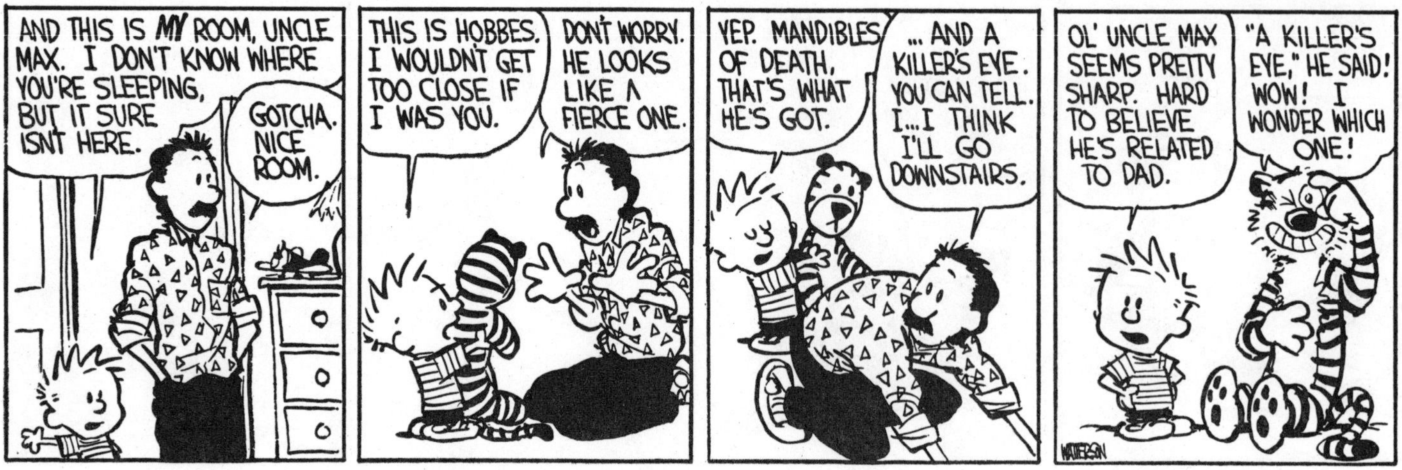
AND THIS IS *MY* ROOM, UNCLE MAX. I DON'T KNOW WHERE YOU'RE SLEEPING, BUT IT SURE ISN'T HERE.
GOTCHA. NICE ROOM.
THIS IS HOBBES. I WOULDN'T GET TOO CLOSE IF I WAS YOU.
DON'T WORRY. HE LOOKS LIKE A FIERCE ONE.
YEP. MANDIBLES OF DEATH, THAT'S WHAT HE'S GOT.
... AND A KILLER'S EYE. YOU CAN TELL. I...I THINK I'LL GO DOWNSTAIRS.
OL' UNCLE MAX SEEMS PRETTY SHARP. HARD TO BELIEVE HE'S RELATED TO DAD.
"A KILLER'S EYE," HE SAID! WOW! I WONDER WHICH ONE!

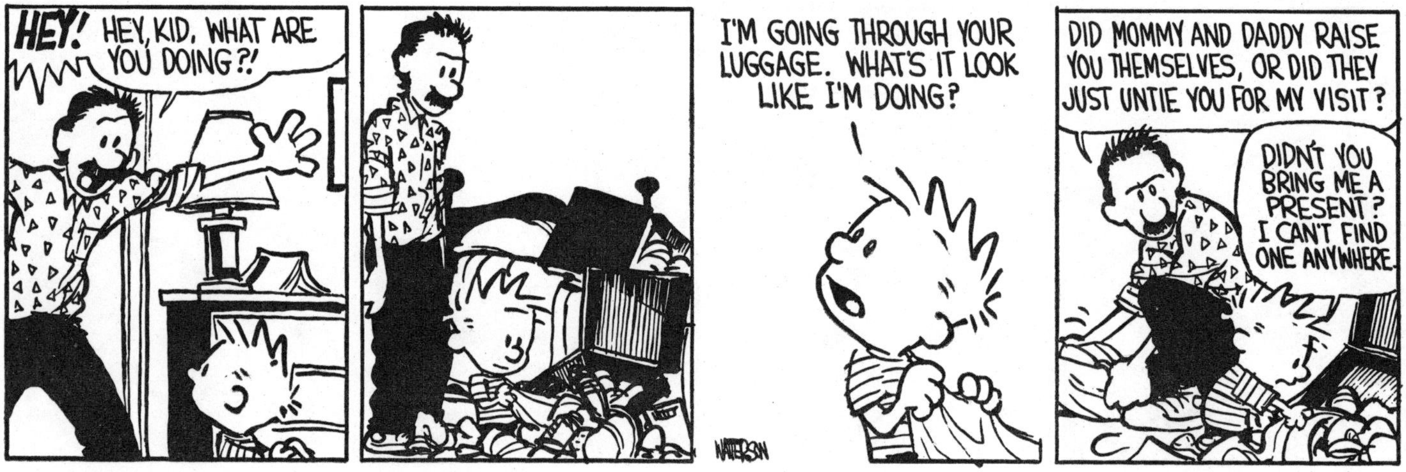
HEY!
HEY, KID, WHAT ARE YOU DOING?!
I'M GOING THROUGH YOUR LUGGAGE. WHAT'S IT LOOK LIKE I'M DOING?
DID MOMMY AND DADDY RAISE YOU THEMSELVES, OR DID THEY JUST UNTIE YOU FOR MY VISIT?
DIDN'T YOU BRING ME A PRESENT? I CAN'T FIND ONE ANYWHERE.

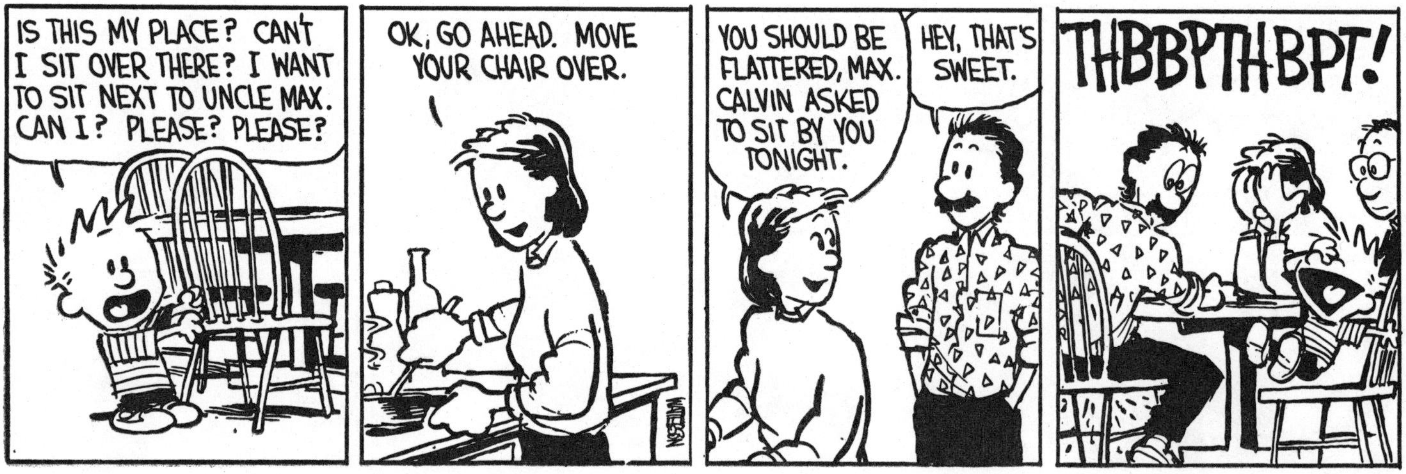
IS THIS MY PLACE? CAN'T I SIT OVER THERE? I WANT TO SIT NEXT TO UNCLE MAX. CAN I? PLEASE? PLEASE?
OK, GO AHEAD. MOVE YOUR CHAIR OVER.
YOU SHOULD BE FLATTERED, MAX. CALVIN ASKED TO SIT BY YOU TONIGHT.
HEY, THAT'S SWEET.
THBBPTHBPT!

Panel 1: DO YOU HAVE ANY KIDS, UNCLE MAX?

Panel 2: ME? NOPE, I'M NOT EVEN MARRIED.

Panel 3: OH.

Panel 4: ...WHAT DIFFERENCE DOES *THAT* MAKE?

KID WATCHES A LOT OF TV, DOES HE?

Panel 5: BOY, CALVIN TAKES THAT STUFFED TIGER EVERYWHERE HE GOES.

YEAH, THEY'RE INSEPARABLE.

Panel 6: DO YOU WORRY ABOUT THAT? I MEAN, SHOULDN'T HE BE PLAYING WITH REAL FRIENDS?

Panel 7: OH, I THINK HE WILL WHEN HE'S READY. DIDN'T YOU EVER HAVE AN IMAGINARY FRIEND?

Panel 8: SOMETIMES I THINK *ALL* MY FRIENDS HAVE BEEN IMAGINARY.

Panel 9: UNCLE MAX, LOOK! I'LL SHOW YOU A MAGIC DISAPPEARING TRICK!

Panel 10: OK, FIRST I'LL NEED AN ORDINARY TWENTY-DOLLAR BILL.

Panel 11: HOW ABOUT IF I LEND YOU A NICKEL INSTEAD?

NO, IT WORKS MUCH BETTER WITH A TWENTY. ...OR A FIFTY, IF YOU HAVE ONE.

Panel 12: I TAKE IT YOU THINK YOUR OL' UNCLE MAX IS A LOW-WATT BULB.

WHY, DID DAD TELL YOU HOW THIS WORKS?

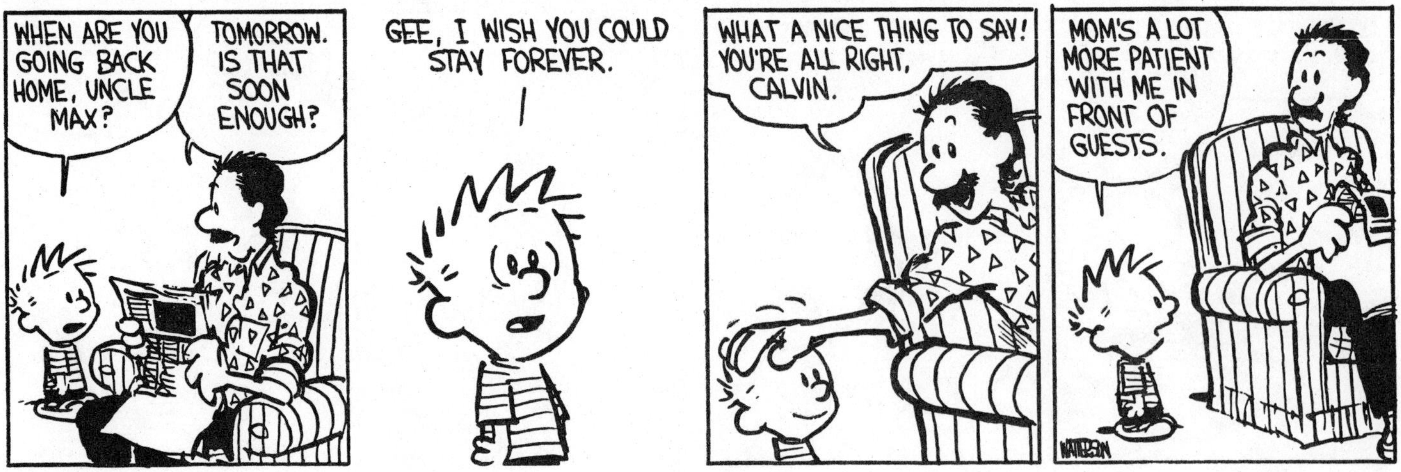
WHEN ARE YOU GOING BACK HOME, UNCLE MAX?
TOMORROW. IS THAT SOON ENOUGH?
GEE, I WISH YOU COULD STAY FOREVER.
WHAT A NICE THING TO SAY! YOU'RE ALL RIGHT, CALVIN.
MOM'S A LOT MORE PATIENT WITH ME IN FRONT OF GUESTS.
WATTERSON

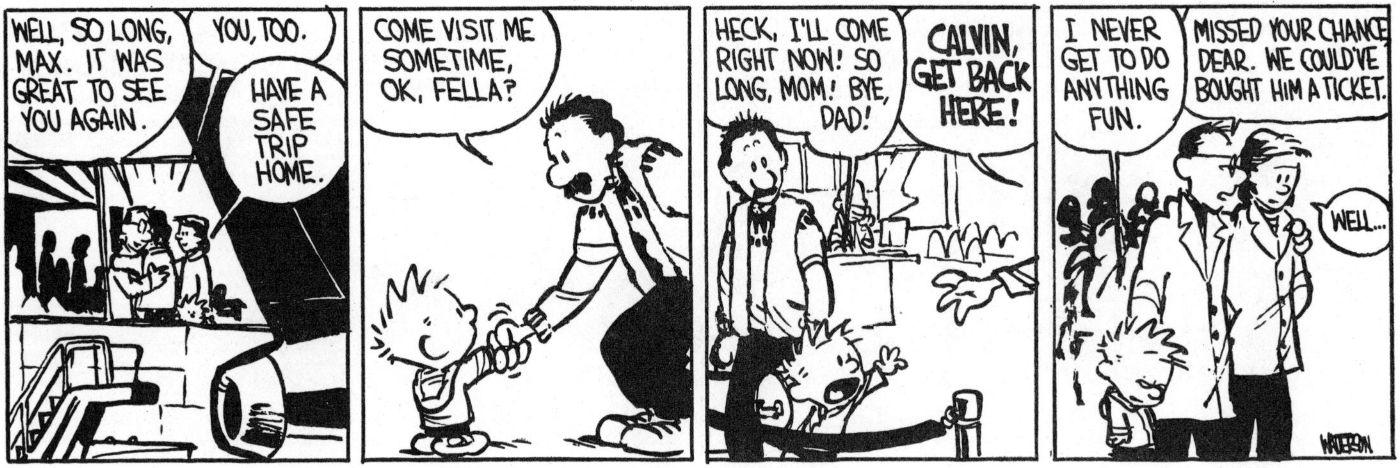
WELL, SO LONG, MAX. IT WAS GREAT TO SEE YOU AGAIN.
YOU, TOO.
HAVE A SAFE TRIP HOME.
COME VISIT ME SOMETIME, OK, FELLA?
HECK, I'LL COME RIGHT NOW! SO LONG, MOM! BYE, DAD!
CALVIN, GET BACK HERE!
I NEVER GET TO DO ANYTHING FUN.
MISSED YOUR CHANCE, DEAR. WE COULD'VE BOUGHT HIM A TICKET.
WELL...
WATTERSON

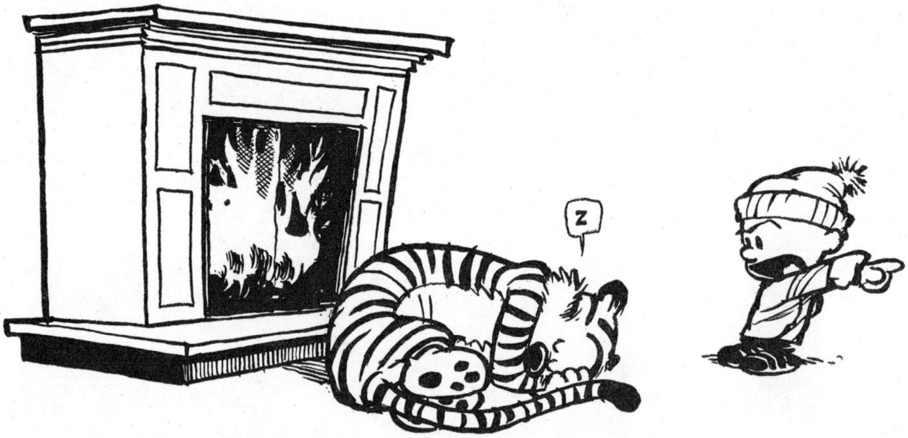
Z

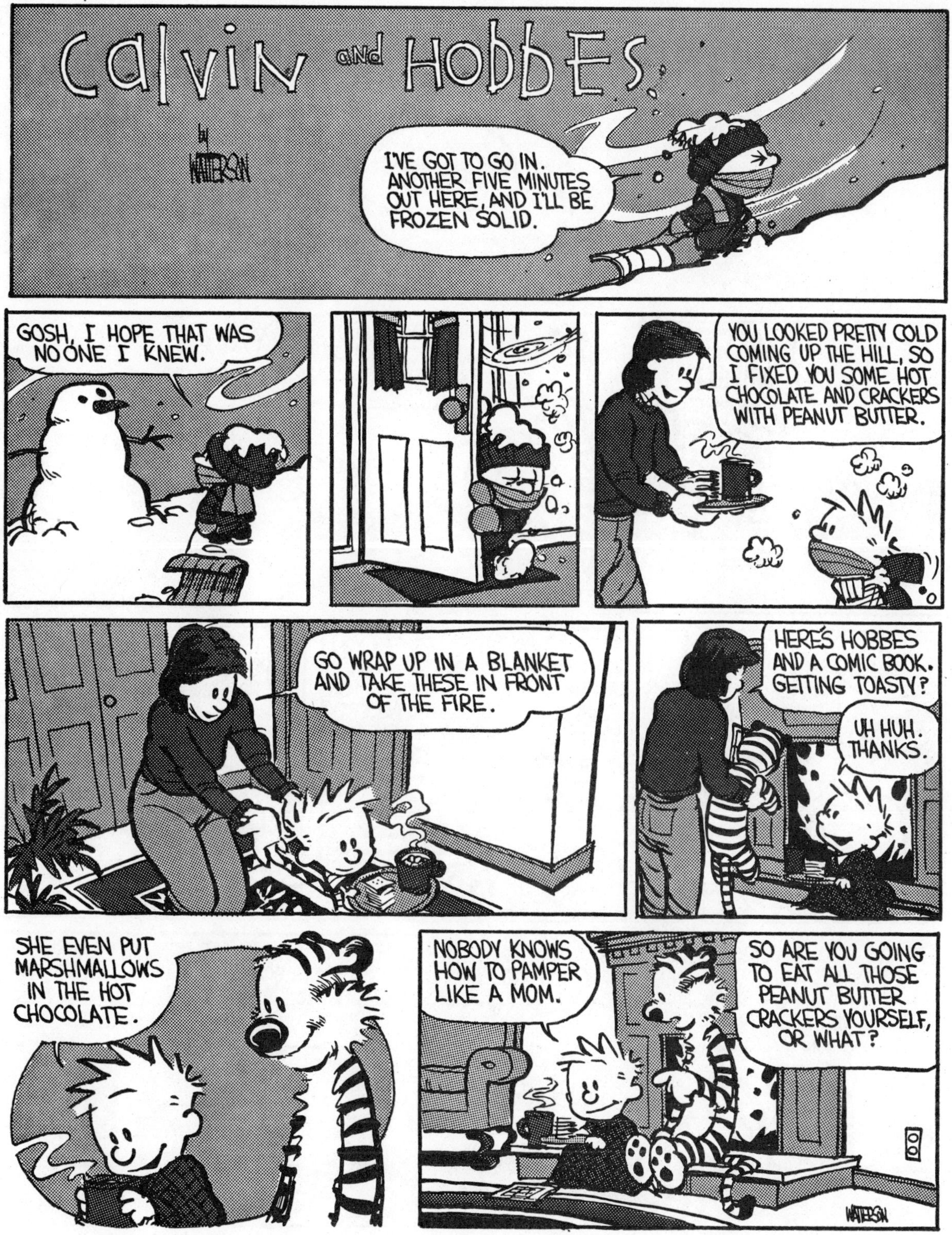
Calvin and HOBBES
by WATTERSON
I'VE GOT TO GO IN. ANOTHER FIVE MINUTES OUT HERE, AND I'LL BE FROZEN SOLID.
GOSH, I HOPE THAT WAS NO ONE I KNEW.
YOU LOOKED PRETTY COLD COMING UP THE HILL, SO I FIXED YOU SOME HOT CHOCOLATE AND CRACKERS WITH PEANUT BUTTER.
GO WRAP UP IN A BLANKET AND TAKE THESE IN FRONT OF THE FIRE.
HERE'S HOBBES AND A COMIC BOOK. GETTING TOASTY?
UH HUH. THANKS.
SHE EVEN PUT MARSHMALLOWS IN THE HOT CHOCOLATE.
NOBODY KNOWS HOW TO PAMPER LIKE A MOM.
SO ARE YOU GOING TO EAT ALL THOSE PEANUT BUTTER CRACKERS YOURSELF, OR WHAT?
WATTERSON

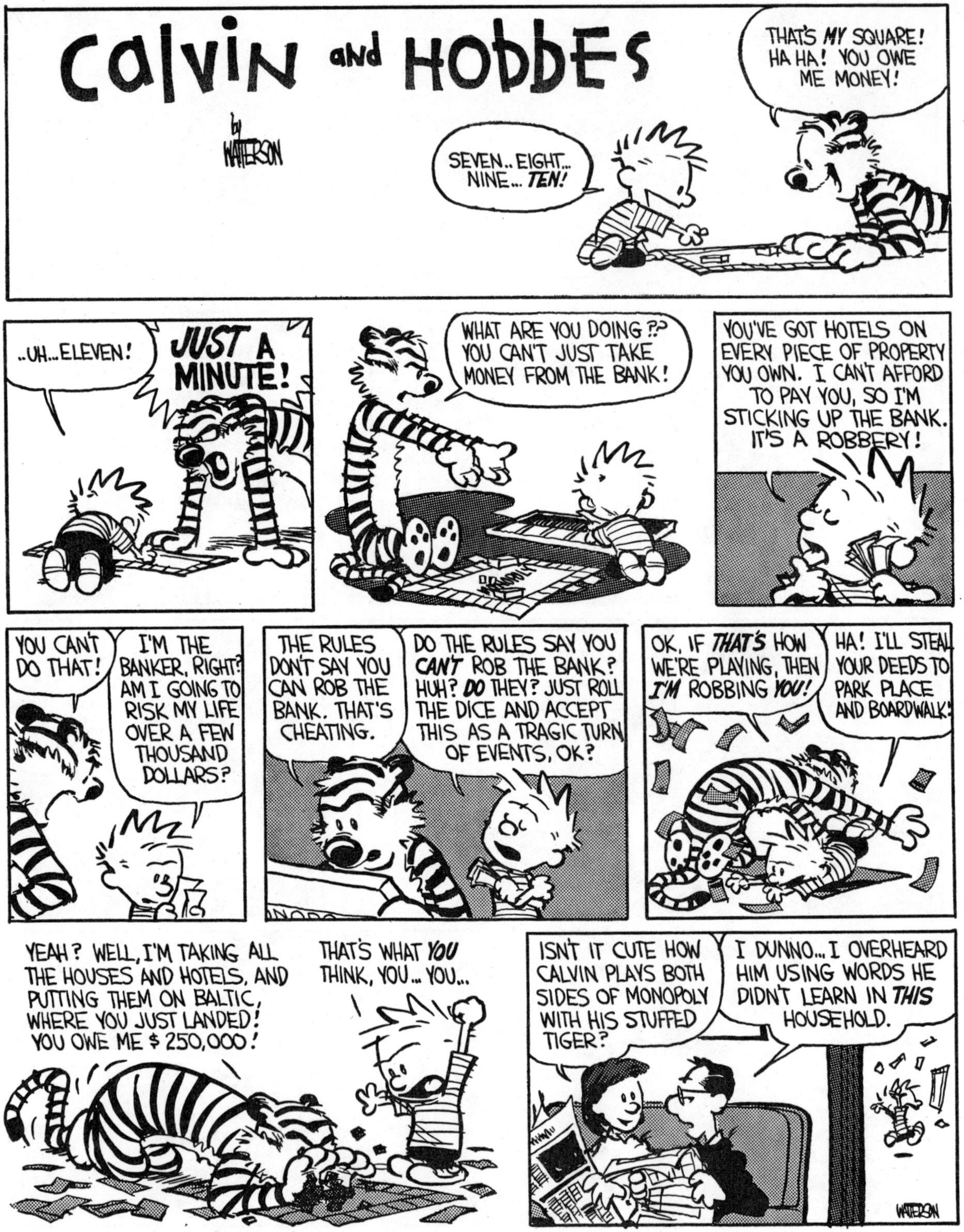
Calvin and HOBBES
by WATTERSON
SEVEN.. EIGHT... NINE... TEN!
THAT'S MY SQUARE! HA HA! YOU OWE ME MONEY!
..UH...ELEVEN!
JUST A MINUTE!
WHAT ARE YOU DOING ?!? YOU CAN'T JUST TAKE MONEY FROM THE BANK!
YOU'VE GOT HOTELS ON EVERY PIECE OF PROPERTY YOU OWN. I CAN'T AFFORD TO PAY YOU, SO I'M STICKING UP THE BANK. IT'S A ROBBERY!
YOU CAN'T DO THAT!
I'M THE BANKER, RIGHT? AM I GOING TO RISK MY LIFE OVER A FEW THOUSAND DOLLARS?
THE RULES DON'T SAY YOU CAN ROB THE BANK. THAT'S CHEATING.
DO THE RULES SAY YOU CAN'T ROB THE BANK? HUH? DO THEY? JUST ROLL THE DICE AND ACCEPT THIS AS A TRAGIC TURN OF EVENTS, OK?
OK, IF THAT'S HOW WE'RE PLAYING, THEN I'M ROBBING YOU!
HA! I'LL STEAL YOUR DEEDS TO PARK PLACE AND BOARDWALK!
YEAH? WELL, I'M TAKING ALL THE HOUSES AND HOTELS, AND PUTTING THEM ON BALTIC, WHERE YOU JUST LANDED! YOU OWE ME $ 250,000!
THAT'S WHAT YOU THINK, YOU... YOU...
ISN'T IT CUTE HOW CALVIN PLAYS BOTH SIDES OF MONOPOLY WITH HIS STUFFED TIGER?
I DUNNO... I OVERHEARD HIM USING WORDS HE DIDN'T LEARN IN THIS HOUSEHOLD.
WATTERSON

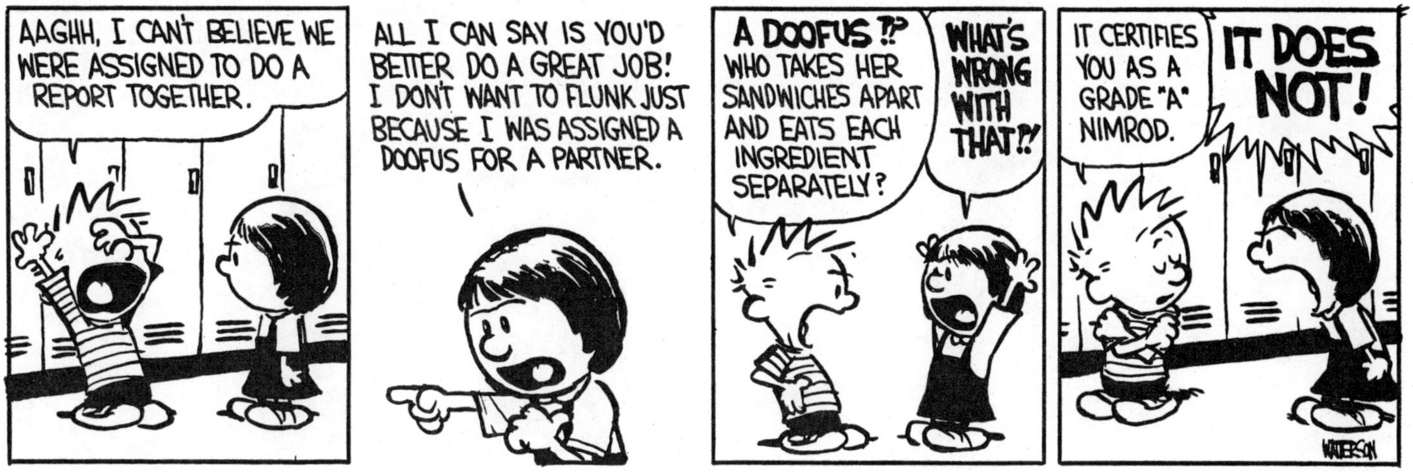
AAGHH, I CAN'T BELIEVE WE WERE ASSIGNED TO DO A REPORT TOGETHER.
ALL I CAN SAY IS YOU'D BETTER DO A GREAT JOB! I DON'T WANT TO FLUNK JUST BECAUSE I WAS ASSIGNED A DOOFUS FOR A PARTNER.
A DOOFUS?!? WHO TAKES HER SANDWICHES APART AND EATS EACH INGREDIENT SEPARATELY?
WHAT'S WRONG WITH THAT?!
IT CERTIFIES YOU AS A GRADE "A" NIMROD.
IT DOES NOT!

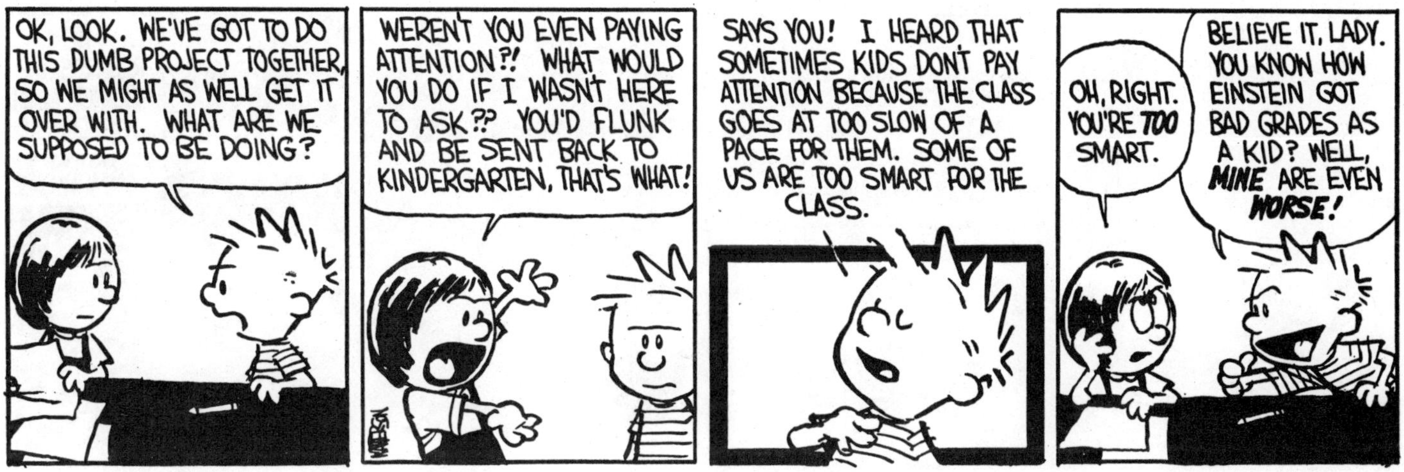
OK, LOOK. WE'VE GOT TO DO THIS DUMB PROJECT TOGETHER, SO WE MIGHT AS WELL GET IT OVER WITH. WHAT ARE WE SUPPOSED TO BE DOING?
WEREN'T YOU EVEN PAYING ATTENTION?! WHAT WOULD YOU DO IF I WASN'T HERE TO ASK?? YOU'D FLUNK AND BE SENT BACK TO KINDERGARTEN, THAT'S WHAT!
SAYS YOU! I HEARD THAT SOMETIMES KIDS DON'T PAY ATTENTION BECAUSE THE CLASS GOES AT TOO SLOW OF A PACE FOR THEM. SOME OF US ARE TOO SMART FOR THE CLASS.
OH, RIGHT. YOU'RE TOO SMART.
BELIEVE IT, LADY. YOU KNOW HOW EINSTEIN GOT BAD GRADES AS A KID? WELL, MINE ARE EVEN WORSE!

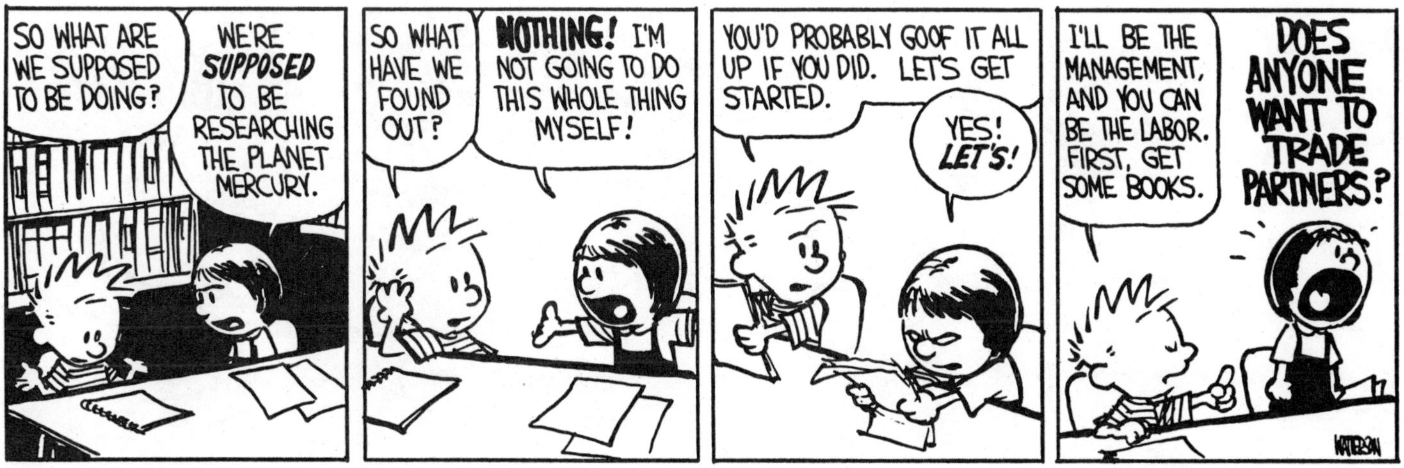
SO WHAT ARE WE SUPPOSED TO BE DOING?
WE'RE SUPPOSED TO BE RESEARCHING THE PLANET MERCURY.
SO WHAT HAVE WE FOUND OUT?
NOTHING! I'M NOT GOING TO DO THIS WHOLE THING MYSELF!
YOU'D PROBABLY GOOF IT ALL UP IF YOU DID. LET'S GET STARTED.
YES! LET'S!
I'LL BE THE MANAGEMENT, AND YOU CAN BE THE LABOR. FIRST, GET SOME BOOKS.
DOES ANYONE WANT TO TRADE PARTNERS?

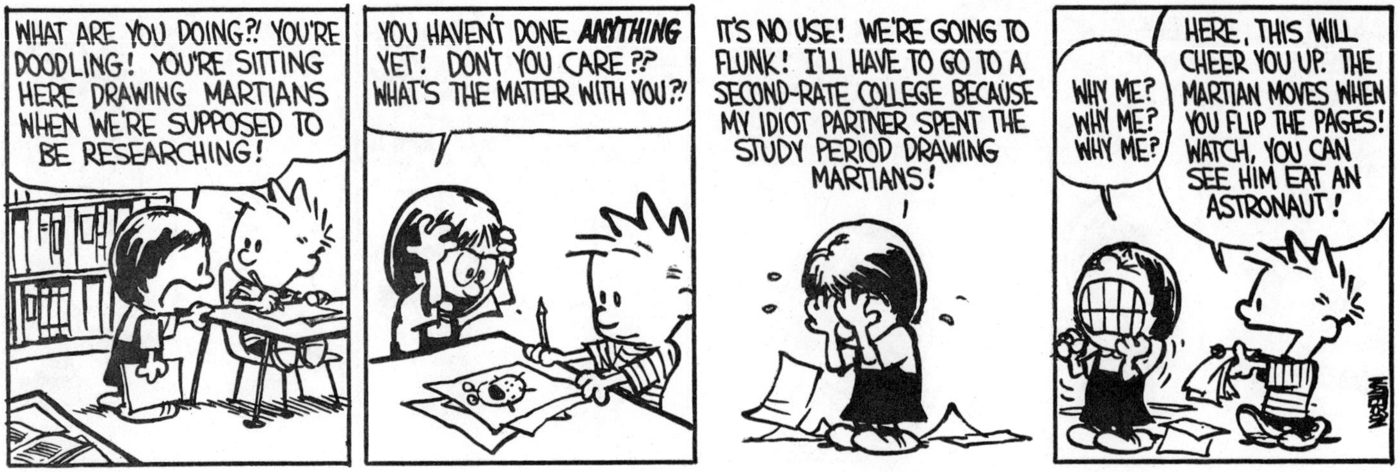
WHAT ARE YOU DOING?! YOU'RE DOODLING! YOU'RE SITTING HERE DRAWING MARTIANS WHEN WE'RE SUPPOSED TO BE RESEARCHING!
YOU HAVEN'T DONE ANYTHING YET! DON'T YOU CARE?? WHAT'S THE MATTER WITH YOU?!
IT'S NO USE! WE'RE GOING TO FLUNK! I'LL HAVE TO GO TO A SECOND-RATE COLLEGE BECAUSE MY IDIOT PARTNER SPENT THE STUDY PERIOD DRAWING MARTIANS!
WHY ME? WHY ME? WHY ME?
HERE, THIS WILL CHEER YOU UP. THE MARTIAN MOVES WHEN YOU FLIP THE PAGES! WATCH, YOU CAN SEE HIM EAT AN ASTRONAUT!

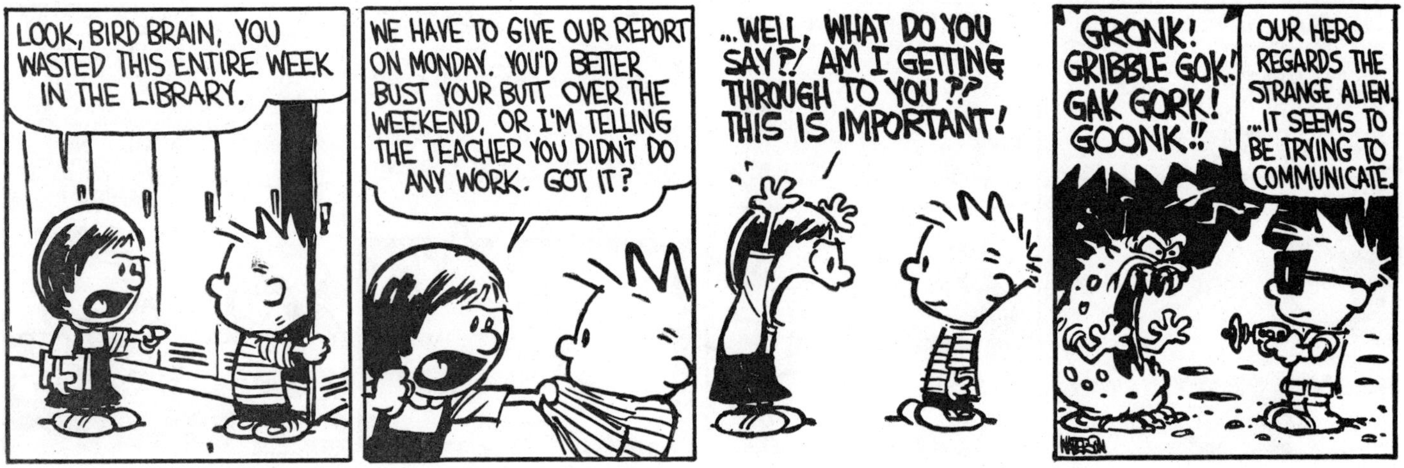
LOOK, BIRD BRAIN, YOU WASTED THIS ENTIRE WEEK IN THE LIBRARY.
WE HAVE TO GIVE OUR REPORT ON MONDAY. YOU'D BETTER BUST YOUR BUTT OVER THE WEEKEND, OR I'M TELLING THE TEACHER YOU DIDN'T DO ANY WORK. GOT IT?
...WELL, WHAT DO YOU SAY?! AM I GETTING THROUGH TO YOU?? THIS IS IMPORTANT!
GRONK! GRIBBLE GOK! GAK GORK! GOONK!!
OUR HERO REGARDS THE STRANGE ALIEN. ...IT SEEMS TO BE TRYING TO COMMUNICATE.

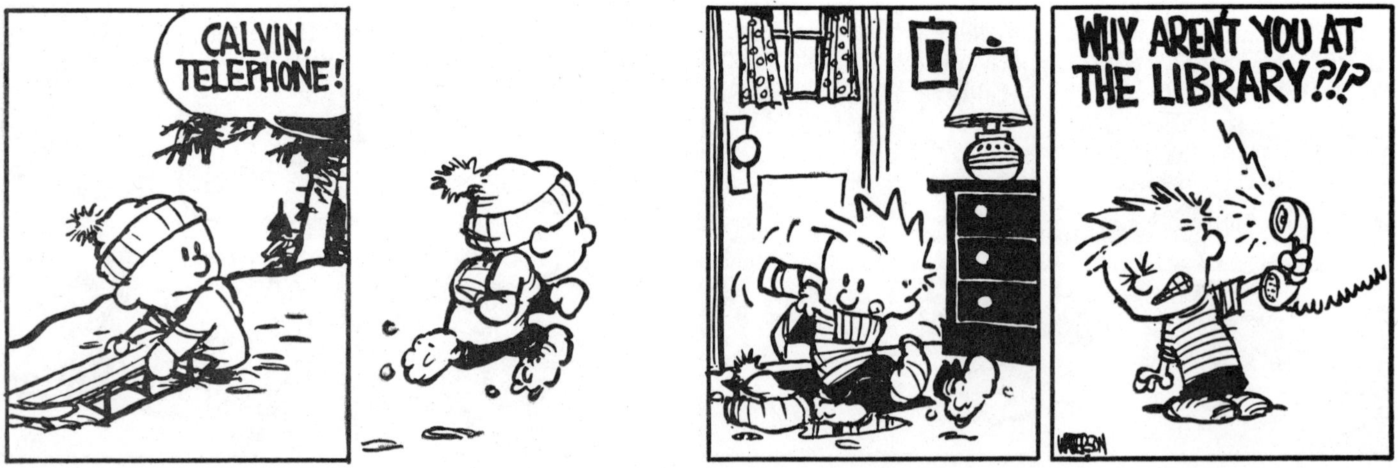
CALVIN, TELEPHONE!
WHY AREN'T YOU AT THE LIBRARY?!?

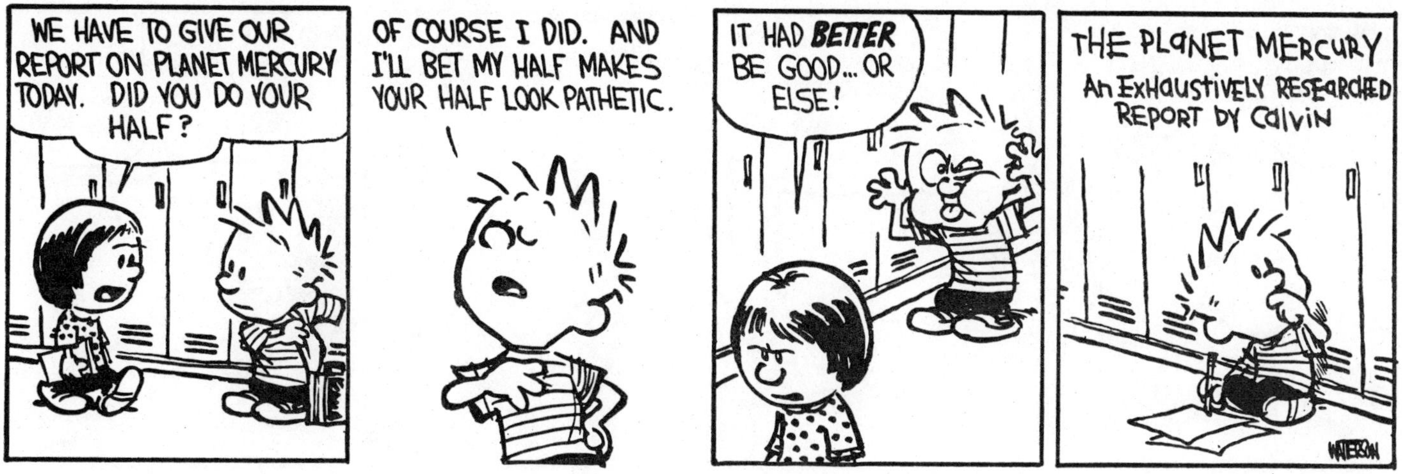
WE HAVE TO GIVE OUR REPORT ON PLANET MERCURY TODAY. DID YOU DO YOUR HALF?
OF COURSE I DID. AND I'LL BET MY HALF MAKES YOUR HALF LOOK PATHETIC.
IT HAD BETTER BE GOOD... OR ELSE!
THE PLANET MERCURY
An Exhaustively Researched Report by Calvin
WATTERSON

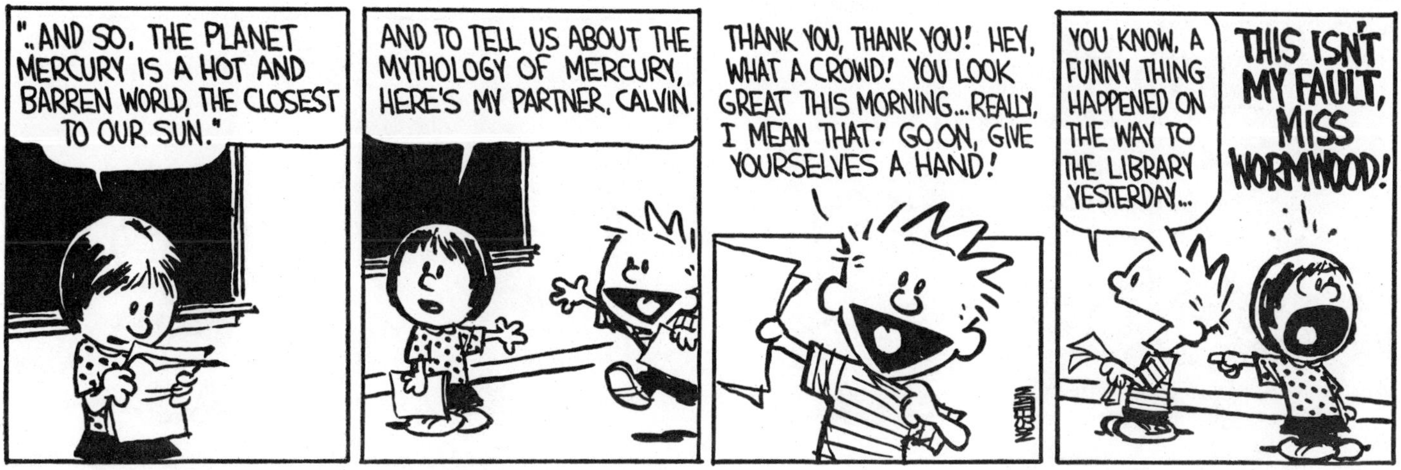
"..AND SO, THE PLANET MERCURY IS A HOT AND BARREN WORLD, THE CLOSEST TO OUR SUN."
AND TO TELL US ABOUT THE MYTHOLOGY OF MERCURY, HERE'S MY PARTNER, CALVIN.
THANK YOU, THANK YOU! HEY, WHAT A CROWD! YOU LOOK GREAT THIS MORNING...REALLY, I MEAN THAT! GO ON, GIVE YOURSELVES A HAND!
WATTERSON
YOU KNOW, A FUNNY THING HAPPENED ON THE WAY TO THE LIBRARY YESTERDAY...
THIS ISN'T MY FAULT, MISS WORMWOOD!

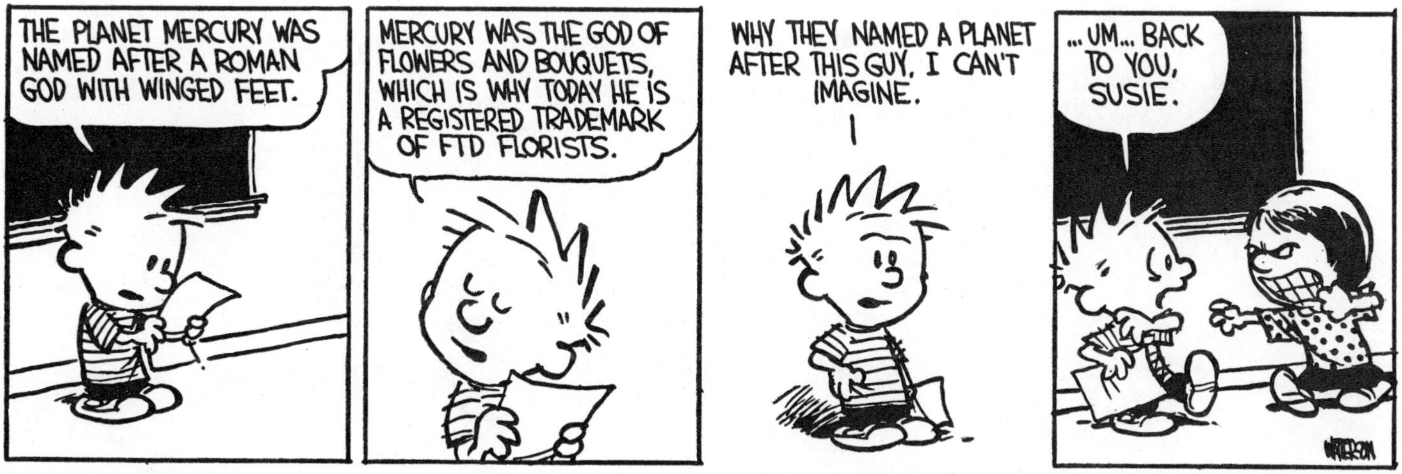
THE PLANET MERCURY WAS NAMED AFTER A ROMAN GOD WITH WINGED FEET.
MERCURY WAS THE GOD OF FLOWERS AND BOUQUETS, WHICH IS WHY TODAY HE IS A REGISTERED TRADEMARK OF FTD FLORISTS.
WHY THEY NAMED A PLANET AFTER THIS GUY, I CAN'T IMAGINE.
...UM... BACK TO YOU, SUSIE.
WATTERSON

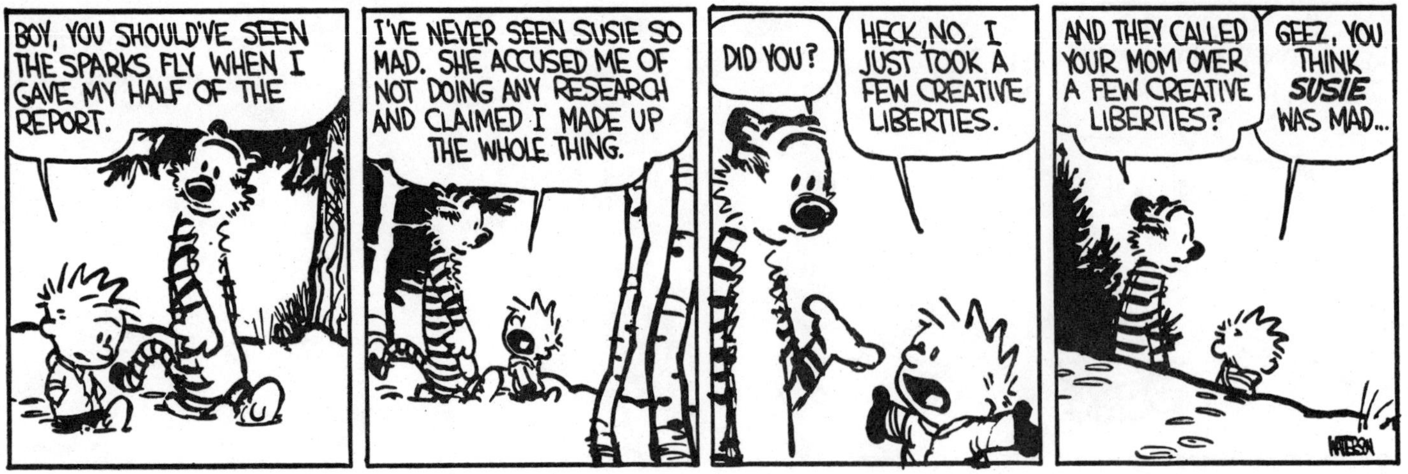
BOY, YOU SHOULD'VE SEEN THE SPARKS FLY WHEN I GAVE MY HALF OF THE REPORT.
I'VE NEVER SEEN SUSIE SO MAD. SHE ACCUSED ME OF NOT DOING ANY RESEARCH AND CLAIMED I MADE UP THE WHOLE THING.
DID YOU?
HECK, NO. I JUST TOOK A FEW CREATIVE LIBERTIES.
AND THEY CALLED YOUR MOM OVER A FEW CREATIVE LIBERTIES?
GEEZ, YOU THINK SUSIE WAS MAD...

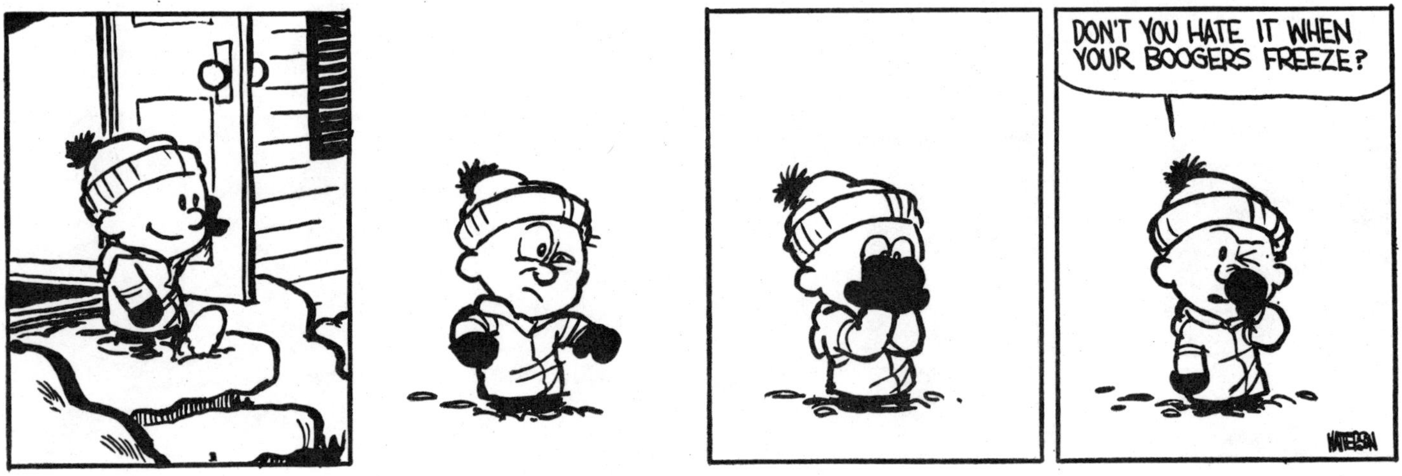
DON'T YOU HATE IT WHEN YOUR BOOGERS FREEZE?

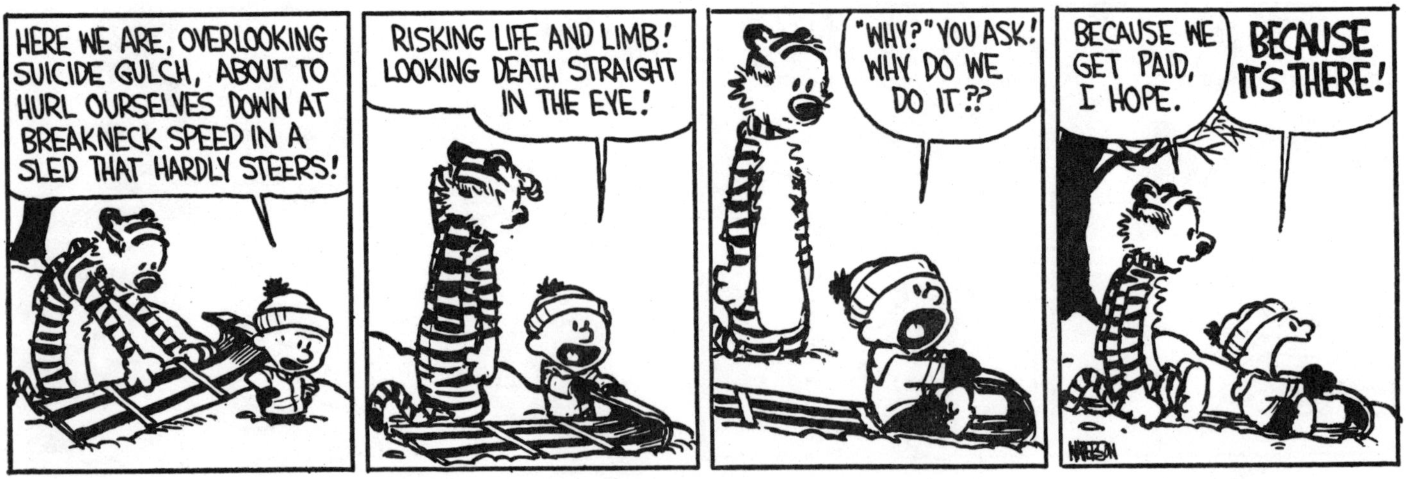
HERE WE ARE, OVERLOOKING SUICIDE GULCH, ABOUT TO HURL OURSELVES DOWN AT BREAKNECK SPEED IN A SLED THAT HARDLY STEERS!
RISKING LIFE AND LIMB! LOOKING DEATH STRAIGHT IN THE EYE!
"WHY?" YOU ASK! WHY DO WE DO IT??
BECAUSE WE GET PAID, I HOPE.
BECAUSE IT'S THERE!

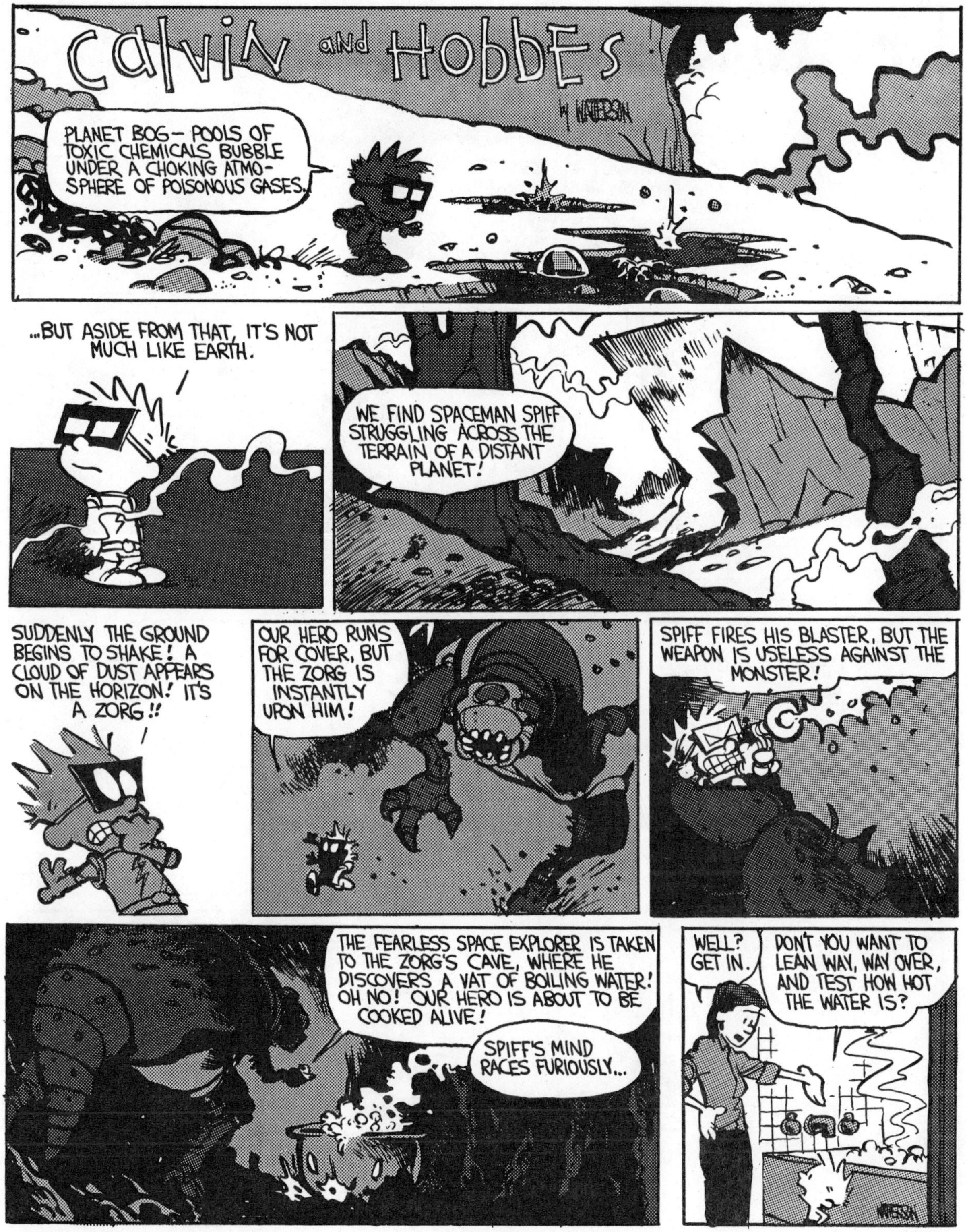
Calvin and Hobbes
by WATTERSON
PLANET BOG— POOLS OF TOXIC CHEMICALS BUBBLE UNDER A CHOKING ATMOSPHERE OF POISONOUS GASES...
...BUT ASIDE FROM THAT, IT'S NOT MUCH LIKE EARTH.
WE FIND SPACEMAN SPIFF STRUGGLING ACROSS THE TERRAIN OF A DISTANT PLANET!
SUDDENLY THE GROUND BEGINS TO SHAKE! A CLOUD OF DUST APPEARS ON THE HORIZON! IT'S A ZORG!!
OUR HERO RUNS FOR COVER, BUT THE ZORG IS INSTANTLY UPON HIM!
SPIFF FIRES HIS BLASTER, BUT THE WEAPON IS USELESS AGAINST THE MONSTER!
THE FEARLESS SPACE EXPLORER IS TAKEN TO THE ZORG'S CAVE, WHERE HE DISCOVERS A VAT OF BOILING WATER! OH NO! OUR HERO IS ABOUT TO BE COOKED ALIVE!
SPIFF'S MIND RACES FURIOUSLY...
WELL? GET IN.
DON'T YOU WANT TO LEAN WAY, WAY OVER, AND TEST HOW HOT THE WATER IS?

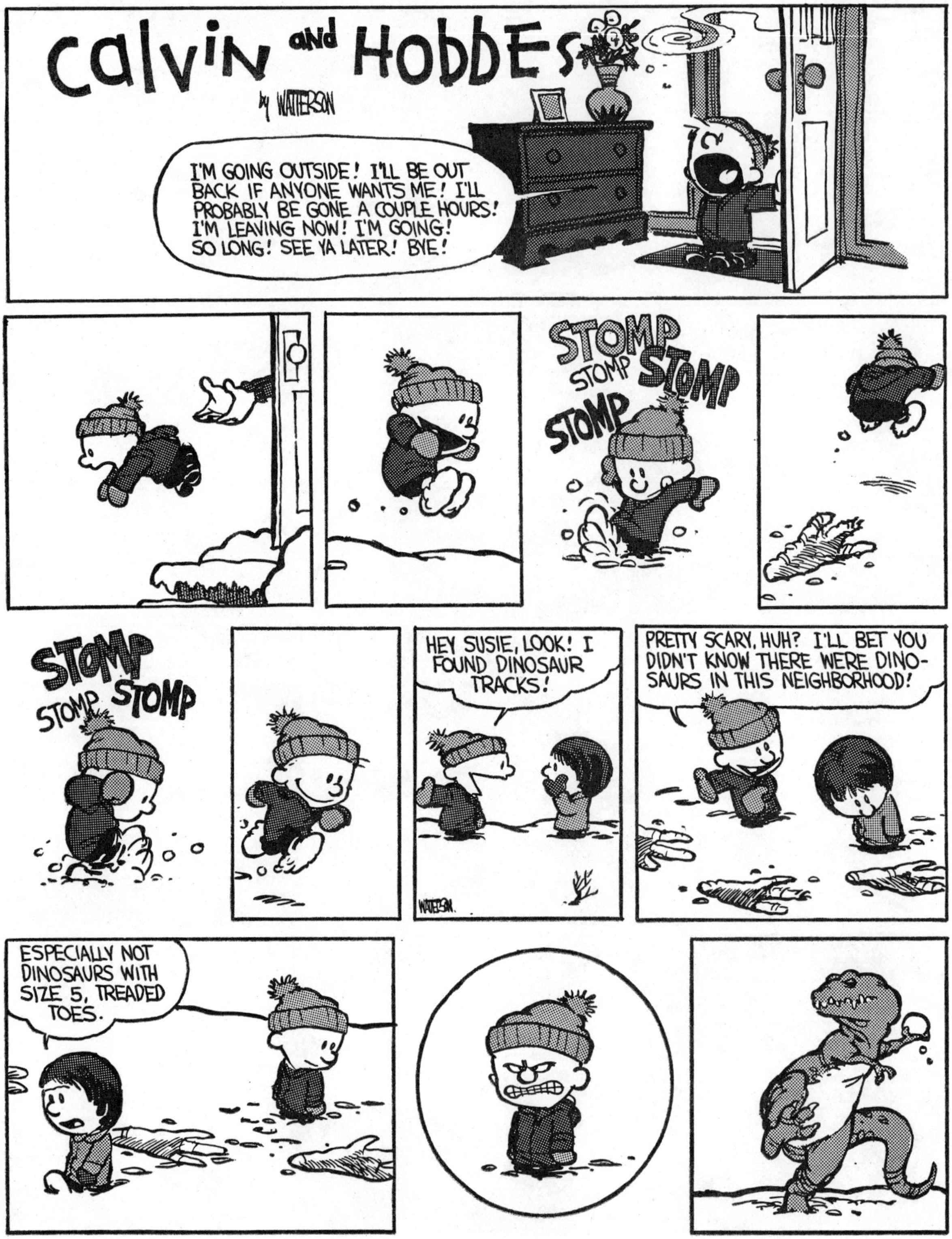
Calvin and HOBBES
by WATTERSON
I'M GOING OUTSIDE! I'LL BE OUT BACK IF ANYONE WANTS ME! I'LL PROBABLY BE GONE A COUPLE HOURS! I'M LEAVING NOW! I'M GOING! SO LONG! SEE YA LATER! BYE!
STOMP STOMP STOMP STOMP
STOMP STOMP STOMP
HEY SUSIE, LOOK! I FOUND DINOSAUR TRACKS!
WATTERSON
PRETTY SCARY, HUH? I'LL BET YOU DIDN'T KNOW THERE WERE DINOSAURS IN THIS NEIGHBORHOOD!
ESPECIALLY NOT DINOSAURS WITH SIZE 5, TREADED TOES.

Panel 1: LOOK, HOBBES, THE LATEST PERFECTION IN TECHNOLOGY.

A WATER PISTOL?

Panel 2: HECK, NO! THIS IS THE NEW, IMPROVED VERSION OF THE TRANSMOGRIFIER.

Panel 3: NOW YOU CAN TRANSMOGRIFY THINGS JUST BY POINTING AT THEM! SAY YOU DON'T LIKE THE COLOR OF YOUR BEDSPREAD. WELL, YOU JUST ZAP IT, AND PRESTO, IT'S AN IGUANA!

Panel 4: ONE CAN CERTAINLY IMAGINE THE MYRIAD OF USES FOR A HAND-HELD IGUANA MAKER.

IT DOESN'T *HAVE* TO BE AN IGUANA. IT CAN BE ANYTHING. SUPPOSE MOM'S GETTING ON OUR NERVES, FOR INSTANCE...

Panel 5: HOW DOES THIS TRANSMOGRIFIER GUN KNOW WHAT TO TRANSMOGRIFY SOMETHING INTO?

TELEPATHY.

Panel 6: THE GUN AUTOMATICALLY READS THE BRAIN WAVES YOU EMIT, AND TURNS THE OBJECT INTO WHATEVER YOU WANT.

Panel 7: THAT'S AMAZING.

WELL, IT TOOK ME ALL MORNING TO INVENT.

Panel 8: SO SAY I'M THINKING ABOUT A BIG SLAB OF GRILLED TUNA NOW...

WATCH WHERE YOU'RE POINTING THAT! WATCH WHERE YOU'RE POINTING THAT!

Panel 9: OK, LET'S TEST THIS TRANSMOGRIFIER GUN.

Panel 10: I WANT TO BE A PTERODACTYL, SO YOU THINK OF ONE AND POINT THE TRANSMOGRIFIER AT ME.

Panel 11: THIS WILL BE GREAT. I'LL TERRORIZE THE NEIGHBORHOOD AWHILE AND THEN YOU CAN TRANSMOGRIFY ME BACK TO A BOY WHEN THE NATIONAL GUARD COMES.

Panel 12: WHAT'S A PTERODACTYL? SOME KIND OF BUG?

NO NO! IT'S A BIG FLYING DINOSAUR! DON'T SHOOT IF YOU DON'T KNOW WHAT IT IS!!

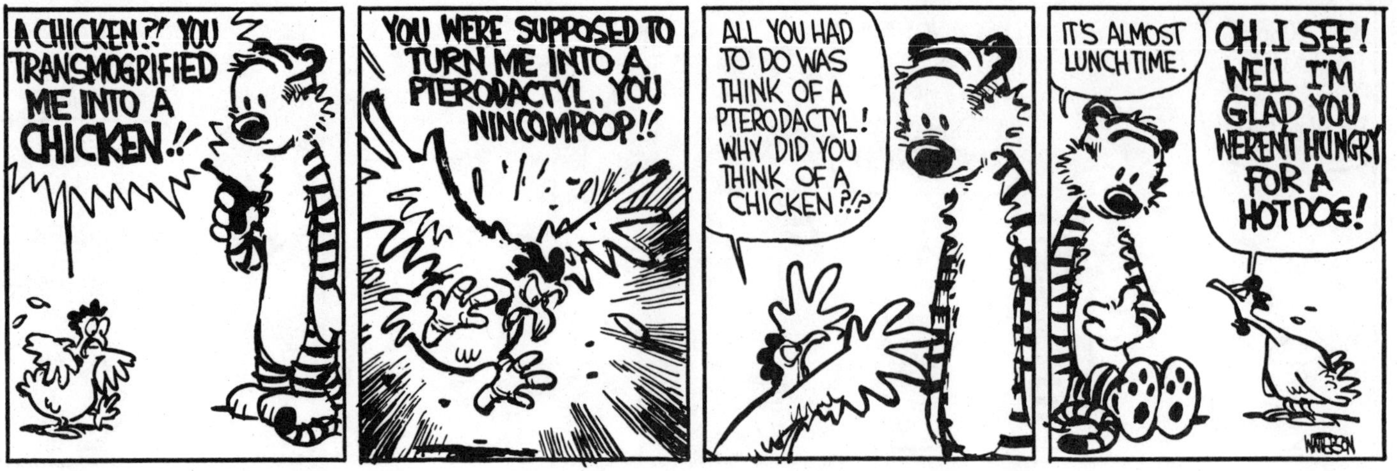
A CHICKEN?! YOU TRANSMOGRIFIED ME INTO A CHICKEN!!
YOU WERE SUPPOSED TO TURN ME INTO A PTERODACTYL, YOU NINCOMPOOP!!
ALL YOU HAD TO DO WAS THINK OF A PTERODACTYL! WHY DID YOU THINK OF A CHICKEN?!?
IT'S ALMOST LUNCHTIME.
OH, I SEE! WELL I'M GLAD YOU WEREN'T HUNGRY FOR A HOT DOG!

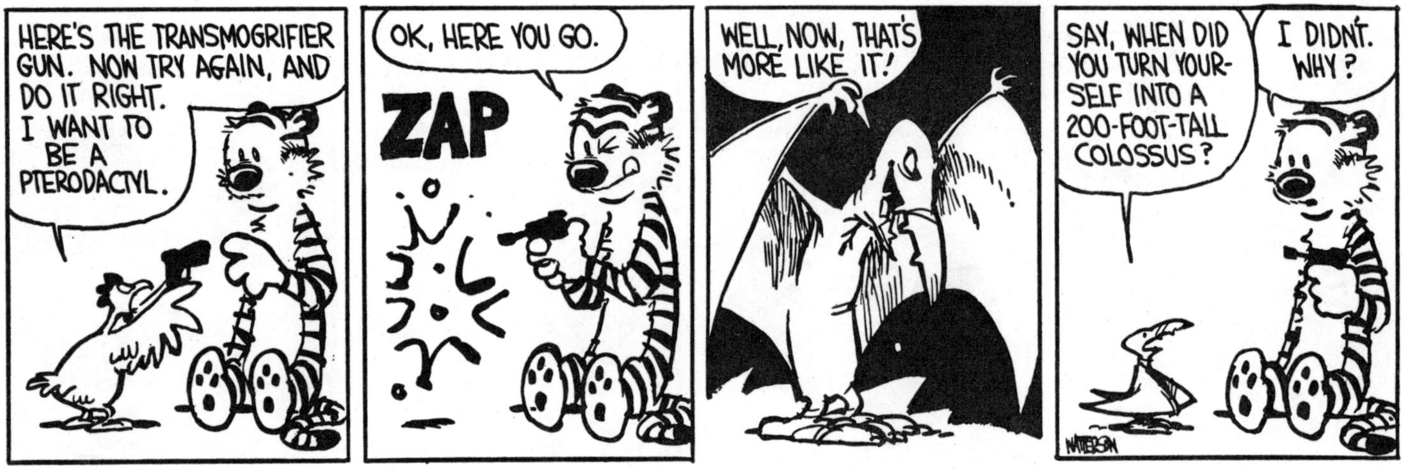
HERE'S THE TRANSMOGRIFIER GUN. NOW TRY AGAIN, AND DO IT RIGHT. I WANT TO BE A PTERODACTYL.
OK, HERE YOU GO.
ZAP
WELL, NOW, THAT'S MORE LIKE IT!
SAY, WHEN DID YOU TURN YOURSELF INTO A 200-FOOT-TALL COLOSSUS?
I DIDN'T. WHY?

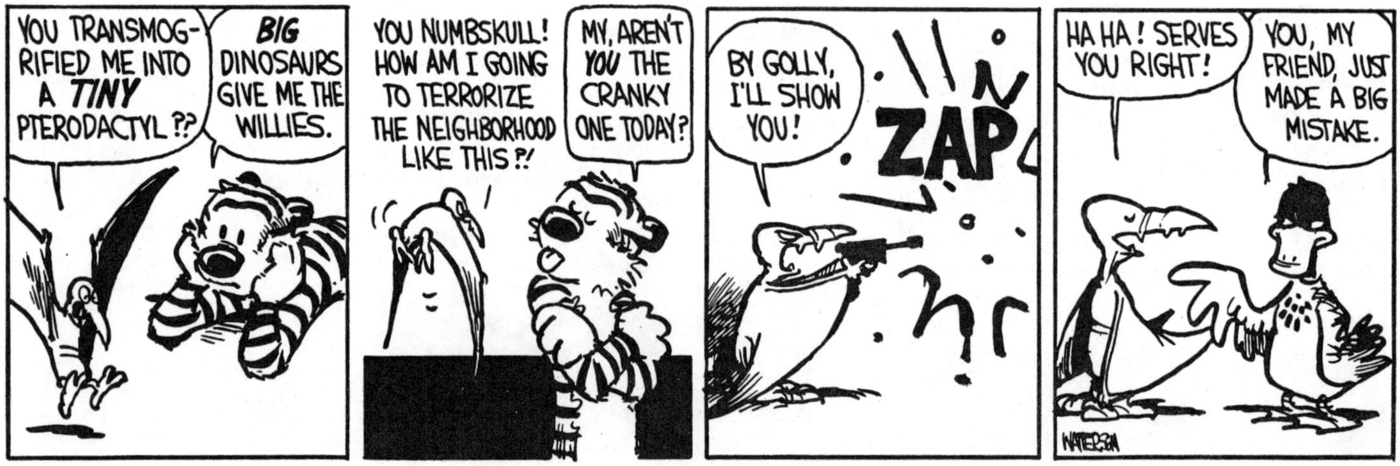
YOU TRANSMOGRIFIED ME INTO A *TINY* PTERODACTYL?!
BIG DINOSAURS GIVE ME THE WILLIES.
YOU NUMBSKULL! HOW AM I GOING TO TERRORIZE THE NEIGHBORHOOD LIKE THIS?!
MY, AREN'T *YOU* THE CRANKY ONE TODAY?
BY GOLLY, I'LL SHOW YOU!
ZAP
HA HA! SERVES YOU RIGHT!
YOU, MY FRIEND, JUST MADE A BIG MISTAKE.

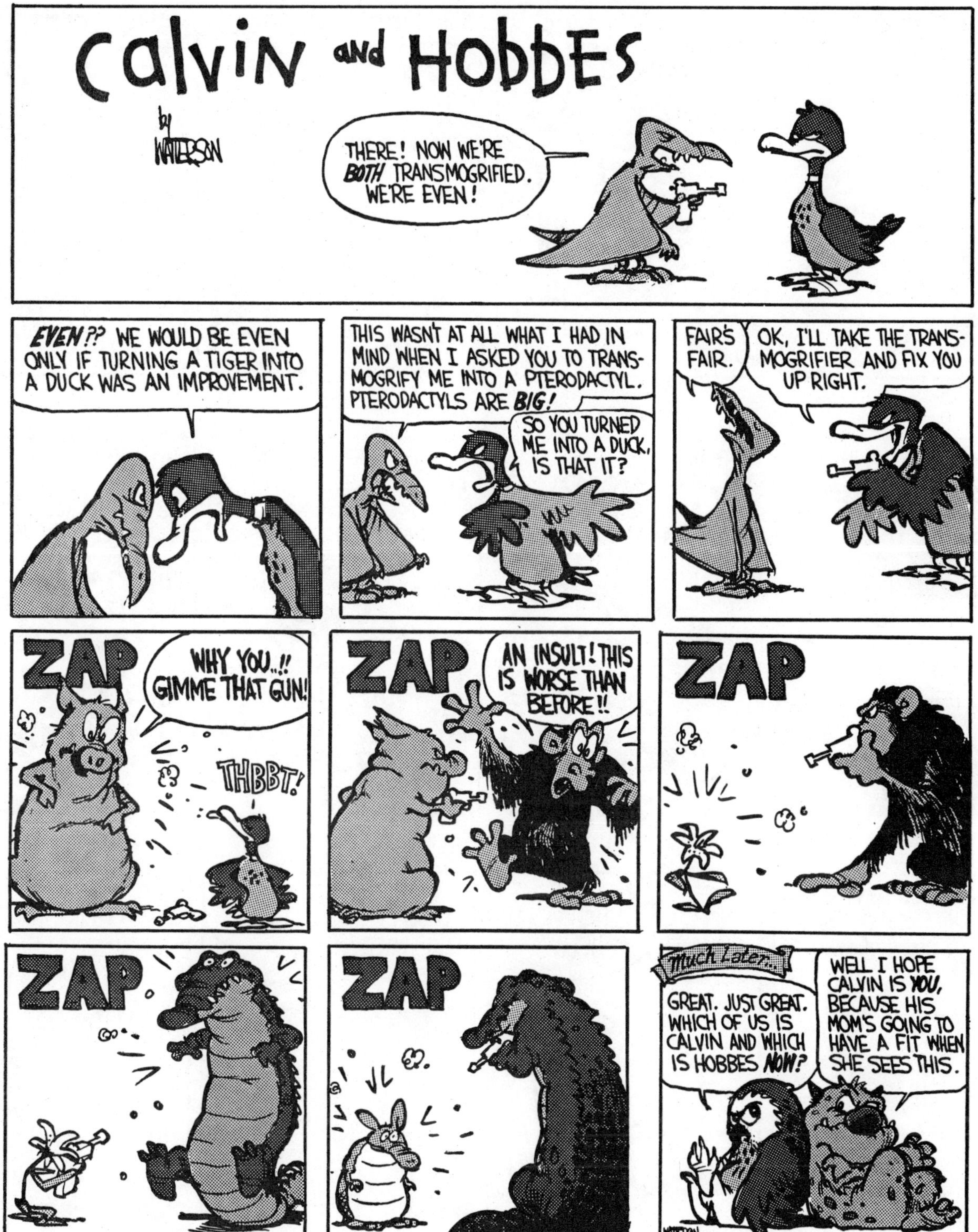
Calvin and HOBBES
by WATTERSON
THERE! NOW WE'RE BOTH TRANSMOGRIFIED. WE'RE EVEN!
EVEN?? WE WOULD BE EVEN ONLY IF TURNING A TIGER INTO A DUCK WAS AN IMPROVEMENT.
THIS WASN'T AT ALL WHAT I HAD IN MIND WHEN I ASKED YOU TO TRANSMOGRIFY ME INTO A PTERODACTYL. PTERODACTYLS ARE BIG!
SO YOU TURNED ME INTO A DUCK, IS THAT IT?
FAIR'S FAIR.
OK, I'LL TAKE THE TRANSMOGRIFIER AND FIX YOU UP RIGHT.
ZAP
WHY YOU..!! GIMME THAT GUN!
THBBT!
ZAP
AN INSULT! THIS IS WORSE THAN BEFORE!!
ZAP
ZAP
ZAP
Much Later...
GREAT. JUST GREAT. WHICH OF US IS CALVIN AND WHICH IS HOBBES NOW?
WELL I HOPE CALVIN IS YOU, BECAUSE HIS MOM'S GOING TO HAVE A FIT WHEN SHE SEES THIS.
WATTERSON

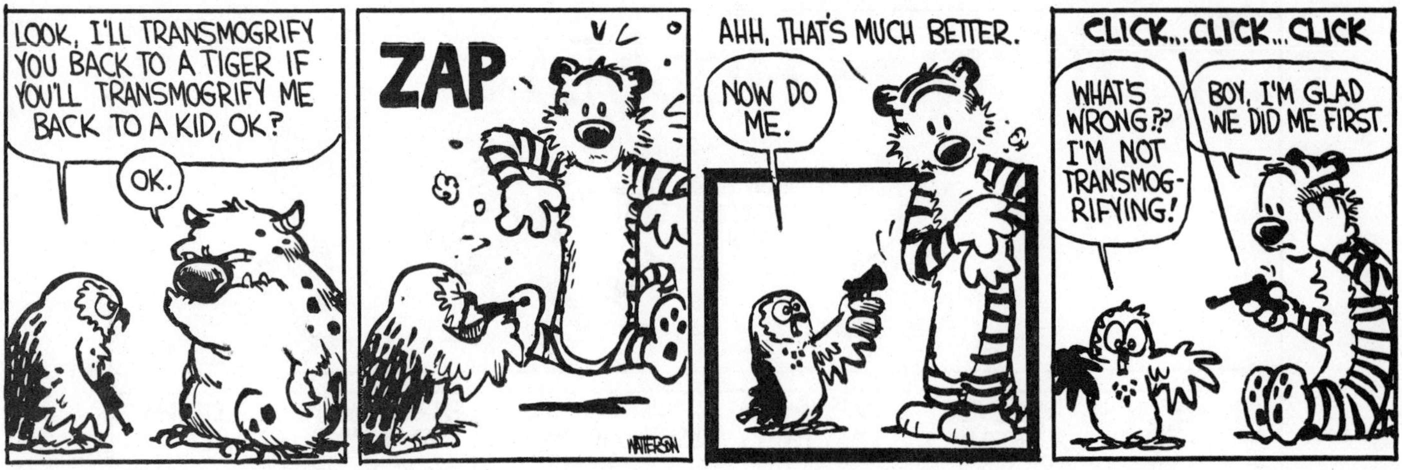
LOOK, I'LL TRANSMOGRIFY YOU BACK TO A TIGER IF YOU'LL TRANSMOGRIFY ME BACK TO A KID, OK?
OK.
ZAP
AHH, THAT'S MUCH BETTER.
NOW DO ME.
CLICK...CLICK...CLICK
WHAT'S WRONG?? I'M NOT TRANSMOG-RIFYING!
BOY, I'M GLAD WE DID ME FIRST.

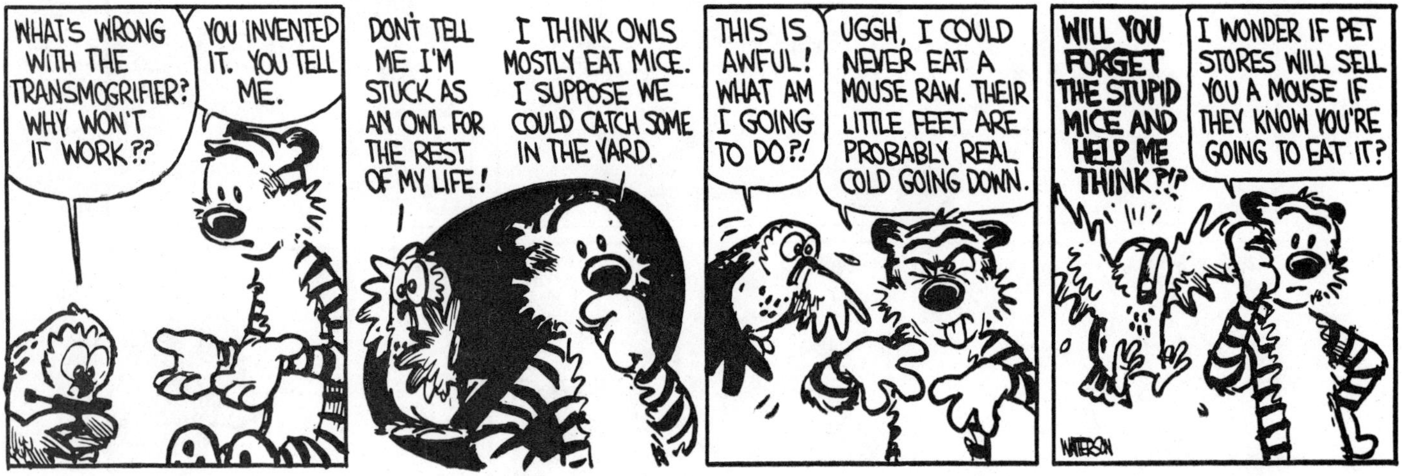
WHAT'S WRONG WITH THE TRANSMOGRIFIER? WHY WON'T IT WORK??
YOU INVENTED IT. YOU TELL ME.
DON'T TELL ME I'M STUCK AS AN OWL FOR THE REST OF MY LIFE!
I THINK OWLS MOSTLY EAT MICE. I SUPPOSE WE COULD CATCH SOME IN THE YARD.
THIS IS AWFUL! WHAT AM I GOING TO DO?!
UGGH, I COULD NEVER EAT A MOUSE RAW. THEIR LITTLE FEET ARE PROBABLY REAL COLD GOING DOWN.
WILL YOU FORGET THE STUPID MICE AND HELP ME THINK?!?
I WONDER IF PET STORES WILL SELL YOU A MOUSE IF THEY KNOW YOU'RE GOING TO EAT IT?

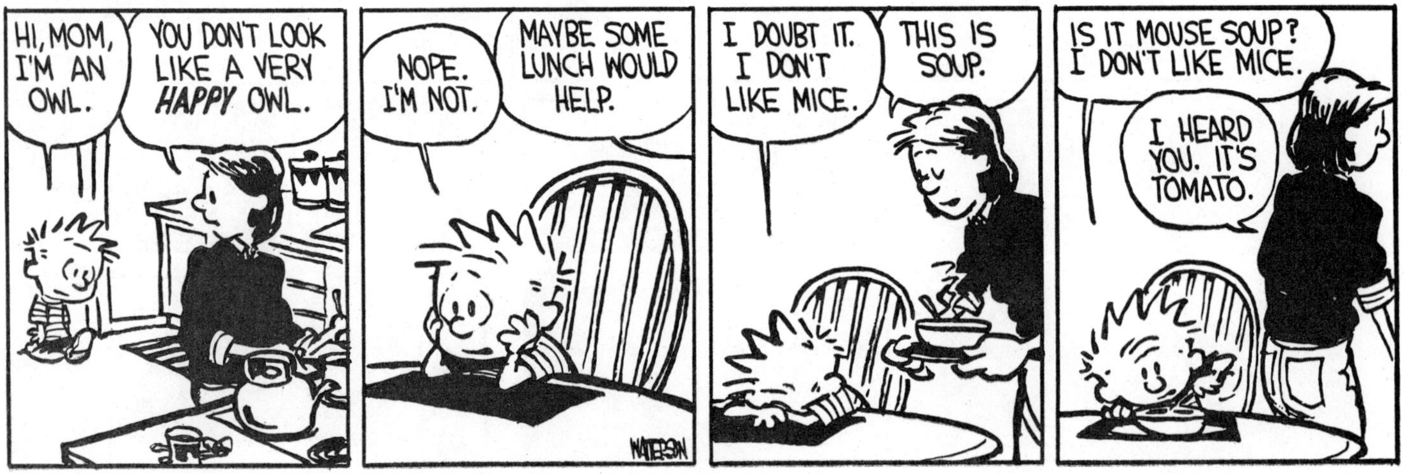
HI, MOM, I'M AN OWL.
YOU DON'T LOOK LIKE A VERY HAPPY OWL.
NOPE. I'M NOT.
MAYBE SOME LUNCH WOULD HELP.
I DOUBT IT. I DON'T LIKE MICE.
THIS IS SOUP.
IS IT MOUSE SOUP? I DON'T LIKE MICE.
I HEARD YOU. IT'S TOMATO.

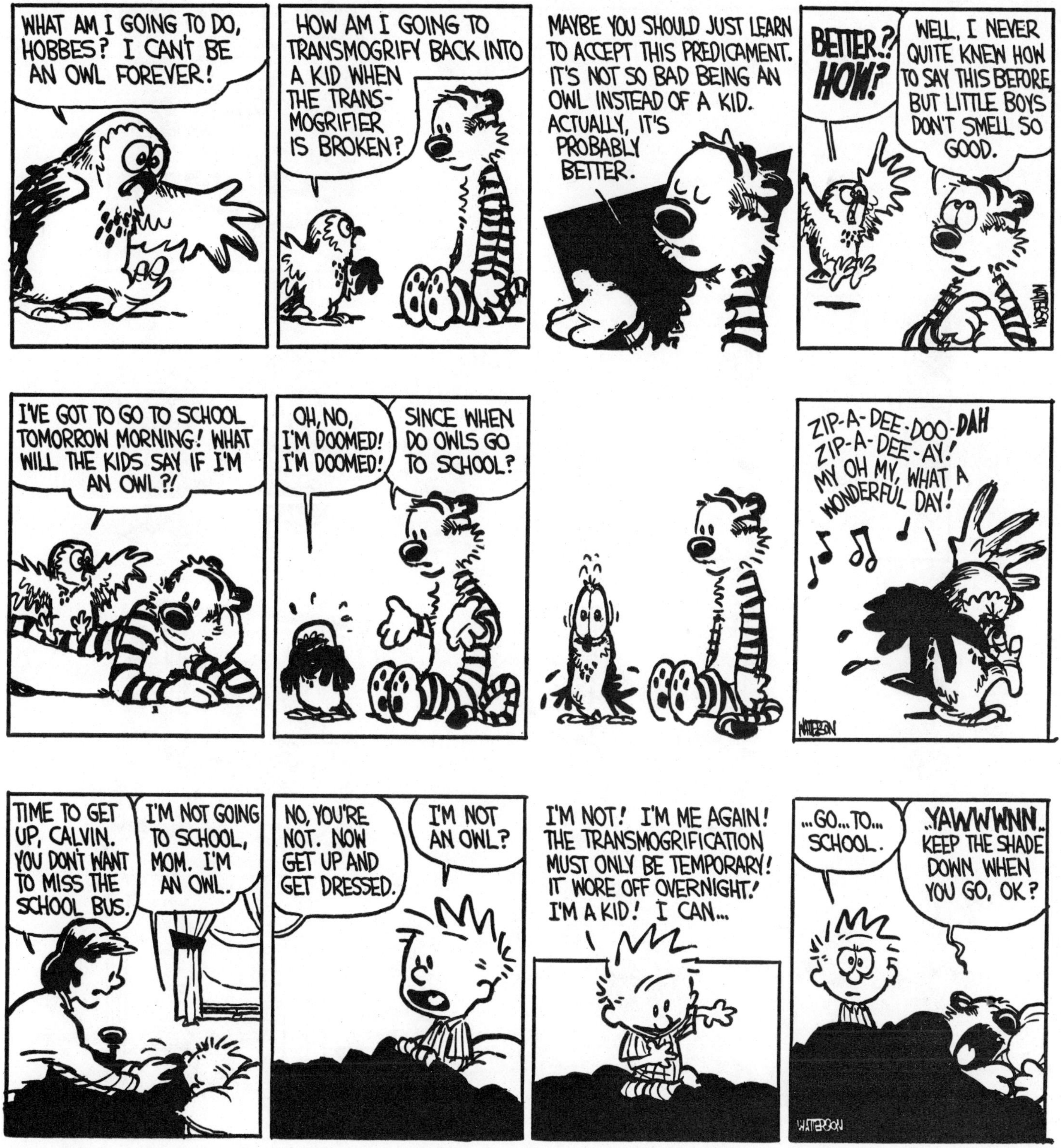
WHAT AM I GOING TO DO, HOBBES? I CAN'T BE AN OWL FOREVER!
HOW AM I GOING TO TRANSMOGRIFY BACK INTO A KID WHEN THE TRANSMOGRIFIER IS BROKEN?
MAYBE YOU SHOULD JUST LEARN TO ACCEPT THIS PREDICAMENT. IT'S NOT SO BAD BEING AN OWL INSTEAD OF A KID. ACTUALLY, IT'S PROBABLY BETTER.
BETTER?! HOW?
WELL, I NEVER QUITE KNEW HOW TO SAY THIS BEFORE, BUT LITTLE BOYS DON'T SMELL SO GOOD.
WATTERSON
I'VE GOT TO GO TO SCHOOL TOMORROW MORNING! WHAT WILL THE KIDS SAY IF I'M AN OWL?!
OH, NO, I'M DOOMED! I'M DOOMED!
SINCE WHEN DO OWLS GO TO SCHOOL?
ZIP-A-DEE-DOO-DAH ZIP-A-DEE-AY! MY OH MY, WHAT A WONDERFUL DAY!
WATTERSON
TIME TO GET UP, CALVIN. YOU DON'T WANT TO MISS THE SCHOOL BUS.
I'M NOT GOING TO SCHOOL, MOM. I'M AN OWL.
NO, YOU'RE NOT. NOW GET UP AND GET DRESSED.
I'M NOT AN OWL?
I'M NOT! I'M ME AGAIN! THE TRANSMOGRIFICATION MUST ONLY BE TEMPORARY! IT WORE OFF OVERNIGHT! I'M A KID! I CAN...
...GO...TO... SCHOOL.
..YAWWWNN.. KEEP THE SHADE DOWN WHEN YOU GO, OK?
WATTERSON

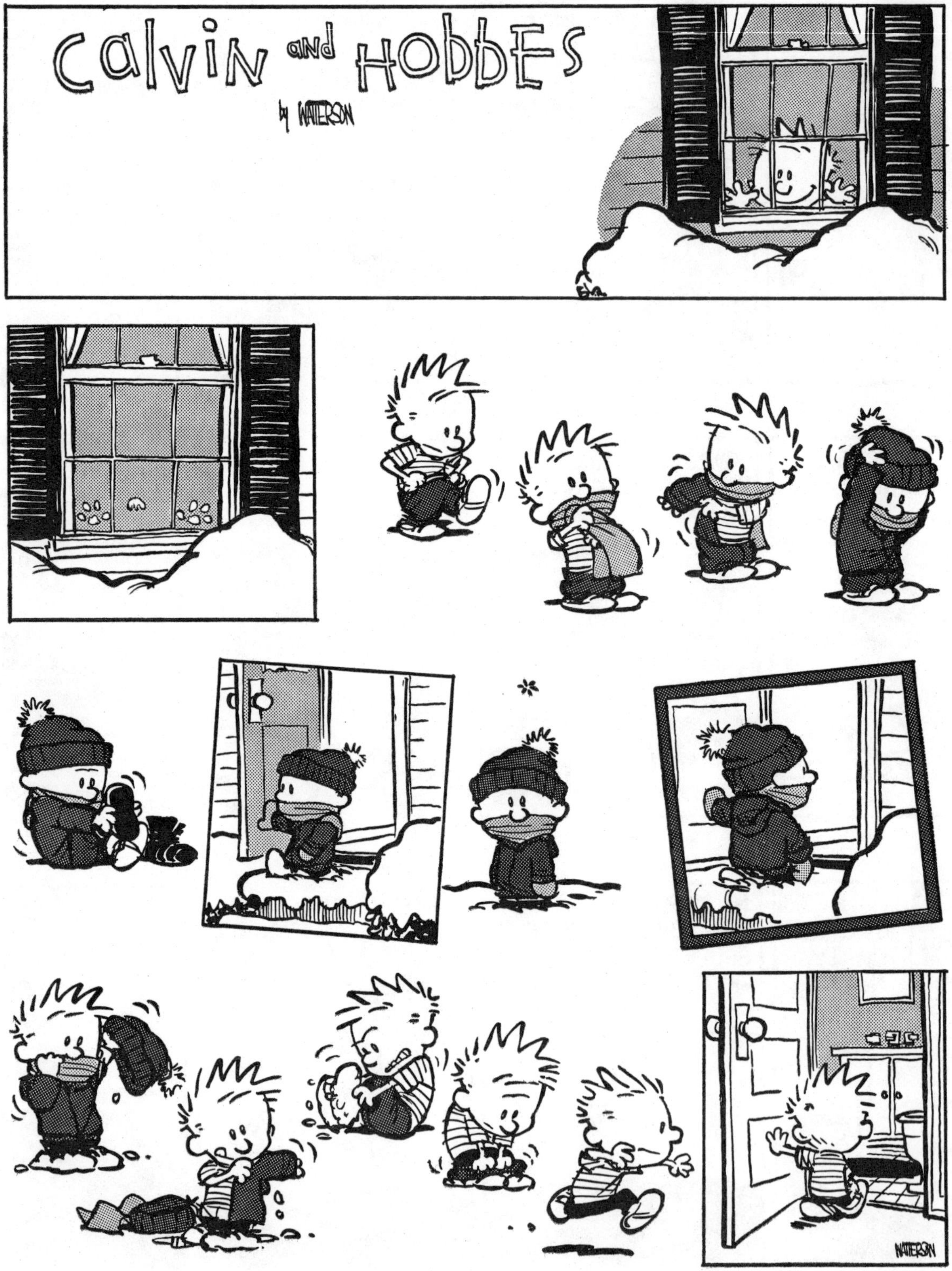
Calvin and HOBBES
by WATTERSON
WATTERSON

The End